The European Tour Yearbook 2004

OFFICIAL  PUBLICATION

Executive Editor
Mitchell Platts

Production Editor
Vanessa O'Brien

Editorial Consultants
Scott Crockett
Chris Plumridge

Picture Editors
David Cannon
Andrew Redington

Art Director
Tim Leney
TC Communications Plc

Print Managed by
London Print & Design Plc

The European Tour Yearbook 2004
is published by The PGA European Tour,
Wentworth Drive, Virginia Water, Surrey GU25 4LX.

Distributed through Aurum Press Ltd.
25 Bedford Avenue
London WC1B 3AT

Loch Lomond, Glasgow, Scotland

Introduction from The European Tour

n winning the Volvo Order of Merit for the first time, Ernie Els not only achieved another significant milestone in his hugely impressive career but he also provided more impetus to The European Tour's fervent mandate to internationalise golf.

In 2003 The European Tour, driven by the desire to take the game to the world and grow partnerships in every corner of the globe, staged no fewer than nine co-sanctioned events with our partners in Asia, Australia and South Africa. Ernie won two of these tournaments - the Heineken Classic in Melbourne and the Johnnie Walker Classic in Perth - in addition to victories in The Barclays Scottish Open at Loch Lomond, the Omega European Masters in Switzerland and the HSBC World Match Play Championship at Wentworth Club in England.

The European Tour's vision that the game should be internationalised must always be balanced by the need to progress through evolution, not revolution. We have always travelled by invitation, and we will continue to do so. Our objective in aligning professional golf worldwide is set, first and foremost, to meet the requirements and aspirations of our Members. Yet in delivering a dynamic and diverse Tour, so strengthening our position in the marketplace, we also sustain and heighten spectator interest by providing the opportunity and incentive for our Members to ply their trade and popularise the game.

Ernie's steadfast commitment to exhibit his world class skills in many different locations - he has won 47 tournaments in nine different countries - has further enhanced the popularity of the game. We welcome the arrival of new players from all corners of the globe as emphasised again on The European Tour International Schedule in 2003 with a record 17 first time winners and no fewer than 17 countries represented on the winner's rostrum.

We congratulate Ernie as we do Darren Clarke who became the second player to win more than one of the World Golf Championships when he triumphed in superb style in the NEC Invitational. Darren finished runner-up in the Volvo Order of Merit followed by Padraig Harrington, Fredrik Jacobson, Ian Poulter, Paul Casey, Lee Westwood and Thomas Björn, who demonstrated his own considerable skills in finishing runner-up in both the 132nd Open Golf Championship and the HSBC World Match Play Championship.

Peter Lawrie became The 2003 Sir Henry Cotton Rookie of the Year and Paul Casey, Padraig Harrington, Fredrik Jacobson, Ian Poulter and Lee Westwood were among the seven multiple winners on The European Tour International Schedule with Fredrik winning three including the season-ending Volvo Masters Andalucia. Bernhard Langer, the European Team Captain for The 35th Ryder Cup Matches in 2004, will share with us the belief that the future is in good hands. We also recognise the magnificent accomplishment of Catrin Nilsmark's European Team in winning the Solheim Cup and Garth McGimpsey's Great Britain and Ireland Team for their success in the Walker Cup. For the first time in history The Ryder Cup, the Solheim Cup and the Walker Cup trophies rest on this side of the Atlantic.

The leading 15 players from the European Challenge Tour, led by Johan Edfors, will now, having secured their cards, compete on The European Tour International Schedule on which, in 2003, no fewer than a record 130 Members earned in excess of £100,000. Our international pedigree was further emphasised by the fact that in 2003 no fewer than 37 countries hosted tournaments on The European Tour, the European Challenge Tour and the European Seniors Tour. The growth and development of the Seniors Tour continued and we congratulate Carl Mason in becoming the fastest player to rack up four victories on the way to record earnings of 350,241 euro for which he received the John Jacobs Trophy ahead of fellow rookie senior professional Bill Longmuir, who won twice.

We trust you will enjoy The 16th Edition of The European Tour Yearbook which reviews another superb season in the history of the Tour.

KENNETH D SCHOFIELD CBE
Executive Director, The European Tour

The best way
to go round the world
in 365 days.

The European Tour. From Taiwan to Dubai via England, Rolex follows The European Tour International Schedule every step of the way – with 48 tournaments across 23 countries through 5 continents.

Rolex Day-Date.
Officially Certified Swiss Chronometer.

ROLEX

Contents

Volvo Order of Merit Winner

seamlessly gifted

Ernie Els

Volvo Order of Merit Winner

There is, of course, no real surprise embroidering the fact that Theodore Ernest Els ended The 2003 European Tour International Schedule as the Number One golfer on the Volvo Order of Merit. Immensely talented and psychologically driven, the South African has more than enough gifts to stamp his authority effortlessly wherever he chooses to play.

On the other hand, however, one is entitled to wonder just why it took this seamlessly gifted man so long to officially confirm his standing among the European elite. The answer, as ever, is complex.

Fifty years ago Gary Player set the template for South African golfers. The Black Knight was not only one of the finest players to step onto a first tee, he also made a virtue out of travelling the globe in search of the victories he knew would establish his reputation as well as his fortune.

Els, too, has followed this rigorous path and although world travel is now swifter than it was for Player, the time it takes to leave, pass immigration, and arrive, is not really any shorter as a result of increased security.

The demands on him as a golfer are global and his instinct has always been to follow the rainbow wherever it may lead. Often this has meant numerous flights across darkened oceans but however draining the journey, Els always seems to manage to arrive with a smile on his face. "Oh, man," he says. "It's a great life. How could I ever complain? Mind you, I sometimes do. But always quietly!"

Arriving optimistically has been the way with him. He properly joined the European scene in 1992, a gangling giant of a young man, all big hands and feet, slightly awkward and gauche as he adjusted to life away from the comfort blanket that was South Africa. Right from the start, however, he was not just impossibly easy going, he was also hugely impressive.

Mark Roe, whose reaction to his disqualification from the 132nd Open Golf Championship at Royal St George's has assured him of a permanent place in the game's history, was happy to speak on behalf of all the players around at the time. Roe, as it happens, played with Els in 1992 during which year the South African made 14 appearances on The European Tour and finished 75th on the Volvo Order of Merit.

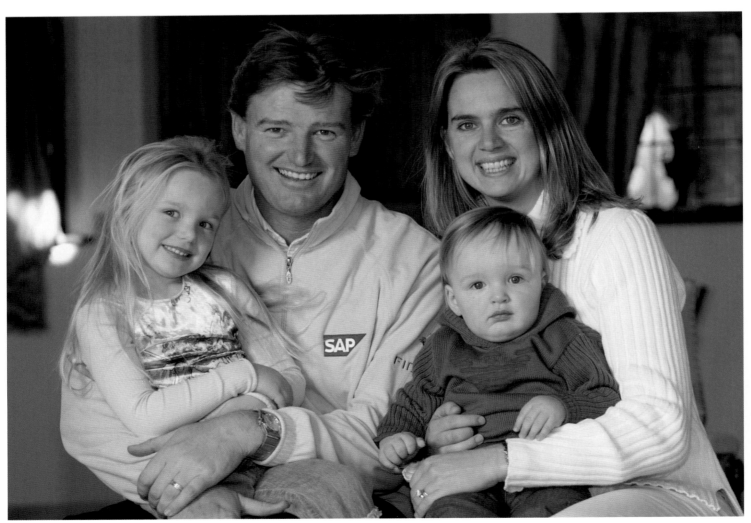

Ernie and Liezl with their children Samantha and Ben

This last sobriquet is universally acknowledged for, when it comes to staying grounded whilst flying high, then Els is indeed a role model. What is beyond doubt too is that this "perfect superstar" made the perfect start to 2003 by winning the opening two events on the US PGA Tour.

When he followed this by returning home to The European Tour and winning the Heineken Classic and the Johnnie Walker Classic before February was out, it seemed that even by the South African's high standards that this was going to be a truly stellar year.

However, just when a player thinks he may have the grand, old game cracked, it tends to bite back. In Els's case the biting was self inflicted and came when he injured his wrist while slapping a punchbag at his English home in the shadow of The European Tour's Wentworth headquarters, and where his wife Liezl, daughter Samantha, and son Ben, offer not just comfort, but reason for all his worldwide endeavour.

He still remembers how he felt about the man who joined him for one of his first rounds on The European Tour. "I had, of course, heard of his reputation as a player in South Africa, how he was supposed to be a star of the future, but you hear that sort of thing all the time, so it was interesting to see him up close," said Roe. "But yes, I was impressed immediately. It was his power, the sheer effortlessness of his swing.

"There was a 600 yard par five that I've never smelled in two shots. Ernie made it with a three iron. And his attitude when he missed a putt or didn't quite make a good swing was wonderful. He just tutted slightly and then focused on what he had to do next. When I came into the clubhouse afterwards I told my mates that I'd just played with a guy who was going to be Number One in the world sooner rather than later.

"Now he has won two US Opens and an Open, finished Number One in Europe and he hasn't changed a bit. Still comes over for a chat, still likes nothing better than a few beers with the lads. He is the perfect superstar."

Volvo Order of Merit Winner

Ernie with his parents, Neels and Hettie

It was not the worst of injuries but it was enough to break his concentration and to release that most debilitating of beasts for the professional golfer, the tiny flying bird of doubt.

It also possibly accounts for the fact that, in 2003, he did not add to his Major Championship tally, although finishing tied sixth, fifth, 18th and fifth in the Masters Tournament, the US Open Championship, the 132nd Open Golf Championship and the US PGA Championship respectively does not exactly add up to failure. Like the one man above him in the World Rankings, Tiger Woods, however, Els has reached that highest of plateaus, the one that encourages critics to judge a player harshly should he not win constantly.

Of course this is unfair, especially in such a sport as golf, so when he took The Barclays Scottish Open in July and the Omega European Masters in September he not only redressed the balance, he established a lead at the top of the Volvo Order of Merit that barricaded him from a late but determined run by Darren Clarke. Els's season, of course, was far from over for as autumn turned to gold so he emulated both Seve Ballesteros and compatriot Player by winning the HSBC World Match Play Championship on the West Course at Wentworth Club for the fifth time.

While Els's shyly modest exterior might suggest to the casual observer that his life has been spent avoiding contact with anything of real importance, unless it came with a course guide, nothing could be further from reality.

At 34, be assured that he is in touch with much that is moving and shaking in the modern world, and not only that, he is bright, articulate and wired. Reassuringly, most of the time, he cannot be fussed to prove any of these facts, preferring instead to lightly polish his image as the gentlest and most subdued of men. He remains, however, restlessly eager to make an ever bigger mark on the game.

"Maybe at my age I'm as good as I can be in terms of technique even if my mind-set could sometimes be a bit better," he says. "So I am where I am now and I know I'm not yet done with Majors, not yet satisfied. I could, maybe should, have had two more by now, but at least I've got three."

The above was related in that calm, reasoned way he carries around with him. It is not an act. For example, he was asked when he last really lost his cool, and for what reason?

After pondering the issue for several seconds, he said: "I don't remember. I don't really lose my temper. I do get irritated sometimes but there is no point in going ballistic is there? I just like to get on with things. If I drop a shot then I just try to get it back at the next hole. That's all you can do."

Such a philosophical outlook might well have something to do with an incident which shaped his life in his formative years. "I was in a bad car crash years ago," recalled Els. "I was in the passenger seat and I had my arm hanging out the window when it happened.

"I was just 20 years old and had finished my military service as had a good friend of mine. Man, we had a hell of a party. The next day we drove back to Johannesburg. I had the window wound down because it was hot but, all of a sudden, my mate lost control.

"We were travelling fast and the car turned upside down and I remember thinking my hand will get ripped off, but all my weight was on that side and I couldn't pull my arm back in.

"I don't know how far we slid like that but it seemed forever. In the end I was lucky but it taught me that life can change very quickly, so I tend to take things as they come...and I try to be careful."

Had that accident turned out differently and robbed the golfing world of Ernie Els, it would have indeed been a tragedy; the fact it did not, more than reason enough to celebrate 'The Big Easy's' good fortune and our own.

Bill Elliott

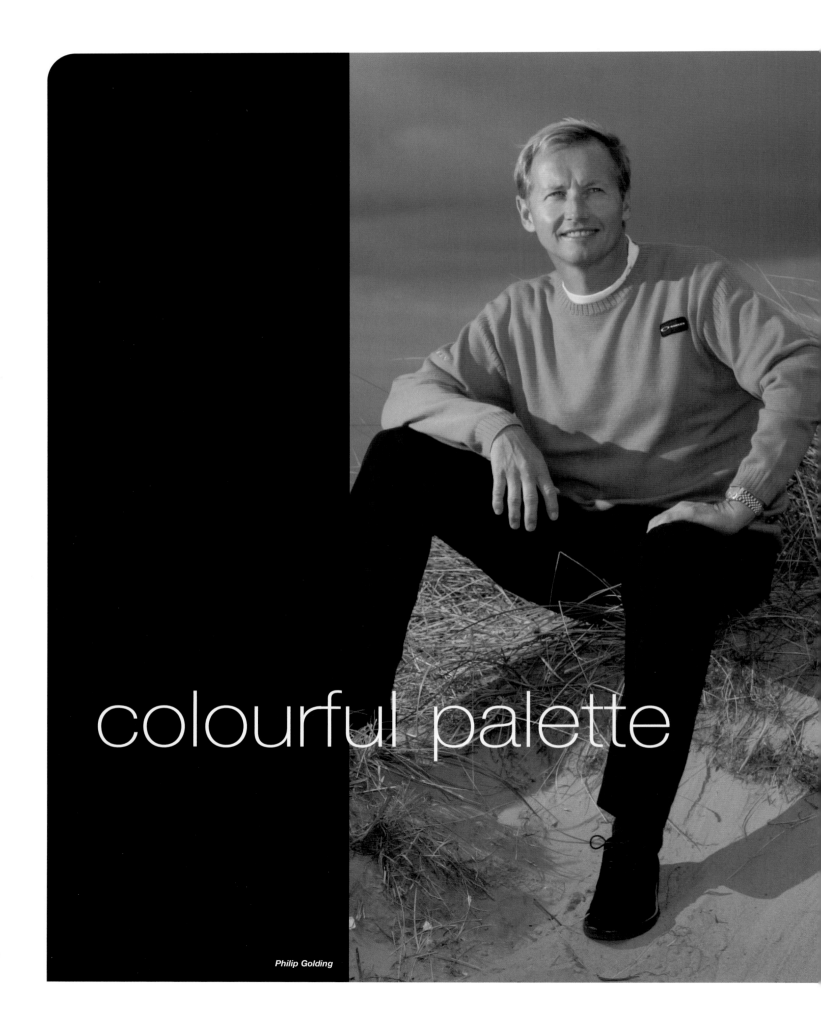

colourful palette

Philip Golding

Professional golf is a tough way to earn a living, focusing, as it does, not just on a man's talent with club and ball, but also on his ability to stand tall and stay calm when the pressure is at its most intense and the nerve endings are screaming a simple adrenaline message, consisting mostly of the words 'run' and 'hide'.

Each year, therefore, The European Tour International Schedule offers the most exquisitely testing of sporting examinations as it travels around the globe. To some, inevitably, this is the modern day equivalent of the rack, a collection of varied sporting fields from which many a broken body and spirit has to be carried. Playing games professionally has always involved this harsh truth.

Yet along with the pain, on an equal basis, there are the pleasures of competing, of testing oneself in the heat of battle, of falling down before getting back up, dusting oneself down and moving on optimistically to the next challenge.

Enjoy these, savour the most difficult moments, learn from errors and The European Tour will reward such effort and fortitude. Certainly as the years have flown and the Tour has grown both in quantity of tournaments and quality of courses - prize money increasing all the while naturally - the opportunity for advancement has been ever-present, while the incentive to work hard and to persevere has never been more apparent.

As evidence of these twin facts a colourful palette of characters emerged from the 2003 season, quite brilliantly led by the proud figure of Philip Golding, whose victory in the Open de France at Le Golf National, Paris, France, embroidered so much of the above.

Fredrik Jacobson

To say Golding was, until that Sunday in June, something of an unsung hero would be to understate the case. Consider this: the fair haired Englishman first tried for his card at the Qualifying School in 1983 but it was not until his tenth visit, in 1993, that he secured his passport to the Tour. Five more trips came before his 16th visit was made in November 2002 and that was only after his wife Sally persuaded him to give it one more try.

So it was at 40 years and 11 months that Golding made par at the final hole of Le Golf National to win and illuminate the 2003 season brilliantly for the scores of players who work so hard to qualify for the Tour before striving to stay on it. His victory, more possibly than any other over a fascinating twelve months, endorsed the possibilities eternally available on The European Tour, as well as the validity of the Challenge Tour, on which, in 2003, Johan Edfors led the European Challenge Tour Rankings, as a route to such riches.

For while the Englishman's gala moment came on The European Tour it was the Challenge Tour that prepared him for it and where he had won three titles in the 1990s. "That's the beauty of The European Tour," Golding reflected. "You are given the chance, be it through the Qualifying School or the Challenge Tour, to perform on the regular Tour. It's maybe taken me a little longer than most to fulfill my ambitions but it goes to show that it's never too late to win." Quite so. Opportunity and Incentive brought to vivid and reassuring life by a doggedly determined character.

Where Golding goes now and how he builds on this remarkable success remains to be seen. One thing, however, is certain, it will not be to the Qualifying School for the foreseeable future. Hopefully he will emulate the likes of Paul Casey, Fredrik Jacobson and Ian Poulter, three young players who not only found form in 2003, but held on to this elusive beast throughout the season.

Ian Poulter and Justin Rose

The Year in Retrospect

Paul Casey

Jacobson, at one time a promising ice-hockey player in his native Sweden, continued to both wear clothes considered cool and to impress, with his calmly considered approach to playing aggressive golf, by taking the Omega Hong Kong Open at the Hong Kong Golf Club, and then adding the Algarve Open de Portugal at Vale do Lobo, Portugal, in April. As his *coup de grâce*, Jacobson won the season-ending Volvo Masters Andalucia at Club de Golf Valderrama, Spain, and catapulted himself at that time into the top twenty in the Official World Golf Ranking. It was quite a year for the charismatic Swede, who also finished the top points scorer in The Seve Trophy even if Great Britain & Ireland did win against Continental Europe at Campo de Golf Parador El Saler Valencia, Spain.

Aggressively entertaining golf also came from the English duo of Casey and Poulter. Casey, an outstanding amateur in the late 1990s, was irresistible as he became the final Benson and Hedges International Open champion at The De Vere Belfry, Sutton Coldfield, England, in May, three months after winning the ANZ Championship at New South Wales Golf Club, Sydney, Australia.

Poulter, meanwhile, became almost as famous for his flamboyant hairstyles as he did for the swashbuckling golf that took him to victories in The Celtic Manor Resort Wales Open at The Celtic Manor Resort, City of Newport, Wales, in June and then the inaugural Nordic Open at Simon's Golf Club, Copenhagen, Denmark, two months later.

Europe's outstanding multiple winner in 2003 was, of course, Ernie Els. The genial South African was in imperious form at the beginning of the year when he won the Heineken Classic on the challenging acres of Royal Melbourne Golf Club, Victoria, Australia, before plundering the Johnnie Walker Classic at Lake Karrinyup Country Club, Perth, Australia, a fortnight later with a European Tour record low score of 29 under par 259.

There was a lull as we waited for Els's third European Tour title, but it eventually came as he unrolled his signature smooth swing in mid-summer during The Barclays Scottish Open at Loch Lomond, Glasgow, Scotland. Two months later, high in the Alps at Crans-sur-Sierre, Crans-Montana, Switzerland, he took his fourth title of the year, the Omega European Masters.

It was a victory that built a barricade around 'The Big Easy's' position at the top of the Volvo Order of Merit, protecting Els from an imposing chasing pack.

Leading that pack was Darren Clarke who illuminated another high-earning year with victory in the World Golf Championships - NEC Invitational at Firestone Country Club, Akron, Ohio, and who in doing so became only the second man, after American Tiger Woods who won the WGC-Accenture Match Play at La Costa Resort & Spa, Carlsbad, California, in March, to have triumphed more than once in WGC events. Woods made a successful defence of the WGC - American Express Championship later in the year to bring to seven the number of individual World Golf Championships he has won alongside eight Major Championships.

Meanwhile, three weeks after his American odyssey, Ulsterman Clarke showed he was a big man in more ways than one when he played in the Challenge Tour's inaugural Benmore Developments Northern Ireland Masters at Clandeboye Golf Club, Belfast, Northern Ireland, won by two shots, and gave the 35,877 euro cheque to his own charitable foundation for others to enjoy.

Another Irishman hoping to win on home soil during the year was Padraig Harrington but it was not to be, Phillip Price of Wales, taking the honours in the Smurfit European Open at The K Club, Dublin, Ireland, at the beginning of July while New Zealand's Michael Campbell won the Nissan Irish Open at Portmarnock Golf Club, Dublin, Ireland, at the end of the same month.

The triumphant Great Britain and Ireland Walker Cup Team

Harrington, however, continued to achieve a degree of consistency envied by others. He won the BMW Asian Open at Ta Shee Golf & Country Club, Taiwan, and the Deutsche Bank - SAP Open TPC of Europe at Gut Kaden, Hamburg, Germany, along the way to becoming one of seven multiple winners on The 2003 European Tour International Schedule.

Harrington was not alone in wishing he could have struck a similar rich vein of form in the Major Championships, but here curiosity prevailed with four first time Major winners in one season for the first time since 1969.

They were led by Canadian Mike Weir in the Masters Tournament at Augusta National, Georgia, USA, before three Americans enjoyed success at the highest level. Jim Furyk won the US Open Championship at Olympia Fields Country Club, Matteson, Illinois, USA, before two rank outsiders in Ben Curtis at the 132nd Open Golf Championship at Royal St George's Golf Club, Sandwich, Kent, England, and Shaun Micheel at the US PGA Championship at Oak Hill Country Club, Rochester, New York, USA, triumphed. For Curtis and Micheel read Opportunity and Incentive again.

Curtis, Furyk and Micheel were all winning for the first time on The European Tour International Schedule, with Golding and Jacobson emulating them, as elsewhere a fresh posse of new champions emerged so that by the end of the season no fewer than 17 golfers had enjoyed that euphoric feeling of capturing a first European Tour title.

There was first time European Tour glory on home turf for Trevor Immelman, whose South African Airways Open win at Erinvale Golf Club, Cape Town, South Africa, more than slightly pleased his home crowd. England's Mark Foster finally achieved what many felt he would years ago when he prevailed in the dunhill championship at Houghton

Golf Club, Johannesburg, South Africa; Lian-Wei Zhang helped China produce its first European Tour victor in the Caltex Masters, presented by Carlsberg, Singapore 2003, in steamy conditions at Laguna National Golf & Country Club, Singapore; and Robert-Jan Derksen of The Netherlands held off a glittering field at the Dubai Desert Classic, Emirates Golf Club, Dubai at the beginning of March.

The end of March saw no let up in first time winners as Welshman Bradley Dredge won the Madeira Island Open at Santo da Serra, Madeira; England's Kenneth Ferrie won the Canarias Open de España at Golf Costa Adeje, Tenerife; Greg Owen, another Englishman, won The Daily Telegraph Damovo British Masters at the Marriott Forest of Arden, Warwickshire, England; Australia's Brett Rumford won the Aa St Omer Open at Aa St Omer Golf Club, St Omer, France; Denmark's Søren Kjeldsen won The Diageo Championship at Gleneagles at The Gleneagles Hotel, Perthshire, Scotland and Marcus Fraser, of Australia, won the BMW Russian Open at Le Meridien Moscow Golf and Country Club, Moscow, Russia. Then KJ Choi struck a mighty blow for Korean golf by winning the Linde German Masters at Gut Lärchenhof, Cologne, Germany, as summer finally ebbed away. Choi's win in Cologne was historic in that it was the first by a Korean player on The European Tour International Schedule and the history books were opened again when Maarten Lafeber became the first home winner of the Dutch Open for 56 years with his win at Hilversumsche Golf Club, Hilversum, The Netherlands. In 2003 players from no fewer than 17 countries recorded victories on The European Tour International Schedule.

In Cologne, Lee Westwood picked up a gold bar, his prize for a hole in one, but in reality the end of the rainbow had arrived three weeks earlier in Germany for the Englishman when he won the BMW International Open at Golfclub München Nord-Eichenried, Munich, Germany, ending a barren spell that had lasted three years but which to some had seemed terminal. "I think I've just proved something to a few people," he said. And he had.

The victorious European Solheim Cup Team

Fit for Golf?

These days it is no longer sufficient to rely on talent and the desire to win. The right training and the right skills are important factors in performance. However, a balanced diet is also very much part of the package. Nestlé Nutrition will provide golf professionals and enthusiasts with information and up-to-date advice on sports nutrition, innovative foods and beverage products, giving them the winning edge.

Please come and ask for your free copy of the "Fit for golf" booklet at the upcoming Tour Event.

It was as if the blue touchpaper had suddenly been lit for Westwood for, a mere four weeks later, he produced another memorable triumph, holding off Els to win the dunhill links championship at the Old Course, St Andrews, Scotland, after having laid the foundations for his one shot success earlier in the week at Carnoustie and Kingsbarns.

There were trumpet calls, too, for Ignacio Garrido, whose stunning victory in the Volvo PGA Championship at Wentworth Club, Surrey, England, reminded us that here is a player of rare subtlety and for whom victory anywhere, any time is a possibility. Later in the year Miguel Angel Jiménez edged out Spanish compatriot José Maria Olazábal to win the Turespaña Mallorca Classic at Pula Golf Club, Mallorca, in Spain in which country the next week at Club de Campo, on the outskirts of Madrid, Argentina's Ricardo Gonzalez triumphed in the Telefonica Open de Madrid.

Elsewhere India's Arjun Atwal followed his debut victory in 2002 by winning the Carlsberg Malaysian Open at The Mines Resort & Golf Club, Kuala Lumpur, Malaysia. Other players on the up were South Africa's Darren Fichardt, who triumphed in the Qatar Masters at Doha Golf Club, Qatar; the reliable Mathias Grönberg of Sweden, who claimed the 60th Italian Open Telecom Italia at Gardagolf, Brescia, Italy; and the ever-improving Australian Adam Scott who won the Scandic Carlsberg Scandinavian Masters at Barsebäck Golf & Country Club, Malmo, Sweden, where little more than one month later, Europe's women triumphed spectacularly over the United States in the Solheim Cup only one week after the amateurs of Great Britain and Ireland proved too strong for their American rivals at Ganton Golf Club, England, and won the Walker Cup for a record breaking third time in a row. So, for the first time, The Ryder Cup, following Europe's win in 2002, the Solheim Cup and the Walker Cup were resting on this side of the Atlantic.

Even getting older has its compensations in the world of golf with the European Seniors Tour increasing in strength and in depth and, of course, in opportunities to play.

Bill Longmuir, who spent the winter honing his skills at his friend Greg Norman's home in Florida, certainly hit the ground running when he won his third event, the Ryder Cup Wales Seniors Open at Royal St David's Golf Club, Wales. The Scot followed up that success with another victory, in the De Vere PGA Seniors Championship at De Vere Carden Park, England, a win which cemented his second place in the Seniors Tour Order of Merit, behind another Tour rookie, Carl Mason, of England, who won a record 350,241 euro (£244,222).

Mason almost won the Senior British Open, presented by MasterCard, at the Westin Turnberry Resort, Scotland, succumbing

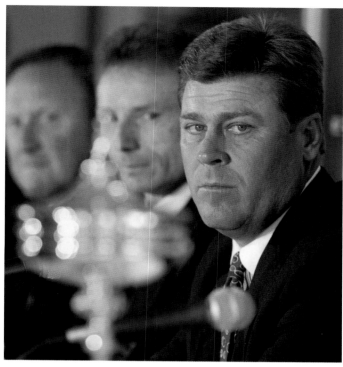

The Captains meet Richard Hills, The Ryder Cup Director, in Detroit where Bernhard Langer and Hal Sutton gave their first press conference at Oakland Hills Country Club ahead of The 35th Ryder Cup Matches.

only to five time Major winner Tom Watson in a play-off, but more than made up for that elsewhere with four victories in The Mobile Cup at Stoke Park, England, The Daily Telegraph/Turismo Andaluz Seniors Match Play Championship at Los Flamingos, Spain, the Merseyside English Seniors Open at Hillside Golf Club, England, and the Estoril Seniors Tour Championship at Oitavos Golf Club, Portugal, the last three in consecutive appearances.

Elsewhere, Retief Goosen remained the definition of understated consistency and won the Trophée Lancôme at Saint-Nom-La-Bretèche, Paris, France, into the bargain, although a third successive Harry Vardon Trophy, awarded annually to the leading player in the Volvo Order of Merit, was not to be his as South African compatriot Els, who claimed a record-equalling fifth title in the HSBC World Match Play Championship, climbed to the top with winnings of 2,975,374 euro (£2,074,458).

There is, perhaps, no finer example of a golfer standing tall and staying calm than Els although, in fairness, the words "run" and "hide" would not meet with his approval. Ernie Els is the epitome of a truly international sportsman and, for that, golf can rejoice in the masterly skills and immense joy he exhibits in playing the game in all corners of the globe as offered by The European Tour International Schedule.

Bill Elliott

Padraig Harrington

dangerous observation

Søren Hansen

The joy of winning The 34th Ryder Cup Matches triggered emotive celebrations for followers of European golf, and for Padraig Harrington the euphoria of success lingered on as he launched The 2003 European Tour International Schedule by winning the BMW Asian Open at Ta Shee Golf & Country Club on the outskirts of Taipei in Taiwan. This was Harrington's first win on the Asian continent, and his sixth on The European Tour since he turned professional in 1995 after playing no fewer than three Walker Cup matches.

Harrington's calculated progress is consistent with his approach to golf. He visualised that the power and the glory was around the corner when, at the start of the 1990s, he first came to prominence with golf of the highest calibre, challenging the likes of Darren Clarke and Paul McGinley for the top titles in his homeland. Even so, he determined to devote himself to amateur golf and to completing his studies to become a certified accountant.

He valued his education and that manifested itself on the golf course, too, where his maturity enabled him to absorb information and improve his technique in an orderly fashion. The learning process was galvanised by a two day session in May 1991 with Nick Faldo and David Leadbetter although at that time his trusted coach was Walter Sullivan at the Grange Golf Club, on the outskirts of Dublin.

Harrington also benefited from remaining an amateur because in Ireland the big events attract huge galleries so his game prospered as he learned to cope with distractions and develop his course management.

So by the time he turned professional, at the ripe old age of 24, and 20 years after hitting his first shots with a cut down eight iron, Harrington was conditioned to what life would be like on the professional circuit. He was a class act arriving in a brave new world, prepared only to look to the future and not to live in the past, and with his modest attitude and engaging smile there was universal belief that he was a real talent.

Some observers, however, suggested that he lacked the killer instinct to become a true champion. Indeed in 2002 they were still pointing to such things because of his record that season of only one win - the dunhill links championship the week after The 34th Ryder Cup Matches - from ten top ten finishes and a further seven top 20 finishes on The European Tour International Schedule. They should have known better.

Maarten Lafeber

BMW Asian Open Ta Shee Golf & Country Club ·Taiwan

the course

Club selection is examined because there is elevation on most holes from tee to the firm and tricky greens, and the choice is made all the more difficult when the wind blows. An excellent and challenging venue for the BMW Asian Open which is jointly-sanctioned by The European Tour and the Asian PGA Tour.

Ian Woosnam

Harrington is a slave to the game. His devotion to the practice range is legendary; his determination to succeed reflected by the time he also spends on personal fitness. Harrington does not drink alcohol, although he did sip a glass of champagne as he digested the importance of this first triumph in Asia.

Sometimes a break from your normal schedule is essential. Yet it was a deviation from his customary routine that might have soured the moment for Harrington. Put quite simply he took his eyes off the ball, and peered instead at a leaderboard as he hit the stretch in the final round.

"I don't watch leaderboards at all but I looked at one when I got to the 15th green because my round had got a bit static and I was looking for something to get it going," he explained. "Unfortunately it had the reverse effect and all of a sudden I got defensive.

"Before I looked at the board I was thinking I would need to get to 17 or 18 under but then I saw the nearest to me was on 14 under so that's probably why I became defensive. It can be very dangerous to watch scoreboards!"

The irony was that the defensive thoughts which so abruptly invaded the mind led to a situation on the last green which did much to silence those who doubted his ability to deliver the killer blow.

He found himself with a ten foot putt in fast fading light for victory and confidently rammed the ball into the sanctuary of the hole. This was not the way Harrington had thought the BMW Asian Open would end but, in the circumstances, it proved a point.

Tobias Dier

From the start the tournament had unfolded in a way which is, perhaps, more in keeping with Harrington's mode. He stuck to the tails of the leaders, massaging his confidence with a crispness in his play that was clear to all, and an opening flawless 66 enabled him to share second place with Maarten Lafeber, of The Netherlands, and Germany's Sven Strüver, one behind India's Jyoti Randhawa. Harrington had 18 birdie putts and holed six of them which, in the wind and rain, was a tribute to his outstanding striking.

Lafeber, joint third in the 2001 Caltex Singapore Masters, has a liking for Asia which he continued to demonstrate with a second successive 66 to move four shots clear at the halfway stage of South Africa's Trevor Immelman, who collected four birdies and an eagle in his 67, and Harrington (70). This was the third time in six weeks that Lafeber had led at the halfway stage, and he was to remain in pole position with a third round of 71 for 203, one ahead of Harrington and Immelman.

Four birdies in the first seven holes of his final round swept Harrington into the lead, but after glancing at *that* leaderboard, he was required to hole from eight feet to save par at the 16th then dropped a shot at the 17th. So, when he missed the green at the par three 18th and chipped to ten feet, he was obliged to show that when the going gets tough, the tough do indeed get going.

Harrington made no mistake with the putt, denying the fast finishing Randhawa by a single shot, and, after finishing runner-up two years in succession on the Volvo Order of Merit, he was able to quip: "It's great, finally, European Number One!"

Mitchell Platts

final results

Ta Shee Golf & Country Club • Taiwan
November 21-24 • 2002 • Par 72 • 7101 yards • 6492 metres

Pos.	Name		Rd1	Rd2	Rd3	Rd4	Total	Par	Prize Money Euro	£
1	Padraig HARRINGTON	Ire	66	70	68	69	273	-15	247967.10	158328.08
2	Jyoti RANDHAWA	Ind	65	75	70	64	274	-14	165304.80	105547.84
3	Andrew PITTS	USA	67	70	69	70	276	-12	76869.79	49081.70
	Maarten LAFEBER	NL	66	66	71	73	276	-12	76869.79	49081.70
	Trevor IMMELMAN	SA	69	67	68	72	276	-12	76869.79	49081.70
6	Thongchai JAIDEE	Thai	71	67	70	69	277	-11	52073.08	33248.89
7	Ian WOOSNAM	Wal	71	69	68	70	278	-10	36227.99	23131.73
	Rick GIBSON	Can	72	69	69	68	278	-10	36227.99	23131.73
	Søren HANSEN	Den	71	68	70	69	278	-10	36227.99	23131.73
	Daniel CHOPRA	Swe	71	73	67	67	278	-10	36227.99	23131.73
11	Wook-Soon KANG	Kor	74	68	68	69	279	-9	26482.88	16909.43
	Arjun ATWAL	Ind	72	73	69	65	279	-9	26482.88	16909.43
13	Simon YATES	Scot	67	71	71	71	280	-8	22391.43	14297.03
	Henrik NYSTRÖM	Swe	67	75	67	71	280	-8	22391.43	14297.03
	Gregory HANRAHAN	USA	73	72	68	67	280	-8	22391.43	14297.03
	Ted OH	Kor	71	71	68	70	280	-8	22391.43	14297.03
17	Tony JOHNSTONE	Zim	71	70	72	68	281	-7	18895.09	12064.60
	James KINGSTON	SA	68	70	71	72	281	-7	18895.09	12064.60
	Dean ROBERTSON	Scot	70	74	71	66	281	-7	18895.09	12064.60
	Kim FELTON	Aus	69	72	70	70	281	-7	18895.09	12064.60
21	Sam TORRANCE	Scot	73	67	72	70	282	-6	16812.17	10734.64
	Barry LANE	Eng	70	69	74	69	282	-6	16812.17	10734.64
	Adrian PERCEY	Aus	68	69	73	72	282	-6	16812.17	10734.64
24	Marc FARRY	Fr	70	73	70	70	283	-5	14803.63	9452.18
	Kenneth FERRIE	Eng	71	70	73	69	283	-5	14803.63	9452.18
	Simon HURD	Eng	71	70	75	67	283	-5	14803.63	9452.18
	David PARK	Wal	69	74	71	69	283	-5	14803.63	9452.18
	Jarmo SANDELIN	Swe	67	74	70	72	283	-5	14803.63	9452.18
	Wei-Tze YEH	Tpe	69	71	74	69	283	-5	14803.63	9452.18
30	Arjun SINGH	Ind	68	70	73	73	284	-4	12150.39	7758.08
	Jean-François LUCQUIN	Fr	69	73	72	70	284	-4	12150.39	7758.08
	Des TERBLANCHE	SA	67	75	73	69	284	-4	12150.39	7758.08
	Andrew COLTART	Scot	72	71	71	70	284	-4	12150.39	7758.08
	John DALY	USA	70	74	70	70	284	-4	12150.39	7758.08
	Tobias DIER	Ger	71	70	72	71	284	-4	12150.39	7758.08
36	Sven STRÜVER	Ger	66	74	72	73	285	-3	10265.84	6554.78
	Søren KJELDSEN	Den	71	70	73	71	285	-3	10265.84	6554.78
	Anthony WALL	Eng	70	72	71	72	285	-3	10265.84	6554.78
	Patrik SJÖLAND	Swe	72	71	71	71	285	-3	10265.84	6554.78
	Alastair FORSYTH	Scot	73	71	70	71	285	-3	10265.84	6554.78
41	José Maria OLAZÁBAL	Sp	73	72	70	71	286	-2	8331.69	5319.82
	Derek FUNG	HK	71	73	71	71	286	-2	8331.69	5319.82
	Jamie SPENCE	Eng	71	73	73	69	286	-2	8331.69	5319.82
	Julien VAN HAUWE	Fr	68	74	76	68	286	-2	8331.69	5319.82
	Jonathan LOMAS	Eng	72	71	73	70	286	-2	8331.69	5319.82
	Wen Teh LU	Tpe	73	72	73	68	286	-2	8331.69	5319.82
	Vijay KUMAR	Ind	71	74	70	71	286	-2	8331.69	5319.82
	Pablo DEL OLMO	Mex	72	71	72	71	286	-2	8331.69	5319.82
49	Miguel Angel JIMÉNEZ	Sp	73	69	77	68	287	-1	6695.11	4274.86
	Fran QUINN	USA	68	74	71	74	287	-1	6695.11	4274.86
	Kevin NA	Kor	71	67	74	75	287	-1	6695.11	4274.86
52	Peter BAKER	Eng	71	71	75	71	288	0	5802.43	3704.88
	Charlie WI	Kor	70	72	77	69	288	0	5802.43	3704.88
	Anthony KANG	Kor	69	75	71	73	288	0	5802.43	3704.88
55	Rafael PONCE	Ecu	70	72	75	72	289	1	4798.16	3063.65
	Ter-Chang WANG	Tpe	73	72	74	70	289	1	4798.16	3063.65
	Mikko ILONEN	Fin	70	71	77	71	289	1	4798.16	3063.65
	Ted PURDY	USA	71	72	74	72	289	1	4798.16	3063.65
59	Thavorn WIRATCHANT	Thai	70	72	76	72	290	2	4091.46	2612.41
	Danny ZARATE	Phil	74	71	74	71	290	2	4091.46	2612.41
	John E MORGAN	Eng	74	70	79	67	290	2	4091.46	2612.41
	Chun-Hsing CHUNG	Tpe	73	72	73	72	290	2	4091.46	2612.41
63	Tze-Chung CHEN	Tpe	72	73	72	74	291	3	3570.73	2279.92
	Peter LAWRIE	Ire	71	72	72	76	291	3	3570.73	2279.92
	Sushi ISHIGAKI	Jpn	71	72	72	76	291	3	3570.73	2279.92
66	Stephen DODD	Wal	71	73	76	72	292	4	3273.17	2089.93
67	Clay DEVERS	USA	71	72	75	75	293	5	2911.13	1858.77
	Fredrik JACOBSON	Swe	75	70	75	73	293	5	2911.13	1858.77
	Ahmad Dan BATEMAN	Can	72	72	73	76	293	5	2911.13	1858.77
	Gary RUSNAK	USA	73	72	77	71	293	5	2911.13	1858.77
71	Thammanoon SRIROT	Thai	73	71	73	78	295	7	2230.50	1424.18
	Gustavo ROJAS	Arg	72	73	74	76	295	7	2230.50	1424.18
73	Mike CUNNING	USA	72	72	79	77	300	12	2226.00	1421.31

Fredrik Jacobson

sumptuous course

1	Fredrik JACOBSON Swe	260	-16
2	Jorge BERENDT Arg	262	-14
	Henrik NYSTROM Swe	262	-14
4	Stephen DODD Wal	263	-13
	Søren KJELDSEN Den	263	-13
	Gary ORR Scot	263	-13
7	Tony JOHNSTONE Zim	264	-12
8	Craig KAMPS SA	265	-11
	Thomas LEVET Fr	265	-11
	Jyoti RANDHAWA Ind	265	-11

Success can be viewed in many ways. For example, most young men who had earned over 1.7 million euro (£1.1 million) in their chosen profession over the past three years would have every reason to congratulate themselves on having made it. Not Fredrik Jacobson.

In the world of professional golf, making money is something, but winning is everything. Every player who tees up on a Thursday morning wants the trophy in their hands come Sunday night, and the 28 year old Monaco-based Swede is no exception.

A sparkling amateur career which brought wins across Europe was, in the view of many observers, merely the aperitif to a sumptuous main course of professional victories. Jacobson, however, went hungry until, at long last, he feasted on the Omega Hong Kong Open.

Six times in his European Tour career Jacobson had had to stand aside in second place while a fellow competitor took the honours. Not all had been disappointments. He was rightly proud of battling to a play-off with Lee Westwood in the 1998 Belgacom Open, a performance which saved his Tour card in the last counting event. He also fought bravely in the 2001 Linde German Masters,

Gary Orr

matching local hero Bernhard Langer's closing 67 before succumbing by a solitary shot.

But some had rankled. An untidy ending to the final round of the 2000 Murphy's Irish Open allowed fellow countryman Patrik Sjöland to pocket the title, while another disappointing finish to regulation play in The 2002 Barclays Scottish Open let Eduardo Romero catch him before the Argentine triumphed in the resultant play-off.

The week before Hong Kong, Jacobson was finishing his final round in the BMW Asian Open, the first counting event on the 2003 Volvo Order of Merit, just as eventual winner Padraig Harrington was teeing off. Fittingly, if the Swede needed any inspiration, here was exactly the man to give it to him.

Like Jacobson, an exemplary amateur record had preceded the Irishman's move to the professional ranks but recently he, too, had endured a number of near misses, seven top eight finishes in 2002 to be exact, before triumphing at the dunhill links championship and carrying that form to the Ta Shee Golf & Country Club in Taiwan.

And so it was to be, finally, for Jacobson, too, an excellent final round of 64 for a 16 under par total of 260 on the altered Hong Kong Golf Club layout, good enough for a two shot winning margin over nearest challengers Jorge Berendt of Argentina and fellow countryman Henrik Nystrom.

The Swede revealed that a new, strong focus had helped elevate him to the winners' podium. "I didn't watch any leaderboards and I felt better than I have ever done before on the final day," he said. "I was really happy I stuck with my game plan."

Henrik Bjornstad

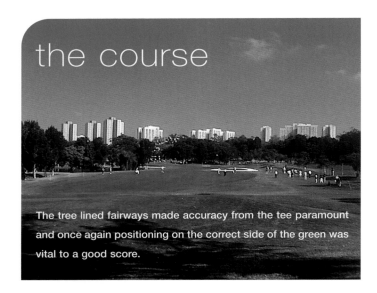

the course

The tree lined fairways made accuracy from the tee paramount and once again positioning on the correct side of the green was vital to a good score.

Tony Johnstone

Ironically, it would have made little difference if Jacobson had glanced at the leaderboards on the opening day, for he would not have seen his name, an inauspicious one under par 68 leaving him outside the top 40, five shots adrift of unheralded Indian golfer Amandeep Johl.

In the lead-up to the event, star attractions Nick Faldo and defending champion José Maria Olazábal had been ferried to their respective press conferences by helicopter after a sightseeing trip over Hong Kong, but at the end of the first round it was Johl who was flying high.

Another player who grabbed the early attention was Shih-Kai Lo who, by virtue of winning the Hong Kong Amateur Stroke Play Championship, had qualified to compete, thus becoming the youngest golfer to play in an event in European Tour history at the tender age of 13 years and 280 days.

Jorge Berendt

Nick Faldo

The previous record had been held by Sergio Garcia, who at 15 years and 45 days played in the 1995 Turespaña Open Mediterrania and made the cut. Although the Taiwanese schoolboy could not match that feat, his two rounds of 73 did enough to suggest his is a name we might be hearing more of in the future.

Into the second round, and perhaps not surprisingly, the pressure of the spotlight told on Johl and the 33 year old from New Delhi slipped back, the lead shared, incredibly, by seven players on nine under par 129, Henrik Bjornstad, Stephen Dodd, Klas Eriksson, Tony Johnstone, Mårten Olander, Jyoti Randhawa and Ter-Chang Wang.

Of the seven, only Welshman Dodd maintained the position come Saturday night, the 36 year old from Cardiff joined at the head of affairs on 12 under par 195 by Berendt and Nystrom. More importantly, however, in a group of players one shot behind, Jacobson had moved into a challenging position thanks to excellent rounds of 65 and 63 following his opening 68.

The Swede continued his forward momentum in the final round thanks to an outward half of 30 and although he dropped a shot at the 11th, he bounced back with birdies at the 12th and 14th and, with victory in sight, carded four successive pars for a 64 to confirm his two shot winning margin.

"I'm now in my eighth season so it is nice to have a win after so many near misses," said Jacobson, adding, "It's good to have the first one done."

It was a comment which suggested there are more to come and who are we to argue. After all, success does breed success.

Scott Crockett

final results

Hong Kong Golf Club • Hong Kong
November 28 - December 1 • 2002 • Par 69 • 6466 yards • 5913 metres

Pos.	Name		Rd1	Rd2	Rd3	Rd4	Total	Par	Prize Money Euro	£
1	Fredrik JACOBSON	Swe	68	65	63	64	260	-16	113385.30	71618.70
2	Jorge BERENDT	Arg	68	65	62	67	262	-14	60821.68	38417.41
	Henrik NYSTROM	Swe	64	68	63	67	262	-14	60821.68	38417.41
4	Søren KJELDSEN	Den	65	70	63	65	263	-13	29225.98	18460.30
	Stephen DODD	Wal	64	65	66	68	263	-13	29225.98	18460.30
	Gary ORR	Scot	67	66	63	67	263	-13	29225.98	18460.30
7	Tony JOHNSTONE	Zim	64	65	67	68	264	-12	21031.47	13284.32
8	Thomas LEVET	Fr	65	65	69	66	265	-11	15716.74	9927.32
	Jyoti RANDHAWA	Ind	67	62	69	67	265	-11	15716.74	9927.32
	Craig KAMPS	SA	68	63	66	68	265	-11	15716.74	9927.32
11	Nick FALDO	Eng	68	65	66	67	266	-10	10679.42	6745.55
	Mårten OLANDER	Swe	65	64	70	67	266	-10	10679.42	6745.55
	Rick GIBSON	Can	67	65	68	66	266	-10	10679.42	6745.55
	Jamie SPENCE	Eng	68	65	64	69	266	-10	10679.42	6745.55
	Arjun SINGH	Ind	65	66	65	70	266	-10	10679.42	6745.55
	Nicolas COLSAERTS	Bel	68	64	69	65	266	-10	10679.42	6745.55
	Boonchu RUANGKIT	Thai	65	69	62	70	266	-10	10679.42	6745.55
	Matthew BLACKEY	Eng	66	67	65	68	266	-10	10679.42	6745.55
19	Andrew MARSHALL	Eng	68	64	68	68	268	-8	8411.92	5313.31
	Henrik BJORNSTAD	Nor	67	62	69	70	268	-8	8411.92	5313.31
	Gerald ROSALES	Phil	70	64	68	66	268	-8	8411.92	5313.31
22	Maarten LAFEBER	NL	67	64	69	69	269	-7	7651.00	4832.68
	Jean-François LUCQUIN	Fr	68	67	66	68	269	-7	7651.00	4832.68
	Adrian PERCEY	Aus	66	67	70	66	269	-7	7651.00	4832.68
	Dean ROBERTSON	Scot	65	68	67	69	269	-7	7651.00	4832.68
26	Lian-Wei ZHANG	PRC	67	66	67	70	270	-6	6492.06	4100.65
	Barry LANE	Eng	66	67	67	70	270	-6	6492.06	4100.65
	Anders HANSEN	Den	72	65	64	69	270	-6	6492.06	4100.65
	Clay DEVERS	USA	66	64	73	67	270	-6	6492.06	4100.65
	Wook-Soon KANG	Kor	67	64	68	71	270	-6	6492.06	4100.65
	Wen Teh LU	Tpe	68	69	65	68	270	-6	6492.06	4100.65
	Kevin NA	Kor	69	64	68	69	270	-6	6492.06	4100.65
33	Chris WILLIAMS	Eng	68	66	70	67	271	-5	5298.00	3346.43
	Vivek BHANDARI	Ind	68	67	68	68	271	-5	5298.00	3346.43
	Danny CHIA	Mal	68	66	69	68	271	-5	5298.00	3346.43
	Simon YATES	Scot	67	69	68	67	271	-5	5298.00	3346.43
	Johan RYSTRÖM	Swe	69	66	65	71	271	-5	5298.00	3346.43
	Gary RUSNAK	USA	66	67	69	69	271	-5	5298.00	3346.43
	Pablo DEL OLMO	Mex	64	71	66	70	271	-5	5298.00	3346.43
40	Marc FARRY	Fr	70	65	68	69	272	-4	4244.42	2680.95
	Peter LAWRIE	Ire	68	65	68	71	272	-4	4244.42	2680.95
	Søren HANSEN	Den	66	65	66	75	272	-4	4244.42	2680.95
	Adam MEDNICK	Swe	67	67	67	71	272	-4	4244.42	2680.95
	Ter-Chang WANG	Tpe	65	64	72	71	272	-4	4244.42	2680.95
	Stephen GALLACHER	Scot	69	66	67	70	272	-4	4244.42	2680.95
	Mikko ILONEN	Fin	69	65	64	74	272	-4	4244.42	2680.95
	Do-Kyu PARK	Kor	68	68	66	70	272	-4	4244.42	2680.95
48	Klas ERIKSSON	Swe	65	64	69	75	273	-3	3120.60	1971.10
	Thammanoon SRIROT	Thai	67	67	70	69	273	-3	3120.60	1971.10
	Peter HEDBLOM	Swe	72	63	68	70	273	-3	3120.60	1971.10
	Thomas BJÖRN	Den	68	64	68	73	273	-3	3120.60	1971.10
	Rafael PONCE	Ecu	66	71	65	71	273	-3	3120.60	1971.10
	Amandeep JOHL	Ind	63	71	71	68	273	-3	3120.60	1971.10
	Ahmad Dan BATEMAN	Can	67	66	69	71	273	-3	3120.60	1971.10
	Thongchai JAIDEE	Thai	67	70	66	70	273	-3	3120.60	1971.10
56	José Maria OLAZÁBAL	Sp	69	65	67	73	274	-2	2347.98	1483.08
	Chi-Huang TSAI	Tpe	70	65	66	73	274	-2	2347.98	1483.08
	Massimo FLORIOLI	It	71	64	67	72	274	-2	2347.98	1483.08
59	Mike CUNNING	USA	68	69	66	72	275	-1	2102.14	1327.80
	Chawalit PLAPHOL	Thai	68	69	68	70	275	-1	2102.14	1327.80
61	Peter BAKER	Eng	66	69	68	73	276	0	1856.31	1172.52
	Jarmo SANDELIN	Swe	69	66	69	72	276	0	1856.31	1172.52
	Lee S JAMES	Eng	70	67	68	71	276	0	1856.31	1172.52
	Matthew CORT	Eng	66	71	66	73	276	0	1856.31	1172.52
	Yong-Eun YANG	Kor	70	62	70	74	276	0	1856.31	1172.52
66	José Manuel LARA	Sp	67	69	70	71	277	1	1540.23	972.87
	Aaron MEEKS	USA	72	65	68	72	277	1	1540.23	972.87
	James KINGSTON	SA	65	70	71	71	277	1	1540.23	972.87
	Ted OH	Kor	69	68	72	68	277	1	1540.23	972.87
70	Alessandro TADINI	It	71	66	67	74	278	2	1208.57	763.38
	Simon WAKEFIELD	Eng	66	69	69	74	278	2	1208.57	763.38
72	Ross BAIN	Scot	66	70	69	74	279	3	1049.50	662.91
73	Danny ZARATE	Phil	69	68	71	73	281	5	1046.50	661.01
74	David DIXON	Eng	69	66	75	72	282	6	1043.50	659.12
75	Taimur HUSSAIN	Pak	70	67	72	74	283	7	1040.50	657.22
76	Unho PARK	Aus	71	64	71	RTD	206	-1		

Trevor Immelman

cape of good hope

1	Trevor **IMMELMAN** SA	274	-14
2	Tim **CLARK** SA	274	-14
3	Jean **HUGO** SA	277	-11
	Bobby **LINCOLN** SA	277	-11
	Charl **SCHWARTZEL** SA	277	-11
	Tjaart **VAN DER WALT** SA	277	-11
	Bradford **VAUGHAN** SA	277	-11
8	Andrew **COLTART** Scot	278	-10
	Brian **DAVIS** Eng	278	-10
	Stephen **DODD** Wal	278	-10
	Rolf **MUNTZ** NL	278	-10
	Gary **MURPHY** Ire	278	-10
	Justin **ROSE** Eng	278	-10

Gary Murphy

Karma...fate...destiny...call it what you will, but there was an eerie sense of inevitability over the outcome of a tournament - the South African Airways Open - which meant the world to Trevor Immelman. Wealthy beyond the dreams of most young men of his age, proud owner of new homes in London and Orlando which he shares with his childhood sweetheart, Carminita, at 23 Immelman seemed to have it all. Well, almost.

From a meteoric rise through the amateur ranks in South Africa, to a successful conversion to the professional game, Immelman had been feted in his native country as the next major golfing talent to follow in the illustrious footsteps of Ernie Els, Retief Goosen and Gary Player.

But as he flew into Cape Town from Lake Nona, where he is now a close neighbour of the aforementioned Els, a tiny voice kept nagging away at the back of Immelman's mind. Despite the trappings of success, he still was not a winner on The European Tour International Schedule. In fact, of the leading 15 golfers on the 2002 Volvo Order of Merit (he finished 14th) Immelman was the only one not to have stepped onto the winners' podium on The European Tour.

As fate would have it, however, the 2003 South African Airways Open offered Immelman the opportunity to begin his year among his home comforts. Erinvale Golf Club is situated in the suburban town of Somerset West, headquarters of the Sunshine Tour and also Immelman's birthplace. It was there, 17 years earlier, after his first eye-opening golfing experience, that five year old Trevor rushed home and breathlessly informed his parents, Johan and June, that he wanted to become the best golfer in the world.

With that mission in mind, Erinvale became his second home for several years as he tramped the lush fairways of the Player-designed course, dreaming, as youngsters do, about one day winning his national championship, the second oldest Open in the world.

Fast forward to January 12, 2003. One stroke behind tournament leader and defending champion, Tim Clark, Immelman knew his moment had arrived. Every time he looked up he saw not only a familiar face, but a face that he could put a name to. Everyone at Erinvale knew the young man with the cheeky grin, who honed his game at the Club and who was accorded Honorary Membership during his stellar amateur career.

At that precise moment, destiny came calling. After carving his tee shot at the 72nd hole into the rough, within 18 inches of a pesky bush, Immelman checked his yardage with his experienced caddie, Neil Wallace. Precisely 180 yards to the flag, every chance of a 'flier'. Selecting his wedge, Immelman applied brute force and propelled the ball onto the green, 12 feet behind the cup.

Tim Clark

the course

Nestling in the lea of the imposing Helderbeg Mountains, Erinvale Golf Club posed a stiff test of golf which was also pleasing on the eye. The back nine, on a higher elevation than the outward half, offered the most spectacular views but the harder finish.

The putt was by no means a formality, but Immelman had been there before. Literally hundreds of times. He knew that green like the back of his hand, knew the nuances, the breaks, the speed. Destiny again.

"I turned to Neil and said to him: 'two cups outside the right edge'. I'd made that putt so many times before I didn't need to read it. It was just a case of getting the pace right," he later recalled.

Sure enough, the ball dropped, dead centre, dead weight, into the hole for the most important birdie three of his young life. The roar could have been heard at the top of Table Mountain as the galleries rose to acclaim the putt and Immelman responded with a passable impersonation of Tiger Woods's 'fist pump' routine.

A round of 67 and a 14 under par total of 274. A play-off now looked likely. Immelman inhaled deeply as he waited for events to unravel, trying, in his own words, "to bring my heart rate down to 1000 beats a minute!"

Just behind, another favourite son of the Cape, Jean Hugo, had lost a winning chance and the opportunity for the headline writer's dream. There would be no *Victor Hugo* after a penalty shot at the 16th followed by a double bogey at the 17th dropped the man from Stellenbosch into a tie for third.

Clark, though, had a birdie putt at the last to win and emulate Player, the last person to defend the title successfully in 1977.

Andrew Coltart

Rolf Muntz

The ball slid agonisingly across the hole, leaving Clark tied with Immelman and unquestionably ruing the five fluffed chips at the 16th hole in the third round which, in all probability, cost him the title. Few golfers rack up a nine and still win.

Cometh the hour, cometh the man. Back to the 18th tee the two gladiators went and Clark, a gritty competitor, knocked his approach to ten feet. A hush fell over Erinvale as Immelman assessed his 169 yard second shot, took out a nine iron and, from the centre of the fairway, hit a shot of radar precision to within nine inches of the cup. Not for the first time that week, destiny beckoned.

Clark, almost inevitably, missed the putt and Immelman tapped in, leaving him hugging family and friends and cradling the glittering prize he had craved so much as a youngster.

"I've been dreaming about this moment for so long and for it to happen at home, in front of my home crowd, people I've known for ever, I don't have words to describe it," said the emotional champion.

"When I hit the approach in the play-off I knew it was all over the pin and I could see people jumping and I knew it had come close. I said to Neil I hope it's a tap-in because I don't think I could handle a five footer right now! The closer we got to the hole the closer it got and anyone could have holed that little putt. It was as if it was meant to be."

Destiny, you might say.

Gordon Simpson

final results

Erinvale Golf Club • Cape Town • South Africa
January 9 - 12 • 2003 • Par 72 • 7087 yards • 6479 metres

Pos.	Name		Rd1	Rd2	Rd3	Rd4	Total	Par	Prize Money Euro	£
1	Trevor IMMELMAN	SA	70	71	66	67	274	-14	121669.50	79000.00
2	Tim CLARK	SA	67	67	71	69	274	-14	88556.90	57500.00
3	Bradford VAUGHAN	SA	69	71	68	69	277	-11	34621.90	22480.00
	Tjaart VAN DER WALT	SA	69	76	64	68	277	-11	34621.90	22480.00
	Jean HUGO	SA	66	73	65	73	277	-11	34621.90	22480.00
	Bobby LINCOLN	SA	71	68	69	69	277	-11	34621.90	22480.00
	Charl SCHWARTZEL	SA	75	69	68	65	277	-11	34621.90	22480.00
8	Gary MURPHY	Ire	71	67	71	69	278	-10	14900.66	9675.00
	Brian DAVIS	Eng	71	69	67	71	278	-10	14900.66	9675.00
	Justin ROSE	Eng	72	69	66	71	278	-10	14900.66	9675.00
	Stephen DODD	Wal	71	73	67	67	278	-10	14900.66	9675.00
	Rolf MUNTZ	NL	68	70	69	71	278	-10	14900.66	9675.00
	Andrew COLTART	Scot	68	69	73	68	278	-10	14900.66	9675.00
14	David HOWELL	Eng	69	72	67	71	279	-9	10934.85	7100.00
	Ian HUTCHINGS	SA	75	68	64	72	279	-9	10934.85	7100.00
	Louis OOSTHUIZEN	SA	73	70	70	66	279	-9	10934.85	7100.00
17	Hennie OTTO	SA	72	72	67	69	280	-8	9972.28	6475.00
	James KINGSTON	SA	67	72	71	70	280	-8	9972.28	6475.00
19	Raphaël JACQUELIN	Fr	72	72	68	69	281	-7	8824.89	5730.00
	Philip GOLDING	Eng	71	70	64	76	281	-7	8824.89	5730.00
	Per NYMAN	Swe	69	73	69	70	281	-7	8824.89	5730.00
	Bradley DREDGE	Wal	71	72	69	69	281	-7	8824.89	5730.00
	Alastair FORSYTH	Scot	73	67	71	70	281	-7	8824.89	5730.00
24	Steve WEBSTER	Eng	72	72	67	71	282	-6	7739.10	5025.00
	Paul LAWRIE	Scot	72	72	69	69	282	-6	7739.10	5025.00
	Brett LIDDLE	SA	72	72	69	69	282	-6	7739.10	5025.00
	Richard STERNE	SA	74	72	68	68	282	-6	7739.10	5025.00
28	Peter BAKER	Eng	75	67	70	71	283	-5	7046.05	4575.00
	Nick DOUGHERTY	Eng	72	66	73	72	283	-5	7046.05	4575.00
30	Jean-Francois REMESY	Fr	71	70	74	69	284	-4	6314.49	4100.00
	Mark MCNULTY	Zim	74	67	71	72	284	-4	6314.49	4100.00
	Ryan REID	SA	72	74	69	69	284	-4	6314.49	4100.00
	Scott DUNLAP	USA	70	74	69	71	284	-4	6314.49	4100.00
	Simon HURD	Eng	71	68	75	70	284	-4	6314.49	4100.00
	Graeme MCDOWELL	N.Ire	75	71	67	71	284	-4	6314.49	4100.00
36	Scott DRUMMOND	Scot	70	76	67	72	285	-3	5390.42	3500.00
	Ian GARBUTT	Eng	69	77	66	73	285	-3	5390.42	3500.00
	David DRYSDALE	Scot	68	72	75	70	285	-3	5390.42	3500.00
	David PARK	Wal	73	70	73	69	285	-3	5390.42	3500.00
	André CRUSE	SA	76	68	71	70	285	-3	5390.42	3500.00
	Craig LILE	USA	75	71	67	72	285	-3	5390.42	3500.00
42	Peter LAWRIE	Ire	68	69	77	72	286	-2	4312.34	2800.00
	Nicolas COLSAERTS	Bel	73	70	73	70	286	-2	4312.34	2800.00
	Marcel SIEM	Ger	72	70	72	72	286	-2	4312.34	2800.00
	Keith HORNE	SA	74	69	70	73	286	-2	4312.34	2800.00
	Markus BRIER	Aut	72	73	73	68	286	-2	4312.34	2800.00
	Iain PYMAN	Eng	68	73	69	76	286	-2	4312.34	2800.00
	Steve VAN VUUREN	SA	71	70	68	77	286	-2	4312.34	2800.00
	Gary BIRCH JNR	Eng	73	70	70	73	286	-2	4312.34	2800.00
50	Tony JOHNSTONE	Zim	73	72	70	72	287	-1	3011.79	1955.56
	Marc FARRY	Fr	74	68	74	71	287	-1	3011.79	1955.56
	Anders HANSEN	Den	71	71	74	71	287	-1	3011.79	1955.56
	Dean VAN STADEN	SA	73	73	70	71	287	-1	3011.79	1955.56
	Ian POULTER	Eng	72	70	70	75	287	-1	3011.79	1955.56
	Roger WESSELS	SA	74	72	70	71	287	-1	3011.79	1955.56
	Des TERBLANCHE	SA	71	71	72	73	287	-1	3011.79	1955.56
	Matthew BLACKEY	Eng	78	67	70	72	287	-1	3011.79	1955.56
	Lewis ATKINSON	Eng	71	72	72	72	287	-1	3011.79	1955.56
59	Ian KEENAN	Eng	70	72	74	72	288	0	2271.68	1475.00
	Andrew BUTTERFIELD	Eng	73	72	71	72	288	0	2271.68	1475.00
	Simon DYSON	Eng	75	66	75	72	288	0	2271.68	1475.00
	Jaco VAN ZYL	SA	72	73	71	72	288	0	2271.68	1475.00
63	Ulrich VAN DEN BERG	SA	75	71	68	75	289	1	2002.16	1300.00
	Mark PILKINGTON	Wal	73	71	73	72	289	1	2002.16	1300.00
	Jamie DONALDSON	Wal	75	67	70	77	289	1	2002.16	1300.00
66	Lee S JAMES	Eng	75	70	70	75	290	2	1771.14	1150.00
	David CARTER	Eng	75	70	70	75	290	2	1771.14	1150.00
	Sandeep GREWAL	Eng	75	67	75	73	290	2	1771.14	1150.00
69	Nic HENNING	SA	72	71	70	78	291	3	1617.13	1050.00
	Peter KARMAS (AM)	SA	75	71	76	69	291	3		
71	Titch MOORE	SA	74	71	65	82	292	4	1347.56	874.97
	Nico LE GRANGE	SA	72	72	74	74	292	4	1347.56	874.97
73	Grant MULLER	SA	70	72	75	76	293	5	1150.50	747.02
	John BELE	SA	73	73	73	74	293	5	1150.50	747.02
75	Mark MOULAND	Wal	75	70	70	79	294	6	1143.00	742.15
	Johan RYSTRÖM	Swe	75	71	70	78	294	6	1143.00	742.15
	Padraig DOOLEY	Ire	70	76	72	76	294	6	1143.00	742.15
78	Tim RICE	Ire	75	71	72	77	295	7	1137.00	738.25
79	Callie SWART	SA	75	70	73	78	296	8	1132.50	735.33
	Warren ABERY	SA	74	68	78	76	296	8	1132.50	735.33
81	Benn BARHAM	Eng	77	68	78	77	300	12	1128.00	732.41

Mark Foster

friends reunited

1	Mark FOSTER Eng	273	-15
2	Anders HANSEN Den	273	-15
	Trevor IMMELMAN SA	273	-15
	Paul LAWRIE Scot	273	-15
	Doug McGUIGAN Scot	273	-15
	Bradford VAUGHAN SA	273	-15
7	Justin ROSE Eng	275	-13
	Richard STERNE SA	275	-13
9	Paul CASEY Eng	276	-12
	Ian POULTER Eng	276	-12
	Steen TINNING Den	276	-12

t cannot be easy living in the shadow of your best friend, but Mark Foster embraced the role behind Lee Westwood without a trace of envy or self-admonition. Both were born and raised in the Nottinghamshire town of Worksop, forming both a tight bond and a healthy competitive rivalry during their formative years through their mutual passion for golf.

Two years older than Foster, Westwood won the British Youths Championship in 1993 and turned professional a few months before his younger friend won the first of his two English Amateur Championships with an English Amateur Stroke Play Championship sandwiched in between for good measure.

Foster was a rising star in the amateur game, playing for Great Britain and Ireland in the victorious 1995 Walker Cup Team at Royal Porthcawl alongside future European Tour winners Padraig Harrington and David Howell, as Westwood was carving a name for himself as a professional. It seemed only a matter of time before Foster would join the professional ranks and provide his mate with a serious challenge to be considered Worksop's finest.

However it did not quite work out like that. Westwood's career ignited and took off into orbit. Foster's stalled on the launch pad.

Raphaël Jacquelin

The man affectionately known as 'Fozzy' secured a European Tour card at the Qualifying School Finals in 1996 but played only eight tournaments after suffering a back injury which required surgery.

From there, Foster's career was the equivalent of climbing a greasy pole. Fully fit again, he missed the cut at the 1999 Qualifying School Finals and was first reserve in 2000 but did not hit a shot in anger. Meanwhile, Westwood had become a multiple winner on The European Tour International Schedule, earning his Ryder Cup spurs and various other accolades around the world with wins in Australia, China, Japan, South Africa and the United States.

By 2002, however, Foster had established himself. Winner of the European Challenge Tour Rankings in 2001, he was a fully exempt Member of The European Tour in 2002 and kept his card by finishing 93rd on the Volvo Order of Merit. So it was, by rights, he lined up alongside Westwood in the dunhill championship at Houghton Golf Club in Johannesburg.

For years, Foster had been on hand to congratulate or commiserate with Westwood after a tournament, offering a handshake or an arm around the shoulder. However as Foster played his way into only the second six-man play-off in European Tour history, it was payback time.

Paul Lawrie, with a round of 65, was the first player to finish on 273, 15 under par, soon after defending champion Justin Rose, also with a 65, had come up just short on 275. A bold defence, but too little, too late.

Then Trevor Immelman, winner of the South African Airways Open the previous week, eagled the last to get to 15 under before Anders

Dean Robertson

the course

Houghton Golf Club, in the leafy suburbs of Johannesburg, was once again in immaculate condition. The parkland course, made trickier by the growth of thicker rough, provided a fair but testing examination, hence a winning score five shots more than in 2002.

Paul Lawrie

Hansen, the 2002 Volvo PGA Championship winner, repeated the feat. The trio were joined by Doug McGuigan, the leader with two holes remaining, who finished double bogey, birdie, before Bradford Vaughan and Foster both made par at the last after having had one shot at winning the title.

Foster, facing the greatest test of his career against the quintet, was nervously hitting a few practice putts as the final cards were handed in. A familiar figure shuffled across the green and offered a few words of advice.

"Whatever you do, enjoy it," said Westwood, a veteran of two successful sudden-death play-offs. Foster responded that he would try. "No," retorted Westwood. "You have to make sure you enjoy it." Lee and his father, John, wished him good luck and left 27 year old Foster to his own devices.

Enjoy it he did, as one of the most enthralling finishes to a European Tour event unfolded over Houghton's 18th hole.

The play-off was gripping and full of possibilities. Could Immelman become the first person to win back to back play-offs since Nick Faldo 20 years earlier? Could Hansen or Immelman emulate Peter Baker, who in 1988 eagled the 72nd hole then beat Faldo with another eagle at the first extra hole in a play-off for the Benson and Hedges International Open at Fulford? Could Lawrie, the 2001 dunhill links champion at St Andrews, become the first winner of both tournaments sponsored by the luxury goods company?

The answer was no for them all. After Hansen and McGuigan were eliminated with par fives at the first play-off hole, Immelman, Lawrie and Vaughan had all played three shots second time round when Foster lined up his 40 foot putt for eagle. Minutes earlier his 12 footer for eagle to win on the first play-off hole had narrowly missed. This time was different though.

A triumphant clenched fist salute greeted the ball's disappearance underground and Immelman and Lawrie were gracious enough to acknowledge that the right man had won. Foster, who had required medication at the crack of dawn that day to combat the effects of dehydration, could only muster a contented smile.

So did that make him officially Worksop's Number One he was asked mischievously at the post-tournament press conference? "Nowhere near," he replied. "Lee's a legend...and I can tell you I always value his support."

That's what friends are for!

Gordon Simpson

Anders Hansen

final results

Houghton Golf Club • Johannesburg • South Africa
January 16 - 19 • 2003 • Par 72 • 7284 yards • 6542 metres

Pos.	Name		Rd1	Rd2	Rd3	Rd4	Total	Par	Prize Money Euro	£
1	Mark FOSTER	Eng	70	66	69	68	273	-15	120573.80	79000.00
2	Anders HANSEN	Den	70	65	69	69	273	-15	47359.54	31030.00
	Bradford VAUGHAN	SA	70	66	66	71	273	-15	47359.54	31030.00
	Trevor IMMELMAN	SA	69	67	70	67	273	-15	47359.54	31030.00
	Paul LAWRIE	Scot	68	73	67	65	273	-15	47359.54	31030.00
	Doug McGUIGAN	Scot	69	67	69	68	273	-15	47359.54	31030.00
7	Justin ROSE	Eng	73	67	70	65	275	-13	20642.53	13525.00
	Richard STERNE	SA	68	67	70	70	275	-13	20642.53	13525.00
9	Ian POULTER	Eng	70	68	68	70	276	-12	15033.56	9850.00
	Steen TINNING	Den	72	69	68	67	276	-12	15033.56	9850.00
	Paul CASEY	Eng	67	76	65	68	276	-12	15033.56	9850.00
12	Per NYMAN	Swe	71	69	69	68	277	-11	11981.06	7850.00
	Bradley DREDGE	Wal	65	68	70	74	277	-11	11981.06	7850.00
	Tim CLARK	SA	68	70	72	67	277	-11	11981.06	7850.00
15	Gary MURPHY	Ire	71	67	71	69	278	-10	10645.59	6975.00
	Scott DUNLAP	USA	67	72	69	70	278	-10	10645.59	6975.00
17	David HOWELL	Eng	72	71	68	68	279	-9	9208.38	6033.33
	Andrew MCLARDY	SA	68	74	66	71	279	-9	9208.38	6033.33
	Andrew MARSHALL	Eng	71	71	68	69	279	-9	9208.38	6033.33
	Stephen DODD	Wal	65	71	71	72	279	-9	9208.38	6033.33
	Mads VIBE-HASTRUP	Den	71	71	69	68	279	-9	9208.38	6033.33
	Michael KIRK	SA	68	74	68	69	279	-9	9208.38	6033.33
23	Raphaël JACQUELIN	Fr	69	71	68	72	280	-8	7669.41	5025.00
	Hennie OTTO	SA	69	69	70	72	280	-8	7669.41	5025.00
	Chris WILLIAMS	Eng	67	72	70	71	280	-8	7669.41	5025.00
	Philip GOLDING	Eng	72	70	67	71	280	-8	7669.41	5025.00
	Jean HUGO	SA	68	70	72	70	280	-8	7669.41	5025.00
	Andrew BUTTERFIELD	Eng	71	69	70	70	280	-8	7669.41	5025.00
29	Mark ROE	Eng	67	67	70	77	281	-7	6422.97	4208.33
	David LYNN	Eng	69	73	67	72	281	-7	6422.97	4208.33
	David PARK	Wal	75	68	71	67	281	-7	6422.97	4208.33
	Lee WESTWOOD	Eng	71	67	71	72	281	-7	6422.97	4208.33
	Michiel BOTHMA	SA	69	73	66	73	281	-7	6422.97	4208.33
	Louis OOSTHUIZEN	SA	66	75	72	68	281	-7	6422.97	4208.33
35	Hendrik BUHRMANN	SA	73	69	68	72	282	-6	5570.81	3650.00
	Richard BLAND	Eng	69	65	72	76	282	-6	5570.81	3650.00
	Ian HUTCHINGS	SA	71	72	68	71	282	-6	5570.81	3650.00
	Iain PYMAN	Eng	71	67	70	74	282	-6	5570.81	3650.00
	Francois DELAMONTAGNE	Fr	74	69	70	69	282	-6	5570.81	3650.00
40	Dean VAN STADEN	SA	71	71	69	72	283	-5	4578.75	3000.00
	Callie SWART	SA	66	74	70	73	283	-5	4578.75	3000.00
	Nicolas VANHOOTEGEM	Bel	72	64	73	74	283	-5	4578.75	3000.00
	Bobby LINCOLN	SA	71	70	71	71	283	-5	4578.75	3000.00
	Simon KHAN	Eng	71	71	71	70	283	-5	4578.75	3000.00
	Simon HURD	Eng	72	71	72	68	283	-5	4578.75	3000.00
	Alastair FORSYTH	Scot	69	72	67	75	283	-5	4578.75	3000.00
	David DIXON	Eng	75	65	70	73	283	-5	4578.75	3000.00
48	Fredrik OREST	Swe	73	70	69	72	284	-4	3357.75	2200.00
	Jean-Francois REMESY	Fr	72	67	73	72	284	-4	3357.75	2200.00
	Mark MCNULTY	Zim	74	68	70	72	284	-4	3357.75	2200.00
	Kenneth FERRIE	Eng	69	73	70	72	284	-4	3357.75	2200.00
	Andrew RAITT	Eng	70	72	74	68	284	-4	3357.75	2200.00
	Markus BRIER	Aut	69	68	72	75	284	-4	3357.75	2200.00
	Jamie DONALDSON	Wal	70	72	71	71	284	-4	3357.75	2200.00
	Martin MARITZ	SA	70	71	71	72	284	-4	3357.75	2200.00
56	Mark MOULAND	Wal	68	75	69	73	285	-3	2594.63	1700.00
	Craig LILE	USA	67	73	72	73	285	-3	2594.63	1700.00
58	Scott DRUMMOND	Scot	68	70	74	74	286	-2	2174.91	1425.00
	John BELE	SA	73	70	73	70	286	-2	2174.91	1425.00
	Tjaart VAN DER WALT	SA	70	72	67	77	286	-2	2174.91	1425.00
	Peter BAKER	Eng	71	69	75	71	286	-2	2174.91	1425.00
	Ryan REID	SA	71	72	72	71	286	-2	2174.91	1425.00
	Simon WAKEFIELD	Eng	72	69	74	71	286	-2	2174.91	1425.00
	Matthew BLACKEY	Eng	69	73	72	72	286	-2	2174.91	1425.00
	Nick DOUGHERTY	Eng	71	72	71	72	286	-2	2174.91	1425.00
66	Paul BROADHURST	Eng	71	70	70	76	287	-1	1793.34	1175.00
	Donald GAMMON	SA	74	69	70	74	287	-1	1793.34	1175.00
68	Bafana HLOPHE	SA	71	72	72	73	288	0	1418.80	929.60
	Mark PILKINGTON	Wal	71	68	73	76	288	0	1418.80	929.60
	Dean ROBERTSON	Scot	72	71	71	74	288	0	1418.80	929.60
	Mikael LUNDBERG	Swe	73	70	76	69	288	0	1418.80	929.60
	Bradley DAVISON	SA	71	69	72	76	288	0	1418.80	929.60
73	Tony JOHNSTONE	Zim	73	67	77	72	289	1	1132.71	742.15
	Wallie COETSEE	SA	73	68	75	73	289	1	1132.71	742.15
	Justin HOBDAY	SA	69	70	71	79	289	1	1132.71	742.15
	Nic HENNING	SA	72	69	70	78	289	1	1132.71	742.15
	Simon DYSON	Eng	68	70	80	71	289	1	1132.71	742.15
78	Johan RYSTRÖM	Swe	76	67	71	78	292	4	1123.79	736.31
79	Ben MASON	Eng	67	76	78	73	294	6	1120.82	734.36
80	Julien CLEMENT	Swi	72	71	77	75	295	7	1117.84	732.41

Caltex Masters, presented by Carlsberg, Singapore 2003
Laguna National Golf & Country Club · Singapore

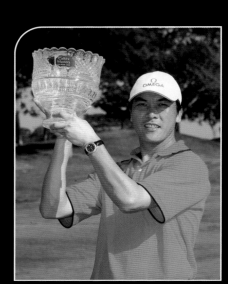

Lian-Wei Zhang

happy new year

1	Lian-Wei ZHANG PRC	278	-10
2	Ernie ELS SA	279	-9
3	Prayad MARKSAENG Thai	280	-8
4	Simon KHAN Eng	281	-7
	Maarten LAFEBER NL	281	-7
6	Rick GIBSON Can	283	-5
	Andrew MARSHALL Eng	283	-5
	Per NYMAN Swe	283	-5
9	Fran QUINN USA	284	-4
10	Arjun ATWAL Ind	285	-3
	Markus BRIER Aut	285	-3
	Thongchai JAIDEE Thai	285	-3
	Jean-François LUCQUIN Fr	285	-3
	Dean ROBERTSON Scot	285	-3
	Simon YATES Scot	285	-3

Two themes dominated the massive advertising hoardings in the bustling city of Singapore. The first heralded the staging of the third Caltex Masters, presented by Carlsberg, Singapore 2003, and prominently featured the face of Ernie Els, the overwhelming favourite. The second proclaimed the onset of the Chinese New Year.

Most people on their way to the impressive Laguna National Golf & Country Club believed the former gave a clear indication of the man destined to pick up the 140,713 euro (£92,747) first prize. As it turned out, the latter was more accurate in pinpointing the nationality of the champion.

Lian-Wei Zhang had played in European Tour events before but had never won, his best finish being fifth in the 2000 Benson and Hedges Malaysian Open. Indeed no Chinese golfer had ever triumphed on The European Tour. Little did we realise we were about to witness history in the making.

It was no surprise that Els was as short priced as 7/4 with some bookmakers. The towering South African came to Asia looking for his fourth consecutive victory, following wins in the Nedbank Challenge at the end of 2002 and in the Mercedes Championships and the Sony Open in Hawaii on the US PGA Tour in 2003.

Stephen Dodd

Simon Khan

Caltex Masters, presented by Carlsberg, Singapore 2003
Laguna National Golf & Country Club · Singapore

the course

Consistently rated one of the outstanding tournament venues in Asia, the Masters Course, designed by Pete Dye's nephew Andy, presented an excellent test for the field. Cunning bunkering allied to water on 11 of the 18 holes, meant caution was often the watchword.

He had also just completed the best year of his life, the Claret Jug in his trophy cabinet after a memorable Open Golf Championship at Muirfield, one of six victories worldwide in addition to the arrival of his new son, Ben. With Tiger Woods sidelined by injury, there was no doubt that, coming to Asia, the reigning Asprey Golfer of the Year was the best golfer on the planet.

An opening round of 69 left Els four shots off the lead, held by Challenge Tour graduate Benn Barham of England and Daniel Chopra of Sweden. But 'order' was restored in round two as Barham and Chopra slipped back with 78 and 77 respectively as the 33 year old South African took a one shot lead at the halfway stage. By the end of play on Saturday, he had doubled that advantage.

Surely it would now simply be a procession for Els on Sunday, a casual stroll through the sweltering humidity to the winners' podium? How wrong we were.

Unquestionably Els was out of sorts in the final round, growing fatigue not helping his attempts to gauge the pace of the greens, and he dropped shots at the eighth, 11th and 14th after early birdies at the second and seventh. But more importantly he had not accounted for the dogged determination and ability of his closest challenger, Zhang. Perhaps none of us had.

The 37 year old former track and field athlete is no stranger to success, having defeated Colin Montgomerie in the old Alfred Dunhill Cup at St Andrews in 1998 and more recently, in October 2002, he held off the challenge of three time Major winner Nick Price to successfully defend his Macau Open title at the fifth play-off hole. But could he do it again on this, his biggest stage?

One man with no doubt was Mitzuo Gyoten, club manager at the Zhuhai International Golf Club, where Zhang first picked up a club. For years, golf had been banned in China under the Cultural Revolution but the 'Open Door' policy of the late 1980s helped change that and when the new club came looking for prospective players, Zhang was one of the first in the queue.

As was the norm, Zhang served his time as a caddie while learning the game and within a short space of time was appointed Caddie Master. His skill on the fairways was developing too and in 1989, he paid his own way to Shenzhen to play in the China Amateur Open. It was only his fourth 72 hole tournament. He won.

Afterwards Gyoten-san said: "To spread golf in China, the sport needs pioneers and leaders and Zhang is one who will be able to contribute to the game's development here. He is honest and diligent, and he has guts."

How appropriate those sentiments were 14 years later in the heat of a Singapore Sunday. A pulled tee shot at the tricky 202 yard 17th cost Zhang a bogey four and saw him drop one shot behind Els with one hole to play. Lesser men would have caved in, Zhang did exactly the opposite.

Richard Green

Andrew Marshall

final results

Laguna National Golf & Country Club • Singapore
January 23 - 26 • 2003 • Par 72 • 7145 yards • 6533 metres

Pos.	Name		Rd1	Rd2	Rd3	Rd4	Total	Par	Prize Money Euro	£
1	Lian-Wei ZHANG	PRC	68	71	69	70	278	-10	140713.20	92747.15
2	Ernie ELS	SA	69	67	70	73	279	-9	93808.81	61831.44
3	Prayad MARKSAENG	Thai	73	67	69	71	280	-8	52851.89	34835.84
4	Maarten LAFEBER	NL	70	72	69	70	281	-7	39005.70	25709.51
	Simon KHAN	Eng	66	73	72	70	281	-7	39005.70	25709.51
6	Rick GIBSON	Can	68	76	71	68	283	-5	25328.38	16694.49
	Andrew MARSHALL	Eng	67	73	73	70	283	-5	25328.38	16694.49
	Per NYMAN	Swe	68	76	67	72	283	-5	25328.38	16694.49
9	Fran QUINN	USA	71	70	71	72	284	-4	18911.86	12465.22
10	Arjun ATWAL	Ind	67	70	76	72	285	-3	14310.53	9432.38
	Jean-François LUCQUIN	Fr	73	69	72	71	285	-3	14310.53	9432.38
	Simon YATES	Scot	68	69	72	76	285	-3	14310.53	9432.38
	Markus BRIER	Aut	69	71	74	71	285	-3	14310.53	9432.38
	Dean ROBERTSON	Scot	70	72	75	68	285	-3	14310.53	9432.38
	Thongchai JAIDEE	Thai	73	71	71	70	285	-3	14310.53	9432.38
16	Jean-Francois REMESY	Fr	73	69	70	74	286	-2	11397.77	7512.52
	James KINGSTON	SA	70	70	72	74	286	-2	11397.77	7512.52
	Daniel CHOPRA	Swe	65	77	72	72	286	-2	11397.77	7512.52
19	Thammanoon SRIROT	Thai	70	69	73	75	287	-1	9709.21	6399.55
	Kenneth FERRIE	Eng	71	73	70	73	287	-1	9709.21	6399.55
	Nick O'HERN	Aus	71	72	69	75	287	-1	9709.21	6399.55
	Mark PILKINGTON	Wal	70	72	69	76	287	-1	9709.21	6399.55
	Mads VIBE-HASTRUP	Den	71	72	71	73	287	-1	9709.21	6399.55
	Ted PURDY	USA	69	71	74	73	287	-1	9709.21	6399.55
25	Mardan MAMAT	Sing	70	70	76	72	288	0	8020.65	5286.59
	Wook-Soon KANG	Kor	71	69	74	74	288	0	8020.65	5286.59
	Jan-Are LARSEN	Nor	71	70	73	74	288	0	8020.65	5286.59
	David LYNN	Eng	73	72	74	69	288	0	8020.65	5286.59
	John BICKERTON	Eng	68	73	73	74	288	0	8020.65	5286.59
	Keng-Chi LIN	Tpe	71	71	72	74	288	0	8020.65	5286.59
	Fredrik WIDMARK	Swe	69	72	72	75	288	0	8020.65	5286.59
32	Stephen LEANEY	Aus	70	75	73	71	289	1	6458.74	4257.10
	Paul BROADHURST	Eng	66	79	75	69	289	1	6458.74	4257.10
	Joon CHUNG	Kor	72	72	73	72	289	1	6458.74	4257.10
	Wei-Tze YEH	Tpe	69	72	75	73	289	1	6458.74	4257.10
	Brad KENNEDY	Aus	75	70	72	72	289	1	6458.74	4257.10
	Eddie LEE	NZ	74	68	73	74	289	1	6458.74	4257.10
38	Kyi Hla HAN	Myan	70	73	72	75	290	2	5318.96	3505.84
	Gary MURPHY	Ire	70	68	81	71	290	2	5318.96	3505.84
	Jyoti RANDHAWA	Ind	70	69	78	73	290	2	5318.96	3505.84
	Stephen DODD	Wal	70	71	73	76	290	2	5318.96	3505.84
	Gustavo ROJAS	Arg	67	74	76	73	290	2	5318.96	3505.84
	David PARK	Wal	67	75	74	74	290	2	5318.96	3505.84
	Wen Teh LU	Tpe	67	77	72	74	290	2	5318.96	3505.84
45	Santiago LUNA	Sp	72	71	78	70	291	3	4136.97	2726.77
	Richard GREEN	Aus	72	72	78	69	291	3	4136.97	2726.77
	Philip ARCHER	Eng	73	72	73	73	291	3	4136.97	2726.77
	Hendrik BUHRMANN	SA	72	73	72	74	291	3	4136.97	2726.77
	Anthony KANG	Kor	71	73	75	72	291	3	4136.97	2726.77
	Chih-Bing LAM	Sing	69	70	72	80	291	3	4136.97	2726.77
	James OH	Kor	71	69	76	75	291	3	4136.97	2726.77
52	Benn BARHAM	Eng	65	78	75	74	292	4	3292.69	2170.28
	Nick DOUGHERTY	Eng	68	74	76	74	292	4	3292.69	2170.28
	Jason KNUTZON	USA	69	74	76	73	292	4	3292.69	2170.28
55	Des TERBLANCHE	SA	72	73	73	75	293	5	2786.12	1836.39
	Gregory HANRAHAN	USA	66	75	74	78	293	5	2786.12	1836.39
	Kevin NA	Kor	70	72	78	73	293	5	2786.12	1836.39
58	Matthew BLACKEY	Eng	72	72	78	72	294	6	2490.62	1641.62
	Craig KAMPS	SA	72	73	77	72	294	6	2490.62	1641.62
60	Andrew PITTS	USA	72	72	76	75	295	7	2237.34	1474.68
	Mårten OLANDER	Swe	71	72	80	72	295	7	2237.34	1474.68
	Gerry NORQUIST	USA	71	70	76	78	295	7	2237.34	1474.68
	Amandeep JOHL	Ind	72	73	75	75	295	7	2237.34	1474.68
64	Soren KJELDSEN	Den	75	69	75	77	296	8	1984.06	1307.73
	Henrik BJORNSTAD	Nor	70	72	76	78	296	8	1984.06	1307.73
66	Jeev Milkha SINGH	Ind	66	71	80	80	297	9	1772.99	1168.61
	Euan LITTLE	Scot	69	74	75	79	297	9	1772.99	1168.61
	Simon WAKEFIELD	Eng	75	69	78	75	297	9	1772.99	1168.61
69	Chris WILLIAMS	Eng	68	76	73	82	299	11	1469.53	968.60
	Julien VAN HAUWE	Fr	70	74	77	78	299	11	1469.53	968.60
	Gary EVANS	Eng	73	71	81	74	299	11	1469.53	968.60
72	Klas ERIKSSON	Swe	74	71	75	80	300	12	1260.00	830.49
	Jarrod MOSELEY	Aus	76	68	79	77	300	12	1260.00	830.49
	Lee S JAMES	Eng	68	74	81	77	300	12	1260.00	830.49
75	Thaworn WIRATCHANT	Thai	73	72	80	77	302	14	1254.00	826.54
76	Pablo DEL OLMO	Mex	71	74	78	80	303	15	1251.00	824.56
77	Eng-Wah POH	Sing	71	72	84	79	306	18	1248.00	822.58
78	Edward LOAR	USA	75	70	78	84	307	19	1245.00	820.61
79	Anders HANSEN	Den	69	71	82	W/D	222	6		

With Els in trouble from the 18th tee and short of the green in two, Zhang's bold drive flirted with the water hazard before a superb nine iron approach landed four feet from the pin. Els pitched to five feet in three, leaving the tournament poised on a knife-edge.

From round one Els had had problems on the greens and his Achilles Heel flinched again when it mattered most, his par effort grazing a spike-mark as it rolled past the edge of the cup. It left Zhang knowing exactly what he needed to do. Two putts for a play-off, one for victory. To the delight of his followers in the crowd, he chose the latter.

All week, the large Chinese population in Singapore had been preparing for the New Year Celebrations which were due to begin as soon as the tournament finished. Already a memorable occasion, Lian-Wei Zhang guaranteed it would now be a party never to be forgotten.

Scott Crockett

Ernie Els

1	Ernie ELS SA	273	-15
2	Nick FALDO Eng	274	-14
	Peter LONARD Aus	274	-14
4	Paul CASEY Eng	276	-12
	Gary EVANS Eng	276	-12
	Stephen GALLACHER Scot	276	-12
	Søren KJELDSEN Den	276	-12
	David LYNN Eng	276	-12
9	Peter FOWLER Aus	278	-10
	Bob FRIEND USA	278	-10

easy does it

Over the years Royal Melbourne Golf Club has been the venue for some stirring clashes featuring the world's greatest golfers. The course, designed in the 1920s by master architect Alister MacKenzie, who was also responsible for Augusta National and Cypress Point, and by local man Alex Russell, is a classic design that has stood the test of time and the advances of modern technology.

Perhaps the golfers of today are using eight and nine irons for approach shots that once demanded four and five irons but the basic qualities of the sandbelt course remain the same. Modern technology has not rendered Royal Melbourne obsolete and hopefully it never will.

One of the delights of the joint-sanctioned events between The European and Australasian Tours is the opportunity they afford European golfers to play classic courses Down Under when the weather in the northern hemisphere is not conducive to tournament play.

Just as the Alfred Dunhill Cup benefited from being played annually over the Old Course at St Andrews, so the added attraction of the Heineken Classic is Royal Melbourne itself, where the tournament moved to in 2002 from The Vines Resort in Perth.

Stephen Gallacher

The course has an illustrious history, having been the venue of the Australian Open on no fewer than 16 occasions. It also saw Peter Thomson, Melbourne's greatest golfer, and Kel Nagle emerge as ten shot winners when the World Cup was played there in 1959 and Rodger Davis land what was then the biggest prize in Australian golf when he edged Fred Couples in a play-off for the 1988 Bicentennial Classic.

The bottom line is you never get a bad winner at a course which, even when the wind is not blowing, can tease and test the best.

The pre-publicity for the 2003 Heineken Classic – 'The Gloves are On!' – promised a fight to the finish and it did indeed feature a memorable conclusion involving the defending champion Ernie Els from South Africa, six times Major winner Nick Faldo from England, and Australia's most consistent player of the previous summer, Peter Lonard. On the final day the outcome was uncertain right to the end before Els, the 2002 Open Golf Champion, ensured a successful defence of the title over a course he readily admits is his all-time favourite.

David Lynn

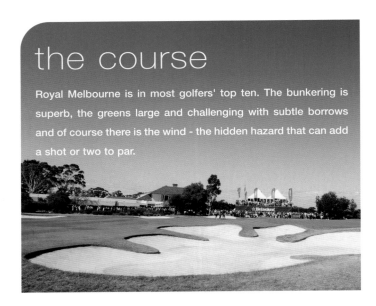

the course

Royal Melbourne is in most golfers' top ten. The bunkering is superb, the greens large and challenging with subtle borrows and of course there is the wind - the hidden hazard that can add a shot or two to par.

For Els it was a continuation of a remarkable run which had begun when he won, for the fourth time, the World Match Play Championship at Wentworth Club, Surrey, England, in October 2002.

Victory in the Nedbank Challenge followed in December before he headed for Hawaii and won the first two events on the US PGA Tour. He was on a roll but mentally tired when he arrived in Singapore the week before the Heineken Classic. There, although leading into the final hole of the Caltex Masters, presented by Carlsberg, Singapore 2003, he was caught and passed in the heat and humidity by Lian-Wei Zhang. At Laguna National Golf & Country Club, Els never quite got to grips with the grainy greens but at Royal Melbourne, despite a slow start which left him ten shots off the pace at halfway and a survivor of the cut by just two, he was more comfortable.

When he found his game at the weekend he was mightily impressive. With rounds of 66 and 65 an inspired Els put Faldo and Lonard to the sword by a shot, as well as a clutch of British players - Paul Casey, Gary Evans, Stephen Gallacher and David Lynn - and the Dane Søren Kjeldsen, who all shared fourth place two shots further back.

Greg Norman, at 47 still hugely competitive but with an uncertain putter, predicted it would take 20 under par to win. In the end 15 under did the job with Norman, living during the week on his new multi-million dollar boat, admitting regret that he was not involved in the nail-biting battle for the title on the final day.

In the last half hour Els, Faldo and Lonard were all potential winners. For a time it looked as if there might be a three-way play-off but in the end Els deserved his one stroke victory.

The 33 year old South African played the most impressive golf and after opening with four birdies in his first five holes, he made further crucial birdies at the 13th and 14th, and a vital par-saving putt at the 16th, which helped him win the day.

Had Faldo, challenging for his first title since the 1997 Nissan Open, snapped up a birdie chance at the 17th, he would have come down

Søren Kjeldsen

Peter Lonard

the last needing a further birdie to have a chance of victory. Lonard needed a par to tie with Els but in the end both he and Faldo pushed their drives, leaving them the most testing of second shots to a pin craftily tucked away in the right-hand corner of the undulating green and protected by a huge bunker.

Faldo sent his approach through the green and knew his chance had gone. Lonard, the reigning Australian PGA champion and MasterCard Masters champion, decided to go for the pin and glory but came up short in the sand with his seven iron.

Els had made par from the same trap with a brilliant recovery; Lonard, less deft, took bogey five. Faldo, from off the green, made par four, meaning it was Ernie's title again.

A glorious week's golf and a stimulating final day ended with *The Big Easy* making it five wins out of seven starts since beating Sergio Garcia in that World Match Play Championship final at Wentworth Club. Certainly the Heineken Classic had lived up to its reputation. The good news is that the event remains at Royal Melbourne Golf Club for the foreseeable future, and, hopefully, Ernie Els will be back to defend in 2004.

Renton Laidlaw

final results

Royal Melbourne Golf Club • Victoria • Australia
January 30 - February 2 • 2003 • Par 72 • 6981 yards • 6395 metres

Pos.	Name		Rd1	Rd2	Rd3	Rd4	Total	Par	Prize Money Euro	£
1	Ernie ELS	SA	70	72	66	65	273	-15	207309.10	137507.53
2	Nick FALDO	Eng	69	71	65	69	274	-14	97608.03	64743.12
	Peter LONARD	Aus	67	72	67	68	274	-14	97608.03	64743.12
4	Søren KJELDSEN	Den	71	67	71	67	276	-12	42613.54	28265.44
	Gary EVANS	Eng	67	73	70	66	276	-12	42613.54	28265.44
	David LYNN	Eng	69	65	73	69	276	-12	42613.54	28265.44
	Stephen GALLACHER	Scot	70	70	71	65	276	-12	42613.54	28265.44
	Paul CASEY	Eng	65	67	74	70	276	-12	42613.54	28265.44
9	Peter FOWLER	Aus	67	72	70	69	278	-10	29944.64	19862.19
	Bob FRIEND	USA	70	73	69	66	278	-10	29944.64	19862.19
11	David BRANSDON	Aus	74	67	71	67	279	-9	23034.34	15278.61
	Stephen ALLAN	Aus	68	68	73	70	279	-9	23034.34	15278.61
	John BICKERTON	Eng	68	70	72	69	279	-9	23034.34	15278.61
14	Brian DAVIS	Eng	70	74	65	71	280	-8	16056.86	10650.47
	Richard GREEN	Aus	69	71	69	71	280	-8	16056.86	10650.47
	David SMAIL	NZ	71	68	69	72	280	-8	16056.86	10650.47
	Nick O'HERN	Aus	71	71	71	67	280	-8	16056.86	10650.47
	Jarrod MOSELEY	Aus	70	72	73	65	280	-8	16056.86	10650.47
	Thomas BJÖRN	Den	70	68	71	71	280	-8	16056.86	10650.47
20	Greg TURNER	NZ	68	73	70	70	281	-7	11747.51	7792.09
	Stephen COLLINS	Aus	69	72	69	71	281	-7	11747.51	7792.09
	Darren FICHARDT	SA	70	74	69	68	281	-7	11747.51	7792.09
	Stephen SCAHILL	NZ	71	69	69	72	281	-7	11747.51	7792.09
	Richard LEE	NZ	69	69	72	71	281	-7	11747.51	7792.09
25	Greg NORMAN	Aus	73	69	69	71	282	-6	8537.10	5662.64
	Ian POULTER	Eng	74	64	71	73	282	-6	8537.10	5662.64
	Søren HANSEN	Den	72	71	68	71	282	-6	8537.10	5662.64
	Jorge BERENDT	Arg	73	68	70	71	282	-6	8537.10	5662.64
	Simon KHAN	Eng	72	72	67	71	282	-6	8537.10	5662.64
	Patrik SJÖLAND	Swe	73	69	69	71	282	-6	8537.10	5662.64
	Eddie LEE	NZ	70	71	72	69	282	-6	8537.10	5662.64
	Steven BOWDITCH	Aus	72	72	69	69	282	-6	8537.10	5662.64
33	Santiago LUNA	Sp	66	74	71	72	283	-5	6334.44	4201.62
	Steve WEBSTER	Eng	68	69	70	76	283	-5	6334.44	4201.62
	Jyoti RANDHAWA	Ind	71	73	69	70	283	-5	6334.44	4201.62
	Lucas PARSONS	Aus	68	73	73	69	283	-5	6334.44	4201.62
	Cameron PERCY	Aus	71	71	70	71	283	-5	6334.44	4201.62
	Paul SHEEHAN	Aus	72	70	72	69	283	-5	6334.44	4201.62
39	Michael LONG	NZ	74	68	73	69	284	-4	4837.21	3208.51
	Charlie WI	Kor	74	70	68	72	284	-4	4837.21	3208.51
	Robert KARLSSON	Swe	69	73	73	69	284	-4	4837.21	3208.51
	David PARK	Wal	75	68	70	71	284	-4	4837.21	3208.51
	Fredrik ANDERSSON	Swe	72	68	73	71	284	-4	4837.21	3208.51
	Jamie DONALDSON	Wal	74	66	74	70	284	-4	4837.21	3208.51
	Andrew TSCHUDIN	Aus	69	73	71	71	284	-4	4837.21	3208.51
46	Kenneth FERRIE	Eng	70	72	71	72	285	-3	3685.49	2444.58
	Niclas FASTH	Swe	68	70	68	79	285	-3	3685.49	2444.58
	Euan WALTERS	Aus	74	70	70	71	285	-3	3685.49	2444.58
49	Scott LAYCOCK	Aus	73	70	73	70	286	-2	2936.88	1948.02
	Tony CAROLAN	Aus	70	74	69	73	286	-2	2936.88	1948.02
	Scott HEND	Aus	72	70	75	69	286	-2	2936.88	1948.02
	Brad KENNEDY	Aus	71	70	76	69	286	-2	2936.88	1948.02
53	Warren BENNETT	Eng	67	74	71	75	287	-1	2517.65	1669.95
	Ian GARBUTT	Eng	68	71	73	75	287	-1	2517.65	1669.95
	Ricardo GONZALEZ	Arg	68	72	76	71	287	-1	2517.65	1669.95
	Brett RUMFORD	Aus	71	70	74	72	287	-1	2517.65	1669.95
	Mahal PEARCE	NZ	71	69	71	76	287	-1	2517.65	1669.95
58	Anthony WALL	Eng	70	70	76	72	288	0	2418.61	1604.25
	Paul LAWRIE	Scot	71	71	74	72	288	0	2418.61	1604.25
	Nick DOUGHERTY	Eng	72	72	74	70	288	0	2418.61	1604.25
61	Gary SIMPSON	Aus	72	72	72	73	289	1	2349.51	1558.42
	Nathan GREEN	Aus	70	73	71	75	289	1	2349.51	1558.42
	David DIAZ	Aus	73	70	72	74	289	1	2349.51	1558.42
64	Arjun ATWAL	Ind	69	72	75	76	290	2	2314.95	1535.50
65	Jean-Francois REMESY	Fr	70	73	73	75	291	3	2274.64	1508.76
	Lee S JAMES	Eng	73	70	74	74	291	3	2274.64	1508.76
67	Mathias GRÖNBERG	Swe	72	69	74	77	292	4	2234.33	1482.02
68	Dean ROBERTSON	Scot	72	72	72	77	293	5	2199.78	1459.10
	Scott GARDINER	Aus	73	71	73	76	293	5	2199.78	1459.10
70	Chris DOWNES	Aus	72	72	76	76	296	8	2165.23	1436.19

Paul Casey

1	Paul CASEY Eng	45 pts
2	Stuart APPLEBY Aus	41 pts
	Nick O'HERN Aus	41 pts
4	Peter LONARD Aus	39 pts
	Jarrod MOSELEY Aus	39 pts
6	Greg TURNER NZ	38 pts
7	Martin DOYLE Aus	37 pts
	Scott HEND Aus	37 pts
9	Robert KARLSSON Swe	35 pts
	Peter SENIOR Aus	35 pts

out of range

David Howell

throughout. Trying to defend his position in the third day at Melbourne he had slipped to a 74. In Sydney, he did not make the same mistake.

In a tournament that rewards aggressive play it was, ironically enough, his brilliant third round that gave him the useful six point cushion he would need in the end. On Saturday in Sydney he powered his way to a brilliant 61, picking up 21 points, and matching the record one day score set at The International which is also a stableford competition launched on the US PGA Tour in 1986. Even more amazingly he did it without hitting a practice shot.

Because of space restrictions at New South Wales Golf Club, the practice range for the week was at a nearby club 20 minutes away. "I just didn't bother to hit any balls all week and it had no adverse effects," said Casey, who formed a useful partnership with Alan Drummond, a plus one amateur from the Woodlands Club in Melbourne who had caddied for Geoff Ogilvy in Europe in the past.

Together Casey and Drummond finished ninth in the dunhill championship in Johannesburg, fourth in Melbourne and then won in Sydney. The Englishman, who went through "at least" ten caddies in 2001, admitted he might have found the right man at last!

When Paul Casey, the 25 year old former Walker Cup player, arrived in Australia he made it clear that his main ambition was to win again...and quickly. In 2001, just weeks after turning professional, he landed The Diageo Championship at Gleneagles, but 2002 had been a frustrating season for someone who, when attending Arizona State University, had beaten many of Phil Mickelson's records.

Casey, who now has a home in Scottsdale where he spends time during the winter honing his game with respected coach Peter Kostis and Chris Doris, who used to work with him at ASU, loves links golf.

"I played a lot of links golf in my amateur days so it was a delight to find myself competing on two Alister MacKenzie courses - Royal Melbourne for the Heineken Classic immediately followed by New South Wales," said Casey after his victory over Stuart Appleby and Nick O'Hern.

The week before he had featured in Melbourne when finishing tied fourth behind Ernie Els after having led at one stage. He had learned much from that experience and in the ANZ Championship, a modified stableford system, he had vowed to stay aggressive

Nick O'Hern

the course

Another Alister MacKenzie gem. Opened in 1928, it remains virtually untouched. Jack Newton and Greg Norman have reshaped a few greens but the tightly laid-out course with several blind shots remains a superb test of a golfer's shot-making and temperament, especially when the wind is whipping off the Tasman Sea.

Drummond's calming influence helped most on Sunday as Casey held off the challenges of Peter Lonard, Jarrod Moseley, Appleby and O'Hern, all of whom put in last day charges that made it far from a victory stroll in the sun.

In the end, the overnight six points lead, a birdie, birdie start and some remarkable putting enabled him to land the first prize of 180,934 euro (£118,133) with 45 points.

Noted as a long hitter, Casey was just as impressive on the greens. When he needed to hole for par he did and never more crucially than on the 17th, a 20 foot putt that kept his title hopes intact.

Lonard's last day challenge, built on seven glorious birdies and an eagle – he holed his second shot at the first – had given the Australian a share of the lead after 13 holes but from the 14th tee he took driver instead of a three wood, pushed the ball into thick rough and made double bogey. In the process, he lost three valuable points and, with it, his chance of winning.

Steve Webster

Robert Karlsson

Meanwhile Appleby, Moseley and O'Hern kept the pressure on Casey but never caught him. Although insisting he never felt nervous and was never worried, Casey did drop shots at the 15th and 16th before making that vital par at the 17th, and a birdie at the last, where Appleby hit the hole with an eagle attempt. In the end Casey won by four points.

After dismal performances Down Under from England's cricketers and tennis players, Casey had achieved his personal goal of a quick win, and restored national pride at the same time.

Renton Laidlaw

Peter Fowler

final results

New South Wales Golf Club • Sydney • Australia
February 6 - 9 • 2003 • Par 72 • 6816 yards • 6232 metres

Pos.	Name		Rd1	Rd2	Rd3	Rd4	Total	Par	Prize Money Euro	£
1	Paul CASEY	Eng	8	10	21	6	45		180934.20	118133.34
2	Stuart APPLEBY	Aus	16	2	15	8	41		85189.84	55621.10
	Nick O'HERN	Aus	10	12	8	11	41		85189.84	55621.10
4	Jarrod MOSELEY	Aus	3	18	3	15	39		44228.35	28877.03
	Peter LONARD	Aus	15	0	8	16	39		44228.35	28877.03
6	Greg TURNER	NZ	4	9	7	18	38		36186.84	23626.67
7	Scott HEND	Aus	4	8	17	8	37		30658.29	20017.03
	Martin DOYLE	Aus	4	7	7	19	37		30658.29	20017.03
9	Peter SENIOR	Aus	10	9	9	7	35		26134.93	17063.70
	Robert KARLSSON	Swe	11	9	11	4	35		26134.93	17063.70
11	Peter FOWLER	Aus	17	2	10	5	34		22114.17	14438.51
12	Klas ERIKSSON	Swe	4	12	5	12	33		17842.12	11649.26
	Søren KJELDSEN	Den	5	7	12	9	33		17842.12	11649.26
	Paul MARANTZ	Aus	8	11	1	13	33		17842.12	11649.26
	Jamie DONALDSON	Wal	4	10	11	8	33		17842.12	11649.26
16	Nick DOUGHERTY	Eng	-2	15	17	2	32		13771.10	8991.26
	Richard LEE	NZ	7	14	4	7	32		13771.10	8991.26
18	Terry PRICE	Aus	10	12	4	5	31		11685.33	7629.44
	Brendan JONES	Aus	8	14	1	8	31		11685.33	7629.44
20	André STOLZ	Aus	5	12	7	6	30		10856.05	7088.00
21	Arjun ATWAL	Ind	3	14	3	9	29		10102.16	6595.78
	Richard BLAND	Eng	3	10	6	10	29		10102.16	6595.78
	Craig PARRY	Aus	14	7	1	7	29		10102.16	6595.78
	Stephen SCAHILL	NZ	11	0	11	7	29		10102.16	6595.78
25	Steve CONRAN	Aus	11	2	8	7	28		8217.43	5365.22
	Gregory HAVRET	Fr	0	13	13	2	28		8217.43	5365.22
	Ricardo GONZALEZ	Arg	6	6	7	9	28		8217.43	5365.22
	Mahal PEARCE	NZ	7	12	-1	10	28		8217.43	5365.22
29	Søren HANSEN	Den	4	15	1	7	27		6835.29	4462.81
	David CARTER	Eng	10	9	-1	9	27		6835.29	4462.81
	Nathan GREEN	Aus	9	13	3	2	27		6835.29	4462.81
32	Steve WEBSTER	Eng	10	2	11	3	26		6131.66	4003.41
	Michael PEARSON	USA	10	6	4	6	26		6131.66	4003.41
34	David HOWELL	Eng	11	6	9	-1	25		5428.02	3544.00
	Mark FOSTER	Eng	8	9	1	7	25		5428.02	3544.00
	Gary EVANS	Eng	7	14	-2	6	25		5428.02	3544.00
	David DRYSDALE	Scot	10	9	-3	9	25		5428.02	3544.00
	Stephen GALLACHER	Scot	0	12	-1	14	25		5428.02	3544.00
39	Jean-Francois REMESY	Fr	10	3	8	3	24		4523.35	2953.33
	Stephen COLLINS	Aus	12	3	6	3	24		4523.35	2953.33
	Cameron PERCY	Aus	5	11	5	3	24		4523.35	2953.33
	Brad KENNEDY	Aus	10	1	8	5	24		4523.35	2953.33
43	Stephen LEANEY	Aus	11	3	7	2	23		3618.68	2362.67
	Marcus CAIN	Aus	10	5	10	-2	23		3618.68	2362.67
	Matthew ECOB	Aus	5	13	1	4	23		3618.68	2362.67
	Jyoti RANDHAWA	Ind	4	10	3	6	23		3618.68	2362.67
	Bradley HUGHES	Aus	7	9	5	2	23		3618.68	2362.67
48	Peter O'MALLEY	Aus	4	7	1	10	22		2739.14	1788.41
	Ignacio GARRIDO	Sp	4	12	10	-4	22		2739.14	1788.41
	Matthew BLACKEY	Eng	12	2	5	3	22		2739.14	1788.41
	Paul SHEEHAN	Aus	5	7	8	2	22		2739.14	1788.41
52	Mike CLAYTON	Aus	9	8	4	0	21		2261.68	1476.67
	Henrik BJORNSTAD	Nor	10	1	5	5	21		2261.68	1476.67
	David LYNN	Eng	6	6	5	4	21		2261.68	1476.67
55	Adam LE VESCONTE	Aus	6	6	4	4	20		2181.26	1424.16
	Patrik SJÖLAND	Swe	-1	15	3	3	20		2181.26	1424.16
57	Raphaël JACQUELIN	Fr	9	8	-3	5	19		2141.05	1397.91
	Douglas LABELLE	USA	-1	12	3	5	19		2141.05	1397.91
59	Paul LAWRIE	Scot	4	7	9	-2	18		2100.85	1371.66
	Shannon JONES	Aus	8	5	3	2	18		2100.85	1371.66
61	Mikko ILONEN	Fin	-2	19	-4	4	17		2060.64	1345.41
	Leigh MCKECHNIE	Aus	1	11	6	-1	17		2060.64	1345.41
63	Ian GARBUTT	Eng	2	10	6	-2	16		2017.09	1316.97
	Jorge BERENDT	Arg	6	7	-3	6	16		2017.09	1316.97
	Raymond RUSSELL	Scot	6	10	-4	4	16		2017.09	1316.97
66	Wayne RILEY	Aus	2	11	0	2	15		1950.07	1273.21
	Adam MEDNICK	Swe	4	9	0	2	15		1950.07	1273.21
	Dean ROBERTSON	Scot	0	14	-6	7	15		1950.07	1273.21
69	Carlos RODILES	Sp	7	4	5	-3	13		1909.86	1246.96
70	Adrian PERCEY	Aus	4	10	-3	0	11		1879.71	1227.28
	Martin MARITZ	SA	6	5	-3	3	11		1879.71	1227.28
72	Tony CAROLAN	Aus	7	4	0	-2	9		1849.55	1207.59
73	David GLEESON	Aus	3	8	-2	-6	3		1829.45	1194.46

Ernie Els

hot century

1	Ernie ELS SA	259	-29
2	Stephen LEANEY Aus	269	-19
	André STOLZ Aus	269	-19
4	Robert ALLENBY Aus	271	-17
	Retief GOOSEN SA	271	-17
	Jean-Francois REMESY Fr	271	-17
	Justin ROSE Eng	271	-17
	David SMAIL NZ	271	-17
9	Niclas FASTH Swe	272	-16
	Craig KAMPS SA	272	-16

Stephen Leaney

Vicente Fernandez in the 1975 Benson and Hedges International Open, and his final 29 under par winning total of 259 was two better than the previous best by Canadian Jerry Anderson at Crans-sur-Sierre in 1984.

The 72 hole total gave the 33 year old South African a unique double, for just a few weeks earlier the winner of the 2002 Open Golf Championship had set a new under par record on the US PGA Tour, shooting a 31 under par total of 261 in the Mercedes Championships on the Plantation Course at Kapalua.

Els was one shot ahead of David Lynn after an opening 64 which was one shot outside the course record established by defending champion Retief Goosen on his way to the title one year earlier. By halfway he was four in front and he was nine clear with a round to go. It was hardly surprising that the report in the local Sunday newspaper read: "When Ernie Els wins today," and not 'if'. *The Big Easy* was so much in control that a second victory in the Johnnie Walker Classic- to follow his first at Hope Island in Queensland in 1997 - was a certainty.

He carded a final round 66 and won by ten shots, a winning margin which bettered by two the domination Goosen had had over the field in 2002. Put simply, the thousands of fans who flocked to Lake Karrinyup Country Club during another brilliantly staged event had been treated to a display by a golfer completely on top of his game both mentally and technically.

When Ernie Els arrived in Perth from a charity shoot out in Bali, the only poser was whether or not the pre-tournament favourite could maintain his magnificent form and claim another success in the Johnnie Walker Classic. How emphatically was that question to be answered!

With two wins on the US PGA Tour, victory in the Heineken Classic at Royal Melbourne Golf Club a fortnight earlier, and a second place finish in the Caltex Masters, presented by Carlsberg, Singapore 2003, Els's brilliant golf had enabled him to be a remarkable 71 under par for his 16 tournament rounds in 2003.

By the end of the week on Australia's west coast, he had moved that particular statistic on to astonishing heights. Having swept the quality field aside in style under a hot sun to record his fourth win in five starts in 2003, he was now the grand total of 100 under par for 20 rounds.

Two weeks earlier Els had squeezed to victory in a nail-biting finish in Melbourne. In Perth he had no such problems. He led from start to finish and was out on his own, breaking two European Tour records in the process and thrilling spectators every bit as much as two other great South Africans, Bobby Locke and Gary Player, had done in years gone by.

Els's 54 hole 23 under par total of 193 after rounds of 64-65-64 beat, by one stroke, the previous best three round under par score set by

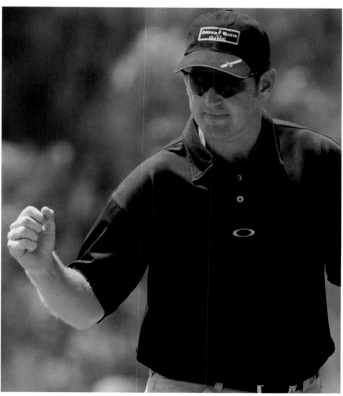

Greg Owen

the course

The delightful Lake Karrinyup layout played very differently from the previous year. Scoring was lower for three main reasons: the rough just off the fairway was much less thick, the greens were softer and the Fremantle Doctor, the prevailing south west wind, hardly blew all week.

Jean-Francois Remesy

Els's performances when winning the Nedbank Golf Challenge in December and throughout January and February represented one of the greatest in-form runs for years. Yet, incredibly in Perth, there was always the feeling he had another gear to move up to if the challenge had materialised from the chasing pack. He ambled round making 28 birdies and three eagles in four rounds without ever breaking sweat.

The bottom line was he knew he was playing better than anyone else on the week and, perhaps even more importantly, they knew it too. If Tiger Woods overwhelms his US PGA Tour colleagues when he tees up in the States, Els did exactly the same to the best of the Australasian, Asian PGA and European Tour players in this tri-sanctioned venture.

Although Els dominated proceedings, there were other fine performances notably from Craig Spence, the 27 year old former Australian Masters champion who showed a welcome return to form after a lean spell. With his wife caddieing, he fired a record equalling 63 in the third round which included eight birdies in a row, thus becoming only the tenth player to achieve such a feat in European Tour history. He also picked up an Omega watch for low round of the week.

Defending champion Goosen went to the turn in the second round in seven under par 29 but even then Els outdid him, carding that mark on the back nine on each of the first two days.

Niclas Fasth

Robert Allenby threatened after a second round 64 but faded and there was no expected challenge from Sergio Garcia who, after having finished third in 2002, missed the cut to the disappointment of many.

Craig Kamps, Stephen Leaney, Jean-Francois Remesy, David Smail, André Stolz, Goosen and Spence were involved in the battle for the minor places. Leaney and Stolz eventually shared second place but quite simply they were merely part of the chorus line in 'The Ernie Els Show'. At seven under par after just seven holes on day one, the writing was on the wall for all the others.

As Leaney said: "If someone had said at the start of the week that I would shoot 19 under par and lose by ten shots, I would have been pretty upset, but what can you do? I can't play any better than that."

Renton Laidlaw

final results

Lake Karrinyup Country Club • Perth • Australia
February 13 - 16 • 2003 • Par 72 • 7014 yards • 6411 metres

Pos.	Name		Rd1	Rd2	Rd3	Rd4	Total	Par	Prize Money Euro	£
1	Ernie ELS	SA	64	65	64	66	259	-29	251263.30	166660.00
2	Stephen LEANEY	Aus	68	67	68	66	269	-19	130946.10	86855.02
	André STOLZ	Aus	68	68	67	66	269	-19	130946.10	86855.02
4	Jean-Francois REMESY	Fr	68	67	67	69	271	-17	54998.71	36480.00
	David SMAIL	NZ	68	71	64	68	271	-17	54998.71	36480.00
	Justin ROSE	Eng	68	69	69	65	271	-17	54998.71	36480.00
	Robert ALLENBY	Aus	69	64	72	66	271	-17	54998.71	36480.00
	Retief GOOSEN	SA	72	65	66	68	271	-17	54998.71	36480.00
9	Niclas FASTH	Swe	74	65	66	67	272	-16	31961.97	21200.00
	Craig KAMPS	SA	71	67	64	70	272	-16	31961.97	21200.00
11	Michael LONG	NZ	71	66	68	69	274	-14	25252.97	16750.00
	Craig SPENCE	Aus	73	68	63	70	274	-14	25252.97	16750.00
	Ignacio GARRIDO	Sp	69	69	68	68	274	-14	25252.97	16750.00
	Nathan GREEN	Aus	73	68	64	69	274	-14	25252.97	16750.00
15	Craig PARRY	Aus	68	69	72	66	275	-13	21257.72	14100.00
	Robert KARLSSON	Swe	69	71	66	69	275	-13	21257.72	14100.00
	Chris DOWNES	Aus	67	73	68	67	275	-13	21257.72	14100.00
18	David HOWELL	Eng	71	69	67	69	276	-12	18430.90	12225.00
	Simon YATES	Scot	72	68	65	71	276	-12	18430.90	12225.00
	Paul MCGINLEY	Ire	67	71	68	70	276	-12	18430.90	12225.00
	Paul CASEY	Eng	71	70	67	68	276	-12	18430.90	12225.00
22	Trevor IMMELMAN	SA	73	68	66	70	277	-11	16584.04	11000.00
	Terry PRICE	Aus	66	71	69	71	277	-11	16584.04	11000.00
	Brett RUMFORD	Aus	67	73	67	70	277	-11	16584.04	11000.00
25	Charlie WI	Kor	72	71	66	69	278	-10	14322.58	9500.00
	Peter O'MALLEY	Aus	67	75	68	68	278	-10	14322.58	9500.00
	Bradley HUGHES	Aus	75	67	65	71	278	-10	14322.58	9500.00
	David LYNN	Eng	65	72	68	73	278	-10	14322.58	9500.00
	Greg OWEN	Eng	69	64	74	71	278	-10	14322.58	9500.00
	Scott GARDINER	Aus	74	69	65	70	278	-10	14322.58	9500.00
	Jamie DONALDSON	Wal	68	71	69	70	278	-10	14322.58	9500.00
32	Tony CAROLAN	Aus	72	70	68	69	279	-9	12061.12	8000.00
	Jarrod MOSELEY	Aus	70	71	68	70	279	-9	12061.12	8000.00
	Paul SHEEHAN	Aus	68	71	69	71	279	-9	12061.12	8000.00
35	Clay DEVERS	USA	70	72	66	72	280	-8	11005.77	7300.00
	Steen TINNING	Den	72	70	69	69	280	-8	11005.77	7300.00
	Henrik BJORNSTAD	Nor	69	71	66	74	280	-8	11005.77	7300.00
38	Ian WOOSNAM	Wal	67	71	75	68	281	-7	9347.37	6200.00
	Marcus NORGREN	Swe	70	71	70	70	281	-7	9347.37	6200.00
	David GILFORD	Eng	71	72	71	67	281	-7	9347.37	6200.00
	Arjun ATWAL	Ind	73	69	68	71	281	-7	9347.37	6200.00
	Nick O'HERN	Aus	74	68	72	67	281	-7	9347.37	6200.00
	Arjun SINGH	Ind	68	71	71	71	281	-7	9347.37	6200.00
	Alastair FORSYTH	Scot	73	69	70	69	281	-7	9347.37	6200.00
	Nick DOUGHERTY	Eng	73	66	74	68	281	-7	9347.37	6200.00
46	Nick FALDO	Eng	68	74	71	69	282	-6	6482.85	4300.00
	Raphaël JACQUELIN	Fr	68	74	67	73	282	-6	6482.85	4300.00
	Søren KJELDSEN	Den	73	67	71	71	282	-6	6482.85	4300.00
	Andrew BONHOMME	Aus	71	70	69	72	282	-6	6482.85	4300.00
	Marcus CAIN	Aus	69	72	67	74	282	-6	6482.85	4300.00
	Jyoti RANDHAWA	Ind	72	69	73	68	282	-6	6482.85	4300.00
	Jonathan LOMAS	Eng	73	70	70	69	282	-6	6482.85	4300.00
	Gary EVANS	Eng	70	71	71	70	282	-6	6482.85	4300.00
	Raymond RUSSELL	Scot	70	70	71	71	282	-6	6482.85	4300.00
	Adam CRAWFORD	Aus	71	72	70	69	282	-6	6482.85	4300.00
	Kevin NA	Kor	71	72	69	70	282	-6	6482.85	4300.00
57	Santiago LUNA	Sp	70	69	72	72	283	-5	4221.39	2800.00
	Peter FOWLER	Aus	70	73	68	72	283	-5	4221.39	2800.00
	Warren BENNETT	Eng	71	68	73	71	283	-5	4221.39	2800.00
	Brian DAVIS	Eng	71	70	70	72	283	-5	4221.39	2800.00
	Thomas BJÖRN	Den	68	74	67	74	283	-5	4221.39	2800.00
	James KINGSTON	SA	72	69	69	73	283	-5	4221.39	2800.00
	Stephen SCAHILL	NZ	70	73	71	69	283	-5	4221.39	2800.00
64	Richard GREEN	Aus	71	69	72	72	284	-4	3467.57	2300.00
	Grant DODD	Aus	71	71	70	72	284	-4	3467.57	2300.00
	Patrik SJÖLAND	Swe	75	67	72	70	284	-4	3467.57	2300.00
67	Andrew PITTS	USA	74	69	70	72	285	-3	2951.20	1957.50
	Darren FICHARDT	SA	70	72	68	75	285	-3	2951.20	1957.50
	Ian POULTER	Eng	74	69	70	72	285	-3	2951.20	1957.50
	John BICKERTON	Eng	70	68	75	72	285	-3	2951.20	1957.50
71	Barry LANE	Eng	74	68	72	72	286	-2	2258.00	1497.71
	Andrew TSCHUDIN	Aus	70	72	70	74	286	-2	2258.00	1497.71
	Eddie LEE	NZ	73	70	73	70	286	-2	2258.00	1497.71
74	Matthew ECOB	Aus	72	71	71	73	287	-1	2250.50	1492.73
	Edward LOAR	USA	72	68	76	71	287	-1	2250.50	1492.73
76	Mardan MAMAT	Sing	69	72	73	74	288	0	2246.00	1489.75
77	Ted OH	Kor	71	72	74	72	289	1	2243.00	1487.76
78	Mark ALLEN	Aus	73	69	72	76	290	2	2238.50	1484.77
	David GLEESON	Aus	71	72	72	75	290	2	2238.50	1484.77
	Michael SIM (AM)	Aus	72	71	71	76	290	2		
81	Anthony WALL	Eng	72	71	71	77	291	3	2234.00	1481.79
	Gary SIMPSON	Aus	72	70	76	73	291	3	2234.00	1481.79

Arjun Atwal

tale of the tiger

1	Arjun ATWAL Ind	260	-24
2	Retief GOOSEN SA	264	-20
	Brad KENNEDY Aus	264	-20
4	Dean ROBERTSON Scot	266	-18
5	Thammanoon SRIROT Thai	267	-17
6	Daniel CHOPRA Swe	268	-16
7	Ted OH Kor	269	-15
8	Patrik SJÖLAND Swe	270	-14
9	Simon DYSON Eng	271	-13
	Simon KHAN Eng	271	-13
	Wen-Chong LIANG PRC	271	-13
	Gerald ROSALES Phil	271	-13
	Wei-Tze YEH Tpe	271	-13

Revered throughout Asia, the tiger is renowned for its strength, courage and killer instinct. In winning the Carlsberg Malaysian Open, Arjun Atwal displayed all these attributes and more as he prowled The Mines Resort & Golf Club in pursuit of his second European Tour title.

There was no escaping the tiger influence at The Mines. Two Bengal White Tigers greeted visitors to the course from their enclosure within the clubhouse while portraits of their golfing namesake, Mr Woods, adorned the walls. Tigers were everywhere and therefore it was fitting that, in Atwal, the only fully exempt Indian golfer on The European Tour, the spirit of the Indian tigers should come to life.

Twelve months previously, the 29 year old from Calcutta had made history when he became the first Indian winner on The European Tour International Schedule with his victory in the Caltex Singapore Masters.

His elevation to a new level was confirmed in Malaysia with a commanding wire-to-wire victory in the event jointly sanctioned by The European Tour and the Asian PGA Tour, his triumph all the more impressive considering Retief Goosen, the two-time Volvo Order of Merit winner, spent the week breathing down his neck.

Atwal demonstrated his prowess with a stunning opening round of nine under par 62, a score which would have beaten the course record by a stroke but for the preferred lies in operation. Two matching halves of 31 placed him on top of the leaderboard where he was joined later in the day by Sweden's Fredrik Andersson.

Goosen emerged as Atwal's main threat on the second day, the South African roaring into life with an outward half of seven under par 29, to take pole position on the day. A back nine of 35 earned Goosen the clubhouse lead on 12 under par 130 before play was suspended as a ferocious tropical thunderstorm hit the course.

Atwal was not fazed. Shaking off the disruption, he returned on Saturday morning to complete a second round 65 to move to 15 under par 127, the lowest 36 hole score of the season, and three strokes clear of Goosen. That had been increased to four by the end of the day before another tropical storm brought a premature end to his third round.

All this was simply the prelude to an enthralling final day. Because of the storm delays the leaders were required to play 28 holes in total, a stiff examination in the stifling heat and humidity. Goosen closed the gap to two shots within minutes of resuming his third

Fredrik Andersson

the course

Designed by Robert Trent Jones Jnr, The Mines Resort & Golf Club is a unique transformation of the world's largest open cast tin mine into a breathtaking golf course, offering a spectacular lake and many typical Trent Jones features.

Paul McGinley

round as Atwal dropped his first, and what was to prove his only, shots of the week when he double bogeyed the ninth.

However, when it looked like Atwal might fall prey to a Goosen charge, the Indian golfer summoned up a courageous shot, finding the green from the tee on the short par four 13th to set up an eagle two and restore his four stroke cushion. Back came Goosen with a brace of birdies to finish his third round before starting his final round with a birdie on the first. Suddenly, the gap was down to one.

Atwal, though, was not to be denied, countering every Goosen attack with a thrust of his own, always keeping his nose in front. As the enthralling contest moved into the home stretch the 13th hole proved decisive when Goosen, still only one behind, pushed his two iron tee shot into the water on his way to a bogey five. Atwal pounced on the slip, converting a birdie on the next hole to pull three strokes clear and put the outcome largely beyond doubt. A chip in for a birdie on the last, a shot that was greeted by thunderous applause from the stands and a clap from the heavens above, was merely the icing on the cake.

Mathias Grönberg

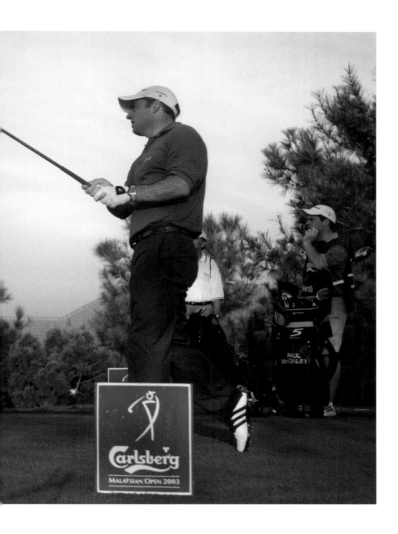

final results

The Mines Resort & Golf Club · Kuala Lumpur · Malaysia
February 20 - 23 · 2003 · Par 71 · 6785 yards · 6204 metres

Pos.	Name		Rd1	Rd2	Rd3	Rd4	Total	Par	Prize Money Euro	£
1	Arjun ATWAL	Ind	62	65	67	66	260	-24	169765.50	113834.20
2	Retief GOOSEN	SA	66	64	66	68	264	-20	88471.05	59323.19
	Brad KENNEDY	Aus	68	66	66	64	264	-20	88471.05	59323.19
4	Dean ROBERTSON	Scot	66	70	64	66	266	-18	50930.58	34150.88
5	Thammanoon SRIROT	Thai	63	69	70	65	267	-17	43189.13	28959.95
6	Daniel CHOPRA	Swe	65	68	66	69	268	-16	35651.41	23905.62
7	Ted OH	Kor	64	67	70	68	269	-15	30558.35	20490.53
8	Patrik SJÖLAND	Swe	68	66	70	66	270	-14	25465.29	17075.44
9	Simon KHAN	Eng	69	67	67	68	271	-13	19170.27	12854.39
	Simon DYSON	Eng	65	70	68	68	271	-13	19170.27	12854.39
	Wei-Tze YEH	Tpe	65	69	72	65	271	-13	19170.27	12854.39
	Gerald ROSALES	Phil	72	68	66	65	271	-13	19170.27	12854.39
	Wen-Chong LIANG	PRC	68	66	66	71	271	-13	19170.27	12854.39
14	Padraig HARRINGTON	Ire	66	66	67	73	272	-12	14973.59	10040.36
	Chawalit PLAPHOL	Thai	70	71	64	67	272	-12	14973.59	10040.36
	Boonchu RUANGKIT	Thai	69	70	69	64	272	-12	14973.59	10040.36
17	Andrew MARSHALL	Eng	71	66	66	70	273	-11	12936.37	8674.33
	Emanuele CANONICA	It	67	66	68	72	273	-11	12936.37	8674.33
	Paul MCGINLEY	Ire	67	69	70	67	273	-11	12936.37	8674.33
	Martin MARITZ	SA	70	69	69	65	273	-11	12936.37	8674.33
21	Arjun SINGH	Ind	67	69	70	68	274	-10	11204.73	7513.20
	Mathias GRÖNBERG	Swe	72	64	71	67	274	-10	11204.73	7513.20
	Fredrik ANDERSSON	Swe	62	69	71	72	274	-10	11204.73	7513.20
	Terry PRICE	Aus	70	70	68	66	274	-10	11204.73	7513.20
	Thongchai JAIDEE	Thai	68	68	70	68	274	-10	11204.73	7513.20
26	Wook-Soon KANG	Kor	66	72	70	67	275	-9	9982.40	6693.57
	Jan-Are LARSEN	Nor	73	65	69	68	275	-9	9982.40	6693.57
	Gary RUSNAK	USA	66	69	70	70	275	-9	9982.40	6693.57
29	Mike CUNNING	USA	70	69	70	67	276	-8	8912.85	5976.41
	Zaw MOE	Myan	70	69	67	70	276	-8	8912.85	5976.41
	Pablo DEL OLMO	Mex	70	67	74	65	276	-8	8912.85	5976.41
	Charl SCHWARTZEL	SA	71	69	67	69	276	-8	8912.85	5976.41
33	Søren KJELDSEN	Den	70	68	71	68	277	-7	7450.42	4995.79
	Thaworn WIRATCHANT	Thai	68	69	73	67	277	-7	7450.42	4995.79
	Prayad MARKSAENG	Thai	68	66	70	73	277	-7	7450.42	4995.79
	Kim FELTON	Aus	74	67	68	68	277	-7	7450.42	4995.79
	Alastair FORSYTH	Scot	71	70	68	68	277	-7	7450.42	4995.79
	David GLEESON	Aus	73	68	71	65	277	-7	7450.42	4995.79
	Mao-Chang SUNG	Tpe	69	70	70	68	277	-7	7450.42	4995.79
40	Kyi Hla HAN	Myan	70	68	71	69	278	-6	5907.95	3961.50
	Mardan MAMAT	Sing	69	70	68	71	278	-6	5907.95	3961.50
	Chris WILLIAMS	Eng	68	69	70	71	278	-6	5907.95	3961.50
	Jean-François LUCQUIN	Fr	70	70	69	69	278	-6	5907.95	3961.50
	Simon YATES	Scot	66	73	68	71	278	-6	5907.95	3961.50
	Anthony KANG	Kor	67	68	73	70	278	-6	5907.95	3961.50
	Stephen SCAHILL	NZ	68	68	71	71	278	-6	5907.95	3961.50
	Marcus FRASER	Aus	67	71	70	70	278	-6	5907.95	3961.50
48	Harmeet KAHLON	Ind	66	75	72	66	279	-5	4889.34	3278.49
	Eddie LEE	NZ	73	68	69	69	279	-5	4889.34	3278.49
50	Ian WOOSNAM	Wal	70	68	74	68	280	-4	3972.59	2663.77
	Andrew PITTS	USA	68	72	70	70	280	-4	3972.59	2663.77
	Brian DAVIS	Eng	73	68	70	69	280	-4	3972.59	2663.77
	Rick GIBSON	Can	69	68	70	73	280	-4	3972.59	2663.77
	Joon CHUNG	Kor	67	69	73	71	280	-4	3972.59	2663.77
	Charlie WI	Kor	72	67	71	70	280	-4	3972.59	2663.77
	Des TERBLANCHE	SA	72	69	71	68	280	-4	3972.59	2663.77
57	Per NYMAN	Swe	73	67	70	71	281	-3	3055.84	2049.05
	Rafael PONCE	Ecu	75	66	72	68	281	-3	3055.84	2049.05
	Jason KNUTZON	USA	70	68	67	76	281	-3	3055.84	2049.05
60	Robert-Jan DERKSEN	NL	69	71	70	72	282	-2	2597.46	1741.70
	Alessandro TADINI	It	65	75	74	68	282	-2	2597.46	1741.70
	V ARUMUGAM	Mal	72	69	70	71	282	-2	2597.46	1741.70
	Gerry NORQUIST	USA	71	69	71	71	282	-2	2597.46	1741.70
	Perlasamy GUNASAGARAN	Mal	66	70	73	73	282	-2	2597.46	1741.70
	Tobias DIER	Ger	73	66	75	68	282	-2	2597.46	1741.70
66	Maarten LAFEBER	NL	73	67	71	72	283	-1	2088.15	1400.19
	Hendrik BUHRMANN	SA	72	69	67	75	283	-1	2088.15	1400.19
	Jorge BERENDT	Arg	69	72	70	72	283	-1	2088.15	1400.19
	Lee S JAMES	Eng	70	69	69	75	283	-1	2088.15	1400.19
70	Simon WAKEFIELD	Eng	70	71	75	68	284	0	1694.64	1136.32
	Sushi ISHIGAKI	Jpn	71	68	73	72	284	0	1694.64	1136.32
72	S MURTHY	Mal	67	69	77	72	285	1	1522.00	1020.56
	Ben MASON	Eng	68	73	71	73	285	1	1522.00	1020.56
	Amandeep JOHL	Ind	68	68	72	77	285	1	1522.00	1020.56
	S SIVACHANDRAN (AM)	Mal	71	69	71	74	285	1		
76	Knud STORGAARD	Den	69	72	73	72	286	2	1513.00	1014.52
	Yu-Shu HSIEH	Tpe	68	73	72	73	286	2	1513.00	1014.52
	Stephen A LINDSKOG	Swe	67	73	73	73	286	2	1513.00	1014.52
79	Mark JAMES	Eng	72	69	72	74	287	3	1504.00	1008.49
	Mohd SHAABAN HUSSIN	Mal	68	72	75	72	287	3	1504.00	1008.49
	Angleo QUE	Phil	72	69	71	75	287	3	1504.00	1008.49
82	Mads VIBE-HASTRUP	Den	73	67	71	80	291	7	1498.00	1004.47
83	David DIXON	Eng	71	70	79	76	296	12	1495.00	1002.45
84	Ted Purdy	USA	69	72	79	W/D	220	7		

The fascinating duel between Atwal and Goosen tended to overshadow other affairs but Brad Kennedy, of Australia, secured his best finish on The European Tour International Schedule when he birdied the last two holes to tie Goosen in second place. This was a particularly outstanding effort by the European Challenge Tour Member who was delighted with his finish.

There was also Dean Robertson. Four years earlier the 32 year old represented Scotland in The World Cup at The Mines Resort & Golf Club. It should have been the start of a glorious spell in his career but it turned out to be the beginning of a nightmare. A mystery virus laid him low for four months and although he returned, he then went on to miss most of the 2002 season with clinical depression. However, a return to The Mines provided a fillip for the 1999 Italian Open champion and he was rewarded with fourth place.

But the week was all about Atwal. As he pounced on his second title it was evident the tiger had earned his stripes.

Rod Williams

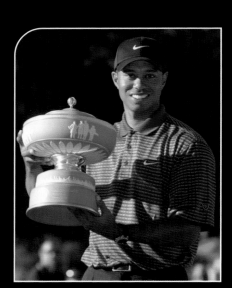

Tiger Woods

california dreaming

Champion – Tiger WOODS USA

Runner-Up – David TOMS USA

Third – Adam SCOTT Aus

Fourth – Peter LONARD Aus

There is nothing like a golf tournament for ending a drought. It does not rain much in southern California and so the cats and dogs variety that descended on La Costa Resort & Spa early in the week of the World Golf Championships - Accenture Match Play represented a sizeable percentage of the area's annual precipitation.

Not that that was a bad thing. Following the upgrading of the course, that included adding 300 yards and thickening the rough, the test offered to the elite 64 man field was strengthened further by the conditions. "There is more of an emphasis on driving the ball long and straight now," said Darren Clarke.

While upsets had dominated proceedings in this event in the past, more themes were allowed to evolve this time. One of them was the performance of Clarke himself, who went close to replicating his stunning success at the Carlsbad course in 2000. Then, the Irishman had beaten Tiger Woods in the final, and while the World Number One made his way towards a possible re-match, Clarke was not doing too badly either.

Encouraged by the changes he had made to both his technique and equipment, Clarke defeated Tim Clark 4 and 3, Davis Love III 7 and 6 and Jim Furyk by one hole on his way to the quarter-finals where

Adam Scott

he was three up on Peter Lonard after eight holes before the Australian mounted a gritty comeback to win at the last. "I can't complain," said Clarke. "It's been a good week but I gave Pete a few chances and he took them."

For the first time the final was between two players seeded in the top ten, Number One Woods and Number Six David Toms, but it was not as if there were no upsets. Ernie Els, coming off a run of four victories in five tournaments in 2003, was one up coming to the last in the first round against New Zealand's Phil Tataurangi but contrived to lose at the 20th. It was also the day Justin Rose defeated 2001 Open Golf Champion David Duval at the 20th and Mike Weir took until the 26th to shake off Loren Roberts, the longest match in the Championship's five year history.

Sergio Garcia also departed on the opening day, despite being three up after 12 holes against defending champion Kevin Sutherland. The 38 year old American had showed considerable grit and determination 12 months ago when he won from the position of 62nd seed and exhibited similar traits against the Spaniard, winning five holes in row to triumph 2 and 1.

A second round victory over Rose extended Sutherland's winning streak in the event to eight matches, but it went no further, Adam Scott ending the run in the third round by 2 and 1.

The 22 year old Australian, who won twice on The European Tour in 2002, showed he was comfortable on the world stage when he gave Woods his hardest match of the week in the semi-finals. Scott has a body shape and a swing that is eerily reminiscent of the World Number One in every department, bar the one on this occasion of holing out putts from four to six feet.

David Toms

the course

The La Costa Resort & Spa was lengthened by some 300 yards and exhibited much thicker rough than in 2002. But the biggest change was the switching of the two nines so that more of the finishing holes were around the clubhouse. It meant the famous par three seventh now became the pivotal 16th.

Peter Lonard

Scott missed four such putts, including one at the 19th, to end the match after an epic tussle. "Adam played beautifully and it was sad it ended like that," said Woods. Scott had led in the early stages and proved resilient when Woods moved one up with three to play. Tiger's tee shot at the short 16th finished a mere 15 inches from the pin but Scott bravely holed from 12 feet for the half before birdieing the 18th to force extra time.

"I didn't feel any nerves after I walked off the first tee and felt I lifted my game for the occasion," said Scott. He went on to face fellow European Tour Member and Australian Lonard in the 18 hole Consolation Match and took third place by one hole after an enthralling contest.

But, once again, a tournament revolved around Woods. He had made a habit of winning WGC events, six in total since 1999, but this was the first time he had claimed the WGC – Accenture Match Play. Given his imperious form, however, he would have won any tournament, anywhere, with any format. In the first five rounds, he had only one bogey, at least as officially recorded.

Though only his third tournament after returning from knee surgery, Woods was magnificent with his putting and, until the final afternoon at least, unerringly precise. Like Clarke, he equalled the biggest winning margin for the tournament with a 7 and 6 win over Stephen Leaney in the third round, then beat Scott Hoch 5 and 4 in the quarter-finals where he was seven under par for 13 holes and looking at another birdie putt when the match was conceded.

The final looked to be progressing as straightforwardly when, after having been four up at lunch, Woods birdied the 19th to move five in front. But Toms displayed plenty of fighting spirit in being the leading American points scorer in The 34th Ryder Cup Matches at The De Vere Belfry and showed similar qualities in reaching the final, despite a night in hospital with food poisoning after the second round.

"I wasn't going to quit, that's not my nature," he said. "We were on national television and I didn't want to embarrass myself by having it end early. It would have been easy to give in but I dug deep and having a chance to win on the back nine kept me going."

In the afternoon, Toms birdied the second, holing from outside Woods, and then the third. Woods then dropped shots at the eighth and ninth and by birdieing the 15th, Toms was only one down. But a poor drive at the 17th proved his eventual downfall.

"This is the hardest of the World Golf Championships to win," said Woods after completing another dream as the winner of all four which sit nicely alongside his Majors 'Grand Slam.' "You have to win

Darren Clarke

six matches to do it. Playing six rounds is physically gruelling but it is even more gruelling mentally because of the ebb and flow of each match. If we had to do this every week, no professional's career would last more than ten years!"

Andy Farrell

final results

La Costa Resort & Spa • Carlsbad • California • USA
February 26 - March 2 • 2003 • Par 72 • 7247 yards • 6628 metres

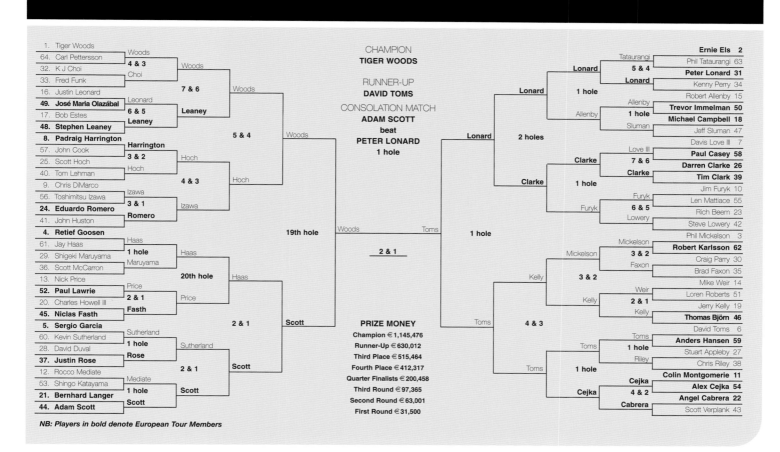

CHAMPION
TIGER WOODS

RUNNER-UP
DAVID TOMS

CONSOLATION MATCH
ADAM SCOTT
beat
PETER LONARD
1 hole

PRIZE MONEY
Champion € 1,145,476
Runner-Up € 630,012
Third Place € 515,464
Fourth Place € 412,317
Quarter Finalists € 200,458
Third Round € 97,365
Second Round € 63,001
First Round € 31,500

NB: Players in bold denote European Tour Members

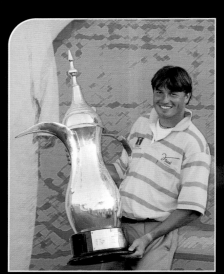

Robert-Jan Derksen

dutch courage

1	Robert-Jan DERKSEN NL	271	-17
2	Ernie ELS SA	272	-16
3	Alastair FORSYTH Scot	274	-14
	David LYNN Eng	274	-14
	Ian WOOSNAM Wal	274	-14
6	Thomas BJÖRN Den	275	-13
	Mikko ILONEN Fin	275	-13
	Kevin NA Kor	275	-13
9	Thongchai JAIDEE Thai	276	-12
	Phillip PRICE Wal	276	-12

Alastair Forsyth

t was to have been the big showdown between Ernie Els and Tiger Woods. Though Woods had had knee surgery in the off-season, he had just returned to the fray in the United States with two wins from three starts. As for Els, he had already bagged four titles worldwide in 2003. All over Dubai, there were striking posters of the world's top two golfers, while the cosmopolitan population of the Gulf State talked of little else.

Woods's last-minute decision not to travel put a momentary damper on things, but there was a truly extraordinary sequel as the unsung Robert-Jan Derksen played to a level which the American would have been happy to call his own. The Dutchman beat Els by a shot.

While Els had been winning tournaments over the first couple of months of the season, Derksen, 29, who was languishing at 593 on the Official World Golf Ranking when he arrived in Dubai, had been chasing around the globe looking for starts.

In January, when he learned he was first reserve for the dunhill championship in Johannesburg, he flew to South Africa but failed to get a spot in the tournament. Precisely the same applied with the Caltex Masters, presented by Carlsberg, Singapore 2003. However, instead of dwelling on his bad luck, he viewed the experiences in a

positive light. Because he had been practising at the venues, he left each time with the feeling he had benefited from another week's golf under his belt.

As January turned into February, he was given an invitation to the Heineken Classic in Melbourne, only to fail to make the cut, while, when it came to his only other outing of the year, the Carlsberg Malaysian Open, he finished in a tie for 60th.

The idea of winning the Dubai Desert Classic, one of the premier titles on The European Tour International Schedule, first entered Derksen's head on the Saturday night. "I was three behind but I thought that if I played well, I would have a chance," he said. Scott Cranfield, his new coach, confirmed as much.

On the Sunday, the winning feeling stirred again when he struck lucky with a 25 yard eagle putt at the 13th. It took him to 16 under the card. Though he did not realise at the time, the eagle was all the more of a turning point due to the fact that Els was having a simultaneous setback at the 12th. The South African's second shot took off from the first cut of rough, his flier leading to a double bogey six and a slide from 16 to 14 under par.

Thomas Björn

the course

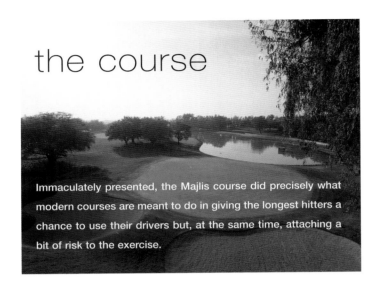

Immaculately presented, the Majlis course did precisely what modern courses are meant to do in giving the longest hitters a chance to use their drivers but, at the same time, attaching a bit of risk to the exercise.

His next stop was short of the water before he tackled his third in front of an audience who simply did not know what to expect. If ever the pressure was going to catch up with the Dutchman, it would surely be now. It never did.

He pitched to four feet and gave himself a talking to before tackling the putt that would change his career. He was enjoying the pressure but, at the same time, he knew he would be even happier when it was over. As such, he had to make sure that he did not rush. "I told myself, 'You've been practising for this moment for ten years so you have to make the most of it.'"

He holed and, try as he might, he could not hold back the tears of joy.

Derksen stuck to his decision not to look at leaderboards though, from the way he played, there was the feeling that he knew, instinctively, what he had to do. Still 16 under leaving the 16th green, he played conservatively at the dog-leg 359 yard 17th, hitting a leisurely iron up the middle instead of making any attempt to cut the corner.

Then, at the 18th, he produced three smart shots instead of trying for the green in two. He explained later, the fact that his drive was a little too far to the right had been the best possible thing. "It stopped me from even thinking of going for the carry," he said.

Out on the course, Els, who had hit back with birdies at the 13th and 15th, knew that he had to birdie one of the last two holes to force a play-off, and both if he were to win outright. The latter seemed an entirely possible scenario. After all, he had driven the 17th the day before and, although he had notched a couple of bogeys at the 18th, it was purely because he had been overly aggressive in looking for eagles rather than birdies.

As it transpired, he pulled his tee shot into the left rough at the 17th en route to a two-putt par. Then, though he hit two grand shots at the last, his ball scampered through the putting surface

Phillip Price

Miguel Angel Jiménez

and left him with a demanding chip back towards the water. To his chagrin, he miscued and left himself with a 25 footer for birdie he failed to make.

When Derksen, whose 271 total was 17 under par, said that the result was the biggest shock of his life, he was not exaggerating. Up until that Sunday afternoon, when he pocketed a cheque for 291,994 euro (£200,000), he had never won anything bigger than the 16,261 euro (£10,384) he collected for finishing in a share of 16th place at the Compass Group English Open in 2002.

You had to admire what he did in the wake of his success. Derksen had long ago decided what he would do in the event of a win. Having seen so many new winners throw themselves into the next event on the schedule and barely pause for breath, he had vowed that he would take time off to enjoy any success with his family back home in The Netherlands.

He did just that and, if ever there were a victory worth savouring, it was this one.

Lewine Mair

final results

Emirates Golf Club • Dubai
March 6 - 9 • 2003 • Par 72 • 7201 yards • 6586 metres

Pos.	Name		Rd1	Rd2	Rd3	Rd4	Total	Par	Prize Money Euro	£
1	Robert-Jan DERKSEN	NL	67	72	67	65	271	-17	291994.00	200000.00
2	Ernie ELS	SA	66	68	69	69	272	-16	194657.80	133330.00
3	Ian WOOSNAM	Wal	69	66	70	69	274	-14	90518.14	62000.00
	David LYNN	Eng	68	66	69	71	274	-14	90518.14	62000.00
	Alastair FORSYTH	Scot	65	69	69	71	274	-14	90518.14	62000.00
6	Thomas BJÖRN	Den	69	66	71	69	275	-13	52558.92	36000.00
	Mikko ILONEN	Fin	67	67	73	68	275	-13	52558.92	36000.00
	Kevin NA	Kor	68	69	68	70	275	-13	52558.92	36000.00
9	Phillip PRICE	Wal	71	67	68	70	276	-12	37141.64	25440.00
	Thongchai JAIDEE	Thai	70	68	67	71	276	-12	37141.64	25440.00
11	Brian DAVIS	Eng	68	72	70	67	277	-11	31184.96	21360.00
	Darren CLARKE	N.Ire	70	69	72	66	277	-11	31184.96	21360.00
13	Mark FOSTER	Eng	73	66	68	72	279	-9	26921.85	18440.00
	Jyoti RANDHAWA	Ind	70	72	69	68	279	-9	26921.85	18440.00
	Jamie DONALDSON	Wal	67	71	72	69	279	-9	26921.85	18440.00
16	Søren KJELDSEN	Den	71	72	71	66	280	-8	23169.72	15870.00
	Gary ORR	Scot	71	69	68	72	280	-8	23169.72	15870.00
	David PARK	Wal	71	69	72	68	280	-8	23169.72	15870.00
	Fredrik ANDERSSON	Swe	68	73	72	67	280	-8	23169.72	15870.00
20	Peter LAWRIE	Ire	72	69	67	73	281	-7	19030.71	13035.00
	Richard BLAND	Eng	72	67	70	72	281	-7	19030.71	13035.00
	Paul LAWRIE	Scot	70	72	69	70	281	-7	19030.71	13035.00
	Bradley DREDGE	Wal	73	69	69	70	281	-7	19030.71	13035.00
	John BICKERTON	Eng	69	71	70	71	281	-7	19030.71	13035.00
	David CARTER	Eng	70	73	70	68	281	-7	19030.71	13035.00
	Mikael LUNDBERG	Swe	69	69	72	71	281	-7	19030.71	13035.00
	Nick DOUGHERTY	Eng	67	69	73	72	281	-7	19030.71	13035.00
28	Steve WEBSTER	Eng	71	71	70	70	282	-6	14383.62	9852.00
	Trevor IMMELMAN	SA	71	68	73	70	282	-6	14383.62	9852.00
	Søren HANSEN	Den	72	71	71	68	282	-6	14383.62	9852.00
	Charlie WI	Kor	70	72	70	70	282	-6	14383.62	9852.00
	Simon YATES	Scot	69	72	68	73	282	-6	14383.62	9852.00
	Ignacio GARRIDO	Sp	72	69	68	73	282	-6	14383.62	9852.00
	Rolf MUNTZ	NL	73	67	74	68	282	-6	14383.62	9852.00
	Greg OWEN	Eng	67	69	74	72	282	-6	14383.62	9852.00
	Tobias DIER	Ger	69	69	76	68	282	-6	14383.62	9852.00
	Shingo KATAYAMA	Jpn	70	68	75	69	282	-6	14383.62	9852.00
38	Maarten LAFEBER	NL	71	69	73	70	283	-5	11387.77	7800.00
	Henrik BJORNSTAD	Nor	70	72	71	70	283	-5	11387.77	7800.00
	Miguel Angel JIMÉNEZ	Sp	68	69	71	75	283	-5	11387.77	7800.00
	Lee WESTWOOD	Eng	70	73	69	71	283	-5	11387.77	7800.00
	Stephen GALLACHER	Scot	69	70	71	73	283	-5	11387.77	7800.00
43	Mark ROE	Eng	71	71	71	71	284	-4	9811.00	6720.00
	Jarrod MOSELEY	Aus	74	68	74	68	284	-4	9811.00	6720.00
	Miles TUNNICLIFF	Eng	70	72	74	68	284	-4	9811.00	6720.00
	Henrik NYSTROM	Swe	70	70	70	74	284	-4	9811.00	6720.00
47	Padraig HARRINGTON	Ire	73	70	71	71	285	-3	8234.23	5640.00
	Paul BROADHURST	Eng	71	70	74	70	285	-3	8234.23	5640.00
	Robert KARLSSON	Swe	76	67	72	70	285	-3	8234.23	5640.00
	Paul MCGINLEY	Ire	72	69	77	67	285	-3	8234.23	5640.00
	Jarmo SANDELIN	Swe	73	69	70	73	285	-3	8234.23	5640.00
52	Peter FOWLER	Aus	72	71	71	72	286	-2	6022.38	4125.00
	Mark O'MEARA	USA	68	72	75	71	286	-2	6022.38	4125.00
	Richard GREEN	Aus	72	70	73	71	286	-2	6022.38	4125.00
	Euan LITTLE	Scot	71	71	73	71	286	-2	6022.38	4125.00
	Paul EALES	Eng	73	69	71	73	286	-2	6022.38	4125.00
	Jonathan LOMAS	Eng	69	70	74	73	286	-2	6022.38	4125.00
	Ian GARBUTT	Eng	73	63	73	77	286	-2	6022.38	4125.00
	Patrik SJÖLAND	Swe	68	74	73	71	286	-2	6022.38	4125.00
60	Mårten OLANDER	Swe	70	71	71	75	287	-1	4730.30	3240.00
	Shaun P WEBSTER	Eng	71	72	72	72	287	-1	4730.30	3240.00
	Simon WAKEFIELD	Eng	71	70	73	73	287	-1	4730.30	3240.00
63	Darren FICHARDT	SA	74	69	73	72	288	0	3854.32	2640.00
	Carlos RODILES	Sp	72	71	71	74	288	0	3854.32	2640.00
	Peter BAKER	Eng	71	72	76	69	288	0	3854.32	2640.00
	Raul BALLESTEROS	Sp	70	72	75	71	288	0	3854.32	2640.00
	Roger WESSELS	SA	68	72	73	75	288	0	3854.32	2640.00
	Francois DELAMONTAGNE	Fr	75	68	72	73	288	0	3854.32	2640.00
	Jamie ELSON	Eng	72	68	74	74	288	0	3854.32	2640.00
70	Nicolas VANHOOTEGEM	Bel	69	74	76	70	289	1	3197.33	2190.00
71	Henrik STENSON	Swe	70	72	72	76	290	2	2626.50	1799.01
	Ian POULTER	Eng	68	70	78	74	290	2	2626.50	1799.01
73	Anders FORSBRAND	Swe	73	70	75	73	291	3	2616.00	1791.82
	Barry LANE	Eng	74	67	78	72	291	3	2616.00	1791.82
	Raphaël JACQUELIN	Fr	69	74	78	70	291	3	2616.00	1791.82
	Sven STRÜVER	Ger	67	69	78	77	291	3	2616.00	1791.82
	Christian CÉVAËR	Fr	72	71	72	76	291	3	2616.00	1791.82
78	Klas ERIKSSON	Swe	70	71	79	73	293	5	2605.50	1784.63
	Mark MCNULTY	Zim	72	70	76	75	293	5	2605.50	1784.63
80	Warren BENNETT	Eng	69	74	79	75	297	9	2601.00	1781.54

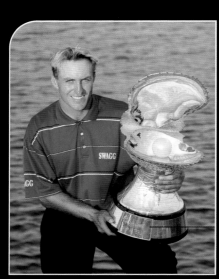

Darren Fichardt

wedded bliss

1	Darren FICHARDT SA	275	-13
2	James KINGSTON SA	275	-13
3	Paul McGINLEY Ire	277	-11
4	David HOWELL Eng	278	-10
5	Peter FOWLER Aus	281	-7
	Peter HEDBLOM Swe	281	-7
7	David PARK Wal	282	-6
8	John BICKERTON Eng	283	-5
	Gary EVANS Eng	283	-5
	Richard GREEN Aus	283	-5

t is a common belief amongst golfers of all levels of competence, that the difference between winning and losing has less to do with technique and technology than it has with the six inches of grey matter between the ears.

Take a casual stroll along any range on The European Tour and you will chance upon countless perfectly grooved swings and watch in wonder as the little white spheroid speeds skywards in a perfect arc.

Strange then, that when some of those swings are put to the ultimate test on the course, wires tend to become crossed and flaws begin to appear. From perfect to imperfect in those few short strides from the range to the first tee. Golf offers constant visual proof that, no matter how pretty it looks, sometimes the results can be pretty ugly.

Darren Fichardt had no real concept of the relevance of the mental game when he turned professional in 1994. The young man from Pretoria in South Africa had knocked off a couple of Northern

James Kingston

Tranvsaal titles in a decent amateur career before plying his trade on the Sunshine Tour in his native country and making a decent fist.

However he had ambitions beyond South Africa. The European Tour beckoned on the horizon but getting there was a different matter. Then, as fate would have it, Fichardt met and fell in love with Natasha, who was to become his girlfriend, his caddie and, in the first week of a new century, his wife.

More importantly, Natasha Fichardt was to become the missing link in her husband's conversion from good professional to maiden European Tour winner in the 2001 Sao Paulo Brazil Open, and finally to outstanding champion in the sixth Qatar Masters.

Although he did not realise it when they met, Natasha was a trained sports psychologist and had an Honours Degree in the subject. She was also to play an influential role in his career from the moment they struck up their initial friendship to, crucially, his decision to play in Qatar during a period when War in the Gulf was imminent.

David Park

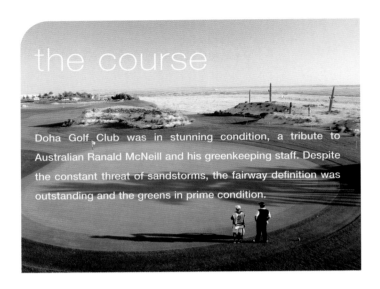

the course

Doha Golf Club was in stunning condition, a tribute to Australian Ranald McNeill and his greenkeeping staff. Despite the constant threat of sandstorms, the fairway definition was outstanding and the greens in prime condition.

It is said that behind every good man is a good woman, and Natasha lent credence to the theory. Her husband was prevaricating about entering the event so she informed him bluntly he was being "a wimp" and to pack his bags and clubs and get on the flight to Qatar.

Fichardt related the tale, a little sheepishly, in the euphoric aftermath of a superb victory, edging out his fellow South African James Kingston with a birdie four at the first hole of a sudden-death play-off. He added tellingly: "I'm really pleased we came now!"

Clearly marrying a psychologist had had the desired effect on a golfer, who although extremely proficient, could be betrayed by mind games. He recounted: "I had led a lot of tournaments in South Africa but had difficulty in finishing them off. It was just down to weakness of the mind.

"Getting married to Natasha was the best thing I ever did. As well as being my caddie for several years, she has been my 'mind doctor'. We work on things together, listening to tapes and so on. I had never thought about working on the mind. She introduced me to that element of the game.

"We work on how to approach a bad shot and go over a round shot by shot. It takes a bit of training and it can't be done overnight but now when I hit a bad shot I just try to calm down and think positive. The best bit of advice she ever gave me was to stay in the present."

Fichardt had more difficulty staying awake on the Saturday morning at Doha. A sandstorm and high winds had caused a seven and a half hour suspension to the first round and the remainder of the week was spent playing 'catch up'. On Saturday at 6.30am, the second round resumed with Fichardt on the second tee. He opened with a birdie three and promptly holed in one with a three iron at the 224 yard third.

John Bickerton

Peter Hedblom

"I think it's fair to say that that kick-started my tournament," he said. "I would have accepted a par-par start so early in the morning but I walked off with a birdie and an eagle."

Earlier, Kingston had moved ahead at the halfway stage, taking over from first round leader David Howell, after rounds of 68 and 67. Fichardt, assisted by his ace, was five behind.

Time constraints then dictated that the field at the 36 hole cut would be reduced from 70 and ties to 50 and ties. A total of 54 players embarked on round three on Saturday afternoon and finished on Sunday morning, with Fichardt and Kingston locked at the top on ten under par 206 after the former's decisive round of 66.

They remained locked together after 72 holes, Kingston having been unable to make a birdie at the last to avoid a play-off. The pair returned to the 18th tee and Kingston made par five again after bunkering his approach. Fichardt, on in two, two putted for a birdie four to atone for his play-off miss the previous year in the Murphy's Irish Open.

For Kingston, at the age of 37, there was the precious consolation prize of knowing he had secured his card to play on The European Tour in 2004. But for Fichardt there were the spoils of victory to consider...and a big hug for the lady who helped make it all possible.

Gordon Simpson

final results

Doha Golf Club • Qatar
March 13 - 16 • 2003 • Par 72 • 7110 yards • 6500 metres

Pos.	Name		Rd1	Rd2	Rd3	Rd4	Total	Par	Prize Money Euro	£
1	Darren FICHARDT	SA	71	69	66	69	275	-13	226983.50	156054.96
2	James KINGSTON	SA	68	67	71	69	275	-13	151316.30	104032.49
3	Paul MCGINLEY	Ire	68	72	70	67	277	-11	85254.98	58614.23
4	David HOWELL	Eng	66	72	72	68	278	-10	68095.04	46816.48
5	Peter FOWLER	Aus	71	67	71	72	281	-7	52705.56	36235.96
	Peter HEDBLOM	Swe	71	71	73	66	281	-7	52705.56	36235.96
7	David PARK	Wal	70	71	71	70	282	-6	40857.02	28089.89
8	Richard GREEN	Aus	71	69	70	73	283	-5	30597.37	21036.20
	Gary EVANS	Eng	73	70	70	70	283	-5	30597.37	21036.20
	John BICKERTON	Eng	73	70	68	72	283	-5	30597.37	21036.20
11	Roger CHAPMAN	Eng	71	69	73	71	284	-4	23470.09	16136.08
	Padraig HARRINGTON	Ire	70	73	76	65	284	-4	23470.09	16136.08
	Gary BIRCH JNR	Eng	70	74	71	69	284	-4	23470.09	16136.08
14	Mårten OLANDER	Swe	69	74	74	68	285	-3	18463.48	12693.95
	Paul BROADHURST	Eng	69	73	70	73	285	-3	18463.48	12693.95
	Philip GOLDING	Eng	68	74	72	71	285	-3	18463.48	12693.95
	Andrew MARSHALL	Eng	73	71	70	71	285	-3	18463.48	12693.95
	Søren HANSEN	Den	71	69	74	71	285	-3	18463.48	12693.95
	Greg OWEN	Eng	72	71	73	69	285	-3	18463.48	12693.95
	David DIXON	Eng	70	68	73	74	285	-3	18463.48	12693.95
21	José Manuel LARA	Sp	69	73	71	73	286	-2	15389.48	10580.53
	Jean-Francois REMESY	Fr	70	68	75	73	286	-2	15389.48	10580.53
	Richard STERNE	SA	70	74	72	70	286	-2	15389.48	10580.53
24	Mark FOSTER	Eng	72	70	74	71	287	-1	13550.91	9316.48
	Julien CLEMENT	Swi	73	70	74	70	287	-1	13550.91	9316.48
	Miles TUNNICLIFF	Eng	70	74	72	71	287	-1	13550.91	9316.48
	Phillip PRICE	Wal	73	71	68	75	287	-1	13550.91	9316.48
	Raymond RUSSELL	Scot	73	69	71	74	287	-1	13550.91	9316.48
	Nick DOUGHERTY	Eng	73	71	71	72	287	-1	13550.91	9316.48
30	Kenneth FERRIE	Eng	71	70	75	72	288	0	11508.06	7911.98
	Henrik STENSON	Swe	71	71	74	72	288	0	11508.06	7911.98
	Gregory HAVRET	Fr	69	75	72	72	288	0	11508.06	7911.98
	Francois DELAMONTAGNE	Fr	70	75	67	76	288	0	11508.06	7911.98
34	Damien MCGRANE	Ire	73	72	71	73	289	1	10214.26	7022.47
	Stuart LITTLE	Eng	74	69	76	70	289	1	10214.26	7022.47
	Kevin NA	Kor	73	72	76	68	289	1	10214.26	7022.47
37	Roger WESSELS	SA	71	74	72	73	290	2	9669.50	6647.94
38	Michael ARCHER	Eng	71	74	75	71	291	3	9124.74	6273.41
	Mikael LUNDBERG	Swe	74	69	75	73	291	3	9124.74	6273.41
	Fredrik WIDMARK	Swe	72	73	73	73	291	3	9124.74	6273.41
41	Søren KJELDSEN	Den	72	73	72	75	292	4	8171.40	5617.98
	Paul DWYER	Eng	71	73	73	75	292	4	8171.40	5617.98
	Ed STEDMAN	Aus	70	75	73	74	292	4	8171.40	5617.98
	Steven BOWDITCH	Aus	70	70	74	78	292	4	8171.40	5617.98
45	Lee S JAMES	Eng	72	73	75	73	293	5	7490.45	5149.81
46	Massimo FLORIOLI	It	72	73	75	74	294	6	7081.88	4868.91
	Sebastien DELAGRANGE	Fr	71	74	77	72	294	6	7081.88	4868.91
48	Malcolm MACKENZIE	Eng	72	72	77	74	295	7	6264.74	4307.12
	Barry LANE	Eng	72	73	79	71	295	7	6264.74	4307.12
	Peter LAWRIE	Ire	73	70	79	73	295	7	6264.74	4307.12
	Nicolas COLSAERTS	Bel	71	73	80	71	295	7	6264.74	4307.12
52	Alvaro SALTO	Sp	73	72	78	73	296	8	5583.79	3838.95
53	Marc FARRY	Fr	69	75	75	78	297	9	5311.41	3651.69
54	Julien VAN HAUWE	Fr	71	74	80	82	307	19	5039.03	3464.42
55	Ian WOOSNAM	Wal	73	73			146	2	3638.22	2501.34
	Anders HANSEN	Den	74	72			146	2	3638.22	2501.34
	Euan LITTLE	Scot	72	74			146	2	3638.22	2501.34
	Greig HUTCHEON	Scot	71	75			146	2	3638.22	2501.34
	Hennie OTTO	SA	72	74			146	2	3638.22	2501.34
	Henrik BJORNSTAD	Nor	73	73			146	2	3638.22	2501.34
	Miguel Angel JIMÉNEZ	Sp	69	77			146	2	3638.22	2501.34
	Per NYMAN	Swe	71	75			146	2	3638.22	2501.34
	Emanuele CANONICA	It	71	75			146	2	3638.22	2501.34
	Ian GARBUTT	Eng	70	76			146	2	3638.22	2501.34
	Thomas NORRET	Den	69	77			146	2	3638.22	2501.34
	Mikko ILONEN	Fin	71	75			146	2	3638.22	2501.34
	Simon DYSON	Eng	70	76			146	2	3638.22	2501.34
	Brett RUMFORD	Aus	75	71			146	2	3638.22	2501.34
69	Tony JOHNSTONE	Zim	74	73			147	3	2065.68	1420.19
	Costantino ROCCA	It	74	73			147	3	2065.68	1420.19
	Andrew PITTS	USA	73	74			147	3	2065.68	1420.19
	Raphaël JACQUELIN	Fr	76	71			147	3	2065.68	1420.19
	Titch MOORE	SA	73	74			147	3	2065.68	1420.19
	Peter BAKER	Eng	75	72			147	3	2065.68	1420.19
	Sam LITTLE	Eng	75	72			147	3	2065.68	1420.19
	Ryan REID	SA	72	75			147	3	2065.68	1420.19
	Jarrod MOSELEY	Aus	74	73			147	3	2065.68	1420.19
	Christian CÉVAËR	Fr	73	74			147	3	2065.68	1420.19
	Rolf MUNTZ	NL	76	71			147	3	2065.68	1420.19
	Simon KHAN	Eng	71	76			147	3	2065.68	1420.19
	Benn BARHAM	Eng	73	74			147	3	2065.68	1420.19
	Simon WAKEFIELD	Eng	73	74			147	3	2065.68	1420.19
	Markus BRIER	Aut	75	72			147	3	2065.68	1420.19
	Mark PILKINGTON	Wal	75	72			147	3	2065.68	1420.19
	David CARTER	Eng	71	76			147	3	2065.68	1420.19
	Lucas PARSONS	Aus	71	76			147	3	2065.68	1420.19
	Doug McGUIGAN	Scot	74	73			147	3	2065.68	1420.19
	Martin MARITZ	SA	72	75			147	3	2065.68	1420.19
	Jamie ELSON	Eng	71	76			147	3	2065.68	1420.19

Bradley Dredge

peak performance

1	Bradley DREDGE Wal	272	-16
2	Fredrik ANDERSSON Swe	280	-8
	Brian DAVIS Eng	280	-8
	Andrew MARSHALL Eng	280	-8
5	Sam LITTLE Eng	281	-7
6	Robert-Jan DERKSEN NL	282	-6
7	Santiago LUNA Sp	283	-5
8	Julien CLEMENT Swi	284	-4
	Andrew COLTART Scot	284	-4
	Mikko ILONEN Fin	284	-4

There is one sure way to look down on your peers on The European Tour International Schedule - climb 1800 feet up a mountain on an island in the North Atlantic Ocean and secure your maiden victory by the not insignificant margin of eight strokes.

When Bradley Dredge realised this lofty ambition by winning the Madeira Island Open, he not only banished the torment of several near-misses, he also revealed his true potential.

For the 29 year old from Tredegar had demonstrated, some six months after watching Phillip Price help Europe win The 34th Ryder Cup Matches at The De Vere Belfry, his own determination to continue the tradition of great Welsh golfers.

The history books resound to the great deeds of the likes of Brian Huggett, Dai Rees and Dave Thomas, although as a teenager Dredge was unquestionably inspired by the exploits of Ian Woosnam.

Indeed Dredge, following an inspirational year on The European Tour International Schedule in which he climbed from 72nd to 18th on the Volvo Order of Merit, had teamed up with Woosnam for Wales in the 2002 WGC - EMC² World Cup. It was another important piece in the jigsaw of his golfing education.

That education had been reinforced by the experience of leading tournaments such as the 2001 Great North Open and the 2003 dunhill championship at the halfway stage, as well as the 2002 Volvo Masters Andalucia entering the final round. In Madeira he catapulted himself into an eight shot lead with a third round of 60.

The fact that preferred lies were in operation after thunderstorms and strong winds must not take anything away from his score. Dredge simply picked up the Santo da Serra course and ripped it to shreds with golf of the highest calibre.

After 16 holes of pure magic, he came to the short 17th 12 under par and with a 59 on the cards. A splendid tee shot and there it was - a ten foot putt to etch a place in golfing folklore. Agonisingly the birdie putt slid just past the hole. He had one more chance, however, this time a swinging downhill putt at the last from 30 feet. Again the putt slid by.

Nevertheless he had equalled the feat of Woosnam, one of nine players to put a score of 60 in The European Tour record books. Coincidentally, Woosnam had also made his score up a mountain, in the 1992 Torras Monte Carlo Open at Mont Agel. "It's not often you get chance to shoot a 59, even on your home course for a few quid," said Dredge. "I really wanted it, but there you go."

Mikko Ilonen

the course

The spectacular Robert Trent Jones Snr course was increased by 162 yards to 6,826 yards for the 2003 event. Removal of a number of trees revealed even more wonderful vistas and more holes to view from the clubhouse.

With a final round of 71 for a 16 under par total of 272, Dredge maintained his eight shot lead – Fredrik Andersson, Brian Davis and Andrew Marshall tied for second – and thereby enjoyed the euphoria of winning for the first time on The European Tour International Schedule.

If the final honours went to Dredge and to Wales, the early plaudits were Spain's and in particular Jesus Maria Arruti, whose father coached José Maria Olazábal at their home San Sebastian club, and

who led the way on day one with a 66. Dutchman Robert-Jan Derksen, watched by his proud father and mother, lay second with a 67 on his return to competitive action following a week's celebration of his superb Dubai Desert Classic triumph. Dredge hovered with a 69.

Arruti kept the lead at halfway after punishing gusts on Friday destroyed many a score but Dredge was about to erupt. This was a defining moment in the Welshman's career and he had good reason to be proud. He had climbed to the top of the mountain, and seen the future.

Julien Clement

Norman Dabell

Brian Davis

Santiago Luna

final results

Santo da Serra • Madeira
March 20 - 23 • 2003 • Par 72 • 6826 yards • 6241 metres

Pos.	Name		Rd1	Rd2	Rd3	Rd4	Total	Par	Prize Money Euro	£
1	Bradley DREDGE	Wal	69	72	60	71	272	-16	100000.00	67789.72
2	Brian DAVIS	Eng	74	70	68	68	280	-8	44740.00	30329.12
	Andrew MARSHALL	Eng	71	70	69	70	280	-8	44740.00	30329.12
	Fredrik ANDERSSON	Swe	73	68	70	69	280	-8	44740.00	30329.12
5	Sam LITTLE	Eng	76	68	68	69	281	-7	25440.00	17245.70
6	Robert-Jan DERKSEN	NL	67	79	68	68	282	-6	21000.00	14235.84
7	Santiago LUNA	Sp	71	72	70	70	283	-5	18000.00	12202.15
8	Julien CLEMENT	Swi	68	76	69	71	284	-4	13480.00	9138.05
	Andrew COLTART	Scot	74	69	70	71	284	-4	13480.00	9138.05
	Mikko ILONEN	Fin	73	70	71	70	284	-4	13480.00	9138.05
11	Marcel SIEM	Ger	70	74	71	70	285	-3	10340.00	7009.46
	Jesus Maria ARRUTI	Sp	66	74	74	71	285	-3	10340.00	7009.46
	Van PHILLIPS	Eng	68	74	67	76	285	-3	10340.00	7009.46
14	Shaun P WEBSTER	Eng	71	75	68	72	286	-2	8460.00	5735.01
	Henrik STENSON	Swe	72	69	71	74	286	-2	8460.00	5735.01
	Paul BROADHURST	Eng	70	72	70	74	286	-2	8460.00	5735.01
	Stuart LITTLE	Eng	77	71	72	66	286	-2	8460.00	5735.01
	Simon HURD	Eng	71	75	72	68	286	-2	8460.00	5735.01
19	Damien MCGRANE	Ire	72	76	69	70	287	-1	7440.00	5043.55
20	Andrew SHERBORNE	Eng	68	77	71	72	288	0	6792.00	4604.28
	Fredrik OREST	Swe	71	75	70	72	288	0	6792.00	4604.28
	Marcello SANTI	It	69	73	72	74	288	0	6792.00	4604.28
	Christopher HANELL	Swe	72	73	72	71	288	0	6792.00	4604.28
	Matthew CORT	Eng	71	72	72	73	288	0	6792.00	4604.28
25	Diego BORREGO	Sp	75	73	71	70	289	1	6060.00	4108.06
	Robert COLES	Eng	79	71	71	68	289	1	6060.00	4108.06
	Ivo GINER	Sp	74	75	67	73	289	1	6060.00	4108.06
28	Carlos RODILES	Sp	71	78	72	69	290	2	5520.00	3741.99
	Christian CÉVAËR	Fr	73	77	72	68	290	2	5520.00	3741.99
	Lucas PARSONS	Aus	75	76	68	71	290	2	5520.00	3741.99
31	Gary MURPHY	Ire	72	74	73	72	291	3	4671.43	3166.75
	Alessandro TADINI	It	73	76	72	70	291	3	4671.43	3166.75
	Peter BAKER	Eng	74	72	71	74	291	3	4671.43	3166.75
	Nicolas COLSAERTS	Bel	73	77	71	70	291	3	4671.43	3166.75
	Nicolas VANHOOTEGEM	Bel	72	77	70	72	291	3	4671.43	3166.75
	Erol SIMSEK	Ger	73	77	70	71	291	3	4671.43	3166.75
	Ben MASON	Eng	73	72	72	74	291	3	4671.43	3166.75
38	Philip GOLDING	Eng	73	74	75	70	292	4	4020.00	2725.15
	Sebastien DELAGRANGE	Fr	72	72	76	72	292	4	4020.00	2725.15
	Mark SANDERS	Eng	75	76	74	67	292	4	4020.00	2725.15
41	Miguel Angel MARTIN	Sp	71	76	70	76	293	5	3540.00	2399.76
	Renaud GUILLARD	Fr	71	80	70	72	293	5	3540.00	2399.76
	Jean-François LUCQUIN	Fr	72	74	72	75	293	5	3540.00	2399.76
	Johan RYSTRÖM	Swe	76	76	70	71	293	5	3540.00	2399.76
	Fernando ROCA	Sp	73	73	71	76	293	5	3540.00	2399.76
46	Daniel SILVA	Port	76	76	72	70	294	6	2880.00	1952.34
	Knud STORGAARD	Den	73	75	74	72	294	6	2880.00	1952.34
	Jean HUGO	SA	73	78	74	69	294	6	2880.00	1952.34
	Stuart CAGE	Eng	73	76	71	74	294	6	2880.00	1952.34
	David DRYSDALE	Scot	73	77	69	75	294	6	2880.00	1952.34
	Markus BRIER	Aut	71	75	74	74	294	6	2880.00	1952.34
52	Philip WALTON	Ire	74	74	73	74	295	7	2160.00	1464.26
	Chris GANE	Eng	73	79	72	71	295	7	2160.00	1464.26
	Neil CHEETHAM	Eng	74	75	73	73	295	7	2160.00	1464.26
	James HEPWORTH	Eng	73	77	70	75	295	7	2160.00	1464.26
	Jarmo SANDELIN	Swe	71	77	69	78	295	7	2160.00	1464.26
	Daren LEE	Eng	74	75	73	73	295	7	2160.00	1464.26
58	Alberto BINAGHI	It	70	77	80	69	296	8	1800.00	1220.21
59	Ilya GORONESKOUL	Fr	72	80	72	73	297	9	1530.00	1037.18
	Gary EMERSON	Eng	73	72	73	79	297	9	1530.00	1037.18
	Peter MITCHELL	Eng	72	79	72	74	297	9	1530.00	1037.18
	Julien VAN HAUWE	Fr	68	78	73	78	297	9	1530.00	1037.18
	Pehr MAGNEBRANT	Swe	73	74	75	75	297	9	1530.00	1037.18
	Raimo SJÖBERG	Swe	71	77	73	76	297	9	1530.00	1037.18
	Marco BERNARDINI	It	73	74	79	71	297	9	1530.00	1037.18
	Stephen BROWNE	Ire	73	77	76	71	297	9	1530.00	1037.18
67	Seve BALLESTEROS	Sp	76	75	71	76	298	10	1175.00	796.53
	Gordon BRAND JNR.	Scot	79	73	74	72	298	10	1175.00	796.53
	Fredrik WIDMARK	Swe	74	74	73	77	298	10	1175.00	796.53
	Richard MCEVOY	Eng	76	76	75	71	298	10	1175.00	796.53
71	Alvaro SALTO	Sp	72	80	72	75	299	11	895.50	607.06
	Jan-Are LARSEN	Nor	73	79	73	74	299	11	895.50	607.06
	Simon WAKEFIELD	Eng	76	74	76	73	299	11	895.50	607.06
	David DIXON	Eng	73	77	75	74	299	11	895.50	607.06
75	Raul BALLESTEROS	Sp	78	73	72	78	301	13	888.00	601.97
76	Edward RUSH	Eng	71	78	75	78	302	14	885.00	599.94
77	Carl SUNESON	Sp	79	72	76	77	304	16	882.00	597.91

Masters Tournament Augusta National · Georgia · USA

sacred days

Mike Weir

1	Mike WEIR Can	281	-7
2	Len MATTIACE USA	281	-7
3	Phil MICKELSON USA	283	-5
4	Jim FURYK USA	284	-4
5	Jeff MAGGERT USA	286	-2
6	Ernie ELS SA	287	-1
	Vijay SINGH Fiji	287	-1
8	Jonathan BYRD USA	288	0
	José Maria OLAZÁBAL Sp	288	0
	Mark O'MEARA USA	288	0
	David TOMS USA	288	0
	Scott VERPLANK USA	288	0

Given that they are locked in by winter for up to six months every year, it is not surprising that Canadian golfers are passionate about their sport. They cling to its vivid reminder of warmer climes, dreaming of April days when the ice finally melts, the greens are no longer covered in carpets of white, and they eventually live up to their name.

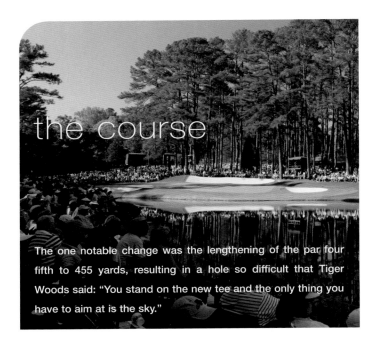

the course

The one notable change was the lengthening of the par four fifth to 455 yards, resulting in a hole so difficult that Tiger Woods said: "You stand on the new tee and the only thing you have to aim at is the sky."

José Maria Olazábal

Just as in northern Europe, the Masters Tournament holds a special place in their hearts, a rite of Spring signalling the start of their own golf season. For many, not even a Claret Jug matches up to the mystique of a Green Jacket.

So imagine what it was like in Canada as the 2003 edition of the Masters Tournament came to its heartstopping conclusion. Imagine one of those sacred days when a nation stops what it is

doing and holds its collective breath. Imagine a couple of hours when even those with no affinity for golf take the phone off the hook and stay glued to the television.

And imagine what it was like at the finish, when one of their own, a man so proud of his roots and the support that stems from them, went from golfing hero to national sporting icon.

No wonder, therefore, that Mike Weir fulsomely thanked Canada and its golf fans in his gracious victory speech. Here was a man like Padraig Harrington, a clean-cut model ambassador who was only too happy to take on the burden of a nation's expectation.

It is not an easy role. It involves countless sacrifices in terms of time and privacy. How much Weir relishes the position, however, was evident when he was asked at the end of 2002 about his relatively disappointing season. "I feel like I have let down Canadian golf fans," he said.

Now he celebrated his moment of redemption, and a nation's joy was summed up by the fact that he had hardly beaten Len Mattiace at the first play-off hole before Prime Minister Jean Chretien was on the other end of his mobile offering congratulations.

Len Mattiace

Augusta National Clubhouse

Weir said that he hoped it would inspire Canadian youngsters to take up the game, and his words revived memories of his own evocative story. Of the boy who used to hit range balls out onto Lake Huron during the winter and who, as a 13 year old, wrote to Jack Nicklaus and asked for advice about his game.

"Should I stick to playing left-handed," Weir wanted to know. "Or should I switch?" Nicklaus's reply was unequivocal. "Left handed is your natural game, and that is the one that you should play." The Golden Bear was as pleased as anyone that this advice should lead all the way to a Green Jacket, that 15 minutes out of a busy day had delivered such a momentous result.

For it was not only Canadians who were cheering their first ever Major Champion, but left handers as well. They had not seen one of their own win a Major since Bob Charles claimed the Open Golf Championship at Royal Lytham & St Annes in 1963, and no left-hander had ever won the Masters Tournament. On two counts, therefore, this was a historic victory.

The history many had expected to see before the event began was Tiger Woods become the first player to win three successive Green Jackets. Like Nick Faldo and Nicklaus, the two previous

players who had a chance to achieve this feat, Woods delivered a strange, out-of-sorts performance that saw him turn in his worst ever first round score of 76 and tie his worst last round of 75. In the end he finished tied 15th, nine shots adrift of Weir.

Retief Goosen

Join the winning team ...

In the days leading up to the tournament, the weather was so bad the event might as well have been staged in Canada, and left the organisers with no option but to put back the first day's play until Friday for the first time since 1939. When golf balls were finally struck it was Darren Clarke who raised hopes of a first Irish victory with a mesmerising first round 66. It was so good that for the first time in 50 years a player was three strokes ahead after the opening round. But no first round leader has gone on to win since Ben Crenshaw in 1984, and unfortunately that jinx would hold for Clarke, who eventually tied for 28th place.

Weir took control with a second round 68 for a four shot lead. He was eventually overhauled by Jeff Maggert on the third day, while the popular Mattiace set a stringent seven under par total by coming out of the pack with an amazing last round 65. Would Weir's nerve hold? Could he play the last six holes in two under par to force a play-off? Would that putting stroke remain true?

Weir answered all those questions to prove a most deserving Masters Champion. And at the end, the greatest American champion of his generation, Woods, slipped the jacket on to the shoulders of a man who will now be known as the greatest Canadian golfer of all.

Derek Lawrenson

Justin Rose and Adam Scott

final results

Augusta National · Georgia · USA
April 10 - 13 · 2003 · Par 72 · 7290 yards · 6666 metres

Pos.	Name		Rd1	Rd2	Rd3	Rd4	Total	Par	Prize Money Euro	£
1	Mike WEIR	Can	70	68	75	68	281	-7	1008312.00	692441.13
2	Len MATTIACE	USA	73	74	69	65	281	-7	604986.90	415464.47
3	Phil MICKELSON	USA	73	70	72	68	283	-5	380917.70	261588.76
4	Jim FURYK	USA	73	72	71	68	284	-4	268883.10	184650.90
5	Jeff MAGGERT	USA	72	73	66	75	286	-2	224069.20	153875.72
6	Vijay SINGH	Fiji	73	71	70	73	287	-1	194660.20	133679.58
	Ernie ELS	SA	79	66	72	70	287	-1	194660.20	133679.58
8	José Maria OLAZÁBAL	Sp	73	71	71	73	288	0	151246.70	103866.10
	Mark O'MEARA	USA	76	71	70	71	288	0	151246.70	103866.10
	Scott VERPLANK	USA	76	73	70	69	288	0	151246.70	103866.10
	David TOMS	USA	71	73	70	74	288	0	151246.70	103866.10
	Jonathan BYRD	USA	74	71	71	72	288	0	151246.70	103866.10
13	Retief GOOSEN	SA	73	74	72	70	289	1	112034.60	76937.86
	Tim CLARK	SA	72	75	71	71	289	1	112034.60	76937.86
15	Tiger WOODS	USA	76	73	66	75	290	2	86826.83	59626.85
	Kyoung-Ju CHOI	Kor	76	69	72	73	290	2	86826.83	59626.85
	Davis LOVE III	USA	77	71	71	71	290	2	86826.83	59626.85
	Angel CABRERA	Arg	76	71	71	72	290	2	86826.83	59626.85
	Paul LAWRIE	Scot	72	72	73	73	290	2	86826.83	59626.85
	Rich BEEM	USA	74	72	71	73	290	2	86826.83	59626.85
21	Ricky BARNES (Am)	USA	69	74	75	73	291	3		
22	Bob ESTES	USA	76	71	74	71	292	4	67220.77	46162.72
23	Brad FAXON	USA	73	71	79	70	293	5	53776.62	36930.18
	Nick PRICE	Zim	70	75	72	76	293	5	53776.62	36930.18
	Scott MCCARRON	USA	77	71	72	73	293	5	53776.62	36930.18
	Chris RILEY	USA	76	72	70	75	293	5	53776.62	36930.18
	Adam SCOTT	Aus	77	72	74	70	293	5	53776.62	36930.18
28	Sergio GARCIA	Sp	69	78	74	73	294	6	40612.55	27889.98
	Fred COUPLES	USA	73	75	69	77	294	6	40612.55	27889.98
	Darren CLARKE	N.Ire	66	76	78	74	294	6	40612.55	27889.98
	Charles HOWELL III	USA	73	72	76	73	294	6	40612.55	27889.98
	Hunter MAHAN (Am)	USA	73	72	73	76	294	6		
33	Nick FALDO	Eng	74	73	75	73	295	7	33960.49	23321.79
	Loren ROBERTS	USA	74	72	76	73	295	7	33960.49	23321.79
	Rocco MEDIATE	USA	73	74	73	75	295	7	33960.49	23321.79
	Kevin SUTHERLAND	USA	77	72	76	70	295	7	33960.49	23321.79
37	Billy MAYFAIR	USA	75	70	77	74	296	8	29549.13	20292.36
	Shingo KATAYAMA	Jpn	74	72	76	74	296	8	29549.13	20292.36
39	Justin ROSE	Eng	73	76	71	77	297	9	25207.79	17311.02
	Craig PARRY	Aus	74	73	75	75	297	9	25207.79	17311.02
	Kenny PERRY	USA	76	72	78	71	297	9	25207.79	17311.02
	Robert ALLENBY	Aus	76	73	74	74	297	9	25207.79	17311.02
	Philip TATAURANGI	NZ	75	70	74	78	297	9	25207.79	17311.02
44	Jeff SLUMAN	USA	75	72	76	75	298	10	21846.75	15002.88
45	Ryan MOORE (Am)	USA	73	74	75	79	301	13		
	Pat PEREZ	USA	74	73	79	75	301	13	20726.40	14233.50
47	John ROLLINS	USA	74	71	80	77	302	14	19606.06	13464.13
48	Jerry KELLY	USA	72	76	77	79	304	16	18485.71	12694.75
49	Craig STADLER	USA	76	73	79	77	305	17	17365.37	11925.37

Fredrik Jacobson

1	Fredrik JACOBSON Swe	283	-5
2	Brian DAVIS Eng	284	-4
	Jamie DONALDSON Wal	284	-4
	Bradley DREDGE Wal	284	-4
5	Greg OWEN Eng	285	-3
6	James KINGSTON SA	287	-1
	Richard STERNE SA	287	-1
8	David LYNN Eng	289	1
	Carlos RODILES Sp	289	1
	Jarmo SANDELIN Swe	289	1
	Marcel SIEM Ger	289	1

sweet music

Jamie Donaldson

With his black, spiky hair and assorted, slightly haphazard facial adornments, Fredrik Jacobson would at first sight to some observers look more like a punk rocker than a professional golfer. But his game is anything but a three-chord thrash – indeed, when the muse is with him, he is capable of producing the most delicate of fugues.

In the Algarve Open de Portugal, Jacobson's instrument of choice was a 58 degree wedge. The record shows that he won on 283, five under par, but of them all, three short shots in the final round turned a simple score into a symphony, an Air on a G Swing in which G equalled Golf.

Each time he played those tiny strokes, there might have been trepidation in his mind. In his hands there was not the slightest hint of even a semi-quaver. The first was at the opening hole and from off the green and 20 yards from the pin, he chipped in for a birdie. On the third he went out of bounds and finished up 15 yards from the hole, again off the putting surface. He was staring at a double-bogey, or worse, but he chipped in again to move on with only a single dropped shot against his name. Sweet, sweet music, and then some.

Jarmo Sandelin

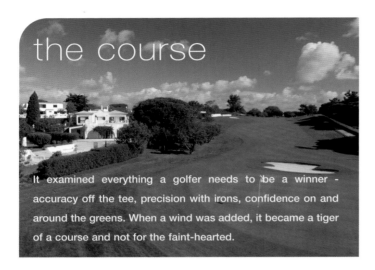

the course

It examined everything a golfer needs to be a winner - accuracy off the tee, precision with irons, confidence on and around the greens. When a wind was added, it became a tiger of a course and not for the faint-hearted.

So far, so good, but with two holes to play, Jacobson faced the possibility of becoming embroiled in a five-man play-off alongside Brian Davis, Jamie Donaldson, Bradley Dredge and Greg Owen. A couple of minutes after missing the 17th green in two, it was all over. He was 35 feet from the flag; if things went wrong now, he would probably have been out of it.

Marcel Siem

Carlos Rodiles

The shot facing him was a potential winner, but it was not easy. He may have required inner strength as his ally, but it was perfect technique and soft hands that sent the ball rolling gently into the hole for an eagle three.

It left him on six under par and two ahead. Owen dropped a shot on the last, but Jacobson still had three to beat. He missed the fairway off the tee, then from short of the green in two he pitched 15 feet beyond the flag. Davis failed with his birdie attempt and Jacobson had two putts for the title. Calmly, he used them both.

After his maiden European Tour victory in the Omega Hong Kong Open in the second event on The 2003 European Tour International Schedule, Jacobson had fallen prey to an injury to

his left wrist that took ten weeks to heal. It was still giving him pain before the tournament but he stuck to his intention to play. How propitious it was he did.

He had a glittering 64 in the first round to lead but slid to a 76 on Friday. However, a 71 in the third round put him back in the mix and eventually he needed no more than a level par 72 to win by a stroke. To his credit, he was perfectly in tune until the final note had been sounded.

Mel Webb

final results

Vale do Lobo • Portugal
April 17 - 20 • 2003 • Par 72 • 7125 yards • 6515 metres

Pos.	Name		Rd1	Rd2	Rd3	Rd4	Total	Par	Prize Money Euro	£
1	Fredrik JACOBSON	Swe	64	76	71	72	283	-5	208330.00	142541.43
2	Brian DAVIS	Eng	70	71	71	72	284	-4	93210.00	63775.20
	Bradley DREDGE	Wal	69	73	74	68	284	-4	93210.00	63775.20
	Jamie DONALDSON	Wal	72	71	73	68	284	-4	93210.00	63775.20
5	Greg OWEN	Eng	66	70	76	73	285	-3	53000.00	36263.12
6	James KINGSTON	SA	72	75	72	68	287	-1	40625.00	27796.02
	Richard STERNE	SA	73	73	69	72	287	-1	40625.00	27796.02
8	Carlos RODILES	Sp	69	71	76	73	289	1	26812.50	18345.38
	Marcel SIEM	Ger	71	68	76	74	289	1	26812.50	18345.38
	David LYNN	Eng	71	72	74	72	289	1	26812.50	18345.38
	Jarmo SANDELIN	Swe	75	67	79	68	289	1	26812.50	18345.38
12	José Manuel LARA	Sp	73	72	74	72	291	3	20250.00	13855.25
	Steve WEBSTER	Eng	72	73	73	73	291	3	20250.00	13855.25
	Gustavo ROJAS	Arg	70	75	74	72	291	3	20250.00	13855.25
	Richard WALKER (AM)	Eng	73	73	74	71	291	3		
16	Maarten LAFEBER	NL	73	73	71	75	292	4	16285.71	11142.84
	Kenneth FERRIE	Eng	74	72	74	72	292	4	16285.71	11142.84
	Rolf MUNTZ	NL	72	70	78	72	292	4	16285.71	11142.84
	Terry PRICE	Aus	76	71	76	69	292	4	16285.71	11142.84
	Ben MASON	Eng	75	69	74	74	292	4	16285.71	11142.84
	Graeme MCDOWELL	N.Ire	70	75	76	71	292	4	16285.71	11142.84
	Charl SCHWARTZEL	SA	72	70	74	76	292	4	16285.71	11142.84
23	Søren KJELDSEN	Den	76	72	73	72	293	5	12812.50	8766.44
	Paul EALES	Eng	77	69	76	71	293	5	12812.50	8766.44
	Jonathan LOMAS	Eng	72	72	75	74	293	5	12812.50	8766.44
	Phillip PRICE	Wal	73	71	72	77	293	5	12812.50	8766.44
	Van PHILLIPS	Eng	70	77	75	71	293	5	12812.50	8766.44
	Matthew BLACKEY	Eng	74	71	73	75	293	5	12812.50	8766.44
	Mikael LUNDBERG	Swe	75	71	72	75	293	5	12812.50	8766.44
	Alastair FORSYTH	Scot	72	72	76	73	293	5	12812.50	8766.44
31	Barry LANE	Eng	72	77	76	69	294	6	10053.57	6878.75
	Søren HANSEN	Den	74	75	76	69	294	6	10053.57	6878.75
	Simon KHAN	Eng	74	74	73	73	294	6	10053.57	6878.75
	Fredrik ANDERSSON	Swe	73	73	73	75	294	6	10053.57	6878.75
	Patrik SJÖLAND	Swe	73	73	73	75	294	6	10053.57	6878.75
	David CARTER	Eng	72	72	75	75	294	6	10053.57	6878.75
	Simon DYSON	Eng	74	72	76	72	294	6	10053.57	6878.75
38	Gordon BRAND JNR.	Scot	72	71	78	74	295	7	8125.00	5559.20
	Malcolm MACKENZIE	Eng	74	75	73	73	295	7	8125.00	5559.20
	Jamie SPENCE	Eng	77	71	73	74	295	7	8125.00	5559.20
	Jean-François LUCQUIN	Fr	76	71	75	73	295	7	8125.00	5559.20
	Charlie WI	Kor	74	75	75	71	295	7	8125.00	5559.20
	Andrew RAITT	Eng	74	70	76	75	295	7	8125.00	5559.20
	Andrew COLTART	Scot	71	71	75	78	295	7	8125.00	5559.20
45	Miles TUNNICLIFF	Eng	73	75	76	72	296	8	7000.00	4789.47
	David DRYSDALE	Scot	76	69	78	73	296	8	7000.00	4789.47
47	Miguel Angel MARTIN	Sp	73	75	72	77	297	9	6375.00	4361.84
	Robert KARLSSON	Swe	73	73	73	78	297	9	6375.00	4361.84
	Mikko ILONEN	Fin	73	72	75	77	297	9	6375.00	4361.84
50	Jesus Maria ARRUTI	Sp	72	77	75	74	298	10	5750.00	3934.21
	Zane SCOTLAND (AM)	Eng	75	72	80	71	298	10		
	Richard MCEVOY	Eng	77	72	74	75	298	10	5750.00	3934.21
53	Jan-Are LARSEN	Nor	73	72	77	77	299	11	4875.00	3335.52
	Ignacio GARRIDO	Sp	78	71	77	73	299	11	4875.00	3335.52
	Benn BARHAM	Eng	75	71	78	75	299	11	4875.00	3335.52
	Lee S JAMES	Eng	71	73	81	74	299	11	4875.00	3335.52
	Nick DOUGHERTY	Eng	74	75	77	73	299	11	4875.00	3335.52
58	Anders HANSEN	Den	71	75	80	74	300	12	4000.00	2736.84
	Euan LITTLE	Scot	70	79	78	73	300	12	4000.00	2736.84
60	Santiago LUNA	Sp	74	75	77	75	301	13	3625.00	2480.26
	Philip GOLDING	Eng	72	76	77	76	301	13	3625.00	2480.26
	Raymond RUSSELL	Scot	76	72	80	73	301	13	3625.00	2480.26
63	Warren BENNETT	Eng	74	73	78	77	302	14	3250.00	2223.68
	Henrik NYSTROM	Swe	74	72	81	75	302	14	3250.00	2223.68
	Mads VIBE-HASTRUP	Den	78	71	73	80	302	14	3250.00	2223.68
66	Roger CHAPMAN	Eng	73	75	80	75	303	15	2812.50	1924.34
	Andrew OLDCORN	Scot	75	72	79	77	303	15	2812.50	1924.34
	David GILFORD	Eng	75	74	77	77	303	15	2812.50	1924.34
	Fredrik WIDMARK	Swe	74	74	78	77	303	15	2812.50	1924.34
70	Mårten OLANDER	Swe	73	75	78	79	305	17	2437.50	1667.76
	Federico BISAZZA	It	74	72	83	76	305	17	2437.50	1667.76
72	Simon WAKEFIELD	Eng	75	72	79	81	307	19	2290.00	1566.84

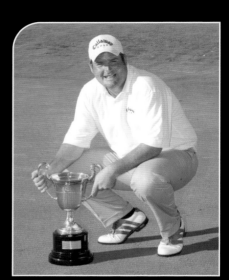

Kenneth Ferrie

reflected glory

1	Kenneth **FERRIE** Eng	266	-22
2	Peter **HEDBLOM** Swe	266	-22
	Peter **LAWRIE** Ire	266	-22
4	Brian **DAVIS** Eng	267	-21
	Mads **VIBE-HASTRUP** Den	267	-21
6	Paul **CASEY** Eng	268	-20
	Gary **EVANS** Eng	268	-20
	Santiago **LUNA** Sp	268	-20
	Charl **SCHWARTZEL** SA	268	-20
10	Markus **BRIER** Aut	269	-19
	Peter **FOWLER** Aus	269	-19
	Richard **GREEN** Aus	269	-19
	Simon **KHAN** Eng	269	-19
	Paul **McGINLEY** Ire	269	-19
	Mårten **OLANDER** Swe	269	-19
	José Maria **OLAZÁBAL** Sp	269	-19
	Phillip **PRICE** Wal	269	-19
	Anthony **WALL** Eng	269	-19

Think of Tenerife and you automatically think of young people having fun. The bars and discotheques of Playa de las Americas continually throb with the sound of youth having its fling.

It was fitting therefore that, across the shimmering bay at Golf Costa Adeje, it was the younger end of The European Tour spectrum that sparkled in the sunshine which blessed all four days of the Canarias Open de España. And no-one prospered more than Kenneth Ferrie.

The 24 year old Englishman became the seventh first time winner on The 2003 European Tour International Schedule when a birdie four was good enough to beat Sweden's Peter Hedblom and Peter Lawrie of Ireland at the second play-off hole after the trio had tied on 22 under par 266.

With idyllic conditions and a course which offered six par fives, low scoring was always on the cards and the players did not disappoint. The first round saw a record number, 133, score under par, while the cut, which fell at six under par 138, was the lowest in European Tour history.

Miguel Angel Jiménez

Peter Lawrie

the course

José Gancedo's 6,814 yard course, with spectacular panoramic mountain and ocean views, offered six par fives which guaranteed low scoring despite the myriad waste areas of palm trees, rocky ravines and volcanic dust.

The more established names such as Sergio Garcia, Paul McGinley, José Maria Olazábal and Phillip Price might have started favourites but from the word go it was the young lions who roared.

South African teenager Charl Schwartzel set a course record 63 on day one which was equalled by Sweden's Mårten Olander then by Switzerland's Julien Clement in round two and England's David Gilford in round three. Finland's Mikko Ilonen, aged 23, matched the 17 year old record of Scotland's Gordon Brand Jnr with four eagles in one round the following day, and 17 year old Spanish amateur champion Pablo Martin featured in a six way tie for the lead after the third round. But all, in the end, stepped aside for Ferrie.

This was the time for Ferrie to step out of the shadows. In his amateur days the powerful Geordie had been a contemporary of

Charl Schwartzel

Mårten Olander

Justin Rose and Garcia. Indeed the record books show the trio developed apace. In 1996 Ferrie won the British Boys Championship, a title claimed the following year by Garcia. In his last three years as an amateur, Ferrie played for England Boys, Youths and Seniors - as did Rose.

It was only when the professional ranks beckoned that their developments differed. After an uncertain start Rose flourished, two victories on The 2002 European Tour International Schedule seeing him finish ninth on the Volvo Order of Merit, while Garcia ended 2002 fourth in the Official World Golf Ranking. They were statistics not lost on Ferrie when he reflected on his success.

"Finishing 112th on the Volvo Order of Merit in 2002 was okay but when I looked at Sergio and Justin it was a wake-up call," he said. "I was determined to dig in, play harder and try to catch them. This is the start."

Tenerife, the *Island of Eternal Spring*, had just seen another career blossom.

Gordon Richardson

final results

Golf Costa Adeje · Tenerife · Spain
April 24 - 27 · 2003 · Par 72 · 6814 yards · 6233 metres

Pos.	Name		Rd1	Rd2	Rd3	Rd4	Total	Par	Prize Money Euro	£
1	Kenneth FERRIE	Eng	67	65	65	69	266	-22	291660.00	201731.94
2	Peter LAWRIE	Ire	67	64	69	66	266	-22	151995.00	105130.10
	Peter HEDBLOM	Swe	64	70	65	67	266	-22	151995.00	105130.10
4	Brian DAVIS	Eng	66	67	65	69	267	-21	80850.00	55921.37
	Mads VIBE-HASTRUP	Den	69	68	65	65	267	-21	80850.00	55921.37
6	Santiago LUNA	Sp	67	64	66	71	268	-20	49175.00	34012.78
	Gary EVANS	Eng	67	69	67	65	268	-20	49175.00	34012.78
	Paul CASEY	Eng	64	65	68	71	268	-20	49175.00	34012.78
	Charl SCHWARTZEL	SA	63	70	67	68	268	-20	49175.00	34012.78
10	Peter FOWLER	Aus	69	65	65	70	269	-19	27650.00	19124.62
	José Maria OLAZÁBAL	Sp	64	67	69	69	269	-19	27650.00	19124.62
	Mårten OLANDER	Swe	63	69	67	70	269	-19	27650.00	19124.62
	Richard GREEN	Aus	67	66	68	68	269	-19	27650.00	19124.62
	Anthony WALL	Eng	68	68	65	68	269	-19	27650.00	19124.62
	Paul MCGINLEY	Ire	66	66	67	70	269	-19	27650.00	19124.62
	Phillip PRICE	Wal	66	68	69	66	269	-19	27650.00	19124.62
	Simon KHAN	Eng	66	65	66	72	269	-19	27650.00	19124.62
	Markus BRIER	Aut	68	68	67	66	269	-19	27650.00	19124.62
19	Sergio GARCIA	Sp	69	67	66	68	270	-18	21000.00	14525.03
	Miguel Angel JIMÉNEZ	Sp	66	67	67	70	270	-18	21000.00	14525.03
	Ricardo GONZALEZ	Arg	68	70	65	67	270	-18	21000.00	14525.03
22	Jamie SPENCE	Eng	69	69	68	65	271	-17	19250.00	13314.61
	Julien VAN HAUWE	Fr	65	69	69	68	271	-17	19250.00	13314.61
	Raymond RUSSELL	Scot	67	67	67	70	271	-17	19250.00	13314.61
	Pablo MARTIN (AM)	Sp	67	66	64	74	271	-17		
26	Shaun P WEBSTER	Eng	64	70	67	71	272	-16	16887.50	11680.55
	Søren HANSEN	Den	64	68	65	75	272	-16	16887.50	11680.55
	Carlos QUEVEDO	Sp	69	65	71	67	272	-16	16887.50	11680.55
	Jarmo SANDELIN	Swe	64	70	68	72	272	-16	16887.50	11680.55
	Ivo GINER	Sp	66	69	67	70	272	-16	16887.50	11680.55
	Mikko ILONEN	Fin	67	65	68	72	272	-16	16887.50	11680.55
32	Klas ERIKSSON	Swe	67	67	71	68	273	-15	12687.50	8775.54
	David GILFORD	Eng	72	65	63	73	273	-15	12687.50	8775.54
	Anders HANSEN	Den	68	70	69	66	273	-15	12687.50	8775.54
	Steve WEBSTER	Eng	67	69	66	71	273	-15	12687.50	8775.54
	Philip GOLDING	Eng	68	67	72	66	273	-15	12687.50	8775.54
	Nicolas COLSAERTS	Bel	65	68	68	72	273	-15	12687.50	8775.54
	Marcel SIEM	Ger	67	71	64	71	273	-15	12687.50	8775.54
	Miles TUNNICLIFF	Eng	64	65	70	74	273	-15	12687.50	8775.54
	James KINGSTON	SA	69	67	68	69	273	-15	12687.50	8775.54
	Stephen SCAHILL	NZ	67	68	68	70	273	-15	12687.50	8775.54
	David PARK	Wal	67	69	70	67	273	-15	12687.50	8775.54
	Martin MARITZ	SA	68	68	67	70	273	-15	12687.50	8775.54
44	Roger CHAPMAN	Eng	68	70	65	71	274	-14	9450.00	6536.26
	José RIVERO	Sp	67	68	69	70	274	-14	9450.00	6536.26
	Gary MURPHY	Ire	68	67	70	69	274	-14	9450.00	6536.26
	Warren BENNETT	Eng	66	68	71	69	274	-14	9450.00	6536.26
	Julien CLEMENT	Swi	69	63	66	76	274	-14	9450.00	6536.26
	Bradley DREDGE	Wal	67	66	68	73	274	-14	9450.00	6536.26
50	Miguel Angel MARTIN	Sp	70	66	70	69	275	-13	7175.00	4962.72
	Mattias ELIASSON	Swe	66	70	68	71	275	-13	7175.00	4962.72
	Mathias GRÖNBERG	Swe	67	66	72	70	275	-13	7175.00	4962.72
	Nicolas VANHOOTEGEM	Bel	67	65	72	71	275	-13	7175.00	4962.72
	Andrew RAITT	Eng	67	70	67	71	275	-13	7175.00	4962.72
	Fredrik WIDMARK	Swe	66	67	67	75	275	-13	7175.00	4962.72
	Jamie DONALDSON	Wal	68	66	67	74	275	-13	7175.00	4962.72
57	Fredrik OREST	Swe	71	66	70	69	276	-12	5191.67	3590.91
	Gary EMERSON	Eng	71	67	74	64	276	-12	5191.67	3590.91
	Andrew MARSHALL	Eng	65	67	70	74	276	-12	5191.67	3590.91
	Jarrod MOSELEY	Aus	71	66	72	67	276	-12	5191.67	3590.91
	Mark PILKINGTON	Wal	67	69	72	68	276	-12	5191.67	3590.91
	Fredrik ANDERSSON	Swe	64	71	66	75	276	-12	5191.67	3590.91
63	Mark ROE	Eng	72	65	69	71	277	-11	4200.00	2905.01
	Robert-Jan DERKSEN	NL	68	70	69	70	277	-11	4200.00	2905.01
	Søren KJELDSEN	Den	68	69	70	70	277	-11	4200.00	2905.01
	Richard STERNE	SA	67	70	68	72	277	-11	4200.00	2905.01
	Graeme MCDOWELL	N.Ire	65	68	68	76	277	-11	4200.00	2905.01
	Alvaro QUIROS (AM)	Sp	70	68	70	69	277	-11		
69	Gordon BRAND JNR.	Scot	65	70	71	72	278	-10	3500.00	2420.84
	Roger WESSELS	SA	68	68	72	70	278	-10	3500.00	2420.84
	Eduardo FERNANDEZ	Sp	69	67	69	73	278	-10	3500.00	2420.84
72	Knud STORGAARD	Den	68	70	69	72	279	-9	2766.50	1913.50
	Francisco CEA	Sp	68	70	66	75	279	-9	2766.50	1913.50
	Dean ROBERTSON	Scot	69	66	73	71	279	-9	2766.50	1913.50
	John BICKERTON	Eng	66	69	71	73	279	-9	2766.50	1913.50
76	Andrew OLDCORN	Scot	64	72	69	75	280	-8	2614.50	1808.37
	Manuel MORENO	Sp	67	69	74	70	280	-8	2614.50	1808.37
78	Nick DOUGHERTY	Eng	71	67	70	73	281	-7	2610.00	1805.25
79	Federico BISAZZA	It	70	67	69	76	282	-6	2607.00	1803.18
80	Fredrik JACOBSON	Swe	70	68	74	71	283	-5	2604.00	1801.10
81	Malcolm MACKENZIE	Eng	70	68	71	75	284	-4	2601.00	1799.03
82	Tomas Jesus MUÑOZ	Sp	68	70	75	72	285	-3	2598.00	1796.95

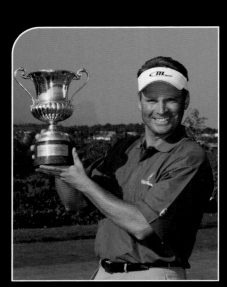

Mathias Grönberg

hunger for success

veryone who wins on The European Tour International Schedule is entitled to believe, for that week at least, he is the *Main Man*. Being the best ahead of 155 of your peers makes you the *Head Honcho*. But no-one ever felt more like the '*Big Cheese*' than Mathias Grönberg.

For, as well as the 183,330 euro (£127,172) first prize and the relief of ending over three winless years, the 33 year old Swede's victory in the 60th Italian Open Telecom Italia saw him receive one of the most unusual prizes of the season, namely his weight in cheese from one of the tournament sponsors, Grana Padano.

Moments after receiving the glittering trophy, Grönberg marched to the Cheese Pavillion, balanced tentatively on the scales, and was informed that 90kg of their finest fromage was now his.

The path to the cheese tent was a well worn one for the man whose last victory on The European Tour came in January 2000 in the South African Open. Every day on his way to and from the practice ground he popped in for a nibble and also indulged on the abundant platefuls available in the Players' Lounge.

Colin Montgomerie

José Manuel Lara

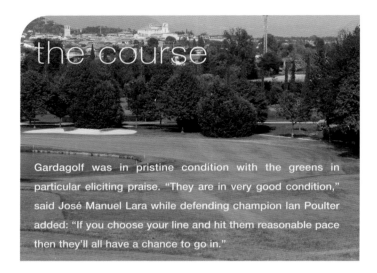

the course

Gardagolf was in pristine condition with the greens in particular eliciting praise. "They are in very good condition," said José Manuel Lara while defending champion Ian Poulter added: "If you choose your line and hit them reasonable pace then they'll all have a chance to go in."

It accounted, in part, for the reason his weight had risen by four kilos from the statistic given at the beginning of the year. "Yes it is slightly more," said a reddening Grönberg. "It is difficult not to do that here with all the great Italian food."

Still, an extra four kilos onto their sponsorship budget was not a bad return for Grana Padano, whose shareholders were understandably twitchy during the final round as the sturdier silhouettes of Ricardo Gonzalez and Colin Montgomerie loomed on the horizon.

Gonzalez, in fact, led by a shot going into the final round before a double bogey six at the seventh marked the beginning of the end of his challenge. The Argentine's closing 70 saw him fall back into a share of second with Spain's José Manuel Lara and Montgomerie, both of whom climbed into the joint runners-up spot with excellent 65s.

It was a score matched by Grönberg who showed it was not just the local dairy produce he was intent on feasting upon. In total during the week, he gorged himself on the immaculately presented Gardagolf layout, claiming 20 birdies and two eagles in total.

His second eagle three, at the 514 yard 11th hole in the final round, was his most significant thrust of the week. After a run of four birdies in five holes from the third, the pitch in from 30 feet propelled him to the top of the leaderboard, his advantage strengthened by the fact that, at exactly the same time in the final group, Gonzalez was running up his double bogey six.

After a consistent 2001 season where he finished 16th on the Volvo Order of Merit, Grönberg's appearances worldwide in 2002 numbered barely in double figures, preferring to spend time at home with wife Tara and their first child Lars. But with family life settled and his appetite for golf returning, Grönberg's visit to Italy was already his ninth tournament of the season and he showed the hunger for success had come with it.

Ricardo Gonzalez

Pierre Fulke

When he won the Smurfit European Open at The K Club in 1998, it was by ten shots and a similar desire to press home his advantage surfaced on the back nine on Sunday at Gardagolf. When a bogey four at the short 14th gave a glimmer of hope to the chasing pack, Grönberg immediately quelled the uprising with birdies at the 15th and 16th.

Although Gonzalez birdied the 16th, Lara birdied the 15th and eagled the 16th and Montgomerie, making his first competitive appearance of the season in Europe, birdied the 15th, 16th and 17th, none could do enough to prevent Grönberg succeeding.

They had played well, battled bravely, but had to be content with second. Hard cheese, lads.

Scott Crockett

final results

Gardagolf • Brescia • Italy
May 1 - 4 • 2003 • Par 72 • 7112 yards • 6505 metres

Pos.	Name		Rd1	Rd2	Rd3	Rd4	Total	Par	Prize Money Euro	£
1	Mathias GRÖNBERG	Swe	71	67	68	65	271	-17	183330.00	127172.96
2	José Manuel LARA	Sp	69	68	71	65	273	-15	82026.66	56900.53
	Colin MONTGOMERIE	Scot	70	67	71	65	273	-15	82026.66	56900.53
	Ricardo GONZALEZ	Arg	67	70	66	70	273	-15	82026.66	56900.53
5	Simon KHAN	Eng	70	72	64	68	274	-14	42570.00	29530.10
	Martin MARITZ	SA	71	71	66	66	274	-14	42570.00	29530.10
7	Pierre FULKE	Swe	68	70	66	71	275	-13	30250.00	20983.92
	Fredrik WIDMARK	Swe	69	65	72	69	275	-13	30250.00	20983.92
9	Marc FARRY	Fr	72	66	68	70	276	-12	20702.00	14360.63
	Peter O'MALLEY	Aus	64	70	70	72	276	-12	20702.00	14360.63
	Emanuele CANONICA	It	72	70	68	66	276	-12	20702.00	14360.63
	Rolf MUNTZ	NL	69	66	69	72	276	-12	20702.00	14360.63
	Gustavo ROJAS	Arg	70	68	68	70	276	-12	20702.00	14360.63
14	Roger WESSELS	SA	70	71	70	66	277	-11	16500.00	11445.77
	James HEPWORTH	Eng	73	70	67	67	277	-11	16500.00	11445.77
16	Barry LANE	Eng	71	68	69	70	278	-10	15180.00	10530.11
	Marcel SIEM	Ger	73	68	67	70	278	-10	15180.00	10530.11
18	Ian POULTER	Eng	74	66	71	68	279	-9	13244.00	9187.14
	Steen TINNING	Den	72	64	70	73	279	-9	13244.00	9187.14
	Jarrod MOSELEY	Aus	74	64	73	68	279	-9	13244.00	9187.14
	Stephen SCAHILL	NZ	71	69	68	71	279	-9	13244.00	9187.14
	Erol SIMSEK	Ger	68	69	69	73	279	-9	13244.00	9187.14
23	Peter FOWLER	Aus	71	71	67	71	280	-8	11770.00	8164.65
	Philip GOLDING	Eng	70	70	72	68	280	-8	11770.00	8164.65
	Matthew CORT	Eng	71	68	71	70	280	-8	11770.00	8164.65
26	Nicolas COLSAERTS	Bel	72	67	73	69	281	-7	10615.00	7363.45
	Gianluca BARUFFALDI	It	71	71	70	69	281	-7	10615.00	7363.45
	Tobias DIER	Ger	68	71	72	70	281	-7	10615.00	7363.45
	David DIXON	Eng	73	69	68	71	281	-7	10615.00	7363.45
30	Philip WALTON	Ire	73	69	70	70	282	-6	8983.33	6231.59
	Sven STRÜVER	Ger	70	67	74	71	282	-6	8983.33	6231.59
	Richard GREEN	Aus	73	68	66	75	282	-6	8983.33	6231.59
	Anthony WALL	Eng	69	70	71	72	282	-6	8983.33	6231.59
	Julien CLEMENT	Swi	70	71	70	71	282	-6	8983.33	6231.59
	Terry PRICE	Aus	74	67	69	72	282	-6	8983.33	6231.59
36	Roger CHAPMAN	Eng	67	76	69	71	283	-5	7260.00	5036.14
	Andrew SHERBORNE	Eng	68	71	71	73	283	-5	7260.00	5036.14
	Mattias ELIASSON	Swe	68	69	74	72	283	-5	7260.00	5036.14
	Denny LUCAS	Eng	73	66	71	73	283	-5	7260.00	5036.14
	Pehr MAGNEBRANT	Swe	71	65	68	79	283	-5	7260.00	5036.14
	Gary CLARK	Eng	66	70	69	78	283	-5	7260.00	5036.14
	Richard STERNE	SA	68	70	71	74	283	-5	7260.00	5036.14
	Steven BOWDITCH	Aus	74	67	72	70	283	-5	7260.00	5036.14
44	Gary EMERSON	Eng	73	69	74	68	284	-4	6050.00	4196.78
	Andrew MARSHALL	Eng	72	70	68	74	284	-4	6050.00	4196.78
	Andrew COLTART	Scot	72	70	69	73	284	-4	6050.00	4196.78
47	Hennie OTTO	SA	73	70	69	73	285	-3	5610.00	3891.56
48	Fredrik OREST	Swe	67	72	76	71	286	-2	4950.00	3433.73
	Raul BALLESTEROS	Sp	69	73	72	72	286	-2	4950.00	3433.73
	Marcello SANTI	It	71	71	70	74	286	-2	4950.00	3433.73
	Neil CHEETHAM	Eng	70	67	77	72	286	-2	4950.00	3433.73
	Matthew BLACKEY	Eng	68	73	73	72	286	-2	4950.00	3433.73
53	Alvaro SALTO	Sp	73	67	72	75	287	-1	3677.14	2550.77
	Jean-Francois REMESY	Fr	71	71	72	73	287	-1	3677.14	2550.77
	Damien MCGRANE	Ire	73	68	74	72	287	-1	3677.14	2550.77
	Sam LITTLE	Eng	70	73	74	70	287	-1	3677.14	2550.77
	Michele REALE	It	71	71	72	73	287	-1	3677.14	2550.77
	Ben MASON	Eng	70	71	70	76	287	-1	3677.14	2550.77
	Brett RUMFORD	Aus	71	70	78	68	287	-1	3677.14	2550.77
60	Gregory HAVRET	Fr	72	71	74	71	288	0	2970.00	2060.24
	David J GEALL	Eng	68	70	80	70	288	0	2970.00	2060.24
	Ivo GINER	Sp	72	68	74	74	288	0	2970.00	2060.24
63	Gary MURPHY	Ire	69	73	70	77	289	1	2640.00	1831.32
	Stuart LITTLE	Eng	68	72	73	76	289	1	2640.00	1831.32
	Charl SCHWARTZEL	SA	72	68	78	71	289	1	2640.00	1831.32
66	Andrea MAESTRONI	It	71	69	77	73	290	2	2365.00	1640.56
	Federico BISAZZA	It	69	69	78	74	290	2	2365.00	1640.56
68	Jesus Maria ARRUTI	Sp	70	72	75	74	291	3	2200.00	1526.10
	Edoardo MOLINARI (AM)	It	71	71	74	75	291	3		
70	Jean HUGO	SA	72	70	75	75	292	4	2090.00	1449.80
71	Simon WAKEFIELD	Eng	70	72	73	78	293	5	2010.00	1394.30

Paul Casey

golden touch

1	Paul CASEY Eng	277	-11
2	Padraig HARRINGTON Ire	281	-7
3	Paul LAWRIE Scot	282	-6
	Rolf MUNTZ NL	282	-6
	Stephen SCAHILL NZ	282	-6
6	Richard S JOHNSON Swe	284	-4
7	Angel CABRERA Arg	285	-3
	Brian DAVIS Eng	285	-3
	David PARK Wal	285	-3
10	Matthew BLACKEY Eng	286	-2
	David DIXON Eng	286	-2
	Simon KHAN Eng	286	-2
	Nick O'HERN Aus	286	-2

Some 32 years after it began, the last Benson and Hedges International Open champion was, in some ways, reassuringly similar to the first.

Back in 1971 it had been the most famous golfer in Europe who stepped forward as the winner, a young Englishman by the name of Tony Jacklin. By then Jacklin had won the 1969 Open Golf Championship and the 1970 US Open Championship.

He was, without question, the classiest act in town and his victory at Fulford offered instant credibility to a company that went on to be the longest and most continuous sponsor on The European Tour International Schedule.

How fitting then that on a bright and breezy Sunday in May another even younger Englishman, Paul Casey, stepped forward to receive the golden trophy that is host to so many of the most illustrious names in golf.

Despite having won the ANZ Championship on The European Tour earlier in the season, Casey, 25, did not carry the same fame into the tournament as Jacklin. For him, Major Championships remain a dream to unfold. But the swaggering manner of his final round echoed much of what encouraged Jacklin himself to step forward all those years ago.

Miles Tunnicliff

As he cradled the cup and glanced at the impressive list of past champions it was entirely unsurprising that Casey's hitherto focused stare was clouded by tears of joy. "Two years ago this was my first tournament as a professional and to stand here now as the last ever champion is a bit overwhelming. This means so much to me," he said.

Casey, it should be stressed, had not started the day as favourite. Instead Padraig Harrington was everyone's idea of a final Benson and Hedges International Open champion, the Irishman tied at ten under par alongside New Zealand's Stephen Scahill and Casey with defending champion Angel Cabrera a stroke behind.

Roger Chapman

Harrington, who had unfathomably failed to sign his card correctly three years earlier while embracing a five shot lead going into the final round, was both an obvious and sentimental favourite.

the course

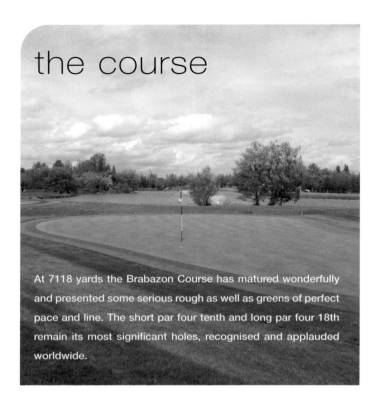

At 7118 yards the Brabazon Course has matured wonderfully and presented some serious rough as well as greens of perfect pace and line. The short par four tenth and long par four 18th remain its most significant holes, recognised and applauded worldwide.

"The only person I've got to fear is myself," he said on the eve of the final round. He was both correct and misguided as events turned out. A place in the top ten of the Official World Golf Ranking on top of a barrowload of sentiment does not count for much when luck and your putter conspire against you.

As Harrington missed a few short putts, Casey holed a few longer challenges and the balance of power tilted so much so that the young Englishman arrived on the 18th tee with a five shot lead. He could have taken eight shots on this troublesome beauty of a hole and still won.

In the end he took five, pitching from the greenside rough before two putting for a title that surely will ignite his career, his winning score of eleven under par 277, four ahead of Harrington with Scotland's Paul Lawrie, who holed in one at the seventh in the final round, Dutchman Rolf Muntz and Scahill tied for third.

Watching all this serious fun were a trio of men without whom, the Benson and Hedges International Open would not have been quite the same, Tournament Director Jim Elkins, Director of Tournament Operations Richard Brown, and George Griffith, whose attention to detail in the hospitality arena has been unparalleled and who is unfamiliar with the concept of a cork remaining in a champagne bottle.

Before Mr Elkins, the man who ran the week was the hugely respected Len Owen, whose concentration was constantly diluted by an impish sense of fun and who, more than anyone, set the abiding, and light, tone for the event, along with his admirable deputy Nick Hill and his good friend Derrick Pillage. Owen set a precedent with his celebrity Pro-Am, for which, as Pillage recalls, "all the celebrities were beating down Len's door to play," and

Stephen Scahill

Bernhard Langer 1981

together they made such a formidable team that much credit must go to Elkins for the wonderful way in which he picked up the baton. No wonder a tear crossed his cheek as Casey caressed the golden trophy.

To all involved, and to the players, to men like Gay Brewer, Billy Casper, Sam Snead and Lee Trevino, all of whom crossed the Atlantic in the early days to help establish the week, to Bernhard Langer who chose to climb a tree by the 17th green at Fulford in 1981 and who thus constructed one of the most famous photographs ever, to all these and more, we in the Media Centre offer our appreciation and thanks.

Whether at Fulford, St Mellion, The Oxfordshire or now, finally, at The De Vere Belfry, the Benson and Hedges International Open was a lot of fun.

Bill Elliott

final results

The De Vere Belfry · Sutton Coldfield · England
May 8 - 11 · 2003 · Par 72 · 7118 yards · 6509 metres

Pos.	Name		Rd1	Rd2	Rd3	Rd4	Total	Par	Prize Money Euro	£
1	Paul CASEY	Eng	71	69	66	71	277	-11	262227.90	183330.00
2	Padraig HARRINGTON	Ire	67	68	71	75	281	-7	174818.60	122220.00
3	Rolf MUNTZ	NL	70	71	69	72	282	-6	81292.13	56833.34
	Paul LAWRIE	Scot	71	72	70	69	282	-6	81292.13	56833.34
	Stephen SCAHILL	NZ	71	70	65	76	282	-6	81292.13	56833.34
6	Richard S JOHNSON	Swe	73	68	79	64	284	-4	55068.86	38500.00
7	Brian DAVIS	Eng	70	74	69	72	285	-3	40593.62	28380.00
	Angel CABRERA	Arg	68	69	70	78	285	-3	40593.62	28380.00
	David PARK	Wal	72	70	74	69	285	-3	40593.62	28380.00
10	Nick O'HERN	Aus	73	74	68	71	286	-2	28203.12	19717.50
	Simon KHAN	Eng	72	70	71	73	286	-2	28203.12	19717.50
	Matthew BLACKEY	Eng	71	76	69	70	286	-2	28203.12	19717.50
	David DIXON	Eng	66	78	68	74	286	-2	28203.12	19717.50
14	Klas ERIKSSON	Swe	75	72	73	67	287	-1	23128.92	16170.00
	José Manuel LARA	Sp	72	68	73	74	287	-1	23128.92	16170.00
	Bradley DREDGE	Wal	73	69	72	73	287	-1	23128.92	16170.00
17	Arjun ATWAL	Ind	71	73	76	68	288	0	19635.98	13728.00
	Jamie SPENCE	Eng	72	71	72	73	288	0	19635.98	13728.00
	Jean VAN DE VELDE	Fr	75	70	70	73	288	0	19635.98	13728.00
	Søren HANSEN	Den	77	70	70	71	288	0	19635.98	13728.00
	Ricardo GONZALEZ	Arg	70	72	70	76	288	0	19635.98	13728.00
22	Gary EMERSON	Eng	75	70	70	74	289	1	16835.34	11770.00
	Paul MCGINLEY	Ire	73	72	71	73	289	1	16835.34	11770.00
	Niclas FASTH	Swe	75	73	66	75	289	1	16835.34	11770.00
	Robert ROCK	Eng	71	73	72	73	289	1	16835.34	11770.00
	Jamie ELSON	Eng	71	69	78	71	289	1	16835.34	11770.00
27	Peter LAWRIE	Ire	74	71	72	73	290	2	14711.25	10285.00
	Colin MONTGOMERIE	Scot	72	70	72	76	290	2	14711.25	10285.00
	Lee WESTWOOD	Eng	72	73	73	72	290	2	14711.25	10285.00
	Daniel GREENWOOD	Eng	79	66	70	75	290	2	14711.25	10285.00
31	Roger CHAPMAN	Eng	71	71	73	76	291	3	12429.83	8690.00
	Henrik STENSON	Swe	68	76	72	75	291	3	12429.83	8690.00
	Richard BLAND	Eng	76	71	70	74	291	3	12429.83	8690.00
	Julien CLEMENT	Swi	71	70	74	76	291	3	12429.83	8690.00
	Markus BRIER	Aut	74	72	71	74	291	3	12429.83	8690.00
	John BICKERTON	Eng	74	71	72	74	291	3	12429.83	8690.00
37	Gordon BRAND JNR.	Scot	69	74	75	74	292	4	10227.07	7150.00
	Jean-Francois REMESY	Fr	71	70	74	77	292	4	10227.07	7150.00
	David GILFORD	Eng	69	75	74	74	292	4	10227.07	7150.00
	Raphaël JACQUELIN	Fr	73	72	72	75	292	4	10227.07	7150.00
	Stephen LEANEY	Aus	69	72	77	74	292	4	10227.07	7150.00
	Mikko ILONEN	Fin	75	67	73	77	292	4	10227.07	7150.00
	John E MORGAN	Eng	73	75	72	72	292	4	10227.07	7150.00
44	Bernhard LANGER	Ger	71	71	74	77	293	5	8024.32	5610.00
	Gary MURPHY	Ire	74	73	70	76	293	5	8024.32	5610.00
	Justin ROSE	Eng	72	75	75	71	293	5	8024.32	5610.00
	Henrik BJORNSTAD	Nor	71	77	73	72	293	5	8024.32	5610.00
	Stephen DODD	Wal	74	73	73	73	293	5	8024.32	5610.00
	Nick DOUGHERTY	Eng	73	75	72	73	293	5	8024.32	5610.00
	Richard STERNE	SA	70	75	73	75	293	5	8024.32	5610.00
51	Santiago LUNA	Sp	73	75	74	72	294	6	5443.95	3806.00
	Eduardo ROMERO	Arg	73	71	74	76	294	6	5443.95	3806.00
	Anthony WALL	Eng	73	72	76	73	294	6	5443.95	3806.00
	Shaun P WEBSTER	Eng	71	74	73	76	294	6	5443.95	3806.00
	David LYNN	Eng	74	74	72	74	294	6	5443.95	3806.00
	David DRYSDALE	Scot	75	72	75	72	294	6	5443.95	3806.00
	Terry PRICE	Aus	73	71	74	76	294	6	5443.95	3806.00
	Mads VIBE-HASTRUP	Den	72	76	67	79	294	6	5443.95	3806.00
	Tobias DIER	Ger	69	76	73	76	294	6	5443.95	3806.00
	Martin MARITZ	SA	71	74	74	75	294	6	5443.95	3806.00
61	Emanuele CANONICA	It	69	72	75	79	295	7	4248.17	2970.00
62	Malcolm MACKENZIE	Eng	72	74	74	76	296	8	3618.81	2530.00
	Peter FOWLER	Aus	72	72	77	75	296	8	3618.81	2530.00
	Marcel SIEM	Ger	70	78	73	75	296	8	3618.81	2530.00
	Miles TUNNICLIFF	Eng	70	75	78	73	296	8	3618.81	2530.00
	Phillip PRICE	Wal	73	72	72	79	296	8	3618.81	2530.00
	Andrew COLTART	Scot	70	75	78	73	296	8	3618.81	2530.00
	Retief GOOSEN	SA	74	73	74	75	296	8	3618.81	2530.00
69	Mark ROE	Eng	72	72	76	77	297	9	2645.37	1849.44
	Johan RYSTRÖM	Swe	74	72	77	74	297	9	2645.37	1849.44
	Ian GARBUTT	Eng	70	77	77	73	297	9	2645.37	1849.44
	David CARTER	Eng	72	73	79	73	297	9	2645.37	1849.44
73	Sandy LYLE	Scot	75	67	75	81	298	10	2352.50	1644.69
	Peter HEDBLOM	Swe	75	69	76	78	298	10	2352.50	1644.69
75	Jorge BERENDT	Arg	71	74	77	77	299	11	2348.00	1641.54
76	Peter MITCHELL	Eng	72	74	74	80	300	12	2345.00	1639.45
77	Alastair FORSYTH	Scot	73	75	81	72	301	13	2342.00	1637.35
78	Charl SCHWARTZEL	SA	72	70	80	80	302	14	2339.00	1635.25
79	Costantino ROCCA	It	71	77	77	78	303	15	2336.00	1633.16
80	Peter SENIOR	Aus	74	74	80	80	308	20	2333.00	1631.06

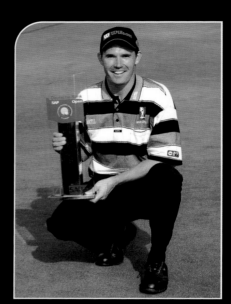

Padraig Harrington

ghostbuster

1	Padraig **HARRINGTON** Ire	269	-19
2	Thomas **BJÖRN** Den	269	-19
3	Retief **GOOSEN** SA	270	-18
4	Niclas **FASTH** Swe	271	-17
5	Paul **CASEY** Eng	272	-16
	Graeme **McDOWELL** N.Ire	272	-16
	Justin **ROSE** Eng	272	-16
8	Darren **CLARKE** N.Ire	273	-15
	Paul **LAWRIE** Scot	273	-15
	Greg **OWEN** Eng	273	-15

Golf courses are a lot like people. Some are born great, some are ordinary and remain so, while some might appear matter of fact on the surface but have a level of greatness thrust upon them as they grow into maturity. The circumstances surrounding Padraig Harrington's victory at Gut Kaden suggested that this course, amidst flat fields north of Hamburg, will forever have an aura about it as it basks in its new found reputation as the place where the affable Irishman may have come of age. The 450,000 euro (£322,474) he won may not have been the richest prize of his career to date, but it was far and away the most significant.

Indeed, there was considerable significance in what happened in Germany over four damp days in May. For once, little of it had to do with Tiger Woods's presence even though his appearance was enhanced by a vivid orange Lamborghini that was put at his disposal for the week.

In the end though, the fact that the American was competing in Germany for the fifth year in succession was overshadowed because

Thomas Levet

Graeme McDowell

the course

Sprawling over pasture land 15 miles north of Hamburg, one of the newer courses on The European Tour showed, on holes such as the par four 13th, that it is not necessary for a par four to be long for it to be difficult.

Woods could only finish tied 29th, his worst ever finish as a professional in an event on European soil. His first two rounds of 69-71 were, respectively, four and five strokes worse than Harrington's and though he matched the Irishman's scores on Saturday and Sunday, the damage had been done.

The eclipsing of Woods was yet another sign of the improvement in standards on The European Tour. It is doubtful if the World Number One would have been moved to the margins of an event a few years earlier, but now that the Tour has become so strong in depth, what had been unthinkable had come to pass.

On the last afternoon of a tournament in which Woods had only three bogeys, his play was far less important than the performance of the wavy haired Irishman with the ready smile.

Harrington, 31, has become the leading British and Irish player so quickly it is easy to forget that he only turned professional at the end

Thomas Björn

of 1995. Furthermore, because of his cheerful demeanour, courtesy and charm, he has made more friends than most. It is said you learn far more about a man from his behaviour in defeat than in victory and Harrington has borne this out.

Prior to this victory he had come second no less that 19 times in stroke play and match play tournaments, 17 times since the start of the 1999 season. It is said that no-one remembers who finishes second. Yet everyone in golf knew about Harrington and his near misses. He had a record that was on everyone's lips for the wrong reasons. However there were not many ifs and buts about Harrington's tenth victory as a professional other than it came in a one hole play-off with Thomas Björn. Harrington had led after the first, second and third rounds, but in the end he won with a display of nerve and character.

His rounds of 65-66-70-68 totalled 19 under par 269 and although there were nervous moments throughout a long and exciting final

afternoon, when five men were in with a chance, it was Harrington who triumphed.

Harrington's challengers were Niclas Fasth, the talented Swede who made his Ryder Cup debut in 2002, Retief Goosen, the 2001 and 2002 Volvo Order of Merit winner, Graeme McDowell, the promising Irishman in his second season as a professional, and Björn. Goosen used all his experience to remain a threat until the end, driving well and putting beautifully when the rest of his golf was anything but. Fasth had an electric start to his last round, being six under par after six holes before slipping back, while McDowell just failed to keep pace with the scintillating golf that was being played around him, of which Björn's 63, that set the mark of 19 under par, was typical.

Björn finished 40 minutes ahead of Harrington, who birdied the par five 15th to draw level but who was not able to birdie the par five 17th to pull clear. Harrington was clearly feeling the pressure and,

Christian Cévaër

having found the last green, left the putt he needed to hole to force a play-off with Björn some ten feet short of the cup.

In the hearts and minds of many who were watching there was a sinking feeling. Harrington looked as though he was about to come second once more. But he bravely holed the putt, the ball bolting into the middle of the hole, and when he had a four foot putt to win the play-off on the same hole a few minutes later, he holed that too.

"This was really important to me," he said. "I had led all last week [in the Benson and Hedges International Open at The De Vere Belfry where he eventually finished second] and all this week. It would have been a real dent to my confidence not to have come out on top today. Last week I thought to myself: Am I back to my old situation? Am I not converting?"

He might have been then, seven days earlier, but he was not in Germany. He had, he hoped, laid to rest a few ghosts.

John Hopkins

final results

Gut Kaden • Hamburg • Germany
May 15 - 18 • 2003 • Par 72 • 7215 yards • 6598 metres

Pos.	Name		Rd1	Rd2	Rd3	Rd4	Total	Par	Prize Money Euro	£
1	Padraig HARRINGTON	Ire	65	66	70	68	269	-19	450000.00	322474.31
2	Thomas BJÖRN	Den	71	70	65	63	269	-19	300000.00	214982.87
3	Retief GOOSEN	SA	65	69	70	66	270	-18	169020.00	121121.35
4	Niclas FASTH	Swe	68	69	68	66	271	-17	135000.00	96742.29
5	Justin ROSE	Eng	72	68	67	65	272	-16	96660.00	69267.48
	Paul CASEY	Eng	70	66	69	67	272	-16	96660.00	69267.48
	Graeme MCDOWELL	N.Ire	70	65	68	69	272	-16	96660.00	69267.48
8	Darren CLARKE	N.Ire	67	69	69	68	273	-15	60660.00	43469.54
	Paul LAWRIE	Scot	70	66	69	68	273	-15	60660.00	43469.54
	Greg OWEN	Eng	70	69	67	67	273	-15	60660.00	43469.54
11	Thomas LEVET	Fr	71	67	68	68	274	-14	49680.00	35601.16
12	Nick FALDO	Eng	70	67	70	68	275	-13	42727.50	30618.94
	Marc FARRY	Fr	70	70	69	66	275	-13	42727.50	30618.94
	Peter LAWRIE	Ire	67	69	71	68	275	-13	42727.50	30618.94
	David PARK	Wal	71	70	70	64	275	-13	42727.50	30618.94
16	Anthony WALL	Eng	71	70	64	71	276	-12	35707.50	25588.34
	Gregory HAVRET	Fr	70	70	68	68	276	-12	35707.50	25588.34
	Andrew COLTART	Scot	68	67	70	71	276	-12	35707.50	25588.34
	Alastair FORSYTH	Scot	70	67	72	67	276	-12	35707.50	25588.34
20	Robert-Jan DERKSEN	NL	70	69	68	70	277	-11	28920.00	20724.35
	Søren KJELDSEN	Den	71	68	71	67	277	-11	28920.00	20724.35
	Peter BAKER	Eng	67	69	71	70	277	-11	28920.00	20724.35
	Nicolas COLSAERTS	Bel	70	70	69	68	277	-11	28920.00	20724.35
	Miles TUNNICLIFF	Eng	69	68	70	70	277	-11	28920.00	20724.35
	John BICKERTON	Eng	72	69	68	68	277	-11	28920.00	20724.35
	David CARTER	Eng	69	70	68	70	277	-11	28920.00	20724.35
	Stephen GALLACHER	Scot	71	67	68	71	277	-11	28920.00	20724.35
	Mads VIBE-HASTRUP	Den	71	67	66	73	277	-11	28920.00	20724.35
29	Tiger WOODS	USA	69	71	70	68	278	-10	23220.00	16639.67
	Stephen LEANEY	Aus	72	70	68	68	278	-10	23220.00	16639.67
	Carlos RODILES	Sp	72	69	69	68	278	-10	23220.00	16639.67
	Robert KARLSSON	Swe	68	67	71	72	278	-10	23220.00	16639.67
	Gustavo ROJAS	Arg	69	69	72	68	278	-10	23220.00	16639.67
34	Peter FOWLER	Aus	72	68	70	69	279	-9	18360.00	13156.95
	Klas ERIKSSON	Swe	72	65	72	70	279	-9	18360.00	13156.95
	Raphaël JACQUELIN	Fr	68	68	73	70	279	-9	18360.00	13156.95
	Jean VAN DE VELDE	Fr	72	67	69	71	279	-9	18360.00	13156.95
	Colin MONTGOMERIE	Scot	69	69	68	73	279	-9	18360.00	13156.95
	Henrik BJORNSTAD	Nor	70	72	67	70	279	-9	18360.00	13156.95
	Johan RYSTRÖM	Swe	71	68	72	68	279	-9	18360.00	13156.95
	Emanuele CANONICA	It	71	71	69	68	279	-9	18360.00	13156.95
	Stephen SCAHILL	NZ	72	70	69	68	279	-9	18360.00	13156.95
	Simon WAKEFIELD	Eng	70	69	69	71	279	-9	18360.00	13156.95
44	Anders HANSEN	Den	68	70	69	73	280	-8	15120.00	10835.14
	Nick DOUGHERTY	Eng	73	68	69	70	280	-8	15120.00	10835.14
46	David HOWELL	Eng	71	71	69	70	281	-7	12960.00	9287.26
	David DRYSDALE	Scot	74	68	70	69	281	-7	12960.00	9287.26
	Fredrik WIDMARK	Swe	70	71	66	74	281	-7	12960.00	9287.26
	Martin MARITZ	SA	71	71	68	71	281	-7	12960.00	9287.26
	Jamie ELSON	Eng	71	70	69	71	281	-7	12960.00	9287.26
	Kevin NA	Kor	69	68	71	73	281	-7	12960.00	9287.26
52	Nick O'HERN	Aus	69	73	68	72	282	-6	10260.00	7352.41
	Peter O'MALLEY	Aus	69	66	74	73	282	-6	10260.00	7352.41
	Fredrik JACOBSON	Swe	71	68	74	69	282	-6	10260.00	7352.41
	Mark PILKINGTON	Wal	74	68	72	68	282	-6	10260.00	7352.41
56	Warren BENNETT	Eng	68	69	76	70	283	-5	8010.00	5740.04
	Steen TINNING	Den	72	70	68	73	283	-5	8010.00	5740.04
	Miguel Angel JIMÉNEZ	Sp	68	71	71	73	283	-5	8010.00	5740.04
	Jarrod MOSELEY	Aus	72	66	74	71	283	-5	8010.00	5740.04
	Benn BARHAM	Eng	68	70	75	70	283	-5	8010.00	5740.04
	Mikael LUNDBERG	Swe	70	71	72	70	283	-5	8010.00	5740.04
62	Gary EMERSON	Eng	73	68	72	71	284	-4	6885.00	4933.86
	Stuart LITTLE	Eng	74	68	69	73	284	-4	6885.00	4933.86
64	Bernhard LANGER	Ger	72	70	70	73	285	-3	6075.00	4353.40
	Ronan RAFFERTY	N.Ire	74	68	74	69	285	-3	6075.00	4353.40
	Richard GREEN	Aus	74	67	73	71	285	-3	6075.00	4353.40
	Nicolas VANHOOTEGEM	Bel	71	69	73	72	285	-3	6075.00	4353.40
68	Marcel SIEM	Ger	72	69	75	71	287	-1	5150.00	3690.54
	Christian CÉVAËR	Fr	68	71	75	73	287	-1	5150.00	3690.54
	Mikko ILONEN	Fin	72	70	74	71	287	-1	5150.00	3690.54
71	Steve WEBSTER	Eng	76	66	72	74	288	0	4045.50	2899.04
	Philip GOLDING	Eng	74	67	70	77	288	0	4045.50	2899.04
	Simon KHAN	Eng	72	70	69	77	288	0	4045.50	2899.04
	Markus BRIER	Aut	69	72	73	74	288	0	4045.50	2899.04
75	Jonathan LOMAS	Eng	70	72	76	73	291	3	4038.00	2893.67
76	Jochen LUPPRIAN	Ger	70	70	74	78	292	4	4035.00	2891.52
77	Gary BIRCH JNR	Eng	71	69	78	80	298	10	4032.00	2889.37

Volvo PGA Championship Wentworth Club · Surrey · England

psychological conquest

Ignacio Garrido

1	Ignacio GARRIDO Sp		270	-18
2	Trevor IMMELMAN SA		270	-18
3	Mathias GRÖNBERG Swe		273	-15
4	Ernie ELS SA		274	-14
5	Kenneth FERRIE Eng		275	-13
	Barry LANE Eng		275	-13
7	Søren KJELDSEN Den		276	-12
	Thomas LEVET Fr		276	-12
9	Paul CASEY Eng		277	-11
	Nick FALDO Eng		277	-11
	Colin MONTGOMERIE Scot		277	-11
	Gary ORR Scot		277	-11
	Phillip PRICE Wal		277	-11

Scaling Everest is all well and good, but coming back down to earth is what it is all about. Ignacio Garrido, coincidentally almost 50 years on from the day that two men "stood on top of the world" for the first time, climbed his ultimate summit when, with his own brand of courage and strength, he won the Volvo PGA Championship at Wentworth Club, Surrey, England.

the course

Chris Kennedy's greenkeeping team ensured that the superb West Course, which Ernie Els rates among the best in the world, provided another fair and examining challenge.

There is no way we can compare the West Course with the south-west face of Everest. Nevertheless just as the phlegmatic Edmund Hillary, a bee-keeper, swiftly returned to normality after his descent from 29,035 feet of ice, rock and snow so Garrido, whose passions include studying insects, was remarkably composed after his ascent of the Burma Road.

Garrido had secured his place in history with only his second win on The European Tour International Schedule. His first, coincidentally, had arrived in the then Volvo sponsored German Open in 1997. "You could say Volvo is my brand," he joked. With that win Garrido appeared to have established his base camp especially as later that year he made his debut in The Ryder Cup Matches. Moreover, he demonstrated his ability under pressure on the second morning at Club de Golf Valderrama. Partnering José Maria Olazábal against Tom Lehman and Phil Mickelson in the fourballs, he produced a match-saving bunker shot at the 17th with the water yawning in front of him. "The second greatest bunker shot I have ever seen," said Lehman.

Such success had been predictable. His father, Antonio, won five times on The European Tour between 1972 and 1986 and, with Seve Ballesteros, won the World Cup of Golf in 1977. Ballesteros and Garrido made history by becoming, in 1979, the first Continental players to compete in The Ryder Cup Matches.

Trevor Immelman

Peter Alliss, who played in eight Ryder Cup Matches before becoming one of the BBC's most respected television commentators, was given the accolade of Honorary Life Membership of The European Tour. Alliss (right) was presented with the award by Ken Schofield, Executive Director of The European Tour, during the Volvo PGA Championship at Wentworth Club.

RED Restaurant

VOLVO

for life

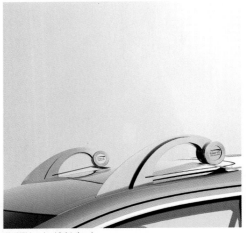

4X4/SUV Award and Safety Award
Institute of Vehicle Engineers Motor Show Design Awards

Truck of the Year in North America
North American Car of the Year Jury

Most Important Foreign Innovation
Auto Zeitung Magazine

Best in Class - Most Versatile
American Woman Road & Travel

Best New Large SUV
Kiplingers Personal Finance

World's Most Stylish Multifunctional Vehicle
L'Automobile più Bella del Mondo

Offroad Car of the Year
Car & Driver Magazine

Truck of Texas
Texas Auto Writers Association

Traffic Safety Achievement Award
World Traffic Safety Symposium
Manufacturer's Award

Urban Truck of the Year
The Urban Wheel Awards

SUV of the Year Award/Mudfest Champion
North West Automotive Press Association

Best 4X4 Car of the Year
What Car? Magazine

69

Nick Dougherty (left) is presented with the Sir Henry Cotton Rookie of the Year Award for 2002 by Retief Goosen.

The young Ignacio was surrounded by experts. José Maria Cañizares and Manuel Piñero were family friends. Golf, however, was not always first on the agenda. He was dispatched every summer as a teenager to stay with families in Hampshire in England. Garrido recalled: "My father was very cruel because he would not let me take my clubs! He told me I had to study first. Now that I study psychology myself, I know why he did and why I did it."

It was, Garrido revealed, simply a case of getting his mind straight that made winning at Wentworth Club possible after five years in the relative wilderness. Samantha Head, a professional on the women's tour, and his girlfriend, had given him a book called Seven Spiritual Laws of Success by Deepak Chopra. "Sam had been telling me from the beginning of the year that my golf was fine, I just needed a better mind. She told me to practice less and read more. The book, basically, is telling you to enjoy yourself. Enjoy life. Enjoy the good and the bad."

In truth there were other reasons. He thanked his father. He thanked his uncle, German Garrido, another former European Tour player. He thanked Alvaro Rogado, his manager. He thanked

Miguel Angel Jiménez for his support. He thanked David Wood, an English professional, for helping him obtain rhythm and increase his confidence with the putter. He thanked Ernie Els, his partner on the last day when 21,961 spectators increased the total attendance to 62,264, for encouraging him all the way. And he thanked Domingo Hospital, who played on The European Tour for many years. "He has been teaching me," Garrido explained. "He gave me two or three things to work on. My job was to focus only on those things. Then six months later he told me that I should have my feet like I am skiing. To open my feet a little in the stance. Sounds easy, but I could write a book about that change."

Garrido admitted that his plan for 2003, having finished 89th and 65th in the Volvo Order of Merit in 2001 and 2002 respectively, was simply to get into the Volvo Masters Andalucia comfortably and maybe have a couple of top ten finishes along the way. Well, the 2003 Volvo PGA Championship, the 49th edition of the Tour's flagship event, changed all that.

Garrido started with a solid 70 as Darren Clarke set the pace with a 66 – one ahead of Alastair Forsyth, Thongchai Jaidee and James

Since 1781 **Asprey** London, New York, Beverly Hills www.asprey.com

LONDON

THE A CHAIN

Robert Rock

Kingston. Clarke did not scar his card with a bogey and he reached every green except one in the regulation number of strokes. Clarke stayed out in front with a second round of 69 for a nine under par score of 135 which was one ahead of Niclas Fasth, who followed a 69 with 67, and two ahead of Kenneth Ferrie, Søren Hansen, Robert Rock and Ian Woosnam.

Rock was the big noise so to speak. The 26 year old teaching professional from the Swingers Golf Centre in Lichfield, whose competitive action was mostly reserved for regional events in the Midlands, was playing in only his fourth European Tour event. As his name rose up the leader board so interest gravitated towards him. But Rock said: "Apart from the spectators and the TV it felt like a normal game."

There was a changing of the guard on the third day. Clarke shot level par, but still seven players overtook him. Trevor Immelman catapulted himself to the head of affairs with a 64 on a lovely, calm day. He had only 23 putts and put himself two shots ahead of Fasth with Els and Garrido sharing third place. Els said of South African compatriot Immelman: "I think the way Trevor is going he could be a world star. Coming from a small nation like ours, I can say definitely that he's going to be the next superstar in South Africa."

Paul Eales (left) is presented with a magnum of Moët & Chandon champagne for his hole in one at the second hole in the final round by James Cockeram, Managing Director of Moët Hennessy Europe.

Ken Schofield, Executive Director of The European Tour, welcomes a party of Special Olympics Athletes to the Volvo PGA Championship at Wentworth Club. The European Tour and the Special Olympics have formed a partnership to help open the eyes of the world to an increasing understanding of Special Olympics.

To win on the West Course – the Harry Colt masterpiece superbly prepared again by Chris Kennedy, the Golf Courses Manager – is, of course, never easy especially with such a title at stake in addition to a 583,330 euro (£414,555) first prize. It becomes a more formidable task when those breathing down your neck also include Paul Casey, winner of the Benson and Hedges International Open two weeks earlier, Nick Faldo and Colin Montgomerie.

Immelman would parry each and every thrust with one exception. 'Nacho' Garrido had not known a moment like this since those days in 1997 when his eloquent English matched the brilliance of his game as he described his pride in following in the footsteps of his father. He had, after all, become only the second son to follow father into a Ryder Cup Team. Percy Alliss played in three teams starting in 1933; Peter followed by making his debut 20 years later. Garrido had caddied for his father in the 1985 Volvo PGA Championship when Antonio finished 12th at Wentworth Club. He had won the Brabazon Trophy on leave from his national service, beating many aspiring Walker Cup golfers. He had played for Spain in the Eisenhower Trophy. He was labelled by some observers as the

most promising young player in Europe but, after 1997, he had moved back into the supporting cast. Indeed Garrido teed up on the last day of the 2003 Volvo PGA Championship in 123rd place on the Volvo Order of Merit and 228th in the Official World Golf Ranking.

You would never have guessed it as he went out in 32 then made three birdies in a row from the tenth. He was ahead now, looking down from the top of the mountain, and when he holed from 30 feet at the 16th for another birdie he knew he was a finger touch away from glory. The two closing par fives offer birdie opportunities at Wentworth Club which proved beyond Garrido so Immelman, with birdies at the 15th and 17th, came to the last one behind. He found the green in two but his 80 foot putt for victory touched the hole refusing to disappear. They returned to the 18th tee and, as so often happens, Immelman was on in two, but Garrido still won. He did so with a fabulous chip from the side of the green, leaving the ball two feet from the hole (shades of Valderrama) from where he holed after Immelman had taken three putts and so completed his psychological conquest.

Garrido had followed in the footsteps of compatriots Seve Ballesteros, José Maria Olazábal and Manuel Piñero by winning the Volvo PGA Championship and he had recorded the 124th victory by a Spanish player since The European Tour was born in 1972. He delivered a wonderful speech at the prize giving, displaying an honesty and modesty that truly reflects his character, and, yes, in that euphoric vacuum which follows surprise success he was able to come straight back down to earth. "Winning this tournament is far more than I thought I could achieve, really," he said. There were many at Wentworth Club who felt certain, as the curtain came down on another superb Volvo PGA Championship, that he will have climbed another mountain or two by the time the 50th edition unfolds in 2004.

Mitchell Platts

Barry Lane

final results

Wentworth Club • Surrey • England
May 22 - 25 • 2003 • Par 72 • 7072 yards • 6468 metres

Pos.	Name		Rd1	Rd2	Rd3	Rd4	Total	Par	Prize Money Euro	£
1	Ignacio GARRIDO	Sp	70	69	66	65	270	-18	583330.00	414555.97
2	Trevor IMMELMAN	SA	69	69	64	68	270	-18	388880.00	276365.91
3	Mathias GRÖNBERG	Swe	72	67	67	67	273	-15	219100.00	155708.11
4	Ernie ELS	SA	69	69	67	69	274	-14	175000.00	124367.50
5	Barry LANE	Eng	72	68	68	67	275	-13	135450.00	96260.45
	Kenneth FERRIE	Eng	70	67	70	68	275	-13	135450.00	96260.45
7	Søren KJELDSEN	Den	68	72	69	67	276	-12	96250.00	68402.13
	Thomas LEVET	Fr	74	69	66	67	276	-12	96250.00	68402.13
9	Nick FALDO	Eng	71	68	68	70	277	-11	65870.00	46811.93
	Colin MONTGOMERIE	Scot	69	70	69	69	277	-11	65870.00	46811.93
	Phillip PRICE	Wal	71	69	67	70	277	-11	65870.00	46811.93
	Gary ORR	Scot	69	72	66	70	277	-11	65870.00	46811.93
	Paul CASEY	Eng	70	72	64	71	277	-11	65870.00	46811.93
14	Eduardo ROMERO	Arg	72	71	65	70	278	-10	48358.33	34366.88
	David GILFORD	Eng	70	69	71	68	278	-10	48358.33	34366.88
	Paul EALES	Eng	74	69	67	68	278	-10	48358.33	34366.88
	Darren CLARKE	N.Ire	66	69	72	71	278	-10	48358.33	34366.88
	Niclas FASTH	Swe	69	67	68	74	278	-10	48358.33	34366.88
	Kevin NA	Kor	69	70	68	71	278	-10	48358.33	34366.88
20	Peter FOWLER	Aus	70	71	70	68	279	-9	40716.67	28936.17
	Stephen LEANEY	Aus	69	73	65	72	279	-9	40716.67	28936.17
	Adam SCOTT	Aus	68	73	71	67	279	-9	40716.67	28936.17
23	Sandy LYLE	Scot	75	68	67	70	280	-8	36400.00	25868.44
	Henrik BJORNSTAD	Nor	71	71	71	67	280	-8	36400.00	25868.44
	John BICKERTON	Eng	72	69	71	68	280	-8	36400.00	25868.44
	Robert ROCK	Eng	69	68	70	73	280	-8	36400.00	25868.44
	Martin MARITZ	SA	71	71	68	70	280	-8	36400.00	25868.44
28	Mårten OLANDER	Swe	73	67	69	72	281	-7	31675.00	22510.52
	Peter HEDBLOM	Swe	69	74	69	69	281	-7	31675.00	22510.52
	Stephen DODD	Wal	71	72	69	69	281	-7	31675.00	22510.52
	Mikko ILONEN	Fin	69	70	72	70	281	-7	31675.00	22510.52
32	Ronan RAFFERTY	N.Ire	69	72	72	69	282	-6	26031.25	18499.67
	Mark MCNULTY	Zim	69	71	68	74	282	-6	26031.25	18499.67
	Justin ROSE	Eng	68	73	70	71	282	-6	26031.25	18499.67
	Miles TUNNICLIFF	Eng	69	73	71	69	282	-6	26031.25	18499.67
	Emanuele CANONICA	It	71	69	69	73	282	-6	26031.25	18499.67
	Paul MCGINLEY	Ire	70	69	71	72	282	-6	26031.25	18499.67
	Fredrik JACOBSON	Swe	72	69	70	71	282	-6	26031.25	18499.67
	Andrew COLTART	Scot	68	71	70	73	282	-6	26031.25	18499.67
40	Gordon BRAND JNR.	Scot	68	70	68	77	283	-5	21700.00	15421.57
	Henrik STENSON	Swe	71	72	70	70	283	-5	21700.00	15421.57
	Alastair FORSYTH	Scot	67	71	71	74	283	-5	21700.00	15421.57
	Jamie DONALDSON	Wal	69	71	68	75	283	-5	21700.00	15421.57
44	Ian WOOSNAM	Wal	68	69	72	75	284	-4	18900.00	13431.69
	Jean VAN DE VELDE	Fr	71	70	70	73	284	-4	18900.00	13431.69
	James KINGSTON	SA	67	76	67	74	284	-4	18900.00	13431.69
	Raymond RUSSELL	Scot	74	67	73	70	284	-4	18900.00	13431.69
48	José Maria OLAZÁBAL	Sp	68	71	74	72	285	-3	15750.00	11193.08
	Ricardo GONZALEZ	Arg	69	73	70	73	285	-3	15750.00	11193.08
	David DRYSDALE	Scot	72	71	71	71	285	-3	15750.00	11193.08
	Matthew BLACKEY	Eng	70	73	71	71	285	-3	15750.00	11193.08
	Michael CAMPBELL	NZ	69	74	69	73	285	-3	15750.00	11193.08
53	Sam TORRANCE	Scot	70	71	70	75	286	-2	12250.00	8705.73
	Jean-Francois REMESY	Fr	73	69	75	69	286	-2	12250.00	8705.73
	Anders HANSEN	Den	70	72	70	74	286	-2	12250.00	8705.73
	Peter BAKER	Eng	68	73	70	75	286	-2	12250.00	8705.73
	Henrik NYSTROM	Swe	73	69	74	70	286	-2	12250.00	8705.73
58	Roger CHAPMAN	Eng	71	69	79	68	287	-1	9625.00	6840.21
	Santiago LUNA	Sp	72	71	71	73	287	-1	9625.00	6840.21
	Greg TURNER	NZ	72	70	71	74	287	-1	9625.00	6840.21
	Steen TINNING	Den	74	69	70	74	287	-1	9625.00	6840.21
	Pierre FULKE	Swe	71	72	70	74	287	-1	9625.00	6840.21
	Greg OWEN	Eng	68	71	73	75	287	-1	9625.00	6840.21
64	Peter SENIOR	Aus	68	73	76	71	288	0	7700.00	5472.17
	Darren FICHARDT	SA	69	73	77	69	288	0	7700.00	5472.17
	Nick O'HERN	Aus	73	69	71	75	288	0	7700.00	5472.17
	Mikael LUNDBERG	Swe	72	69	73	74	288	0	7700.00	5472.17
	Thongchai JAIDEE	Thai	67	72	76	73	288	0	7700.00	5472.17
69	Carlos RODILES	Sp	70	73	73	73	289	1	6520.00	4633.58
	Søren HANSEN	Den	69	68	77	75	289	1	6520.00	4633.58
71	Arjun ATWAL	Ind	68	74	72	77	291	3	5250.00	3731.03
72	Barry AUSTIN	Eng	73	68	77	74	292	4	5245.50	3727.83
	David ORR	Scot	72	71	75	74	292	4	5245.50	3727.83
74	Christian CÉVAËR	Fr	73	70	77	75	295	7	5241.00	3724.63
75	Ben WILLMAN	Eng	73	68	77	79	297	9	5238.00	3722.50

The Celtic Manor Resort Wales Open
The Celtic Manor Resort · City of Newport · Wales

swallow song

Ian Poulter

1	Ian POULTER Eng	270	-18
2	Darren FICHARDT SA	273	-15
	Jonathan LOMAS Eng	273	-15
	Jarrod MOSELEY Aus	273	-15
5	Andrew COLTART Scot	275	-13
	Mark McNULTY Zim	275	-13
7	Peter FOWLER Aus	276	-12
	Santiago LUNA Sp	276	-12
	Phillip PRICE Wal	276	-12
10	Jamie DONALDSON Wal	278	-10
	Bradley DREDGE Wal	278	-10
	Fredrik JACOBSON Swe	278	-10
	Iain PYMAN Eng	278	-10
	Jarmo SANDELIN Swe	278	-10

A victory on The European Tour International Schedule can often bring a lump to the throat, but Ian Poulter had one even before he began his first round in The Celtic Manor Resort Wales Open. In fact, he had two and he claimed they felt as big as cricket balls.

the course

In a few years, professionals will be spared the spectacular but daunting climb up the slopes of the Usk Valley which contain the Wentwood Hills's final six holes. Work has already started on reshaping the course in good time for it to host The 2010 Ryder Cup Matches.

Tonsilitis is the medical term for the condition he took with him to the spectacular Wentwood Hills course, but anyone who witnessed the Englishman's arrival would have diagnosed alongside it, a serious case of flamboyance.

He roared up to the luxurious hotel in a red, open-topped Ferrari, fashioning a personalised number plate, with his tousled hair streaked red in honour of Arsenal's victory in the FA Cup Final at the nearby Millennium Stadium in Cardiff 12 days earlier.

However, no-one could see the most vividly red part of his ensemble - his throat. One sight of it might have persuaded tournament officials to allow him to withdraw.

But Poulter had long been a martyr to his tonsils and since he had won the Moroccan Open in 2001 with the same glands inflamed, he felt it was worth the effort. He played in the Pro-Am on Wednesday and went straight to bed afterwards, downing a dose of the antibiotics that are his constant companions on Tour.

He felt no better the following morning when he reported for his 8.30am tee-time but was determined to give his recently refurbished swing another outing. What transpired was as big a surprise to the 2000 Sir Henry Cotton Rookie of the Year as it was to anyone else.

Jarrod Moseley

Several big names were kept away by injury and other commitments but there were many whose chances were rated better than those of Poulter who had narrowly missed qualifying for The 2001 European Ryder Cup Team but who had not enjoyed the best of starts to the 2003 season as he worked on his swing realignment.

Undisputed favourite was Colin Montgomerie, who had been showing signs of improvement in his build up to the US Open Championship, and who had certainly brought plenty of confidence with him. "Having won the English, Scottish and Irish

Jonathan Lomas

Nick O'Hern

Opens I thought this was a great opportunity to complete the set," said the Scot who had come fresh from a top ten finish in the Volvo PGA Championship the previous week.

This was fighting talk from the man who knew there was a strong Welsh contingent bidding to keep the title at home for the first time. One was Ian Woosnam, who had also played encouraging golf at Wentworth Club, and another was Ryder Cup hero Phillip Price, this week a local hero as his house is no more than a ten minutes drive from the course.

So few eyes were on Poulter as he began to fashion the first of four exceptional rounds during which he was never headed at the top of the leaderboard. His 65 on that first day saw him share the lead with Australia's Nick O'Hern and he confessed at his press conference that he had gone out with no expectations other than it would hurt every time he swallowed.

But his tonsils turned out to be his best friends. He had taken five weeks out of his season earlier in the year in order to re-fashion his swing under the guidance of David Leadbetter. In six events since then he had made only one cut. "Perhaps, I'd been trying too hard," he said. "Today, I didn't try hard at all. I was only swinging at 80 per cent and I hit some great shots."

Jarmo Sandelin

final results

The Celtic Manor Resort • City of Newport • Wales
May 29 - June 1 • 2003 • Par 72 • 7355 yards • 6727 metres

Pos.	Name		Rd1	Rd2	Rd3	Rd4	Total	Par	Prize Money Euro	£
1	Ian POULTER	Eng	65	67	68	70	270	-18	347360.00	250000.00
2	Darren FICHARDT	SA	68	67	70	68	273	-15	155413.50	111853.34
	Jarrod MOSELEY	Aus	74	67	63	69	273	-15	155413.50	111853.34
	Jonathan LOMAS	Eng	66	71	68	68	273	-15	155413.50	111853.34
5	Mark MCNULTY	Zim	69	67	69	70	275	-13	80656.99	58050.00
	Andrew COLTART	Scot	68	69	67	71	275	-13	80656.99	58050.00
7	Santiago LUNA	Sp	68	69	70	69	276	-12	53771.32	38699.99
	Peter FOWLER	Aus	67	72	68	69	276	-12	53771.32	38699.99
	Phillip PRICE	Wal	68	66	68	74	276	-12	53771.32	38699.99
10	Bradley DREDGE	Wal	71	69	67	71	278	-10	36264.38	26100.00
	Fredrik JACOBSON	Swe	71	68	64	75	278	-10	36264.38	26100.00
	Jarmo SANDELIN	Swe	67	73	68	70	278	-10	36264.38	26100.00
	Iain PYMAN	Eng	73	67	68	70	278	-10	36264.38	26100.00
	Jamie DONALDSON	Wal	68	71	68	71	278	-10	36264.38	26100.00
15	Roger CHAPMAN	Eng	74	68	67	70	279	-9	29386.65	21150.00
	Jean-Francois REMESY	Fr	68	72	69	70	279	-9	29386.65	21150.00
	Richard GREEN	Aus	67	70	72	70	279	-9	29386.65	21150.00
18	Peter LAWRIE	Ire	68	75	67	70	280	-8	25913.05	18650.00
	Christian CÉVAËR	Fr	71	72	65	72	280	-8	25913.05	18650.00
	Terry PRICE	Aus	71	71	68	70	280	-8	25913.05	18650.00
21	Barry LANE	Eng	69	71	66	75	281	-7	22925.76	16500.00
	Arjun ATWAL	Ind	75	68	72	66	281	-7	22925.76	16500.00
	David DRYSDALE	Scot	68	70	73	70	281	-7	22925.76	16500.00
	Stephen GALLACHER	Scot	70	72	69	70	281	-7	22925.76	16500.00
	Graeme MCDOWELL	N.Ire	70	72	72	67	281	-7	22925.76	16500.00
26	Sven STRÜVER	Ger	68	72	71	71	282	-6	19799.52	14250.00
	Steve WEBSTER	Eng	70	70	69	73	282	-6	19799.52	14250.00
	Nick O'HERN	Aus	65	72	70	75	282	-6	19799.52	14250.00
	Paul BROADHURST	Eng	72	70	72	68	282	-6	19799.52	14250.00
	Stephen DODD	Wal	70	71	71	70	282	-6	19799.52	14250.00
31	David HOWELL	Eng	70	69	71	73	283	-5	16226.67	11678.57
	Alessandro TADINI	It	69	70	73	71	283	-5	16226.67	11678.57
	Philip GOLDING	Eng	72	69	69	73	283	-5	16226.67	11678.57
	Diego BORREGO	Sp	71	72	69	71	283	-5	16226.67	11678.57
	Greg OWEN	Eng	74	68	70	71	283	-5	16226.67	11678.57
	Patrik SJÖLAND	Swe	72	69	69	73	283	-5	16226.67	11678.57
	Nick DOUGHERTY	Eng	72	70	72	69	283	-5	16226.67	11678.57
38	Malcolm MACKENZIE	Eng	67	73	70	74	284	-4	13963.87	10050.00
	Carlos RODILES	Sp	68	70	76	70	284	-4	13963.87	10050.00
	Martin MARITZ	SA	74	68	70	72	284	-4	13963.87	10050.00
41	Anthony WALL	Eng	72	70	72	71	285	-3	11879.71	8550.00
	Jean-François LUCQUIN	Fr	69	74	68	74	285	-3	11879.71	8550.00
	Julien CLEMENT	Swi	71	72	70	72	285	-3	11879.71	8550.00
	Emanuele CANONICA	It	71	70	70	74	285	-3	11879.71	8550.00
	David PARK	Wal	70	72	74	69	285	-3	11879.71	8550.00
	Alastair FORSYTH	Scot	67	73	75	70	285	-3	11879.71	8550.00
	Robert ROCK	Eng	70	71	73	71	285	-3	11879.71	8550.00
48	Marc FARRY	Fr	73	70	73	70	286	-2	8545.06	6150.00
	Mårten OLANDER	Swe	74	67	70	75	286	-2	8545.06	6150.00
	Gregory HAVRET	Fr	68	73	74	71	286	-2	8545.06	6150.00
	Richard BLAND	Eng	72	69	71	74	286	-2	8545.06	6150.00
	Julien VAN HAUWE	Fr	68	75	72	71	286	-2	8545.06	6150.00
	Ian GARBUTT	Eng	72	71	77	66	286	-2	8545.06	6150.00
	Ricardo GONZALEZ	Arg	67	71	72	76	286	-2	8545.06	6150.00
	Stephen SCAHILL	NZ	71	69	72	74	286	-2	8545.06	6150.00
	Simon WAKEFIELD	Eng	69	71	72	74	286	-2	8545.06	6150.00
57	Sandy LYLE	Scot	70	70	76	71	287	-1	5731.44	4125.00
	Klas ERIKSSON	Swe	68	72	74	73	287	-1	5731.44	4125.00
	Fredrik OREST	Swe	70	73	70	74	287	-1	5731.44	4125.00
	Anders HANSEN	Den	73	70	71	73	287	-1	5731.44	4125.00
	Maarten LAFEBER	NL	72	70	73	72	287	-1	5731.44	4125.00
	Peter BAKER	Eng	74	69	73	71	287	-1	5731.44	4125.00
	Jesus Maria ARRUTI	Sp	68	69	76	74	287	-1	5731.44	4125.00
	David DIXON	Eng	72	69	74	72	287	-1	5731.44	4125.00
65	Philip ARCHER	Eng	67	73	70	78	288	0	4585.15	3300.00
	Barry AUSTIN	Eng	68	74	73	73	288	0	4585.15	3300.00
	Michael CAMPBELL	NZ	69	73	70	76	288	0	4585.15	3300.00
68	Henrik BJORNSTAD	Nor	73	67	72	77	289	1	3978.43	2863.33
	Miles TUNNICLIFF	Eng	70	70	74	75	289	1	3978.43	2863.33
	Simon HURD	Eng	70	72	74	73	289	1	3978.43	2863.33
71	Euan LITTLE	Scot	73	70	74	73	290	2	3124.50	2248.75
	Nicolas COLSAERTS	Bel	69	73	69	79	290	2	3124.50	2248.75
73	Robert-Jan DERKSEN	NL	70	73	72	76	291	3	3115.50	2242.27
	Raphaël JACQUELIN	Fr	74	69	75	73	291	3	3115.50	2242.27
	Shaun P WEBSTER	Eng	72	71	74	74	291	3	3115.50	2242.27
	Jamie SPENCE	Eng	71	71	71	78	291	3	3115.50	2242.27
77	Gary MURPHY	Ire	69	74	77	74	294	6	3106.50	2235.79
	Fredrik WIDMARK	Swe	69	73	80	72	294	6	3106.50	2235.79
79	Benn BARHAM	Eng	73	69	78	76	296	8	3102.00	2232.55

He continued to do so and found the strength to beat off two determined challenges on his way to the trophy. Neither came from Montgomerie who struggled so much on the greens that he drove 130 miles home on Thursday evening to get a new putter. That didn't work either and he missed the cut.

The challenge from Price came on the second day when the Welshman produced a solid 66 to lie two shots behind Poulter. A course record 63 in the third round by Jarrod Moseley of Australia brought him into the reckoning but Poulter, despite one or two wobbles, kept his rivals at bay and broke their hearts when he scored the only eagle of the tournament on the testing 621 yard 11th hole in the final round.

"Yes, my throat's a lot better," he said, when he celebrated moving from 135th to 14th on the Volvo Order of Merit. He might have even managed a song in the Ferrari on the way home.

Peter Corrigan

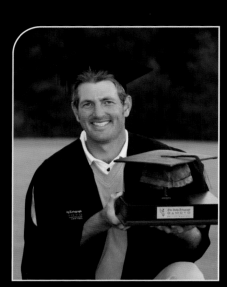

Greg Owen

1	Greg OWEN Eng	274	-14
2	Christian CÉVAËR Fr	277	-11
	Ian POULTER Eng	277	-11
4	Darren CLARKE N.Ire	280	-8
	Robert ROCK Eng	280	-8
	Anthony WALL Eng	280	-8
7	Jorge BERENDT Arg	281	-7
	Stephen GALLACHER Scot	281	-7
	Raphaël JACQUELIN Fr	281	-7
	David LYNN Eng	281	-7

merry master

There was a new look to the British Masters this year. New sponsors in The Daily Telegraph and Damovo; new promoters in International Sports Management; a new venue in the Marriott Forest of Arden; a new golf exhibition initiative, and a brand new S-Type 200 Jaguar for Argentine Jorge Berendt for finishing nearest the pin at the 18th hole on the final day.

It was only fitting then that the tournament, too, should have a new champion, if not a new face. Greg Owen, from Sherwood Forest territory, has been one of the merry men of the circuit for a number of years without ever being able to capture one of the game's biggest prizes. Indeed there were plenty of occasions, not too many birdies before he finally became a champion, when Owen wondered if he would ever burst in to rob the rich.

Owen had begun to debate with himself if he had what it took to be a winner. When he lost a three shot lead in Portugal in April, the despair was almost unbearable. Family and friends may not have had to take his shoelaces from him or keep him away from cliff edges, high bridges or the medicine cabinet, but the last thing he wanted to do for a while was play golf.

The 31 year old, who ironically was once on promoter Andrew 'Chubby' Chandler's ISM books before joining Barry Hearn's Matchroom Golf stable, was decanted out of his vat of self-pity by caddie Richard Hill and his coach from Coxmoor Golf Club, David Ridley. They convinced him that he was not made of jelly, but the right stuff. They told him to turn the negatives into positives the next time opportunity knocked. They told him not only to get a grip of his club, but also reality. They told him that one day it would happen for him.

That day came sooner than they and definitely Owen might have predicted. What is more, the squash and fitness fanatic found himself in exactly the same position he had been during the Algarve Open de Portugal - pursued by the pack. This time, however, he did not

Darren Clarke

the course

The Arden Course had never been in better condition. Proof came from seven time Volvo Order of Merit winner Colin Montgomerie who asked for a late invitation because he knew it would offer excellent preparation for the following week's US Open Championship.

Stephen Gallacher

buckle under the pressure of expectancy and nerves, even though his closest challenger was no less a figure than Ian Poulter, who seven days previously had been crowned prince of The Celtic Manor Resort Wales Open.

Poulter is one of those players who does not back off. If he were a dog the only way anybody would get a bone from his jaws would be to drag out his teeth with it and even then it would be a tough task for a Tug of War team. Owen bared his own teeth to the challenge and passed his Masters degree with a first.

Owen did it thanks to a career best three iron - a shot over water to the 71st hole many were aghast to see him take on and one he placed in his all-time top three alongside the one that produced an albatross in The 130th Open Golf Championship at Royal Lytham & St Annes, and the one which yielded an eagle in the US PGA Championship at Hazeltine National in 2002.

The safe play to protect his lead without overdue stress would have

been to lay up, but Owen sensed fate had already taken over this day and dealt him a winning hand.

When Richard Hill passed him a three iron, he took it without hesitation. The next time he saw the ball was when it finished ten feet from the hole for a birdie that meant he would be wearing the event's cape and mortarboard to show that he was the Master of 2003.

Typically, Owen did not forget the tutors when he started to sing his songs of praise afterwards. His caddie of five years, he admitted, was brilliant. "He's dedicated to me and his job, what more could I ask?" Coach Ridley was also amongst the many singled out.

It had been Ridley who had not offered a shoulder for Owen to cry on after the pain of Portugal, but a reminder that his job was as a professional golfer. There were going to be days that would not go to plan, he told him, no matter how well he played. "When I came back from Portugal, I did not want to play golf I just wanted to

The Daily Telegraph

Read a bestseller...

The Daily Telegraph

LEWINE MAIR | JUSTIN ROSE | COLIN MONTGOMERIE

BRITAIN'S BEST-SELLING QUALITY DAILY

...every day

telegraph.co.uk

Richard Green

final results

Marriott Forest of Arden • Warwickshire • England
June 5 - 8 • 2003 • Par 72 • 7213 yards • 6595 metres

Pos.	Name		Rd1	Rd2	Rd3	Rd4	Total	Par	Prize Money Euro	£
1	Greg OWEN	Eng	68	68	67	71	274	-14	348312.50	250000.00
2	Ian POULTER	Eng	71	73	63	70	277	-11	181512.60	130279.99
	Christian CÉVAËR	Fr	73	70	66	68	277	-11	181512.60	130279.99
4	Anthony WALL	Eng	72	70	67	71	280	-8	88750.02	63700.00
	Darren CLARKE	N.Ire	71	71	72	66	280	-8	88750.02	63700.00
	Robert ROCK	Eng	73	69	70	68	280	-8	88750.02	63700.00
7	Raphaël JACQUELIN	Fr	70	72	72	67	281	-7	50888.46	36525.00
	Jorge BERENDT	Arg	72	72	67	70	281	-7	50888.46	36525.00
	David LYNN	Eng	66	71	71	73	281	-7	50888.46	36525.00
	Stephen GALLACHER	Scot	69	71	71	70	281	-7	50888.46	36525.00
11	Søren KJELDSEN	Den	70	73	70	69	282	-6	34148.56	24510.00
	Richard GREEN	Aus	70	66	71	75	282	-6	34148.56	24510.00
	Henrik STENSON	Swe	69	74	70	69	282	-6	34148.56	24510.00
	Mathias GRÖNBERG	Swe	73	71	66	72	282	-6	34148.56	24510.00
	Fredrik ANDERSSON	Swe	74	70	68	70	282	-6	34148.56	24510.00
16	Mark ROE	Eng	71	70	69	73	283	-5	25809.96	18525.00
	Darren FICHARDT	SA	72	66	71	74	283	-5	25809.96	18525.00
	Nick O'HERN	Aus	72	70	70	71	283	-5	25809.96	18525.00
	Philip GOLDING	Eng	69	73	69	72	283	-5	25809.96	18525.00
	Marcel SIEM	Ger	66	71	74	72	283	-5	25809.96	18525.00
	Robert KARLSSON	Swe	75	69	69	70	283	-5	25809.96	18525.00
	Ignacio GARRIDO	Sp	67	72	73	71	283	-5	25809.96	18525.00
	Mikael LUNDBERG	Swe	69	69	71	74	283	-5	25809.96	18525.00
24	David HOWELL	Eng	72	71	67	74	284	-4	20794.26	14925.00
	Barry LANE	Eng	73	68	68	75	284	-4	20794.26	14925.00
	Justin ROSE	Eng	69	75	73	67	284	-4	20794.26	14925.00
	Jarrod MOSELEY	Aus	70	73	70	71	284	-4	20794.26	14925.00
	Gary ORR	Scot	72	72	72	68	284	-4	20794.26	14925.00
	Andrew COLTART	Scot	68	73	70	73	284	-4	20794.26	14925.00
30	Peter FOWLER	Aus	65	75	69	76	285	-3	17067.31	12250.00
	David GILFORD	Eng	70	73	71	71	285	-3	17067.31	12250.00
	Peter BAKER	Eng	69	74	68	74	285	-3	17067.31	12250.00
	Gregory HAVRET	Fr	73	71	70	71	285	-3	17067.31	12250.00
	Markus BRIER	Aut	71	72	70	72	285	-3	17067.31	12250.00
	Patrik SJÖLAND	Swe	70	72	71	72	285	-3	17067.31	12250.00
36	Sandy LYLE	Scot	72	71	73	70	286	-2	13584.19	9750.00
	Mårten OLANDER	Swe	75	67	71	73	286	-2	13584.19	9750.00
	Philip ARCHER	Eng	71	73	72	70	286	-2	13584.19	9750.00
	Miguel Angel JIMÉNEZ	Sp	72	70	71	73	286	-2	13584.19	9750.00
	Charlie WI	Kor	72	72	68	74	286	-2	13584.19	9750.00
	Stephen SCAHILL	NZ	73	71	67	75	286	-2	13584.19	9750.00
	Simon WAKEFIELD	Eng	71	71	73	71	286	-2	13584.19	9750.00
	Matthew BLACKEY	Eng	70	68	70	78	286	-2	13584.19	9750.00
	Lee WESTWOOD	Eng	67	76	73	70	286	-2	13584.19	9750.00
45	Gordon BRAND JNR.	Scot	71	73	71	72	287	-1	10240.39	7350.00
	Santiago LUNA	Sp	70	74	71	72	287	-1	10240.39	7350.00
	Costantino ROCCA	It	69	72	73	73	287	-1	10240.39	7350.00
	Brian DAVIS	Eng	72	70	69	76	287	-1	10240.39	7350.00
	Henrik BJORNSTAD	Nor	73	71	69	74	287	-1	10240.39	7350.00
	Iain PYMAN	Eng	71	72	73	71	287	-1	10240.39	7350.00
	Jamie DONALDSON	Wal	70	71	68	78	287	-1	10240.39	7350.00
52	Mark JAMES	Eng	71	72	67	78	288	0	7941.52	5700.00
	Peter LAWRIE	Ire	69	74	70	75	288	0	7941.52	5700.00
	Euan LITTLE	Scot	72	71	72	73	288	0	7941.52	5700.00
	Jean-François LUCQUIN	Fr	69	71	73	75	288	0	7941.52	5700.00
56	Mark MOULAND	Wal	74	70	69	76	289	1	6090.49	4371.43
	Robert-Jan DERKSEN	NL	70	73	73	73	289	1	6090.49	4371.43
	Gary EMERSON	Eng	71	72	78	68	289	1	6090.49	4371.43
	James KINGSTON	SA	72	70	70	77	289	1	6090.49	4371.43
	Matthew CORT	Eng	69	72	75	73	289	1	6090.49	4371.43
	Mikko ILONEN	Fin	75	67	72	75	289	1	6090.49	4371.43
	Brett RUMFORD	Aus	71	70	69	79	289	1	6090.49	4371.43
63	Fernando ROCA	Sp	73	70	72	75	290	2	4911.21	3525.00
	Adam MEDNICK	Swe	72	69	74	75	290	2	4911.21	3525.00
	Bradley DREDGE	Wal	72	72	70	76	290	2	4911.21	3525.00
	Robert COLES	Eng	76	68	76	70	290	2	4911.21	3525.00
67	Fredrik OREST	Swe	71	73	75	72	291	3	4089.19	2935.00
	Damien MCGRANE	Ire	75	67	74	75	291	3	4089.19	2935.00
	Paul EALES	Eng	72	72	74	73	291	3	4089.19	2935.00
	Raymond RUSSELL	Scot	66	77	75	73	291	3	4089.19	2935.00
71	Klas ERIKSSON	Swe	71	71	74	76	292	4	3132.00	2247.98
	Jarmo SANDELIN	Swe	67	76	68	81	292	4	3132.00	2247.98
	Gary BIRCH JNR	Eng	72	69	76	75	292	4	3132.00	2247.98
74	Jesus Maria ARRUTI	Sp	66	76	76	76	294	6	3126.00	2243.67
75	Ivo GINER	Sp	73	69	73	83	298	10	3123.00	2241.52

spend time with my little girl," he said. Ridley shook him out of it and Owen stopped feeling sorry for himself.

At the start of the week, Owen's CV offered no better than a string of third place finishes, but with the words of his caddie and coach ringing in his ears, he knew he was better than third rate.

The Daily Telegraph Damovo British Masters allowed him the chance to prove he was first class. He did it with the style that prompted his former manager Chandler to say: "If one of my stable couldn't win it then I can think of nobody better than Greg to become our champion."

Just champion, that's Owen.

Martin Hardy

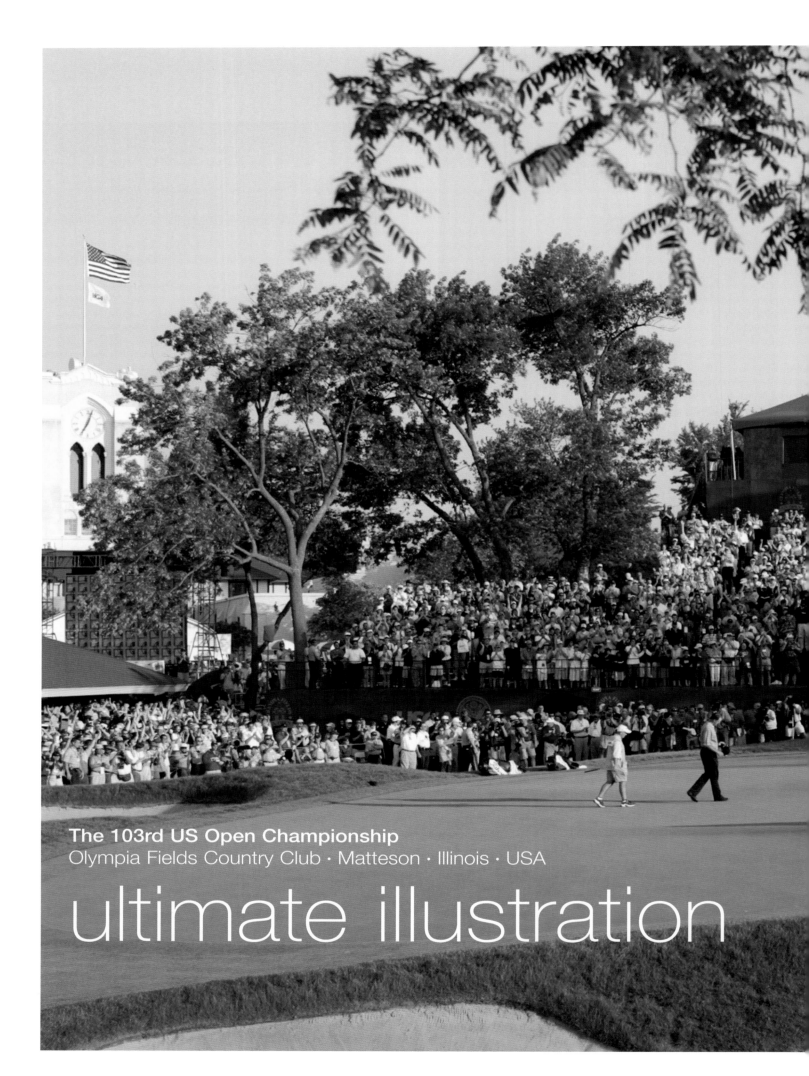

The 103rd US Open Championship
Olympia Fields Country Club · Matteson · Illinois · USA

ultimate illustration

Jim Furyk

1	Jim FURYK USA		272	-8
2	Stephen LEANEY Aus		275	-5
3	Kenny PERRY USA		279	-1
	Mike WEIR Can		279	-1
5	Ernie ELS SA		280	0
	Fredrik JACOBSON Swe		280	0
	Nick PRICE Zim		280	0
	Justin ROSE Eng		280	0
	David TOMS USA		280	0
10	Padraig HARRINGTON Ire		281	1
	Jonathan KAYE USA		281	1
	Cliff KRESGE USA		281	1
	Billy MAYFAIR USA		281	1
	Scott VERPLANK USA		281	1

After finishing first in sand saves one year, Eamonn Darcy was asked about his bunker technique for the purposes of a magazine instruction feature. "Well, there isn't much to it," he said. "I get into the bunker, I place my feet – and then I hit it."

the course

A classically traditional course, rightfully restored to the US Open Championship rota after 75 years. Let down by the weather on the first two days, Olympia Fields Country Club played hard and fast over the weekend to show its true quality.

The Irishman's brevity might not have been much use for a writer with several pages to fill but in skipping the detail he had raised the important point that too much knowledge can be a dangerous thing. Understanding every nuance leads to changing what comes naturally, when some players would indeed be better off just hitting it.

Perhaps the ultimate illustration came during an intriguing week at the first US Open Championship to be held at Olympia Fields Country Club on the outskirts of Chicago since 1928. In the days leading up to the event, the unusual three-tier practice ground was filled with perfect swing after perfect swing. Then you came to Jim Furyk.

Now if Furyk had a pound for every time some 'expert' recommended changing his unorthodox swing, every time he heard some wisecrack about his unique action, his riches would have doubled.

Instead he ignored them all in that kindly, understated manner of his. He drew upon examples such as Arnold Palmer and Lee Trevino to hammer home the fact that desire and self-belief are more important than textbook technique. He concentrated on grooving his unusual method to the point where it could withstand the pressures of the game at the highest level.

Nick Price

Stephen Leaney

Players seeking perfect swings say they are making changes because they want consistency, but how about Furyk's consistency? He came to Chicago having registered ten top tens in 14 starts. Since the US Open Championship is by common consent the Major that places the most emphasis on accuracy, everyone agreed in the build-up that Furyk possessed the hallmark of a Champion. So much for perfect technique - compliments don't get much bigger than that.

Furyk justified it with the performance of his career. Leading from the front is the hardest way to win your first Major, but he took a three stroke lead into the final day's play and never at any stage looked like losing it.

Indeed it was a remarkable showing from both players in the final group, for alongside him was the hitherto unheralded Australian Stephen Leaney. On television on Saturday night a rather smug conclusion from a 30 second interview was reached that Leaney looked terrified, and would struggle the following day. He certainly made that verdict look foolish as he pulled away from some of the best players in the world to finish runner-up and register his best finish in a Major Championship.

As the event drew towards its conclusion, and the course hardened up and showed some fearsome teeth, two more players trained in the all-encompassing arena of The European Tour seized their chance to impress a new audience. Anyone who paid attention to Fredrik Jacobson's victory in the Algarve Open de Portugal in April knew all about his skills around the greens. Here he gave another vivid demonstration in what has to go down as one of the best performances by a professional playing in his first event in the United States.

Illustrating the point was the company Jacobson kept. Alongside him in joint fifth position were three proven Major Champions in Ernie Els, Nick Price and David Toms. The fifth member of this quintet was Justin Rose, playing in just his third American Major, and doing enough to suggest that before his career is through, the 22 year old will have lifted this trophy.

A compelling sub-plot to Furyk's masterclass was the performance of Tom Watson. Taking inspiration from caddie Bruce Edwards, who suffers from an aggressive form of multiple sclerosis from which there is no known cure, Watson shot 65 on the first day, which in 30 US Open Championship appearances, just happened to be the best opening round of his career in this Major Championship.

Official Supplier

# of The European Tour ...
They count on us ... So can you.

Along with superb shotmaking and tight competition, what makes a European Tour event so memorable are the stunning golf landscapes where championships are contested. The dedicated teams of managers, superintendents and greenkeepers who create these lush, challenging courses count on Toro—and so can you. The same equipment, irrigation systems and support Toro provides to its partners at European Tour sites is available to golf courses everywhere. Whether large or small, new or old, every golf course with the desire to provide memorable golf experiences has a willing partner in this pursuit: Toro. Count on it.

©2003 The Toro Company

 David Garland, Director of Tour Operations, The European Tour (pictured above)

"Not only did Toro have a full and diverse range of equipment that we required, and the majority of the Tour's top venues were already committed Toro users, but the endorsements and plaudits we received from the Course Superintendent's, in our opinion the men who really count, were so numerous the decision was easy."

Chris Kennedy, Director and Golf Courses Manager, The Wentworth Club, England (pictured above)

"We prepare for three televised golf tournaments annually and since coming to Wentworth 13 years ago I've done 32 televised golf tournaments using Toro equipment and irrigation. It is simply the best equipment for the preparation of golf tournaments.

Toro is still the only company that has the aeration equipment you can use the day before the tournament. Certainly for tournament presentation, the Toro range of product is second to none."

 Peter Nyberg
General Manager, Kungsangen Golf Club, Sweden

"The best part of Toro is they are so up to date with their new technology. If there's anything our greenkeepers are discussing or may need, they know that Toro is always in the front.

Toro equipment allows the staff to prepare a course to meet the demanding new standards of the tour. Nowadays you need to have such a wide range of equipment to maintain a course, and you know that Toro has the equipment you need."

 Steve Taylor
Course Superintendent, Druids Glen Golf Club, Ireland

"We find the machines give a quality cut. This, coupled with an excellent mechanic, means the machines perform at the highest standard.

The Toro units offer easy maintenance, and I don't just mean easier to work with, I mean they get less and less complicated, easier to work on, easier to set up and adjust."

 Eddie Bullock
Managing Director, Woburn Golf and Country Club, England

"Toro has listened and they've become a part of Woburn Golf and Country Club. They're team members.

... and when things are not going right, that Toro team member is right there, listening and working with you."

 Theuns Van Niekerk
Superintendent, Houghton Golf Club, South Africa

"The service that we get from Toro in South Africa is excellent. If we're in trouble, they'll lend us machines and help us out. They fix things at quite a fast speed. The support is very good."

"There's not one machine in the whole range that I think is inferior to anything else available."

 Jaime Ortiz Patiño
President, Club de Golf Valderrama, Spain

"Having received recommendations from specialists in the field of go maintenance of the quality of Toro equipment, I was fortunate since the day I purchased Valderrama in 1985 to go exclusively with Toro

I do not regret this choice, since the use of Toro equipment has always given me optimum results and their technology is always at the forefront. The durability of Toro equipment makes it more economical in the long run."

 Klaus Peter Sauer
Course Manager, Golf Club St. Leon-Rot, Germany

"The machines are always good, especially the Greensmaster Flex 21. There's no other possibility on the market at the moment to cut sloped greens down as low. You can get better speeds on the greens, which makes the course much tougher.

When they deliver the machinery, they always have the time to demonstrate the equipment to my staff.

When they come out from the factory, you see there was a lot of thought put into the machine."

 Bill Warwick
Superintendent, Saint-Nom-La-Bretèche Golf Club, France

"Going into the tournament, I don't worry about equipment. I'm worried more about the golf course and the weather. I don't even have to think about the equipment. I know it's going to be reliable It's one less thing I have to think about. I know it's going to start and work well.

All machines break eventually, every superintendent knows that. Be the support you get when your machine's down, when you need it most, that's what great about Toro. That's why we are Toro. That' why we don't have any other colour here."

www.toro.co

 Count on it.

Justin Rose

At 53, it was hardly surprising that age caught up with him thereafter, but Watson and Edwards continued to hold the galleries spellbound as they celebrated their 30 year partnership and life itself. Edwards said afterwards that if someone had told him in 1973 the path his life would take, with its dreadful denouement, he would not have changed a thing.

And so from a caddie's brave outlook to a US Open Champion's unbending commitment to the unorthodox, the theme of the week became the acceptance that things are rarely perfect. It is how you work with imperfection that decides your fate.

Derek Lawrenson

final results

Olympia Fields Country Club • Matteson • Illinois • USA
June 12 - 15 • 2003 • Par 70 • 7190 yards • 6576 metres

Pos.	Name		Rd1	Rd2	Rd3	Rd4	Total	Par	Prize Money Euro	£
1	Jim FURYK	USA	67	66	67	72	272	-8	923470.80	649741.29
2	Stephen LEANEY	Aus	67	68	68	72	275	-5	555792.60	391047.99
3	Mike WEIR	Can	73	67	68	71	279	-1	291891.20	205370.61
	Kenny PERRY	USA	72	71	69	67	279	-1	291891.20	205370.61
5	Nick PRICE	Zim	71	65	69	75	280	0	158985.80	111860.21
	Justin ROSE	Eng	70	71	70	69	280	0	158985.80	111860.21
	Ernie ELS	SA	69	70	69	72	280	0	158985.80	111860.21
	Fredrik JACOBSON	Swe	69	67	73	71	280	0	158985.80	111860.21
	David TOMS	USA	72	67	70	71	280	0	158985.80	111860.21
10	Padraig HARRINGTON	Ire	69	72	72	68	281	1	106828.50	75163.06
	Scott VERPLANK	USA	76	67	68	70	281	1	106828.50	75163.06
	Billy MAYFAIR	USA	69	71	67	74	281	1	106828.50	75163.06
	Jonathan KAYE	USA	70	70	72	69	281	1	106828.50	75163.06
	Cliff KRESGE	USA	69	70	72	70	281	1	106828.50	75163.06
15	Eduardo ROMERO	Arg	70	66	70	76	282	2	79828.07	56165.93
	Hidemichi TANAKA	Jpn	69	71	71	71	282	2	79828.07	56165.93
	Tim PETROVIC	USA	69	70	70	73	282	2	79828.07	56165.93
	Tom BYRUM	USA	69	69	71	73	282	2	79828.07	56165.93
	Jonathan BYRD	USA	69	66	71	76	282	2	79828.07	56165.93
20	Tiger WOODS	USA	70	66	75	72	283	3	54869.56	38605.46
	Ian LEGGATT	Can	68	70	68	77	283	3	54869.56	38605.46
	Justin LEONARD	USA	66	70	72	75	283	3	54869.56	38605.46
	Robert DAMRON	USA	69	68	73	73	283	3	54869.56	38605.46
	Mark CALCAVECCHIA	USA	68	72	67	76	283	3	54869.56	38605.46
	Vijay SINGH	Fiji	70	63	72	78	283	3	54869.56	38605.46
	Peter LONARD	Aus	72	69	74	68	283	3	54869.56	38605.46
	Jay WILLIAMSON	USA	72	69	69	73	283	3	54869.56	38605.46
28	Tom WATSON	USA	65	72	75	72	284	4	35274.88	24818.92
	Stewart CINK	USA	70	68	72	74	284	4	35274.88	24818.92
	Kirk TRIPLETT	USA	71	68	73	72	284	4	35274.88	24818.92
	Kevin SUTHERLAND	USA	71	71	72	70	284	4	35274.88	24818.92
	Brett QUIGLEY	USA	65	74	71	74	284	4	35274.88	24818.92
	Dicky PRIDE	USA	71	69	66	78	284	4	35274.88	24818.92
	John MAGINNES	USA	72	70	72	70	284	4	35274.88	24818.92
35	Sergio GARCIA	Sp	69	74	71	71	285	5	27834.09	19583.68
	Mark O'MEARA	USA	72	68	67	78	285	5	27834.09	19583.68
	Fred FUNK	USA	70	73	71	71	285	5	27834.09	19583.68
	Angel CABRERA	Arg	72	68	73	72	285	5	27834.09	19583.68
	Brandt JOBE	USA	70	68	76	71	285	5	27834.09	19583.68
	Chad CAMPBELL	USA	70	70	69	76	285	5	27834.09	19583.68
	Chris DIMARCO	USA	72	71	71	71	285	5	27834.09	19583.68
42	Bernhard LANGER	Ger	70	70	73	73	286	6	21378.35	15041.51
	Loren ROBERTS	USA	69	72	74	71	286	6	21378.35	15041.51
	Steve LOWERY	USA	70	72	70	74	286	6	21378.35	15041.51
	Colin MONTGOMERIE	Scot	69	74	71	72	286	6	21378.35	15041.51
	Darren CLARKE	N.Ire	70	69	72	75	286	6	21378.35	15041.51
	Retief GOOSEN	SA	71	72	73	70	286	6	21378.35	15041.51
48	Woody AUSTIN	USA	74	64	76	73	287	7	16267.62	11445.67
	Niclas FASTH	Swe	75	68	73	71	287	7	16267.62	11445.67
	Dan FORSMAN	USA	71	67	73	76	287	7	16267.62	11445.67
	Marco DAWSON	USA	72	71	75	69	287	7	16267.62	11445.67
	Darron STILES	USA	71	68	72	76	287	7	16267.62	11445.67
53	Charles HOWELL III	USA	70	73	74	71	288	8	14539.54	10229.82
	John ROLLINS	USA	73	70	68	77	288	8	14539.54	10229.82
55	Phil MICKELSON	USA	70	70	75	74	289	9	13851.21	9745.52
	Lee JANZEN	USA	72	68	72	77	289	9	13851.21	9745.52
57	Len MATTIACE	USA	69	73	77	71	290	10	13375.79	9411.02
	Trip KUEHNE (Am)	USA	74	67	76	73	290	10		
59	Olin BROWNE	USA	72	70	74	75	291	11	13122.69	9232.94
	Ricky BARNES (Am)	USA	71	71	79	70	291	11		
61	Brian DAVIS	Eng	71	72	74	75	292	12	12663.52	8909.88
	Alex CEJKA	Ger	73	66	76	77	292	12	12663.52	8909.88
	Chris ANDERSON	USA	72	70	78	72	292	12	12663.52	8909.88
64	JP HAYES	USA	70	73	79	71	293	13	12141.93	8542.89
	Jay Don BLAKE	USA	66	77	75	75	293	13	12141.93	8542.89
66	Fred COUPLES	USA	70	72	73	80	295	15	11723.80	8248.70
	Brian HENNINGER	USA	76	67	76	76	295	15	11723.80	8248.70
68	Ryan DILLON	USA	72	68	81	80	301	21	11401.44	8021.90

Brett Rumford

1	Brett RUMFORD Aus	269	-15
2	Ben MASON Eng	274	-10
3	Federico BISAZZA It	278	-6
4	Mattias ELIASSON Swe	279	-5
	Peter HANSON Swe	279	-5
	James HEPWORTH Eng	279	-5
	Damien McGRANE Ire	279	-5
8	Garry HOUSTON Wal	280	-4
	Martin LeMESURIER Eng	280	-4
	Stuart LITTLE Eng	280	-4
	Cesar MONASTERIO Arg	280	-4
	Alvaro SALTO Sp	280	-4

opportunity and incentive

The view from the back window on the first floor of the clubhouse went beyond beautiful. It was the sort of vista that induces a sharp intake of breath, an involuntary gasp at the sheer magnificence of it all. Florence causes it, so do Rome, Madrid and Vienna, but they are made by man. This was, too, to a certain degree, yet the overriding sense was that the rolling hills and a multi-shaded celebration of the colour green was an organic thing, something that had just happened. It was splendid.

St Omer, for it was there that the manifold treats for the visual senses were granted to those who looked on, is a comparative handful of miles from the landing grounds of Dunkirk in World War II. Omaha Beach is an hour away; it is a region of north-west France that will forever remain a living monument to countless brave men.

It was a more humble endeavour in which other courageous young chaps were engaged in four days in the sun in early June. They were not literally fighting for their lives and yet, in a professional sense, they almost were.

Peter Hanson

The Aa St Omer Open was one of three tournaments in 2003 that had dual ranking between The European Tour International Schedule, on which it was making its maiden appearance, and the Challenge Tour, which it had graced for the previous three years. It meant that prize money counted on both circuits and, furthermore, that victory would bring a precious exemption on The European Tour for the remainder of 2003 and throughout 2004.

There was a lot more at stake then, than the money involved. Indeed, a cogent argument could be made that the exemption was more important than the cheque, never mind the pleasure of communing with a blessed slice of nature.

More than half of the field was composed of regulars on the Challenge Tour, being given their chance to play for a much bigger purse than they are used to, on a stunningly photogenic golf course. The contestants were mostly young, mostly fairly inexperienced but all talented and all ambitious. That said, there were still ten former winners of full European Tour titles in the start list, so whoever won would have to beat plenty of good 'uns.

Ben Mason

the course

There was sadness that Johan Dudok van Heel, the distinguished Dutch architect who designed the course, did not see his pride and joy used at the highest level - he passed away two weeks before the tournament started. He would have been proud had he heard the praise that was rightly heaped upon St Omer by the players.

Such men as Paul Broadhurst and Philip Walton, former Ryder Cup players both, Mark Mouland and Andrew Sherborne, all of them with victories to their credit and plenty of miles under their experienced belts, and all there to stake their respective claims. Oh yes, and Brett Rumford, Ben Mason and Federico Bisazza, who just happened to show the experienced hands the way home in first, second and third places respectively.

The performances of the top three underlined the burgeoning skills of the up-and-comers in the Tour ranks and gave further credibility to the Tour's theme of Opportunity and Incentive. The words deserve their capital letters, for they form an integral and vital part of a corporate philosophy whose validity is ably supported by fact.

Rumford deserves pride of place, of course, not only because he won but also because he led from first day to last. He had a two stroke advantage after a marvellous opening 64, had it cut to one in the second round but was three shots ahead going into the final day.

Johan Edfors

Martin LeMesurier

The last time the 25 year old Australian from Perth had led by three after 54 holes was in the 2001 Ericsson Masters in Melbourne, but he bogeyed three of the first six holes and ended up tied for third after Colin Montgomerie made up five strokes on him to win the tournament. There were to be no such hiatuses this time.

Mason, his closest pursuer and playing partner, closed the gap to one after three birdies to Rumford's one in the opening five holes. It was the ensuing stretch that did for Mason however, playing the last 13 holes in one over par for 69 while Rumford negotiated the same piece of real estate in three under for a 67, a total of 269, 15 under par, and victory by five shots.

Long before the end of that run Mason was a beaten man and nowhere was that better illustrated than by the ninth hole, where Rumford was literally two inches from going out of bounds yet still managed to salvage his par five. Mason, meanwhile, did nothing wrong until he missed an eight foot putt for a birdie. It just was not his day – that belonged to a cool, calm and collected Australian.

Mel Webb

final results

Aa St Omer Golf Club • St Omer • France
June 12 - 15 • 2003 • Par 71 • 6799 yards • 6217 metres

Pos.	Name		Rd1	Rd2	Rd3	Rd4	Total	Par	Prize Money Euro	£
1	Brett RUMFORD	Aus	64	70	68	67	269	-15	66660.00	46901.05
2	Ben MASON	Eng	70	69	66	69	274	-10	44440.00	31267.37
3	Federico BISAZZA	It	68	72	68	70	278	-6	25040.00	17617.80
4	Mattias ELIASSON	Swe	66	73	69	71	279	-5	15740.00	11074.45
	Damien MCGRANE	Ire	72	70	69	68	279	-5	15740.00	11074.45
	Peter HANSON	Swe	69	69	70	71	279	-5	15740.00	11074.45
	James HEPWORTH	Eng	70	72	70	67	279	-5	15740.00	11074.45
8	Alvaro SALTO	Sp	68	67	74	71	280	-4	8240.00	5797.55
	Cesar MONASTERIO	Arg	66	73	72	69	280	-4	8240.00	5797.55
	Garry HOUSTON	Wal	68	69	68	75	280	-4	8240.00	5797.55
	Stuart LITTLE	Eng	71	68	71	70	280	-4	8240.00	5797.55
	Martin LEMESURIER	Eng	72	73	68	67	280	-4	8240.00	5797.55
13	Martin ERLANDSSON	Swe	70	69	70	72	281	-3	6146.67	4324.71
	Sebastien BRANGER	Fr	69	69	72	71	281	-3	6146.67	4324.71
	Bjorn PETTERSSON	Swe	68	74	68	71	281	-3	6146.67	4324.71
16	Neil CHEETHAM	Eng	71	72	74	65	282	-2	5400.00	3799.37
	Erol SIMSEK	Ger	71	70	71	70	282	-2	5400.00	3799.37
	Lucas PARSONS	Aus	72	69	73	68	282	-2	5400.00	3799.37
19	Pasi PURHONEN	Fin	73	70	73	67	283	-1	4960.00	3489.79
20	Philip WALTON	Ire	74	70	71	69	284	0	4405.71	3099.80
	Marc PENDARIES	Fr	69	72	71	72	284	0	4405.71	3099.80
	Paul BROADHURST	Eng	69	69	73	73	284	0	4405.71	3099.80
	Michele REALE	It	70	69	72	73	284	0	4405.71	3099.80
	Sion E BEBB	Wal	69	72	72	71	284	0	4405.71	3099.80
	Raphael PELLICIOLI	Fr	74	71	68	71	284	0	4405.71	3099.80
	Allan HOGH	Den	71	72	70	71	284	0	4405.71	3099.80
27	Marco SOFFIETTI	It	72	72	70	71	285	1	3444.44	2423.46
	Philip GOLDING	Eng	74	67	73	71	285	1	3444.44	2423.46
	Pehr MAGNEBRANT	Swe	71	74	69	71	285	1	3444.44	2423.46
	Robert COLES	Eng	70	71	73	71	285	1	3444.44	2423.46
	Gary CLARK	Eng	72	70	71	72	285	1	3444.44	2423.46
	Marco BERNARDINI	It	70	71	73	71	285	1	3444.44	2423.46
	Mark SANDERS	Eng	70	70	74	71	285	1	3444.44	2423.46
	Michael KIRK	SA	69	69	75	72	285	1	3444.44	2423.46
	Gregory BOURDY	Fr	74	70	69	72	285	1	3444.44	2423.46
36	Greig HUTCHEON	Scot	73	72	70	71	286	2	2760.00	1941.90
	Titch MOORE	SA	71	70	74	71	286	2	2760.00	1941.90
	Johan EDFORS	Swe	71	71	73	71	286	2	2760.00	1941.90
	Joakim RASK	Swe	68	74	71	73	286	2	2760.00	1941.90
	Philippe LIMA	Fr	68	74	71	73	286	2	2760.00	1941.90
41	Lionel ALEXANDRE	Fr	70	70	77	70	287	3	2360.00	1660.46
	Michael ARCHER	Eng	70	71	77	69	287	3	2360.00	1660.46
	Jamie LITTLE	Eng	72	70	76	69	287	3	2360.00	1660.46
	Gianluca BARUFFALDI	It	70	71	70	76	287	3	2360.00	1660.46
	Oskar BERGMAN	Swe	72	71	71	73	287	3	2360.00	1660.46
46	Fredrik OREST	Swe	74	71	74	69	288	4	1960.00	1379.03
	Scott DRUMMOND	Scot	72	73	73	70	288	4	1960.00	1379.03
	Denny LUCAS	Eng	67	75	75	71	288	4	1960.00	1379.03
	Christopher HANELL	Swe	70	73	71	74	288	4	1960.00	1379.03
	Simon DYSON	Eng	69	75	72	72	288	4	1960.00	1379.03
51	Marcel HAREMZA	Ger	70	73	74	72	289	5	1520.00	1069.45
	Jean HUGO	SA	71	74	72	72	289	5	1520.00	1069.45
	Paul DWYER	Eng	72	72	71	74	289	5	1520.00	1069.45
	Edward RUSH	Eng	72	71	73	73	289	5	1520.00	1069.45
	Brad KENNEDY	Aus	72	71	73	73	289	5	1520.00	1069.45
	Marcus FRASER	Aus	70	71	74	74	289	5	1520.00	1069.45
57	Alessandro TADINI	It	71	74	73	72	290	6	1120.00	788.02
	Massimo FLORIOLI	It	71	72	74	73	290	6	1120.00	788.02
	David DUPART	Fr	71	74	74	71	290	6	1120.00	788.02
	Kariem BARAKA	Ger	73	72	73	72	290	6	1120.00	788.02
	Thomas NORRET	Den	74	70	75	71	290	6	1120.00	788.02
	Peter GUSTAFSSON	Swe	74	70	75	71	290	6	1120.00	788.02
	Paul MCKECHNIE	Scot	70	75	73	72	290	6	1120.00	788.02
64	Sam LITTLE	Eng	68	76	74	73	291	7	940.00	661.37
	Andrew BEAL	Eng	70	75	72	74	291	7	940.00	661.37
66	Nicolas VANHOOTEGEM	Bel	74	71	71	76	292	8	840.00	591.01
	Michael JONZON	Swe	71	73	74	74	292	8	840.00	591.01
	Nicolas MARIN	Fr	71	73	75	73	292	8	840.00	591.01
69	Dominique NOUAILHAC	Fr	74	71	73	75	293	9	760.00	534.73
70	Raimo SJÖBERG	Swe	71	74	73	76	294	10	670.00	471.40
	Daniel Alfredo VANCSIK	Arg	74	70	77	73	294	10	670.00	471.40
72	Mark MOULAND	Wal	75	70	77	73	295	11	594.00	417.93
	Olivier DAVID	Fr	74	71	73	77	295	11	594.00	417.93
	David J GEALL	Eng	71	71	77	76	295	11	594.00	417.93
75	Stefano REALE	It	74	71	74	77	296	12	586.50	412.65
	Lee S JAMES	Eng	75	70	77	74	296	12	586.50	412.65
77	Jerome GUILLAIN(AM)	Fr	74	70	76	79	299	15		
78	Gary David CULLEN	Ire	70	75	78	77	300	16	582.00	409.49

Søren Kjeldsen

1	Søren KJELDSEN Den	279	-9
2	Alastair FORSYTH Scot	281	-7
3	Paul BROADHURST Eng	282	-6
4	Colin MONTGOMERIE Scot	283	-5
5	Stephen GALLACHER Scot	285	-3
	Miguel Angel MARTIN Sp	285	-3
	Rolf MUNTZ NL	285	-3
8	John BICKERTON Eng	286	-2
	Adam SCOTT Aus	286	-2
10	Stephen DODD Wal	287	-1
	Richard GREEN Aus	287	-1
	Raphaël JACQUELIN Fr	287	-1

written in the wind

Paul Broadhurst

f we had been dutiful enough to read the signs we would have spotted it was written in the wind that Søren Kjeldsen was going to win The Diageo Championship at Gleneagles.

Five times during the early part of the season he had occupied a top 12 position, and two of them had been in his previous two events, the Volvo PGA Championship at Wentworth Club and The Daily Telegraph Damovo British Masters at the Marriott Forest of Arden.

It was a victory on its way, and Kjeldsen was determined to deliver to silence those back home in his native Denmark who kept asking when he was going to follow Thomas Björn, Anders Hansen, Søren Hansen and Steen Tinning onto the winners' rostrum.

Björn, the 'big brother' of the Viking corps, had been helpful to Kjeldsen more than once, advising him only the previous month at Wentworth Club that, as he was a good Sunday shooter, all he had to do was to try and ensure he was in contention at the end of play on Saturday.

However Björn, who himself claimed his maiden European Tour

International Schedule title in Scotland at Loch Lomond in 1996, would not have programmed a pummelling Perthshire wind into the equation.

The first two days of the championship were severely demanding to the sturdiest of men, and at five feet seven inches tall and just ten and a half stone in his spikes, Kjeldsen, at least in a physical sense, could not be described as a Great Dane. However, he amply proved himself to be a Dane great in heart and cool in temperament.

This was his 160th event on Tour and, for a man who in 1997 ran a marathon to test his physical fitness, it was the week his nerve remained firm.

From the moment he returned a level par 72 on the opening day he steadily increased his grip on a tournament that explored the patience, and the arithmetic, of a number of competitors. The wind was so strong during the first two rounds, and some of the rough so punitive, that more than one player reached double figures for one hole.

Come the halfway mark, Kjeldsen was one shot clear of Paul Broadhurst, thanks to a 68 which contained only 24 putts, ten fewer than the number

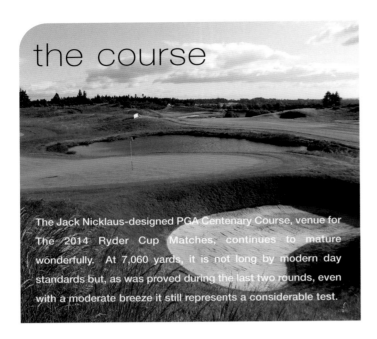

the course

The Jack Nicklaus-designed PGA Centenary Course, venue for The 2014 Ryder Cup Matches, continues to mature wonderfully. At 7,060 yards, it is not long by modern day standards but, as was proved during the last two rounds, even with a moderate breeze it still represents a considerable test.

the final day singles, had not had his troubles to seek since the new century had arrived.

Injured for the bulk of the 2000 season, the 37 year old lost his card at the end of 2001, failed to regain it at the Tour School that year and played largely on invitations in 2002 before succeeding at the Tour School in November, 2002.

"I'm thrilled," said Broadhurst, whose final round 70 saw him finish third and virtually guarantee his playing privileges for 2004. "I can relax and who knows you might even see some good golf from me now. It is a lot of pressure off me and I can look forward to the rest of the season." Ken Schofield spoke for all when he said: "Nice men do come back."

There was pressure on Kjeldsen but thankfully for him, his putter behaved impeccably throughout a third round 67 which opened up a lead of five shots over Alastair Forsyth, whose 69 earned him the distinction of being only one of ten players under par after 54 holes, and Broadhurst with Scott giving impetus to his title defence with a best-of-the-championship 66 to be only one shot further back.

taken by the defending champion Adam Scott whose putter, like the majority of the shivering spectators, remained steadfastly cold throughout the tournament.

A warming sight for all lovers of golf, however, was the performance of Broadhurst. The affable Englishman, who played in The 1991 Ryder Cup Matches at Kiawah Island and beat Mark O'Meara in

Kjeldsen's only concern was how he would react to being the leader on the final day. "I felt really good going into the third round, but I don't know how I will feel in the morning," he said on Saturday night. "I have

Sandy Lyle and Sam Torrance

Alastair Forsyth

final results

The Gleneagles Hotel · Perthshire · Scotland
June 19 - 22 · 2003 · Par 72 · 7060 yards · 6456 metres

Pos.	Name		Rd1	Rd2	Rd3	Rd4	Total	Par	Prize Money Euro	£
1	Søren KJELDSEN	Den	72	68	67	72	279	-9	281928.00	200000.00
2	Alastair FORSYTH	Scot	70	73	69	69	281	-7	187947.30	133330.00
3	Paul BROADHURST	Eng	73	68	71	70	282	-6	105892.20	75120.00
4	Colin MONTGOMERIE	Scot	72	73	69	69	283	-5	84578.40	60000.00
5	Miguel Angel MARTIN	Sp	74	70	70	71	285	-3	60558.13	42960.00
	Rolf MUNTZ	NL	72	70	73	70	285	-3	60558.13	42960.00
	Stephen GALLACHER	Scot	76	71	67	71	285	-3	60558.13	42960.00
8	John BICKERTON	Eng	74	71	71	70	286	-2	40090.16	28440.00
	Adam SCOTT	Aus	72	75	66	73	286	-2	40090.16	28440.00
10	Raphaël JACQUELIN	Fr	74	72	71	70	287	-1	31350.39	22240.00
	Richard GREEN	Aus	74	75	68	70	287	-1	31350.39	22240.00
	Stephen DODD	Wal	72	71	75	69	287	-1	31350.39	22240.00
13	Nicolas COLSAERTS	Bel	76	73	71	68	288	0	26557.62	18840.00
	Paul CASEY	Eng	76	71	68	73	288	0	26557.62	18840.00
15	Steve WEBSTER	Eng	77	71	68	73	289	1	23851.11	16920.00
	Andrew RAITT	Eng	75	71	72	71	289	1	23851.11	16920.00
	Brad KENNEDY	Aus	70	72	74	73	289	1	23851.11	16920.00
18	Sandy LYLE	Scot	73	71	74	72	290	2	20679.42	14670.00
	Philip GOLDING	Eng	75	75	69	71	290	2	20679.42	14670.00
	Paul EALES	Eng	74	74	73	69	290	2	20679.42	14670.00
	Nicolas VANHOOTEGEM	Bel	73	73	71	73	290	2	20679.42	14670.00
22	Peter FOWLER	Aus	77	73	69	72	291	3	17084.84	12120.00
	David GILFORD	Eng	76	74	70	71	291	3	17084.84	12120.00
	Shaun P WEBSTER	Eng	76	72	69	74	291	3	17084.84	12120.00
	Hennie OTTO	SA	74	77	67	73	291	3	17084.84	12120.00
	Gary ORR	Scot	75	68	72	76	291	3	17084.84	12120.00
	Iain PYMAN	Eng	71	74	73	73	291	3	17084.84	12120.00
	Francois DELAMONTAGNE	Fr	72	76	70	73	291	3	17084.84	12120.00
	David ORR	Scot	76	74	72	69	291	3	17084.84	12120.00
	Graeme MCDOWELL	N.Ire	74	77	68	72	291	3	17084.84	12120.00
31	David HOWELL	Eng	77	70	73	72	292	4	13363.39	9480.00
	Peter BAKER	Eng	75	74	71	72	292	4	13363.39	9480.00
	Julien CLEMENT	Swi	78	74	68	72	292	4	13363.39	9480.00
	Miles TUNNICLIFF	Eng	78	69	72	73	292	4	13363.39	9480.00
	Peter O'MALLEY	Aus	76	74	71	71	292	4	13363.39	9480.00
	Gustavo ROJAS	Arg	71	75	74	72	292	4	13363.39	9480.00
37	Mark MOULAND	Wal	75	74	75	69	293	5	11164.35	7920.00
	Jean-Francois REMESY	Fr	74	77	71	71	293	5	11164.35	7920.00
	Jean-François LUCQUIN	Fr	73	77	75	68	293	5	11164.35	7920.00
	Ian GARBUTT	Eng	76	76	69	72	293	5	11164.35	7920.00
	Simon WAKEFIELD	Eng	73	75	70	75	293	5	11164.35	7920.00
	David PARK	Wal	75	75	71	72	293	5	11164.35	7920.00
43	Mark MCNULTY	Zim	75	75	72	72	294	6	9980.25	7080.00
44	Mark JAMES	Eng	76	75	70	74	295	7	8796.15	6240.00
	Alvaro SALTO	Sp	77	72	75	71	295	7	8796.15	6240.00
	Barry LANE	Eng	74	75	73	73	295	7	8796.15	6240.00
	Darren FICHARDT	SA	77	75	70	73	295	7	8796.15	6240.00
	Lee WESTWOOD	Eng	74	74	75	72	295	7	8796.15	6240.00
	Martin MARITZ	SA	74	74	73	74	295	7	8796.15	6240.00
50	Sam TORRANCE	Scot	74	71	73	78	296	8	6597.12	4680.00
	Neil CHEETHAM	Eng	73	71	79	73	296	8	6597.12	4680.00
	Christian CÉVAËR	Fr	75	75	71	75	296	8	6597.12	4680.00
	Roger WESSELS	SA	74	77	68	77	296	8	6597.12	4680.00
	Fredrik ANDERSSON	Swe	78	74	70	74	296	8	6597.12	4680.00
	Mads VIBE-HASTRUP	Den	76	75	71	74	296	8	6597.12	4680.00
	Ben MASON	Eng	76	76	73	71	296	8	6597.12	4680.00
57	Philip WALTON	Ire	74	74	72	77	297	9	4990.13	3540.00
	Paul LAWRIE	Scot	77	71	76	73	297	9	4990.13	3540.00
	Gary CLARK	Eng	79	70	72	76	297	9	4990.13	3540.00
	Zane SCOTLAND	Eng	72	78	71	76	297	9	4990.13	3540.00
61	Gary MURPHY	Ire	73	76	72	77	298	10	4398.08	3120.00
	Julien VAN HAUWE	Fr	79	73	71	75	298	10	4398.08	3120.00
	Russell CLAYDON	Eng	73	79	73	73	298	10	4398.08	3120.00
64	Ross DRUMMOND	Scot	78	73	75	73	299	11	3890.61	2760.00
	Ivo GINER	Sp	71	72	75	81	299	11	3890.61	2760.00
	Thomas NORRET	Den	73	73	71	77	299	11	3890.61	2760.00
67	Andrew MARSHALL	Eng	79	73	73	75	300	12	3309.13	2347.50
	Jean HUGO	SA	75	75	72	78	300	12	3309.13	2347.50
	Jesus Maria ARRUTI	Sp	76	76	73	75	300	12	3309.13	2347.50
	Pierre FULKE	Swe	78	74	75	73	300	12	3309.13	2347.50
71	Gregory HAVRET	Fr	72	75	78	76	301	13	2534.00	1797.62
	Matthew BLACKEY	Eng	74	77	78	72	301	13	2534.00	1797.62
	Marc WARREN	Scot	70	75	75	81	301	13	2534.00	1797.62
74	Santiago LUNA	Sp	75	75	72	80	302	14	2526.50	1792.30
	Mark ROE	Eng	77	75	72	78	302	14	2526.50	1792.30
76	Titch MOORE	SA	76	75	74	78	303	15	2520.50	1788.05
	Sebastien DELAGRANGE	Fr	73	78	75	77	303	15	2520.50	1788.05
78	Philip ARCHER	Eng	74	78	78	75	305	17	2516.00	1784.85
79	Fraser MANN	Scot	74	76	84	77	311	23	2511.50	1781.66
	Adam MEDNICK	Swe	74	75	78	84	311	23	2511.50	1781.66
81	Scott KAMMANN	USA	75	77	79	81	312	24	2507.00	1778.47

had good final rounds, but never started in a good enough position on Sunday, so maybe that will be the difference this week." It was.

He began shakily, missing from three feet to make bogey on the first green, but responded immediately with a birdie at the second. Try as they might, playing partner Forsyth, and Broadhurst, playing in the group immediately in front, could not dislodge his hold on the tournament.

Kjeldsen played the last round rather like US Open Champion Jim Furyk had done the previous week, courageously but carefully. No one got closer to him than two shots, and that was how it ended, Forsyth holing a 15 foot birdie putt on the last green to claim second place ahead of Broadhurst with Colin Montgomerie fourth following successive 69s.

"When I turned professional in 1995, Thomas Björn was the superstar in Danish golf," he said. "He set the standard. Before then no one ever thought a Dane had a chance to play at that level in Europe, let alone the world."

Montgomerie birdied the last two holes for fourth place, a satisfactory conclusion to his competitive days in his 30s. The next day he was back home in Oxshott celebrating his 40th birthday. Kjeldsen, on the other hand, was back in an aeroplane on his way to the next tournament in France, celebrating being the latest Dane to bring home the bacon.

Jock MacVicar

Philip Golding

1	Philip **GOLDING** Eng	273	-15
2	David **HOWELL** Eng	274	-14
3	Peter **O'MALLEY** Aus	275	-13
	Justin **ROSE** Eng	275	-13
5	Brian **DAVIS** Eng	276	-12
	Andrew **OLDCORN** Scot	276	-12
	Simon **WAKEFIELD** Eng	276	-12
8	Bradley **DREDGE** Wal	277	-11
	Pierre **FULKE** Swe	277	-11
	Stephen **GALLACHER** Scot	277	-11
	Barry **LANE** Eng	277	-11

kindred spirit

ad Robert the Bruce been alive today he could not have failed to recognise a kindred spirit in English golfer Philip Golding. The old Scottish King harboured a distrust of anyone residing south of Hadrian's Wall, but in Golding he would have surely identified a man of strong moral fibre, in whose dictionary the word failure did not exist.

Almost seven centuries have elapsed since Robert shivered in his cave watching the legendary spider "try, try and try again" to spin a web, imbuing him with the resolve to reclaim his kingdom. In a golfing context, few professionals have displayed a greater resolve than the man from Bushey in Hertfordshire.

Over the course of two eventful decades Golding pursued the Holy Grail of a victory on The European Tour International Schedule and, following an unwanted record of 16 visits to The European Tour Qualifying School Finals, he arrived at the summit of a life's work by winning the Open de France at Le Golf National in Paris.

Blue eyes, blonde hair and a disarming smile had made Golding one of the most noticeable golfers on The European Tour. But male-model looks are for the catwalks and not an essential aid on the fairways, and Golding's seasonal results were never a pretty sight.

José Maria Olazábal

Nicolas Colsaerts

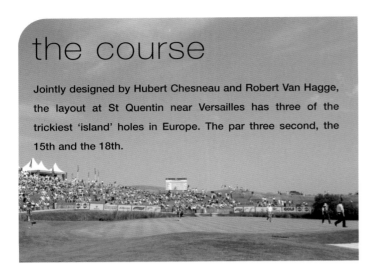

the course

Jointly designed by Hubert Chesneau and Robert Van Hagge, the layout at St Quentin near Versailles has three of the trickiest 'island' holes in Europe. The par three second, the 15th and the 18th.

Peter O'Malley

It took ten years for him to break through and earn a card but gaining a foothold on Tour remained a problem. Like the spider in the cave, every time he made progress, he would lose the thread and have to return to the Qualifying School.

A 63 in the final round of the 59th Italian Open Telecom Italia in 2002 told him he could play a bit, even if, agonisingly, had he carded one shot fewer in the final round he would have amassed enough money to keep his card.

He did, at least, achieve his highest career finish on the Volvo Order of Merit, 119th, and, urged on by his family and in particular by wife Sally, Golding decided to trod the well worn path to the Qualifying School once again. The reward for his 16th visit was third place and the opportunity to play in nearly all the early season events.

He had an encouraging start to 2003, even with a couple of infringements that knocked his results back, like misunderstanding the rules when swapping clubs during a round in Qatar which cost him a four shot penalty.

Unabashed, however, Golding marched onwards and took on a high quality field in Paris in his 201st Tour event, 308 fewer than Malcolm Mackenzie the year before. But just as his fellow Englishman had proved with his own memorable maiden victory in the French capital, life really can begin at 40.

A solid opening 66 showed Golding he had re-found the touch that had earned him his career-best 63 the previous year in Italy. Not even the presence of Ryder Cup team-mates Thomas Björn and Pierre Fulke could faze him as they moved into position for an expected weekend charge.

But when that did not materialise it was Justin Rose in the final round, making his competitive return in Europe after his superb tie for fifth place in the US Open Championship a fortnight earlier, who set the clubhouse target of 13 under par 275 after a swashbuckling closing 65.

It could have been even better for the 22 year old Englishman for, in the first round, he had been penalised for standing on his ball in the rough in the first round while talking to Ian Poulter.

Come the home straight it was another Englishman, the 1999 Dubai Desert Classic winner David Howell, whom Golding had to overcome. After Howell missed his eagle chance on the par five 72nd hole, Golding's dream rested on his own approach to the same putting surface.

David Howell

It is said that, 'Cometh the hour, cometh the man' and Golding proved the old adage to a tee. Faced with 167 yards to the pin over water and with water behind, Golding produced an exquisite six iron second shot to the heart of the green.

Not only did it allow him two putts for birdie and victory, it also led to him winning the award for The Royal Bank of Scotland Shot of the Month for June and the accolade of being named Asprey Golfer of the Month for June, too.

After the euphoria of his thrilling success had sunk in, Golding was left with a perplexing poser: "What to do in November when it's time for The European Tour Qualifying School?"

The answer, of course, was to tee-up the previous week for the first time in the Volvo Masters Andalucia then relax following a season that took him to the heights his resilience and skill fully deserved.

Norman Dabell

final results

Le Golf National • Paris • France
June 26 - 29 • 2003 • Par 72 • 7105 yards • 6496 metres

Pos.	Name		Rd1	Rd2	Rd3	Rd4	Total	Par	Prize Money Euro	£
1	Philip GOLDING	Eng	66	70	68	69	273	-15	416,660.00	290,791.08
2	David HOWELL	Eng	71	65	69	69	274	-14	277,770.00	193,858.39
3	Justin ROSE	Eng	68	69	73	65	275	-13	140,750.00	98,230.80
	Peter O'MALLEY	Aus	70	69	66	70	275	-13	140,750.00	98,230.80
5	Andrew OLDCORN	Scot	69	70	69	68	276	-12	89,500.00	62,462.92
	Brian DAVIS	Eng	68	72	68	68	276	-12	89,500.00	62,462.92
	Simon WAKEFIELD	Eng	70	70	70	66	276	-12	89,500.00	62,462.92
8	Barry LANE	Eng	70	68	67	72	277	-11	53,625.00	37,425.41
	Pierre FULKE	Swe	70	68	67	72	277	-11	53,625.00	37,425.41
	Bradley DREDGE	Wal	67	72	70	68	277	-11	53,625.00	37,425.41
	Stephen GALLACHER	Scot	68	69	69	71	277	-11	53,625.00	37,425.41
12	José Maria OLAZÁBAL	Sp	70	68	69	71	278	-10	40,500.00	28,265.35
	Raphaël JACQUELIN	Fr	70	68	68	72	278	-10	40,500.00	28,265.35
	Thomas BJÖRN	Den	70	64	71	73	278	-10	40,500.00	28,265.35
15	Robert-Jan DERKSEN	NL	68	74	66	71	279	-9	35,250.00	24,601.32
	Stephen LEANEY	Aus	70	70	71	68	279	-9	35,250.00	24,601.32
	Matthew BLACKEY	Eng	71	71	68	69	279	-9	35,250.00	24,601.32
18	Santiago LUNA	Sp	70	70	70	70	280	-8	30,100.00	21,007.08
	Miguel Angel MARTIN	Sp	70	68	70	72	280	-8	30,100.00	21,007.08
	José Manuel LARA	Sp	67	69	71	73	280	-8	30,100.00	21,007.08
	Andrew MARSHALL	Eng	69	74	70	67	280	-8	30,100.00	21,007.08
	Graeme MCDOWELL	N.Ire	70	68	73	69	280	-8	30,100.00	21,007.08
23	Carlos RODILES	Sp	70	69	71	71	281	-7	25,250.00	17,622.22
	Miguel Angel JIMÉNEZ	Sp	67	74	69	71	281	-7	25,250.00	17,622.22
	Nicolas COLSAERTS	Bel	66	70	73	72	281	-7	25,250.00	17,622.22
	Marcel SIEM	Ger	74	69	64	74	281	-7	25,250.00	17,622.22
	Stephen DODD	Wal	72	67	71	71	281	-7	25,250.00	17,622.22
	Stephen SCAHILL	NZ	74	67	72	68	281	-7	25,250.00	17,622.22
	Martin MARITZ	SA	73	70	67	71	281	-7	25,250.00	17,622.22
30	Ian POULTER	Eng	75	68	67	72	282	-6	20,107.14	14,032.97
	Jarrod MOSELEY	Aus	69	72	73	68	282	-6	20,107.14	14,032.97
	Paul MCGINLEY	Ire	71	72	69	70	282	-6	20,107.14	14,032.97
	Ignacio GARRIDO	Sp	71	72	68	71	282	-6	20,107.14	14,032.97
	Raymond RUSSELL	Scot	71	70	69	72	282	-6	20,107.14	14,032.97
	John BICKERTON	Eng	69	71	68	74	282	-6	20,107.14	14,032.97
	David CARTER	Eng	71	69	70	72	282	-6	20,107.14	14,032.97
37	Gordon BRAND JNR.	Scot	70	73	67	73	283	-5	16,000.00	11,166.56
	Marc FARRY	Fr	68	73	70	72	283	-5	16,000.00	11,166.56
	Søren KJELDSEN	Den	71	71	67	74	283	-5	16,000.00	11,166.56
	Ilya GORONESKOUL	Fr	76	67	69	71	283	-5	16,000.00	11,166.56
	Richard BLAND	Eng	72	67	70	74	283	-5	16,000.00	11,166.56
	Julien VAN HAUWE	Fr	74	68	70	71	283	-5	16,000.00	11,166.56
	Alastair FORSYTH	Scot	68	73	71	71	283	-5	16,000.00	11,166.56
	Richard STERNE	SA	71	71	69	72	283	-5	16,000.00	11,166.56
	Jean-Baptiste GONNET (AM)	Fr	70	71	72	70	283	-5		
46	Gary MURPHY	Ire	68	74	74	68	284	-4	13,250.00	9,247.30
	Peter LAWRIE	Ire	69	73	67	75	284	-4	13,250.00	9,247.30
	Francois DELAMONTAGNE	Fr	69	69	73	73	284	-4	13,250.00	9,247.30
49	Olivier EDMOND	Fr	70	72	72	71	285	-3	11,750.00	8,200.44
	Jean Louis GUEPY	Fr	71	72	72	70	285	-3	11,750.00	8,200.44
	Simon DYSON	Eng	70	69	69	77	285	-3	11,750.00	8,200.44
52	Peter FOWLER	Aus	72	69	70	75	286	-2	9,750.00	6,804.62
	Kenneth FERRIE	Eng	71	72	73	70	286	-2	9,750.00	6,804.62
	Trevor IMMELMAN	SA	71	72	71	72	286	-2	9,750.00	6,804.62
	Jonathan LOMAS	Eng	69	74	74	69	286	-2	9,750.00	6,804.62
	Mathias GRÖNBERG	Swe	72	70	68	76	286	-2	9,750.00	6,804.62
57	Anders HANSEN	Den	70	66	75	76	287	-1	7,833.33	5,466.96
	Gustavo ROJAS	Arg	71	69	73	74	287	-1	7,833.33	5,466.96
	Gary BIRCH JNR	Eng	67	74	71	75	287	-1	7,833.33	5,466.96
60	Ronan RAFFERTY	N.Ire	70	72	71	75	288	0	6,375.00	4,449.17
	Eduardo ROMERO	Arg	75	68	70	75	288	0	6,375.00	4,449.17
	Greg TURNER	NZ	73	69	69	77	288	0	6,375.00	4,449.17
	Arjun ATWAL	Ind	72	71	69	76	288	0	6,375.00	4,449.17
	Henrik STENSON	Swe	71	70	72	75	288	0	6,375.00	4,449.17
	Miles TUNNICLIFF	Eng	74	69	68	77	288	0	6,375.00	4,449.17
	Emanuele CANONICA	It	69	74	74	71	288	0	6,375.00	4,449.17
	Fredrik WIDMARK	Swe	73	69	74	72	288	0	6,375.00	4,449.17
68	Gary ORR	Scot	71	72	74	72	289	1	5,125.00	3,576.79
	David PARK	Wal	72	69	73	75	289	1	5,125.00	3,576.79
70	Darren FICHARDT	SA	71	68	75	76	290	2	4,750.00	3,315.07
71	Sven STRÜVER	Ger	70	72	71	78	291	3	4,160.00	2,903.30
	Ian GARBUTT	Eng	71	71	72	77	291	3	4,160.00	2,903.30
	Eric CHAUDOUET (AM)	Fr	66	77	69	79	291	3		
74	Per NYMAN	Swe	72	69	75	76	292	4	3,742.50	2,611.93
	Mark PILKINGTON	Wal	72	71	74	75	292	4	3,742.50	2,611.93
	Mikko ILONEN	Fin	73	70	74	75	292	4	3,742.50	2,611.93
	Charl SCHWARTZEL	SA	70	68	74	80	292	4	3,742.50	2,611.93
78	Gary EVANS	Eng	72	69	71	82	294	6	3,735.00	2,606.69

the quiet man

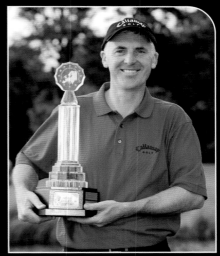

Phillip Price

1	Phillip PRICE Wal	272	-16
2	Alastair FORSYTH Scot	273	-15
	Mark McNULTY Zim	273	-15
4	Gary EVANS Eng	275	-13
5	Darren CLARKE N.Ire	276	-12
	Eduardo ROMERO Arg	276	-12
7	Andrew COLTART Scot	278	-10
	Jarmo SANDELIN Swe	278	-10
9	Angel CABRERA Arg	279	-9
	Barry LANE Eng	279	-9
	Lee WESTWOOD Eng	279	-9

Phillip Price is a quiet man. Reserved and polite on and off the course, he is not one for expansive demonstrations of delight. Mind you, there have not been many occasions in his 14 years as a professional to let his feelings run wild.

the course

The North Course, designated as the venue for The 36th Ryder Cup Matches, gets tougher each year and will present a formidable test for the best from Europe and the United States in 2006. For the 2003 Smurfit European Open it was lengthened to 7,337 yards.

Until, that is, The 34th Ryder Cup Matches at The De Vere Belfry propelled him into the world spotlight. There, the 36 year old from Pontypridd not only enjoyed a marvellous win over Phil Mickelson in the final day's singles as Europe regained the golden chalice, but he also spent the best part of the evening punching the air in delight. In the hotel lounge Lee Westwood, acting as MC, introduced one player after another to roars of approval and, on calling out Phillip Price's name, the Welshman leaned towards his colleague and screamed: "Tell 'em who I beat; tell 'em who I beat."

He may profess to prefer anonymity to adulation – although his achievement at The De Vere Belfry put that on the back-burner – but there could be no denying what victory at The K Club meant to him as the final putt disappeared into the hole.

At The Ryder Cup, the clenched fist and little jig on the 16th green as he dismissed the then World Number Two was about as much emotion as this modest man had released throughout his life on Tour. But the repeat action at the venue for The 36th Ryder Cup Matches in 2006 was a clear indication he was back where he wanted to be. At the top.

"This is where it's at, a four round tournament with all the best players," he said. "The Ryder Cup was different. It is unique and it was nice to have done well there but it really didn't give me that much confidence to deal with a normal tournament. This is where you learn your skills. I was a little short on titles, especially the big ones. The Smurfit European Open is a big tournament and to win it is just fantastic."

Gary Evans

The record books might show it was a wire-to-wire win but it did not come easy. Several times during the four days he had to share the lead but, from day one, he never lost it. Argentinian Angel Cabrera, K Club specialist Darren Clarke, Scotland's Alastair Forsyth, double Volvo Order of Merit winner Retief Goosen and a resurgent Mark McNulty, of Zimbabwe, were amongst those who challenged his authority.

There was, too, the brief, but spectacular, appearance of 18 year old South African Charl Schwartzel with a record eight under par 64 for the extended course in the second round. But in the end, Price saw them all off.

Clarke, perhaps, presented the greatest threat. They set out together on the third day in the lead at nine under par and home hopes were high that the Ulsterman would collect his second victory at The K Club in three years.

But it did not happen for him like it did for the Welshman. Price shot 67 to distance himself by three shots from a pack of five players comprising Jarmo Sandelin, Cabrera, Clarke, Forsyth and McNulty. His destiny was now in his own hands.

Eduardo Romero

Clarke was the first to strike in the final round with a birdie at the second and an eagle at the fourth to share the lead, momentarily, but he could not maintain the momentum as three bogeys, two caused by trips into the water, dampened his challenge. There was another visit to the River Liffey at the 17th but at least he had the consolation of finishing with a spectacular 50 foot putt for an eagle three to share fifth place.

Cabrera also threw down the gauntlet but his challenge eventually evaporated. Now all Price had to do was shake off Forsyth and McNulty. There seemed to be little danger until he took three putts for a bogey on the 17th to drop back alongside his two closest pursuers.

The blip jolted Price from cruise control into overdrive. He needed a birdie at the last, and he was not about to let this chance of glory slip from his grasp. That steel-like nerve which he had displayed at The Ryder Cup would ensure he achieved his goal.

With water all the way down the left and the huge gallery lining the right he followed a perfect drive with a bold four iron that trundled just through the back of the putting surface. From there he chipped beautifully to a couple of feet and calmly rolled it in to the roar of the crowd.

Mark McNulty

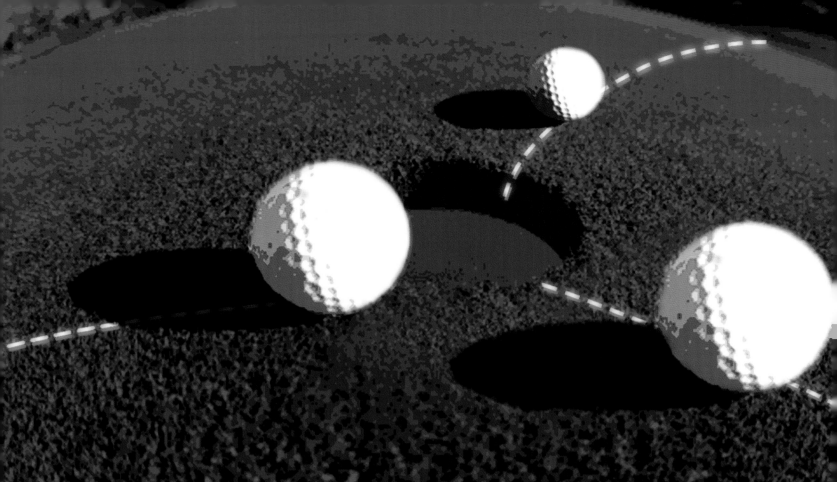

Reuters Performance Data

As the official sponsor of Performance Data on
The European Tour, Reuters provides relevant
and insightful information on player performance,
allowing professionals everywhere to make accurate
and informed decisions.

www.reuters.com

PUTTING ACCURACY FIRST.
Reuters and The European Tour

Lee Westwood

Now we could witness again what is becoming a trademark clenched fist as he revelled in the glory and the acclaim. Forsyth and McNulty shared second place, and McNulty, at the age of 49, was particularly proud of his performance.

The Smurfit European Open trophy, however, was now the property of Phillip Price and, following in the footsteps of the likes of Nick Faldo, Bernhard Langer, Sandy Lyle, Greg Norman and Ian Woosnam, not to mention Darren Clarke and Lee Westwood in recent years, he had every reason to let the world know how he felt.

Colm Smith

final results

The K Club · Dublin · Ireland
July 3 - 6 · 2003 · Par 72 · 7337 yards · 6706 metres

Pos.	Name		Rd1	Rd2	Rd3	Rd4	Total	Par	Prize Money Euro	£
1	Phillip PRICE	Wal	66	69	67	70	272	-16	481,245.20	333,330.00
2	Mark MCNULTY	Zim	68	69	68	68	273	-15	250,793.80	173,710.00
	Alastair FORSYTH	Scot	66	70	69	68	273	-15	250,793.80	173,710.00
4	Gary EVANS	Eng	68	70	69	68	275	-13	144,375.00	100,000.00
5	Eduardo ROMERO	Arg	69	68	71	68	276	-12	111,746.30	77,400.03
	Darren CLARKE	N.Ire	67	68	70	71	276	-12	111,746.30	77,400.03
7	Jarmo SANDELIN	Swe	72	66	67	73	278	-10	79,406.25	55,000.00
	Andrew COLTART	Scot	67	70	70	71	278	-10	79,406.25	55,000.00
9	Barry LANE	Eng	70	70	69	70	279	-9	58,520.00	40,533.33
	Angel CABRERA	Arg	70	69	66	74	279	-9	58,520.00	40,533.33
	Lee WESTWOOD	Eng	70	71	69	69	279	-9	58,520.00	40,533.33
12	Colin MONTGOMERIE	Scot	68	71	73	68	280	-8	49,665.00	34,400.00
13	Carlos RODILES	Sp	73	70	70	68	281	-7	44,371.25	30,733.33
	Raymond RUSSELL	Scot	71	73	67	70	281	-7	44,371.25	30,733.33
	Paul CASEY	Eng	73	71	68	69	281	-7	44,371.25	30,733.33
16	Mark ROE	Eng	71	70	71	70	282	-6	38,981.25	27,000.00
	Raphaël JACQUELIN	Fr	72	70	71	69	282	-6	38,981.25	27,000.00
	Thomas BJÖRN	Den	71	71	72	68	282	-6	38,981.25	27,000.00
19	Roger CHAPMAN	Eng	70	73	72	68	283	-5	34,144.69	23,650.00
	Nick O'HERN	Aus	70	72	70	71	283	-5	34,144.69	23,650.00
	David LYNN	Eng	71	71	70	71	283	-5	34,144.69	23,650.00
	Mikko ILONEN	Fin	69	71	73	70	283	-5	34,144.69	23,650.00
23	Mark JAMES	Eng	72	69	68	75	284	-4	30,463.13	21,100.00
	Bernhard LANGER	Ger	73	67	71	73	284	-4	30,463.13	21,100.00
	Brian DAVIS	Eng	76	66	74	68	284	-4	30,463.13	21,100.00
	Matthew BLACKEY	Eng	73	69	71	71	284	-4	30,463.13	21,100.00
27	Gary MURPHY	Ire	67	75	71	72	285	-3	25,698.75	17,800.00
	Shaun P WEBSTER	Eng	70	76	65	74	285	-3	25,698.75	17,800.00
	Søren HANSEN	Den	67	75	69	74	285	-3	25,698.75	17,800.00
	Rolf MUNTZ	NL	73	69	71	72	285	-3	25,698.75	17,800.00
	John BICKERTON	Eng	71	73	71	70	285	-3	25,698.75	17,800.00
	Retief GOOSEN	SA	66	74	68	77	285	-3	25,698.75	17,800.00
	Charl SCHWARTZEL	SA	72	64	76	73	285	-3	25,698.75	17,800.00
34	Nick FALDO	Eng	75	70	69	72	286	-2	21,656.25	15,000.00
	Mathias GRÖNBERG	Swe	73	65	77	71	286	-2	21,656.25	15,000.00
	David CARTER	Eng	73	73	67	73	286	-2	21,656.25	15,000.00
37	Klas ERIKSSON	Swe	69	72	67	79	287	-1	18,191.25	12,600.00
	Anders HANSEN	Den	73	73	71	70	287	-1	18,191.25	12,600.00
	Darren FICHARDT	SA	74	71	69	73	287	-1	18,191.25	12,600.00
	Miguel Angel JIMÉNEZ	Sp	74	72	73	68	287	-1	18,191.25	12,600.00
	Paul MCGINLEY	Ire	72	73	70	72	287	-1	18,191.25	12,600.00
	Stephen SCAHILL	NZ	69	71	74	73	287	-1	18,191.25	12,600.00
	Bradley DREDGE	Wal	75	70	71	71	287	-1	18,191.25	12,600.00
	Fredrik ANDERSSON	Swe	67	74	69	77	287	-1	18,191.25	12,600.00
	Niclas FASTH	Swe	70	75	73	69	287	-1	18,191.25	12,600.00
46	Richard GREEN	Aus	73	73	68	74	288	0	14,437.50	10,000.00
	Andrew RAITT	Eng	69	73	74	72	288	0	14,437.50	10,000.00
	Richard STERNE	SA	74	70	71	73	288	0	14,437.50	10,000.00
	Jamie DONALDSON	Wal	71	70	77	70	288	0	14,437.50	10,000.00
50	Sandy LYLE	Scot	72	73	70	74	289	1	11,550.00	8,000.00
	Steve WEBSTER	Eng	73	71	73	72	289	1	11,550.00	8,000.00
	Anthony WALL	Eng	74	72	73	70	289	1	11,550.00	8,000.00
	Julien CLEMENT	Swi	73	72	74	70	289	1	11,550.00	8,000.00
	Miles TUNNICLIFF	Eng	74	68	76	71	289	1	11,550.00	8,000.00
	Stephen GALLACHER	Scot	71	74	70	74	289	1	11,550.00	8,000.00
56	David GILFORD	Eng	73	73	69	75	290	2	8,720.25	6,040.00
	Stephen LEANEY	Aus	74	71	73	72	290	2	8,720.25	6,040.00
	Nicolas COLSAERTS	Bel	75	69	70	76	290	2	8,720.25	6,040.00
	Nicolas VANHOOTEGEM	Bel	74	71	72	73	290	2	8,720.25	6,040.00
	Brett RUMFORD	Aus	75	71	72	72	290	2	8,720.25	6,040.00
61	David HOWELL	Eng	71	74	74	72	291	3	6,504.09	4,505.00
	Padraig HARRINGTON	Ire	73	73	73	72	291	3	6,504.09	4,505.00
	Mårten OLANDER	Swe	71	71	73	76	291	3	6,504.09	4,505.00
	Damien MCGRANE	Ire	73	72	73	73	291	3	6,504.09	4,505.00
	Arjun ATWAL	Ind	76	70	74	71	291	3	6,504.09	4,505.00
	Greg OWEN	Eng	70	74	72	75	291	3	6,504.09	4,505.00
	David DRYSDALE	Scot	74	72	69	76	291	3	6,504.09	4,505.00
	Mark PILKINGTON	Wal	72	72	77	70	291	3	6,504.09	4,505.00
	Ben MASON	Eng	72	72	74	73	291	3	6,504.09	4,505.00
	Graeme MCDOWELL	N.Ire	69	73	73	76	291	3	6,504.09	4,505.00
71	Andrew OLDCORN	Scot	73	72	73	74	292	4	4,326.50	2,996.71
	Ian WOOSNAM	Wal	74	70	75	73	292	4	4,326.50	2,996.71
	Michael CAMPBELL	NZ	70	75	70	77	292	4	4,326.50	2,996.71
	Mikael LUNDBERG	Swe	73	73	68	78	292	4	4,326.50	2,996.71
75	Stephen DODD	Wal	70	73	75	75	293	5	4,319.00	2,991.52
76	Gustavo ROJAS	Arg	71	75	78	71	295	7	4,316.00	2,989.44
77	Andrew MARSHALL	Eng	75	71	71	79	296	8	4,313.00	2,987.36
78	Costantino ROCCA	It	72	73	77	75	297	9	4,310.00	2,985.28
79	Peter HEDBLOM	Swe	72	73	75	79	299	11	4,307.00	2,983.20

The Barclays Scottish Open Loch Lomond · Glasgow · Scotland

nice accomplishment

Ernie Els

1	Ernie ELS SA		267	-17
2	Darren CLARKE N.Ire		272	-12
	Phillip PRICE Wal		272	-12
4	Gary MURPHY Ire		274	-10
5	Gary EVANS Eng		275	-9
	Peter LONARD Aus		275	-9
	Ian POULTER Eng		275	-9
8	Iain PYMAN Eng		276	-8
	Mark ROE Eng		276	-8
10	Paul CASEY Eng		277	-7
	Bradley DREDGE Wal		277	-7
	Alastair FORSYTH Scot		277	-7
	Charl SCHWARTZEL SA		277	-7

On returning from a restorative two week break with his family at their Wentworth home, Ernie Els was sure of a couple of things: his swing was in smooth working order, and he wanted to focus on playing his best golf at Loch Lomond rather than utilise the tournament merely as a tune-up for the 132nd Open Golf Championship at Royal St George's the following week.

the course

It is a measure of the esteem in which Loch Lomond is held that, despite the rain, Phil Mickelson was full of praise. "They've done a great job in making this tournament unique," observed the American. "It is a wonderful course and a terrific venue."

As it turned out, Els's golf was close to his peerless best and his overall approach to the tournament was just right. The South African showed the way over the Jay Morrish and Tom Weiskopf masterpiece – he won 'wire to wire' because he yoked together the twin giants of physical strength and mental toughness.

In order to become the first golfer to win twice at Loch Lomond, Els was confident his technique was solid after visiting the range every other day during his summer holiday. But he also understood that what went on in his head during The Barclays Scottish Open was crucial. As the winner of the 2002 Open Golf Championship at Muirfield, Els appreciated how easy it would be to become consumed by thoughts of defending the Claret Jug.

One of the strategies he had learned in working with psychologist Jos Vanstiphout was the importance of not getting ahead of yourself. He decided to stay in the moment at Loch Lomond, do his job, and let everything else take care of itself.

As an old hand on the Bonnie Banks, Els appreciated the benefit of getting off to a flier. Tom Lehman showed the rest a clean pair of heels with a 65 on the road to victory in 1997 while Retief Goosen went even lower with an opening 62 in 2001.

While Els's 64 in the demanding, wet weather which caused a four hour morning delay might not have been quite as emphatic as Goosen's declaration of intent two years earlier, it was convincing enough to persuade most onlookers that his run of outstanding performances in Scotland was about to continue.

Raphaël Jacquelin

Iain Pyman

On Friday, the three time Major winner kept up the good work. He completed 29 holes without the blemish of a dropped shot before carding a bogey five on the 12th in the second round. Otherwise it was a near flawless display in sodden conditions, his 67 confirming the Open Champion was the man to beat.

By Saturday, when the depression of wet weather lifted, it was evident Els could see the finishing line. He added a second consecutive 67 to take a five shot lead into the final round. Not that Els was taking anything for granted. His swing was still close to perfection but he had to stay in the zone. "There's a lot of thinking going on," he admitted. "I have to be patient and stick to my guns."

With Ryder Cup team-mates Darren Clarke and Phillip Price waiting for Els to show a glimpse of weakness, the scene was set for a compelling last day. As it turned out, the leader did falter slightly at the start of the closing round but had the presence of mind to inform his long-serving caddie, Ricci Roberts, on the fourth tee, that they were going to turn things around.

"There was a little battle within myself but I overcame it," he said. "It's tough to play in the lead from day one and that's something I'll learn from. When you sleep on a lead you don't want to back off, you don't want to do something stupid.

"You have to play a game within yourself and I won that battle this week. I made some nice putts and that was encouraging. To win with the pressure of leading is also a nice accomplishment. My rhythm is back."

In finishing with a 69 for a 17 under par total of 267, Els completed a five stroke success over Clarke and Price. The in-form duo shared the runners-up spot after shooting respective 69s for 272. After his success in the Smurfit European Open, Price continued to tap into a rich vein of form, performing solidly on a course which many believed would favour players with more power in their armoury than the precise Welshman.

He felt deep down, however, that unless Els faltered in the early stages he was more or less uncatchable. That was how it turned out,

Caddies aren't the only
ones with good advice.

BARCLAYS
FLUENT IN FINANCE

Andrew Oldcorn

final results

Loch Lomond • Glasgow • Scotland
July 10 - 13 • 2003 • Par 71 • 7095 yards • 6486 metres

Pos.	Name		Rd1	Rd2	Rd3	Rd4	Total	Par	Prize Money Euro	£
1	Ernie ELS	SA	64	67	67	69	267	-17	532,888.90	366,660.00
2	Phillip PRICE	Wal	67	68	68	69	272	-12	277,708.00	191,080.00
	Darren CLARKE	N.Ire	69	70	64	69	272	-12	277,708.00	191,080.00
4	Gary MURPHY	Ire	70	69	68	67	274	-10	159,869.60	110,000.00
5	Ian POULTER	Eng	70	68	68	69	275	-9	114,466.60	78,760.00
	Gary EVANS	Eng	71	71	68	65	275	-9	114,466.60	78,760.00
	Peter LONARD	Aus	70	68	68	69	275	-9	114,466.60	78,760.00
8	Mark ROE	Eng	72	68	71	65	276	-8	75,778.19	52,140.00
	Iain PYMAN	Eng	69	71	67	69	276	-8	75,778.19	52,140.00
10	Bradley DREDGE	Wal	69	68	70	70	277	-7	57,313.25	39,435.00
	Alastair FORSYTH	Scot	72	69	66	70	277	-7	57,313.25	39,435.00
	Paul CASEY	Eng	69	74	68	66	277	-7	57,313.25	39,435.00
	Charl SCHWARTZEL	SA	75	68	67	67	277	-7	57,313.25	39,435.00
14	David HOWELL	Eng	66	73	70	69	278	-6	44,177.30	30,396.67
	Anders HANSEN	Den	72	69	72	65	278	-6	44,177.30	30,396.67
	Kenneth FERRIE	Eng	72	72	68	66	278	-6	44,177.30	30,396.67
	Nick O'HERN	Aus	72	72	65	69	278	-6	44,177.30	30,396.67
	David LYNN	Eng	70	70	70	68	278	-6	44,177.30	30,396.67
	Lee WESTWOOD	Eng	71	72	67	68	278	-6	44,177.30	30,396.67
20	Brian DAVIS	Eng	71	70	69	69	279	-5	36,690.07	25,245.00
	Raphaël JACQUELIN	Fr	72	70	68	69	279	-5	36,690.07	25,245.00
	Paul MCGINLEY	Ire	73	71	67	68	279	-5	36,690.07	25,245.00
	Rolf MUNTZ	NL	72	70	72	65	279	-5	36,690.07	25,245.00
24	Eduardo ROMERO	Arg	72	73	68	67	280	-4	32,293.66	22,220.00
	Peter O'MALLEY	Aus	67	76	62	75	280	-4	32,293.66	22,220.00
	Benn BARHAM	Eng	72	70	69	69	280	-4	32,293.66	22,220.00
	Tim CLARK	SA	68	68	71	73	280	-4	32,293.66	22,220.00
	Martin MARITZ	SA	67	71	70	72	280	-4	32,293.66	22,220.00
29	José Manuel LARA	Sp	73	69	72	67	281	-3	27,017.96	18,590.00
	Jean-Francois REMESY	Fr	71	71	72	67	281	-3	27,017.96	18,590.00
	Søren HANSEN	Den	74	71	67	69	281	-3	27,017.96	18,590.00
	Marcel SIEM	Ger	69	73	69	70	281	-3	27,017.96	18,590.00
	Thomas BJÖRN	Den	72	70	67	72	281	-3	27,017.96	18,590.00
	Niclas FASTH	Swe	73	71	71	66	281	-3	27,017.96	18,590.00
35	Maarten LAFEBER	NL	74	69	69	70	282	-2	22,701.48	15,620.00
	Shaun P WEBSTER	Eng	72	68	67	75	282	-2	22,701.48	15,620.00
	Scott HENDERSON	Scot	70	71	71	70	282	-2	22,701.48	15,620.00
	Phil MICKELSON	USA	76	68	70	68	282	-2	22,701.48	15,620.00
	Raymond RUSSELL	Scot	70	72	71	69	282	-2	22,701.48	15,620.00
40	Andrew OLDCORN	Scot	71	71	72	69	283	-1	19,184.35	13,200.00
	Greg TURNER	NZ	71	71	75	66	283	-1	19,184.35	13,200.00
	Stephen LEANEY	Aus	74	70	72	67	283	-1	19,184.35	13,200.00
	Nicolas COLSAERTS	Bel	69	71	71	72	283	-1	19,184.35	13,200.00
	Simon KHAN	Eng	73	70	70	70	283	-1	19,184.35	13,200.00
	Fredrik ANDERSSON	Swe	70	72	72	69	283	-1	19,184.35	13,200.00
46	José Maria OLAZÁBAL	Sp	73	72	71	68	284	0	15,986.96	11,000.00
	Paul EALES	Eng	68	73	71	72	284	0	15,986.96	11,000.00
	Julien CLEMENT	Swi	69	74	69	72	284	0	15,986.96	11,000.00
	Robert KARLSSON	Swe	71	69	69	75	284	0	15,986.96	11,000.00
50	Robert-Jan DERKSEN	NL	71	72	68	74	285	1	11,606.53	7,986.00
	Colin MONTGOMERIE	Scot	71	70	72	72	285	1	11,606.53	7,986.00
	Gregory HAVRET	Fr	70	74	70	71	285	1	11,606.53	7,986.00
	Richard BLAND	Eng	72	71	69	73	285	1	11,606.53	7,986.00
	Stephen DODD	Wal	72	73	72	68	285	1	11,606.53	7,986.00
	Andrew COLTART	Scot	75	68	70	72	285	1	11,606.53	7,986.00
	Henrik NYSTROM	Swe	73	71	73	68	285	1	11,606.53	7,986.00
	Terry PRICE	Aus	67	68	72	78	285	1	11,606.53	7,986.00
	Brett RUMFORD	Aus	67	72	72	74	285	1	11,606.53	7,986.00
	John ROLLINS	USA	70	75	76	64	285	1	11,606.53	7,986.00
60	Roger CHAPMAN	Eng	73	70	68	75	286	2	8,153.35	5,610.00
	Miguel Angel JIMÉNEZ	Sp	72	72	71	71	286	2	8,153.35	5,610.00
	Ian GARBUTT	Eng	70	69	75	72	286	2	8,153.35	5,610.00
	Gary ORR	Scot	73	72	70	71	286	2	8,153.35	5,610.00
	David CARTER	Eng	74	70	72	70	286	2	8,153.35	5,610.00
	Carl PETTERSSON	Swe	69	72	68	77	286	2	8,153.35	5,610.00
66	Klas ERIKSSON	Swe	70	74	68	75	287	3	6,714.52	4,620.00
	Richard GREEN	Aus	71	74	72	70	287	3	6,714.52	4,620.00
	Stephen GALLACHER	Scot	73	70	74	70	287	3	6,714.52	4,620.00
69	Steve WEBSTER	Eng	70	73	73	72	288	4	5,571.18	3,833.31
	Jarmo SANDELIN	Swe	71	68	75	74	288	4	5,571.18	3,833.31
	Graeme MCDOWELL	N.Ire	71	71	72	74	288	4	5,571.18	3,833.31
72	Emanuele CANONICA	It	71	71	77	70	289	5	4,791.50	3,296.84
	Tobias DIER	Ger	71	74	69	75	289	5	4,791.50	3,296.84
74	Sandy LYLE	Scot	73	72	74	74	293	9	4,787.00	3,293.75
75	Julien VAN HAUWE	Fr	69	76	74	75	294	10	4,784.00	3,291.68
76	Gordon BRAND JNR.	Scot	71	72	74	78	295	11	4,781.00	3,289.62
77	Ricardo GONZALEZ	Arg	72	73	77	74	296	12	4,778.00	3,287.55
78	Peter HEDBLOM	Swe	68	72	74	DISQ	214	1		
	John DALY	USA	74	66	77	W/D	217	4		

even if the winner looked vulnerable for a moment or two when he bogeyed the second and failed to birdie the par five third.

Clarke, alongside Els in the last group, made fours on those early holes and would have been a more serious challenger if he had maintained the pressure on the World Number Two. "In truth though I didn't swing the club well enough to mount a real challenge," the Irishman admitted honestly, adding: "Ernie was in control for most of the day."

In fact, Ernie was in control for the whole tournament.

Mike Aitken

132nd Open Golf Championship
Royal St George's Golf Club · Sandwich · Kent · England

sight and sound

Ben Curtis

1	Ben **CURTIS** USA	283	-1
2	Thomas **BJÖRN** Den	284	0
	Vijay **SINGH** Fiji	284	0
4	Davis **LOVE III** USA	285	1
	Tiger **WOODS** USA	285	1
6	Brian **DAVIS** Eng	286	2
	Fredrik **JACOBSON** Swe	286	2
8	Nick **FALDO** Eng	287	3
	Kenny **PERRY** USA	287	3
10	Gary **EVANS** Eng	288	4
	Sergio **GARCIA** Sp	288	4
	Retief **GOOSEN** SA	288	4
	Hennie **OTTO** SA	288	4
	Phillip **PRICE** Wal	288	4

After some years of concern in certain quarters that, thanks to Tiger Woods's supremacy, the grand, old game of golf had become a tad predictable when it came to the biggest occasions, the 132nd Open Golf Championship at Royal St George's contrived to produce what was, beyond question or debate, one of the very best Opens of recent times.

PADRAIG HARRINGTON	V	PADRAIG HARRINGTON
THOMAS BJÖRN	V	THOMAS BJÖRN
LUKE DONALD	V	LUKE DONALD
SERGIO GARCIA	V	SERGIO GARCIA
COLIN MONTGOMERIE	V	COLIN MONTGOMERIE
DARREN CLARKE	V	DARREN CLARKE
ADAM SCOTT	V	ADAM SCOTT
IAN POULTER	V	IAN POULTER
PHILLIP PRICE	V	PHILLIP PRICE
ERNIE ELS	V	ERNIE ELS

The 2004 European Tour will see the players up against some tough opposition.

There is only one person you have to beat to win. Yourself. Focus, determination and a will to make it happen is what singles out all great players from the rest of the field. And like them we don't just talk a good game, we play a good game. Which is why The Royal Bank of Scotland are delighted to provide banking services to players, officials and exhibitors as official bank to The European Tour.

Make it happen

The Royal Bank of Scotland

Brian Davis

Of course there have been unexpected Champions before when this particular glittering circus has hit town, in this case to Sandwich on the Kent coast, but nothing like this. Alf Perry for example, a Surrey club professional who had to plead to be excused tee-peg selling duties at Leatherhead to play in the 1935 Championship at Muirfield, was a surprise winner even in his own house.

So, too, was Kel Nagle when the genial Australian thwarted Arnold Palmer during the Centenary Open at St Andrews in 1960. More recently, Paul Lawrie's wonderful performance at Carnoustie in 1999 caused a few eyebrows to be raised in the golfing firmament, particularly across the Atlantic.

Yet even these three Champions came to the Open with some previous form. Each had walked the walk and swung the swing on many practice grounds. Each, in other words, had learned the hard way how to operate as a professional golfer which is infinitely more difficult, demanding and different than the, mostly, fun game we amateurs enjoy.

Ben Curtis's victory, however, was different. How different? Well, what is ice compared to sand, bread to rock or the 396th ranked golfer in the world when stood alongside Thomas Björn, Davis Love III, Vijay Singh or Woods? One is simply not comparable to the others. Or it shouldn't be.

Yet, when push came to shove in this most contrary of Opens, Curtis shoved harder than anyone else, stood taller, and made more putts. Quite extraordinary. Even some time later, simply unbelievable.

As ever the devil is in the detail. Curtis qualified for the Championship because he finished 13th in the Western Open on the US PGA Tour and so gained entry via one of the 'mini-leaderboards' the Royal and Ancient Golf Club have established around the world to encourage far-flung professionals to support the biggest and best Major of them all. It was Curtis's highest finish yet in his rookie year and if he had not qualified for the Open, he was not planning to fly the Atlantic to try his luck this side of the Pond.

Instead he was going to stay in Kent, Ohio, and help fiancée Candace plan their wedding. Once qualified, however, the couple decided to embark on a bit of an adventure. Their plan was simple: Ben would play in the Open, where his ambition was to make the cut, and at some point they would visit London and take in the sights.

London was achieved on the Monday of Open week, "the neatest bit" according to Candace, was "seeing Buckingham Palace in the flesh." By Friday her partner had made the cut. By Saturday he had moved into a share of third place. Twenty four hours later he was the Champion Golfer for 2003. Simple really. Rome, at its height, did not move as swiftly as this.

How did he do it? Well, obviously, he played well, his nerve held, he putted sublimely, he chipped well and he benefitted, as all Champions do, from the misfortune and miscalculations of others.

Woods had miscalculated early, hauling his driver from the bag instead of his four wood when he stood on the first tee on the first morning and, as a result, he lost his ball in the deep rough some 20 yards to the right of the fairway. He was buggied back to the tee, whacked his ball into the rough again and eventually exited the par four hole with a seven. Three shots dropped, confidence diluted, scene set for the remarkable drama to come.

Mark Roe

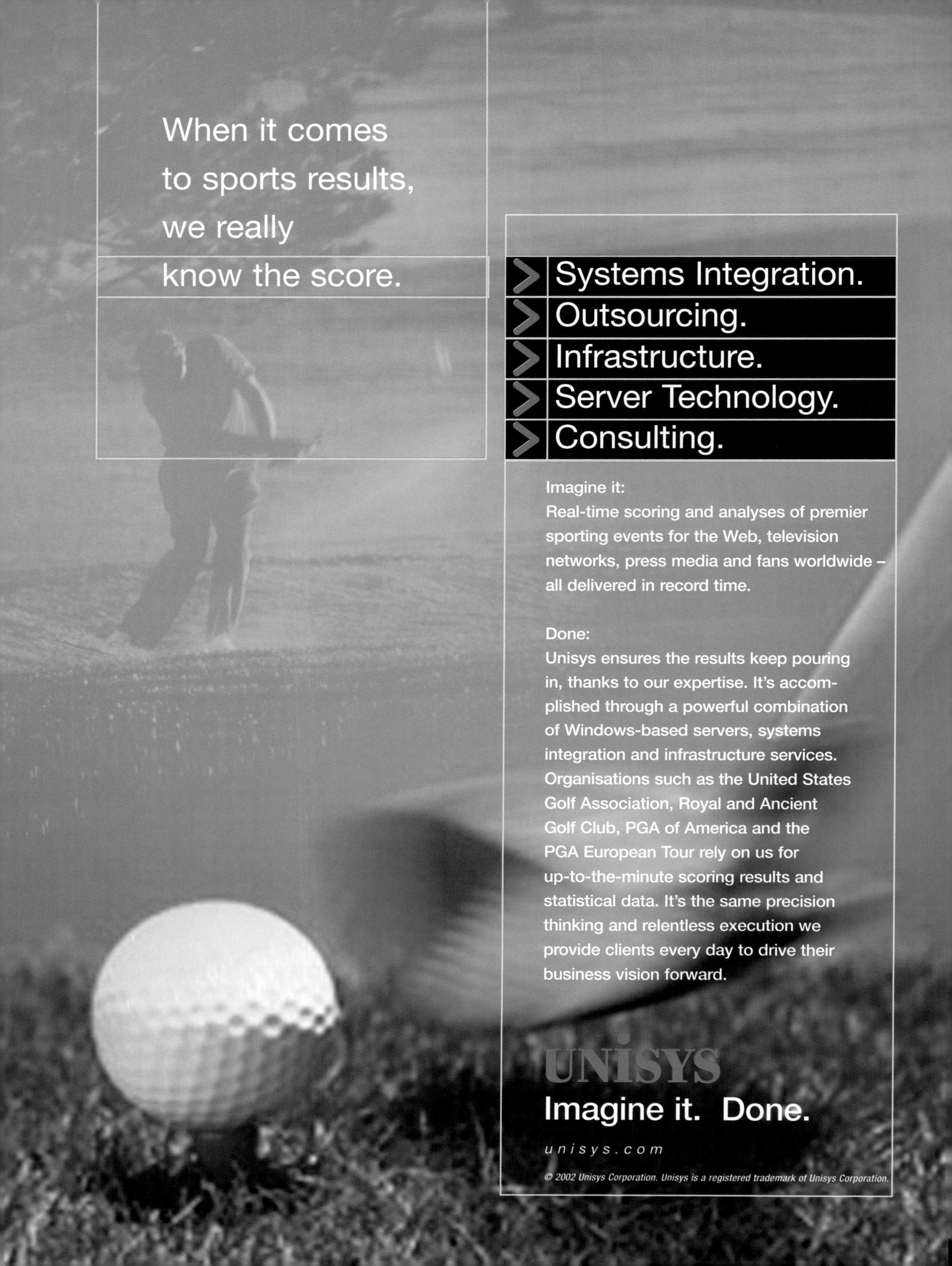

When it comes
to sports results,
we really
know the score.
Systems Integration.
Outsourcing.
Infrastructure.
Server Technology.
Consulting.
Imagine it:
Real-time scoring and analyses of premier sporting events for the Web, television networks, press media and fans worldwide – all delivered in record time.
Done:
Unisys ensures the results keep pouring in, thanks to our expertise. It's accomplished through a powerful combination of Windows-based servers, systems integration and infrastructure services. Organisations such as the United States Golf Association, Royal and Ancient Golf Club, PGA of America and the PGA European Tour rely on us for up-to-the-minute scoring results and statistical data. It's the same precision thinking and relentless execution we provide clients every day to drive their business vision forward.
UNISYS
Imagine it. Done.
unisys.com
© 2002 Unisys Corporation. Unisys is a registered trademark of Unisys Corporation.

John Jacobs (right), founding father of The European Tour, receives the Michael Williams Outstanding Services Award from Michael's widow Judy and John Hopkins, Chairman of the Association of Golf Writers. The award was presented at the AGW's Annual Dinner which preceded the 132nd Open Golf Championship at Royal St George's Golf Club.

Hours later a determined teenager searched for an hour, found the ball - the first the World Number One had ever lost in a Major Championship - stuck it on a website and was rewarded when someone paid him £7,500. Which, incidentally, was only £750 less than what England's Mark Roe eventually earned from his week in the south of England.

Roe was disqualified alongside third round playing partner Jesper Parnevik, yet it could have been he who picked up the Claret Jug, for the Englishman played the round of his life on the Saturday, a course record equalling 67, to move to within two shots of leader Björn.

The amiably eccentric golfer, who now spends as much time dealing in antiques and memorabilia as he does on the practice ground, had never been this close to the ultimate glory. He was excited at the prospect. Too excited perhaps? Or maybe too distracted?

He and the equally eccentric Swede had enjoyed appearing on the first tee together so much that they forgot to exchange scorecards. Such a simple act. Such an elementary error. Such a severe penalty. Both were disqualified. Everyone was upset. Peter Dawson, Secretary of the R&A, said: "We like to think we have procedures in place but we are looking at them very hard."

Gary Evans

Sergio Garcia

Retief Goosen

Hennie Otto

Phillip Price

the course

Since the last Open Golf Championship at Royal St George's in 1993, the tees at nine holes were pushed back to add 246 yards and thus take the course to the modern minimum length of 7106 yards. It was the most radical tinkering yet of an Open venue.

Fredrik Jacobson

While Parnevik and Roe suffered, there was delight elsewhere for The European Tour contingent whose fantastic showing saw ten Members finish in the top 14 come Sunday night.

Pick of the bunch, outside joint runners up Björn and Singh, was England's Brian Davis who made the cut right on the mark of eight over par 150 but who posted the best weekend aggregate of 136 after successive 68s to finish in a tie for sixth, his best ever finish in a Major Championship.

Alongside Davis was Sweden's Fredrik Jacobson, who followed up his superb showing in the US Open Championship at Olympia Fields Country Club where he tied for fifth, with another strong performance, carding matching one under par rounds of 70 over the weekend for 286.

In the final round, Love III, in the form of his life as he approached forty years of age, was paired with Denmark's Björn in the final group. The European led the American by a stroke on the first tee. A few holes later the gap was increased as Love III, perhaps trying

too hard, bogeyed his way into the meat of the round.

Up ahead Curtis was doing well but few were noticing. Instead the focus was on Singh and Woods. The Fijian had the edge. The American struck the ball beautifully at times from tee to green but his putter was infested with something nasty.

Suddenly Björn was ahead. A very good golfer, he always has had the potential to be great. But he, too, was to miscalculate. In a deep bunker at the short 16th he watched the ball twice trundle back to his feet after failing by inches to hit its intended target. In the end he did remarkably well to make a double bogey five.

Singh also miscalculated at this demanding hole, aiming for the flag instead of the heart of the green, the left-to-right wind doing the rest, his ball nestling in a bunker from where he dropped a vital shot. Up ahead Curtis, who had dropped a flurry of shots himself on the inward half, was regrouping. He drove sublimely down the last but his approach was charged with too much adrenalin and his ball careered over the back of the green.

Nick Faldo

Greg Norman

It was a tough chip to get close in the circumstances and he did not manage it, leaving himself a curling twelve footer for par. After considering the putt for what seemed like only a couple of seconds he stepped up and holed it, politely mini-punching the air as it dropped. It was, he believed, the difference between finishing second and third in his first ever Major, his first ever experience of a tough links, his first visit to Britain. Ignorance was never more blissful.

"Ladies and Gentlemen," said Secretary Dawson an hour later. "The Champion Golfer for 2003 is Ben Curtis of the United States of America." And Ben stepped up to receive the most coveted trophy in the game.

"Wow," he said. Wow, Ben, does not get close. Not close at all. Let's start with fantastic and work our way up. Eventually we might find a suitable word to cover this incredible achievement.

Bill Elliott

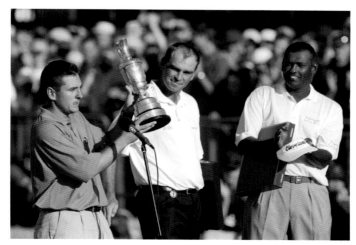

Ben Curtis, Thomas Björn and Vijay Singh

final results

Royal St George's Golf Club • Sandwich • Kent • England
July 17 - 20 • 2003 • Par 71 • 7106 yards • 6496 metres

Pos.	Name		Rd1	Rd2	Rd3	Rd4	Total	Par	Prize Money Euro	£
1	Ben CURTIS	USA	72	72	70	69	283	-11	1,010,800.00	700,000.00
2	Vijay SINGH	Fiji	75	70	69	70	284	0	498,180.00	345,000.00
	Thomas BJÖRN	Den	73	70	69	72	284	0	498,180.00	345,000.00
4	Tiger WOODS	USA	73	72	69	71	285	1	267,140.00	185,000.00
	Davis LOVE III	USA	69	72	72	72	285	1	267,140.00	185,000.00
6	Brian DAVIS	Eng	77	73	68	68	286	2	194,218.00	134,500.00
	Fredrik JACOBSON	Swe	70	76	70	70	286	2	194,218.00	134,500.00
8	Nick FALDO	Eng	76	74	67	70	287	3	141,151.00	97,750.00
	Kenny PERRY	USA	74	70	70	73	287	3	141,151.00	97,750.00
10	Sergio GARCIA	Sp	73	71	70	74	288	4	98,192.00	68,000.00
	Hennie OTTO	SA	68	76	75	69	288	4	98,192.00	68,000.00
	Gary EVANS	Eng	71	75	70	72	288	4	98,192.00	68,000.00
	Phillip PRICE	Wal	74	72	69	73	288	4	98,192.00	68,000.00
	Retief GOOSEN	SA	73	75	71	69	288	4	98,192.00	68,000.00
15	Stuart APPLEBY	Aus	75	71	71	72	289	5	71,237.34	49,333.34
	Pierre FULKE	Swe	77	72	67	73	289	5	71,237.34	49,333.34
	Chad CAMPBELL	USA	74	71	72	72	289	5	71,237.34	49,333.34
18	Greg NORMAN	Aus	69	79	74	68	290	6	60,648.00	42,000.00
	Tom WATSON	USA	71	77	73	69	290	6	60,648.00	42,000.00
	Ernie ELS	SA	78	68	72	72	290	6	60,648.00	42,000.00
	Mathias GRÖNBERG	Swe	71	74	73	72	290	6	60,648.00	42,000.00
22	Peter FOWLER	Aus	77	73	70	71	291	7	47,531.67	32,916.67
	Padraig HARRINGTON	Ire	75	73	74	69	291	7	47,531.67	32,916.67
	Kyoung-Ju CHOI	Kor	77	72	72	70	291	7	47,531.67	32,916.67
	Thomas LEVET	Fr	71	73	74	73	291	7	47,531.67	32,916.67
	Angel CABRERA	Arg	75	73	70	73	291	7	47,531.67	32,916.67
	J.L. LEWIS	USA	78	70	72	71	291	7	47,531.67	32,916.67
28	Andrew OLDCORN	Scot	72	74	73	73	292	8	37,544.00	26,000.00
	Mark FOSTER	Eng	73	73	72	74	292	8	37,544.00	26,000.00
	Nick PRICE	Zim	74	72	72	74	292	8	37,544.00	26,000.00
	Mike WEIR	Can	74	76	71	71	292	8	37,544.00	26,000.00
	Paul MCGINLEY	Ire	77	73	69	73	292	8	37,544.00	26,000.00
	S K HO	Kor	70	73	72	77	292	8	37,544.00	26,000.00
34	Gary MURPHY	Ire	73	74	73	73	293	9	27,115.11	18,777.78
	Stewart CINK	USA	75	75	75	68	293	9	27,115.11	18,777.78
	Scott MCCARRON	USA	71	74	73	75	293	9	27,115.11	18,777.78
	Bob ESTES	USA	77	71	76	69	293	9	27,115.11	18,777.78
	Adam MEDNICK	Swe	76	72	76	69	293	9	27,115.11	18,777.78
	José COCERES	Arg	77	70	72	74	293	9	27,115.11	18,777.78
	Duffy WALDORF	USA	76	73	71	73	293	9	27,115.11	18,777.78
	Shingo KATAYAMA	Jpn	76	73	73	71	293	9	27,115.11	18,777.78
	Marco RUIZ	Par	73	71	75	74	293	9	27,115.11	18,777.78
43	Robert ALLENBY	Aus	73	75	74	72	294	10	20,577.00	14,250.00
	Rich BEEM	USA	76	74	75	69	294	10	20,577.00	14,250.00
	Tom BYRUM	USA	77	72	71	74	294	10	20,577.00	14,250.00
46	Brad FAXON	USA	77	73	70	75	295	11	17,132.03	11,864.29
	Anthony WALL	Eng	75	74	71	75	295	11	17,132.03	11,864.29
	Mathew GOGGIN	Aus	76	72	70	77	295	11	17,132.03	11,864.29
	Ian POULTER	Eng	78	72	70	75	295	11	17,132.03	11,864.29
	Fred COUPLES	USA	71	75	71	78	295	11	17,132.03	11,864.29
	Markus BRIER	Aut	76	71	74	74	295	11	17,132.03	11,864.29
	Tom LEHMAN	USA	77	73	72	73	295	11	17,132.03	11,864.29
53	Mark MCNULTY	Zim	79	71	77	69	296	12	14,728.80	10,200.00
	Raphaël JACQUELIN	Fr	77	71	72	76	296	12	14,728.80	10,200.00
	Trevor IMMELMAN	SA	77	73	72	74	296	12	14,728.80	10,200.00
	David LYNN	Eng	73	76	71	76	296	12	14,728.80	10,200.00
	Michael CAMPBELL	NZ	78	72	74	72	296	12	14,728.80	10,200.00
	Rory SABBATINI	SA	79	71	75	71	296	12	14,728.80	10,200.00
59	Skip KENDALL	USA	73	76	73	75	297	13	13,790.20	9,550.00
	Craig PARRY	Aus	73	73	76	75	297	13	13,790.20	9,550.00
	Darren CLARKE	N.Ire	75	75	71	76	297	13	13,790.20	9,550.00
	Peter LONARD	Aus	73	73	70	81	297	13	13,790.20	9,550.00
	Phil MICKELSON	USA	74	72	73	78	297	13	13,790.20	9,550.00
	Alastair FORSYTH	Scot	74	70	78	75	297	13	13,790.20	9,550.00
65	Mark O'MEARA	USA	73	77	77	71	298	14	13,068.20	9,050.00
	Stephen LEANEY	Aus	74	76	78	70	298	14	13,068.20	9,050.00
	Len MATTIACE	USA	74	75	74	75	298	14	13,068.20	9,050.00
	Charles HOWELL III	USA	71	76	77	74	298	14	13,068.20	9,050.00
69	Katsuyoshi TOMORI	Jpn	72	77	75	76	300	16	12,707.20	8,800.00
70	John ROLLINS	USA	72	76	78	75	301	17	12,562.80	8,700.00
71	Chris SMITH	USA	74	73	76	79	302	18	12,418.40	8,600.00
72	Ian WOOSNAM	Wal	73	75	80	75	303	19	12,201.80	8,450.00
	John DALY	USA	75	74	74	80	303	19	12,201.80	8,450.00
74	Mark ROE	Eng	77	70	DISQ		147	5	11,913.00	8,250.00
	Jesper PARNEVIK	Swe	72	75	DISQ		147	5	11,913.00	8,250.00

Michael Campbell

1	Michael CAMPBELL	NZ	277	-11
2	Thomas BJÖRN	Den	277	-11
	Peter HEDBLOM	Swe	277	-11
4	David LYNN	Eng	279	-9
	Greg OWEN	Eng	279	-9
6	Sven STRÜVER	Ger	280	-8
7	Robert KARLSSON	Swe	282	-6
	Peter LONARD	Aus	282	-6
9	Raymond RUSSELL	Scot	283	-5
	Greg TURNER	NZ	283	-5

the homecoming

There is nothing quite as therapeutic to unscramble the mind in troubled times, as the peace and solitude of a drive in the family car. Certainly, the short journey to collect his two young sons from school one clear, sunny day in June provided a seminal moment in the shaping of Michael Campbell's career.

The New Zealander – to borrow a motoring metaphor – had been idling in neutral for several months, having opted to concentrate on the US PGA Tour for the first half of 2003. However, back in his adopted home town of Brighton as a precursor to a few weeks of competition on The European Tour International Schedule, Campbell engaged the gears in his car – and his mind – to analyse his unhappy predicament.

Consider this. In the previous three seasons on The European Tour International Schedule, Campbell had finished fourth, 12th and eighth on the Volvo Order of Merit, accumulating 4,384,419 euro in prize money and five prestigious titles.

In six months on the US PGA Tour in 2003, the 34 year old Kiwi missed seven cuts, was disqualified for signing for an incorrect score after shooting a first round 89 in The Players Championship, withdrew from the Bay Hill Invitational due to a shoulder injury and lost in the first round of the World Golf Championships – Accenture Match Play. He lay moribund in 209th place on the US PGA Tour Money List and his earnings had all but dried up.

Hardly surprising then, that Campbell was at a low ebb when he returned 'home' to be with his wife Julie and their two young boys, Thomas and Jordan. However, the sight of England's south coast, he admitted, was like a huge weight being lifted off his shoulders. Technically, home was 12,000 miles away in New Zealand, but Brighton was where he felt at ease with himself and his surroundings.

In the time it took to collect his sons, Campbell had made his decision. He was going to abandon his American odyssey and play full-time on The European Tour once again. As decisions go, this was

David Lynn

the course

Portmarnock, according to Thomas Björn, is the "finest links golf course on earth." The majestic tract of links land, just north of Dublin, offered as true and fair a test as can be found anywhere. In one word - awesome.

as shrewd as they come. Within a month, vindication was at hand when he collected the Nissan Irish Open at Portmarnock Golf Club. Just for good measure, it was achieved in front of his thrilled parents, Tom and Maria.

Campbell struck a majestic eight iron from 145 yards to within a foot at the first play-off hole against Denmark's Thomas Björn and Peter Hedblom of Sweden to seal his sixth title on The European

Ian Woosnam

Tour after the trio had finished regulation play, over one of the world's great links, on 11 under par 277.

"I never doubted myself. I always knew I would come back," said Campbell. "I've been down before and didn't enjoy it. I knew I had the determination and support of family and friends to turn my career around. Fortunately, both my caddie and my manager persuaded me to play at Portmarnock. I was going to take the week off but they convinced me to enter just before the deadline."

On reflection, Campbell confessed that the relentless grind of travelling from city to city, hotel room to hotel room, in the United States had been a punishing routine to undertake with a wife, two young children and two nannies in tow.

"The hardest thing was spending 12 weeks on the road. Never again," he admitted. "It was frustrating. I played ten events in America and didn't make a cut, which put a big dent in my ego. By the tenth or 11th week everyone was getting pretty ratty. It's hard to stay in a foreign country in those circumstances.

"I am a creature of comfort and six wins confirms how happy I feel playing on The European Tour. We have a great house in Brighton and returning there felt like coming home. If the family are happy, then I'm happy. Julie and I have plenty of friends here and I know everyone on The European Tour. It is far more harmonious here than in the States."

The week before travelling to Ireland, Campbell played all four rounds in the 132nd Open Golf Championship - an encouraging

Peter Hedblom

sign. Four days at Portmarnock saw the signs point to glory as he shot rounds of 66-69-71-71 to join Björn – the first round leader with a course record 64 – and the fast-finishing Hedblom, before completing the job one hole later.

Spare a thought for Björn, however. The great Dane, still aching from narrowly missing out in the 132nd Open Golf Championship at Royal St George's, had to accept second place once more. As Campbell generously observed, Björn is a class player whose day would come again. But for the new champion, it was the happiest of homecomings.

Welcome back, Michael.

Gordon Simpson

final results

Portmarnock Golf Club · Dublin · Ireland
July 24 - 27 · 2003 · Par 72 · 7363 yards · 6733 metres

Pos.	Name		Rd1	Rd2	Rd3	Rd4	Total	Par	Prize Money Euro	£
1	Michael CAMPBELL	NZ	66	69	71	71	277	-11	300,000.00	212,497.70
2	Peter HEDBLOM	Swe	70	71	68	68	277	-11	156,340.00	110,739.63
	Thomas BJÖRN	Den	64	74	68	71	277	-11	156,340.00	110,739.63
4	David LYNN	Eng	69	65	72	73	279	-9	83,160.00	58,904.36
	Greg OWEN	Eng	68	71	68	72	279	-9	83,160.00	58,904.36
6	Sven STRÜVER	Ger	71	71	69	69	280	-8	63,000.00	44,624.52
7	Robert KARLSSON	Swe	69	69	69	75	282	-6	49,500.00	35,062.12
	Peter LONARD	Aus	71	68	69	74	282	-6	49,500.00	35,062.12
9	Greg TURNER	NZ	71	71	69	72	283	-5	38,160.00	27,029.71
	Raymond RUSSELL	Scot	71	73	68	71	283	-5	38,160.00	27,029.71
11	Gary MURPHY	Ire	74	68	70	72	284	-4	28,740.00	20,357.28
	Paul BROADHURST	Eng	67	74	71	72	284	-4	28,740.00	20,357.28
	Miguel Angel JIMÉNEZ	Sp	73	68	71	72	284	-4	28,740.00	20,357.28
	Peter O'MALLEY	Aus	70	69	72	73	284	-4	28,740.00	20,357.28
	Lee WESTWOOD	Eng	70	72	69	73	284	-4	28,740.00	20,357.28
	John BICKERTON	Eng	71	72	72	69	284	-4	28,740.00	20,357.28
17	Shaun P WEBSTER	Eng	72	71	67	75	285	-3	22,110.00	15,661.08
	Gary EMERSON	Eng	68	71	72	74	285	-3	22,110.00	15,661.08
	Simon KHAN	Eng	68	73	70	74	285	-3	22,110.00	15,661.08
	Mark PILKINGTON	Wal	76	67	69	73	285	-3	22,110.00	15,661.08
	Brett RUMFORD	Aus	72	71	70	72	285	-3	22,110.00	15,661.08
	Charl SCHWARTZEL	SA	71	71	70	73	285	-3	22,110.00	15,661.08
23	Peter FOWLER	Aus	70	73	70	73	286	-2	17,370.00	12,303.62
	Alvaro SALTO	Sp	70	72	71	73	286	-2	17,370.00	12,303.62
	José Maria OLAZÁBAL	Sp	70	73	72	71	286	-2	17,370.00	12,303.62
	Peter LAWRIE	Ire	70	68	71	77	286	-2	17,370.00	12,303.62
	Ian POULTER	Eng	70	71	69	76	286	-2	17,370.00	12,303.62
	Jarrod MOSELEY	Aus	70	72	71	73	286	-2	17,370.00	12,303.62
	Christian CÉVAËR	Fr	72	71	70	73	286	-2	17,370.00	12,303.62
	James KINGSTON	SA	73	69	71	73	286	-2	17,370.00	12,303.62
	Luke DONALD	Eng	68	74	69	75	286	-2	17,370.00	12,303.62
	Ben MASON	Eng	69	71	70	76	286	-2	17,370.00	12,303.62
33	Malcolm MACKENZIE	Eng	70	72	73	72	287	-1	13,920.00	9,859.89
	Paul MCGINLEY	Ire	74	66	76	71	287	-1	13,920.00	9,859.89
	Andrew RAITT	Eng	70	72	70	75	287	-1	13,920.00	9,859.89
36	Jean-Francois REMESY	Fr	69	75	71	73	288	0	11,700.00	8,287.41
	Maarten LAFEBER	NL	72	69	71	76	288	0	11,700.00	8,287.41
	Arjun ATWAL	Ind	70	74	70	74	288	0	11,700.00	8,287.41
	Jean HUGO	SA	70	73	71	74	288	0	11,700.00	8,287.41
	Jean-Francois LUCQUIN	Fr	72	68	70	78	288	0	11,700.00	8,287.41
	Nicolas COLSAERTS	Bel	72	72	73	71	288	0	11,700.00	8,287.41
	Ian GARBUTT	Eng	72	70	71	75	288	0	11,700.00	8,287.41
	Markus BRIER	Aut	71	71	69	77	288	0	11,700.00	8,287.41
	Matthew BLACKEY	Eng	75	67	71	75	288	0	11,700.00	8,287.41
45	Mark ROE	Eng	69	74	72	74	289	1	9,720.00	6,884.93
	Peter BAKER	Eng	72	70	71	76	289	1	9,720.00	6,884.93
47	Damien MCGRANE	Ire	72	70	76	72	290	2	8,460.00	5,992.44
	Jesus Maria ARRUTI	Sp	73	71	72	74	290	2	8,460.00	5,992.44
	Phillip PRICE	Wal	68	76	71	75	290	2	8,460.00	5,992.44
	Darren CLARKE	N.Ire	75	68	72	75	290	2	8,460.00	5,992.44
	Fredrik ANDERSSON	Swe	71	73	73	73	290	2	8,460.00	5,992.44
52	David GILFORD	Eng	70	74	75	72	291	3	6,840.00	4,844.95
	Didier DE VOOGHT	Bel	71	73	74	73	291	3	6,840.00	4,844.95
	Patrik SJÖLAND	Swe	73	70	73	75	291	3	6,840.00	4,844.95
	Terry PRICE	Aus	73	70	77	71	291	3	6,840.00	4,844.95
56	Carlos RODILES	Sp	69	75	72	76	292	4	5,340.00	3,782.46
	Simon WAKEFIELD	Eng	70	73	77	72	292	4	5,340.00	3,782.46
	David PARK	Wal	71	72	70	79	292	4	5,340.00	3,782.46
	Lee S JAMES	Eng	71	72	72	77	292	4	5,340.00	3,782.46
	Damian MOONEY	N.Ire	70	74	75	73	292	4	5,340.00	3,782.46
	Stephen GALLACHER	Scot	68	73	76	75	292	4	5,340.00	3,782.46
62	Henrik BJORNSTAD	Nor	74	70	72	77	293	5	4,590.00	3,251.21
	Søren HANSEN	Den	72	72	71	78	293	5	4,590.00	3,251.21
64	Klas ERIKSSON	Swe	72	68	77	77	294	6	4,230.00	2,996.22
	Euan LITTLE	Scot	72	71	72	79	294	6	4,230.00	2,996.22
66	Ian WOOSNAM	Wal	72	70	75	78	295	7	3,690.00	2,613.72
	Steve WEBSTER	Eng	71	73	72	79	295	7	3,690.00	2,613.72
	Jamie SPENCE	Eng	71	71	77	76	295	7	3,690.00	2,613.72
	Nick DOUGHERTY	Eng	71	71	77	76	295	7	3,690.00	2,613.72
70	Robert COLES	Eng	74	69	78	75	296	8	3,280.00	2,323.31
71	Sandy LYLE	Scot	72	71	75	79	297	9	2,697.00	1,910.35
	Jonathan LOMAS	Eng	74	69	76	78	297	9	2,697.00	1,910.35
	Simon DYSON	Eng	69	72	74	82	297	9	2,697.00	1,910.35
74	Robert ROCK	Eng	73	71	76	78	298	10	2,691.00	1,906.10
75	Pierre FULKE	Swe	74	70	81	80	305	17	2,688.00	1,903.98

Adam Scott

1	Adam SCOTT Aus	277	-11
2	Nick DOUGHERTY Eng	279	-9
3	Andrew COLTART Scot	280	-8
	Luke DONALD Eng	280	-8
	Robert KARLSSON Swe	280	-8
6	Miguel Angel JIMÉNEZ Sp	281	-7
	Carl PETTERSSON Swe	281	-7
8	Peter HEDBLOM Swe	282	-6
	Fredrik JACOBSON Swe	282	-6
	Jamie SPENCE Eng	282	-6

swivel hips

Gordon Brand Jnr

Never afraid to poke fun at himself as well as others, Lee Trevino was once asked what three things an ageing golfer losers. "His nerve, his memory....and I can't remember the third one," replied the wise-cracking Mexican.

Fortunately for the protagonists involved in the Scandic Carlsberg Scandinavian Masters, it will be a long time before they have to worry about such afflictions. Indeed, while the Barsebäck clubhouse often resembled a crèche as several players brought their young families with them, the leaderboard had a similarly youthful feel to it.

This was no accident however, but a result of the commendable policy of the tournament organisers to invite some of the brightest new stars in the golfing firmament, such as Luke Donald, Kevin Na and Zane Scotland, to Malmo to compete alongside the cream of the existing young talent on The European Tour.

They had no cause to regret the decision as Nick Dougherty, Adam Scott and Donald battled for the title on the final day, with teenagers Charl Schwartzel and Na also signalling their ability to follow in their footsteps.

In the end it was Scott who held the trophy aloft to the adulation of the huge crowds but the 23 year old knew his fourth European Tour International Schedule victory had been a hard fought one on a tough course likened to a US Open Championship venue by third round joint leader Maarten Lafeber.

Dougherty was the first of the young guns to fire, the 21 year old sleeping for 18 hours before his excellent opening round 67 to share the lead with Andrew Coltart and David Gilford, the lengthy lie-in a side-effect of his battle to recover from a bout of glandular fever. Even Dougherty, though, is a relative veteran compared to Korean teenager Na, who was only one shot behind after a 68, the 19 year old still travelling everywhere with his father Yong, who doubles as his caddie, and his mother Annie.

the course

A composite course made up of the two layouts at Barsebäck, the championship course featured three holes alongside the stretch of water which separates Malmo and Copenhagen with the remainder amongst the tall pines. Together they represented a tough test.

Nick Dougherty

Na, however, could not even lay claim to being the youngest player in the field, that honour going to Schwartzel, the highlight of the 18 year old South African's week being a third round 69 which helped him to a share of 16th place overall.

Add in the likes of 22 year old Julien Clement and 21 year old Scotland, both of whom completed all four rounds, it was understandable why former Ryder Cup Captain Mark James felt somewhat out of place as he shared second place at halfway stage at the ripe old age of 49.

The man James and the others chased into the weekend was Nick Faldo protégé Dougherty, who had carded a second round 69 to lead by three shots from three players and by five from Scott. But the Australian was growing in confidence with every round, the hard work put in on the putting green finally paying off as he negotiated the week without a single three putt.

His long game was not too shabby either, the player nicknamed 'Swivel Hips' by his idol and friend Greg Norman needing just 67 blows on Saturday to wipe out the deficit and share the lead with Lafeber going into the last round.

It was a final day which reunited the 2001 Walker Cup partners Donald and Dougherty in the second to last pairing, drawing as many admiring glances from the young ladies in the crowd as the golfing aficionados.

But it was ultimately a final day which belonged to Scott despite briefly losing the lead as Dougherty made a flying start. Having

David Gilford

regrouped, the Australian reasserted his authority with birdies on the 11th and 12th to eventually ease to a two shot victory over the young Englishman.

Dougherty looked set for a share of second with Robert Karlsson, Coltart and Donald but a bold birdie putt from 15 feet on the final hole saw him punch the air with delight as he knew the runners-up spot was his alone. With it, of course, came the knowledge he had secured his playing privileges for the 2004 season.

People like Adam Scott will be there, too. The future of The European Tour is indeed a bright one.

Phil Casey

final results

Barsebäck Golf & Country Club • Malmo • Sweden
July 31 - August 3 • 2003 • Par 72 • 7365 yards • 6735 metres

Pos.	Name		Rd1	Rd2	Rd3	Rd4	Total	Par	Prize Money Euro	£
1	Adam SCOTT	Aus	70	71	67	69	277	-11	316,660.00	225,071.61
2	Nick DOUGHERTY	Eng	67	69	74	69	279	-9	211,110.00	150,050.11
3	Robert KARLSSON	Swe	71	69	71	69	280	-8	98,166.66	69,773.66
	Andrew COLTART	Scot	67	76	69	68	280	-8	98,166.66	69,773.66
	Luke DONALD	Eng	71	68	71	70	280	-8	98,166.66	69,773.66
6	Miguel Angel JIMÉNEZ	Sp	73	70	71	67	281	-7	61,750.00	43,889.89
	Carl PETTERSSON	Swe	69	75	66	71	281	-7	61,750.00	43,889.89
8	Jamie SPENCE	Eng	74	70	69	69	282	-6	42,686.67	30,340.29
	Peter HEDBLOM	Swe	70	70	71	71	282	-6	42,686.67	30,340.29
	Fredrik JACOBSON	Swe	71	70	72	69	282	-6	42,686.67	30,340.29
11	Maarten LAFEBER	NL	68	71	69	75	283	-5	34,960.00	24,848.43
12	Philip ARCHER	Eng	71	70	71	72	284	-4	30,067.50	21,371.00
	Richard S JOHNSON	Swe	71	71	69	73	284	-4	30,067.50	21,371.00
	Adam MEDNICK	Swe	73	69	71	71	284	-4	30,067.50	21,371.00
	Michael CAMPBELL	NZ	70	72	71	71	284	-4	30,067.50	21,371.00
16	Mark ROE	Eng	71	70	71	73	285	-3	23,465.00	16,678.16
	Robert-Jan DERKSEN	NL	73	71	67	74	285	-3	23,465.00	16,678.16
	Mark FOSTER	Eng	74	67	73	71	285	-3	23,465.00	16,678.16
	Sven STRÜVER	Ger	72	71	70	72	285	-3	23,465.00	16,678.16
	Søren KJELDSEN	Den	71	70	70	74	285	-3	23,465.00	16,678.16
	Carlos RODILES	Sp	69	72	73	71	285	-3	23,465.00	16,678.16
	Jamie DONALDSON	Wal	76	69	70	70	285	-3	23,465.00	16,678.16
	Charl SCHWARTZEL	SA	72	72	69	72	285	-3	23,465.00	16,678.16
24	Gordon BRAND JNR.	Scot	73	71	73	69	286	-2	17,765.00	12,626.78
	Bernhard LANGER	Ger	70	71	72	73	286	-2	17,765.00	12,626.78
	Barry LANE	Eng	71	75	71	69	286	-2	17,765.00	12,626.78
	Damien MCGRANE	Ire	73	73	69	71	286	-2	17,765.00	12,626.78
	Henrik STENSON	Swe	73	72	73	68	286	-2	17,765.00	12,626.78
	Gary ORR	Scot	71	71	69	75	286	-2	17,765.00	12,626.78
	Fredrik ANDERSSON	Swe	74	68	75	69	286	-2	17,765.00	12,626.78
	Raymond RUSSELL	Scot	72	70	71	73	286	-2	17,765.00	12,626.78
	Jean Louis GUEPY	Fr	75	71	69	71	286	-2	17,765.00	12,626.78
	Ben MASON	Eng	72	72	73	69	286	-2	17,765.00	12,626.78
34	Mark JAMES	Eng	69	70	72	76	287	-1	14,250.00	10,128.44
	Steve WEBSTER	Eng	70	72	68	77	287	-1	14,250.00	10,128.44
	Simon WAKEFIELD	Eng	70	71	74	72	287	-1	14,250.00	10,128.44
37	David GILFORD	Eng	67	74	75	72	288	0	12,730.00	9,048.07
	Mårten OLANDER	Swe	72	72	72	72	288	0	12,730.00	9,048.07
	Paul BROADHURST	Eng	71	74	74	69	288	0	12,730.00	9,048.07
	Tobias DIER	Ger	72	71	73	72	288	0	12,730.00	9,048.07
	Kevin NA	Kor	68	74	74	72	288	0	12,730.00	9,048.07
42	Richard BLAND	Eng	71	75	69	74	289	1	10,830.00	7,697.61
	Nicolas COLSAERTS	Bel	73	73	73	70	289	1	10,830.00	7,697.61
	Roger WESSELS	SA	72	75	72	70	289	1	10,830.00	7,697.61
	Andrew RAITT	Eng	74	72	72	71	289	1	10,830.00	7,697.61
	Terry PRICE	Aus	71	73	73	72	289	1	10,830.00	7,697.61
47	Jean-Francois REMESY	Fr	72	71	75	72	290	2	8,740.00	6,212.11
	Trevor IMMELMAN	SA	73	74	74	69	290	2	8,740.00	6,212.11
	Jonathan LOMAS	Eng	72	73	76	69	290	2	8,740.00	6,212.11
	Ignacio GARRIDO	Sp	72	72	70	76	290	2	8,740.00	6,212.11
	Stephen SCAHILL	NZ	68	74	78	70	290	2	8,740.00	6,212.11
	Henrik NYSTROM	Swe	73	72	76	69	290	2	8,740.00	6,212.11
53	Brian DAVIS	Eng	71	73	75	72	291	3	6,840.00	4,861.65
	Paul MCGINLEY	Ire	75	72	74	70	291	3	6,840.00	4,861.65
	Jarmo SANDELIN	Swe	71	73	73	74	291	3	6,840.00	4,861.65
	Graeme MCDOWELL	N.Ire	73	72	75	71	291	3	6,840.00	4,861.65
57	Greg TURNER	NZ	69	74	76	73	292	4	5,605.00	3,983.85
	Andrew MARSHALL	Eng	72	74	74	72	292	4	5,605.00	3,983.85
	Ian GARBUTT	Eng	72	71	73	76	292	4	5,605.00	3,983.85
	Bradley DREDGE	Wal	75	71	76	70	292	4	5,605.00	3,983.85
61	Ronan RAFFERTY	N.Ire	73	72	73	75	293	5	4,750.00	3,376.15
	Philip GOLDING	Eng	75	72	75	71	293	5	4,750.00	3,376.15
	Johan RYSTRÖM	Swe	77	70	72	74	293	5	4,750.00	3,376.15
	Christopher HANELL	Swe	75	72	73	73	293	5	4,750.00	3,376.15
	Aaron BADDELEY	Aus	72	74	72	75	293	5	4,750.00	3,376.15
66	Marc FARRY	Fr	74	71	76	73	294	6	3,895.00	2,768.44
	Gary EMERSON	Eng	78	69	76	71	294	6	3,895.00	2,768.44
	Peter BAKER	Eng	73	73	76	72	294	6	3,895.00	2,768.44
	Julien CLEMENT	Swi	75	71	75	73	294	6	3,895.00	2,768.44
70	Gregory HAVRET	Fr	70	75	76	74	295	7	3,055.67	2,171.87
	Simon HURD	Eng	69	73	73	80	295	7	3,055.67	2,171.87
	Greg OWEN	Eng	71	73	74	77	295	7	3,055.67	2,171.87
73	Joakim HAEGGMAN	Swe	73	74	78	71	296	8	2,842.50	2,020.36
	Rolf MUNTZ	NL	76	71	74	75	296	8	2,842.50	2,020.36
75	Arjun ATWAL	Ind	73	68	76	80	297	9	2,836.50	2,016.09
	Zane SCOTLAND	Eng	73	73	77	74	297	9	2,836.50	2,016.09
77	Andrew OLDCORN	Scot	73	74	76	75	298	10	2,832.00	2,012.89
78	Roger CHAPMAN	Eng	74	73	76	76	299	11	2,829.00	2,010.76
79	Warren BENNETT	Eng	74	73	76	77	300	12	2,826.00	2,008.63
80	Mark PILKINGTON	Wal	70	77	85	80	312	24	2,823.00	2,006.50
81	Jarrod MOSELEY	Aus	73	74	WD		147	3		

Ian Poulter

1	Ian POULTER Eng	266	-22
2	Colin MONTGOMERIE Scot	267	-21
3	Stephen GALLACHER Scot	268	-20
	Søren HANSEN Den	268	-20
	Gregory HAVRET Fr	268	-20
6	Brian DAVIS Eng	269	-19
7	David GILFORD Eng	270	-18
8	Miguel Angel JIMÉNEZ Sp	271	-17
	Mårten OLANDER Swe	271	-17
	Patrik SJÖLAND Swe	271	-17
	Steve WEBSTER Eng	271	-17

harlequin personality

hey were, in a modest way, things of beauty. The powers-that-be made an inspired decision when they shipped in a fleet of small electrically-powered scooters for the use of officials during the inaugural Nordic Open. All sorts of people used them, from young officials, who threw them about like Grand Prix racers, to the doctors, who made somewhat more circumspect progress on their errands of mercy. The little machines were the last word in understated elegance – which is more than you could say for the eventual champion.

No matter what claims could be made of Ian Poulter, a charge of understatedness could never be levelled with any hope of a conviction. Poulter is a man who believes fervently that his mission in life is two-fold. Firstly, he must win tournament after tournament and secondly, that he has to bring some colour into the game. In these twin aims, he succeeded handsomely at Simon's Golf Club, 25 miles north of Copenhagen, in the early days of August.

The simple facts were that Poulter won the tournament with a total of 266, 22 under par. But there was so much more to it than that.

Poulter's polychrome hairstyle and his harlequin personality should never be allowed to detract from his considerable qualities as a golfer. His hirsute colour scheme for the week was platinum blonde

and almost black, but his golf for much of four days under a blistering Danish sun was pure gold.

Much had preceded the final acts of the tournament, but ultimately it was distilled into a classic confrontation between fearless kid and grizzled veteran, the new generation and the old, the peacock against the bird of prey that had seen everything a hundred times and more. This time the one with the flashy plumage got away with it, but not before the hungry predator had given the baby bird a thorough working over.

The man who would be king was Poulter and he won the battle on this occasion, edging out Colin Montgomerie for the title. For Poulter, it was the fifth time he had walked forward on The European Tour International Schedule to receive the plaudits. For Montgomerie, it would have been the 28th. Yet it might not have ended that way but for a strange and unaccountable stroke that Montgomerie produced on the 72nd hole.

Poulter had not birdied the par five 17th but Montgomerie had, to narrow the gap to one. Now was his chance, although it did not help that he was forced to wait while David Gilford, with whom Poulter was playing in the penultimate match, and his fellow Englishman finished out on the green up ahead.

Raymond Russell

the course

Colin Montgomerie said that the greens at Simon's Golf Club were as good as he had seen all season - as solid an endorsement a course can get. The rest was pretty good too and the host club could be proud of their maiden adventure on The European Tour International Schedule.

Montgomerie had fought the good fight with all his might in his return to tournament action after he had been forced to pull out of the 132nd Open Golf Championship early in the first round with a hand injury. But the last two holes at Simon's Golf Club are both par fives, holes where tournaments can be won and lost with equal facility.

To be frank, Poulter made a bit of a mess of the 18th, missing the green to the right and fluffing his chip, leaving it 18 feet from the pin. Par was the best he could manage as he completed a 66. If Montgomerie was to push the piece into a play-off, he had three strokes to get the ball in the hole from where he stood in the heart of the fairway following a perfect drive.

He tried to look cool, calm and collected. Very few things can be new to him; he had been here a hundred times before, but an occasional puff of the cheeks and a couple of deep swallows, as he tried to banish the awful dryness in his mouth, betrayed him. When it came to it, so did the stroke he played.

There was no reason why he should not at least have hit the green. Maybe he rushed it a touch? Perhaps the nerves really did get to him? The fact was that he missed the putting surface by a distance,

Colin Montgomerie

Gregory Havret

plunging into a thatch of greenside rough. A horrible lie did not help and he was unable to chip closer than 15 feet.

The great man's putting had not always pleased him during the week and it did not come to his aid in the denouement as he pushed the ball wide of the hole before sinking the final putt in a 68.

It was a dramatic end to a tournament that had seen two Frenchmen, Raphaël Jacquelin and Gregory Havret, lead after the first and second rounds respectively before Søren Hansen, the local boy to whom the host course is a second home, shared the lead with Montgomerie after the third.

The enthusiastic home galleries rooted with unashamed partisanship for Hansen in the final round, but even as he went on to share third spot with Stephen Gallacher, whose 63 was the best score of the final day, and Havret, they had something equally as impressive to cheer at the prize giving.

For say what you like about Ian Poulter, he is not dull – and wouldn't be, even if he had no hair at all.

Mel Webb

final results

Simon's Golf Club • Copenhagen • Denmark
August 7 - 10 • 2003 • Par 72 • 7027 yards • 6426 metres

Pos.	Name		Rd1	Rd2	Rd3	Rd4	Total	Par	Prize Money Euro	£
1	Ian POULTER	Eng	68	67	65	66	266	-22	266,660.00	187,002.53
2	Colin MONTGOMERIE	Scot	70	65	64	68	267	-21	177,770.00	124,666.02
3	Gregory HAVRET	Fr	68	63	69	68	268	-20	82,666.66	57,972.23
	Søren HANSEN	Den	71	66	62	69	268	-20	82,666.66	57,972.23
	Stephen GALLACHER	Scot	71	65	69	63	268	-20	82,666.66	57,972.23
6	Brian DAVIS	Eng	66	68	67	68	269	-19	56,000.00	39,271.51
7	David GILFORD	Eng	66	67	67	70	270	-18	48,000.00	33,661.30
8	Mårten OLANDER	Swe	66	73	65	67	271	-17	34,320.00	24,067.83
	Steve WEBSTER	Eng	66	71	69	65	271	-17	34,320.00	24,067.83
	Miguel Angel JIMÉNEZ	Sp	65	70	68	68	271	-17	34,320.00	24,067.83
	Patrik SJÖLAND	Swe	69	64	68	70	271	-17	34,320.00	24,067.83
12	Julien CLEMENT	Swi	70	70	68	64	272	-16	27,520.00	19,299.14
13	Peter LAWRIE	Ire	69	66	73	65	273	-15	24,586.67	17,242.07
	Henrik BJORNSTAD	Nor	72	69	66	66	273	-15	24,586.67	17,242.07
	Andrew COLTART	Scot	66	69	69	69	273	-15	24,586.67	17,242.07
16	Peter HEDBLOM	Swe	70	68	69	67	274	-14	22,080.00	15,484.20
	Miles TUNNICLIFF	Eng	73	64	68	69	274	-14	22,080.00	15,484.20
18	Mark FOSTER	Eng	69	68	67	71	275	-13	19,560.00	13,716.98
	Maarten LAFEBER	NL	72	69	66	68	275	-13	19,560.00	13,716.98
	Thomas BJÖRN	Den	67	69	72	67	275	-13	19,560.00	13,716.98
	Kevin NA	Kor	70	64	69	72	275	-13	19,560.00	13,716.98
22	Søren KJELDSEN	Den	68	72	69	67	276	-12	17,600.00	12,342.48
	Peter JESPERSEN	Den	68	68	71	69	276	-12	17,600.00	12,342.48
	David PARK	Wal	67	71	68	70	276	-12	17,600.00	12,342.48
25	Raphaël JACQUELIN	Fr	62	72	74	69	277	-11	14,254.55	9,996.39
	Greg TURNER	NZ	67	72	68	70	277	-11	14,254.55	9,996.39
	Alessandro TADINI	It	72	67	70	68	277	-11	14,254.55	9,996.39
	Nicolas COLSAERTS	Bel	73	68	67	69	277	-11	14,254.55	9,996.39
	Peter O'MALLEY	Aus	70	70	67	70	277	-11	14,254.55	9,996.39
	Jorge BERENDT	Arg	70	71	68	68	277	-11	14,254.55	9,996.39
	Stephen SCAHILL	NZ	70	68	74	65	277	-11	14,254.55	9,996.39
	John BICKERTON	Eng	67	70	67	73	277	-11	14,254.55	9,996.39
	Fredrik WIDMARK	Swe	67	70	67	73	277	-11	14,254.55	9,996.39
	Francois DELAMONTAGNE	Fr	67	70	69	71	277	-11	14,254.55	9,996.39
	Marcus FRASER	Aus	68	70	72	67	277	-11	14,254.55	9,996.39
36	Malcolm MACKENZIE	Eng	72	67	67	72	278	-10	10,720.00	7,517.69
	Jamie SPENCE	Eng	69	72	68	69	278	-10	10,720.00	7,517.69
	Peter BAKER	Eng	67	72	70	69	278	-10	10,720.00	7,517.69
	Gustavo ROJAS	Arg	72	69	71	66	278	-10	10,720.00	7,517.69
	Benn BARHAM	Eng	72	66	73	67	278	-10	10,720.00	7,517.69
	Simon DYSON	Eng	71	70	66	71	278	-10	10,720.00	7,517.69
	David DIXON	Eng	70	69	71	68	278	-10	10,720.00	7,517.69
43	Mattias ELIASSON	Swe	72	69	67	71	279	-9	8,480.00	5,946.83
	Damien MCGRANE	Ire	71	69	71	68	279	-9	8,480.00	5,946.83
	Jonathan LOMAS	Eng	69	65	73	72	279	-9	8,480.00	5,946.83
	Christian CÉVAËR	Fr	68	71	69	71	279	-9	8,480.00	5,946.83
	David LYNN	Eng	67	66	73	73	279	-9	8,480.00	5,946.83
	Terry PRICE	Aus	71	69	69	70	279	-9	8,480.00	5,946.83
	Matthew CORT	Eng	68	70	69	72	279	-9	8,480.00	5,946.83
50	David HOWELL	Eng	72	68	70	70	280	-8	6,240.00	4,375.97
	Philip ARCHER	Eng	65	69	71	75	280	-8	6,240.00	4,375.97
	Philip GOLDING	Eng	67	69	72	72	280	-8	6,240.00	4,375.97
	Andrew RAITT	Eng	66	68	74	72	280	-8	6,240.00	4,375.97
	Fredrik ANDERSSON	Swe	70	68	73	69	280	-8	6,240.00	4,375.97
	Raymond RUSSELL	Scot	65	72	71	72	280	-8	6,240.00	4,375.97
	Jean Louis GUEPY	Fr	69	72	70	69	280	-8	6,240.00	4,375.97
57	Barry LANE	Eng	72	66	72	71	281	-7	4,640.00	3,253.93
	Shaun P WEBSTER	Eng	69	68	72	72	281	-7	4,640.00	3,253.93
	Steen TINNING	Den	72	68	71	70	281	-7	4,640.00	3,253.93
	Jean HUGO	SA	71	69	72	69	281	-7	4,640.00	3,253.93
	David CARTER	Eng	69	70	70	72	281	-7	4,640.00	3,253.93
62	Roger CHAPMAN	Eng	68	70	75	69	282	-6	3,680.00	2,580.70
	Miguel Angel MARTIN	Sp	70	70	71	71	282	-6	3,680.00	2,580.70
	Robert-Jan DERKSEN	NL	68	72	72	70	282	-6	3,680.00	2,580.70
	Chris GANE	Eng	70	68	71	73	282	-6	3,680.00	2,580.70
	Marcel SIEM	Ger	73	68	72	69	282	-6	3,680.00	2,580.70
	Per NYMAN	Swe	73	68	70	71	282	-6	3,680.00	2,580.70
	Fernando ROCA	Sp	70	71	74	67	282	-6	3,680.00	2,580.70
69	Klas ERIKSSON	Swe	68	69	76	70	283	-5	2,562.86	1,797.27
	Sven STRÜVER	Ger	68	73	72	70	283	-5	2,562.86	1,797.27
	Michael ARCHER	Eng	69	69	70	75	283	-5	2,562.86	1,797.27
	Jan-Are LARSEN	Nor	68	70	70	75	283	-5	2,562.86	1,797.27
	Robert KARLSSON	Swe	67	72	71	73	283	-5	2,562.86	1,797.27
	Matthew BLACKEY	Eng	72	69	69	73	283	-5	2,562.86	1,797.27
	Tobias DIER	Ger	67	67	73	76	283	-5	2,562.86	1,797.27
76	José Manuel LARA	Sp	73	68	69	74	284	-4	2,382.00	1,670.44
	Stuart LITTLE	Eng	69	70	71	74	284	-4	2,382.00	1,670.44
	Jamie DONALDSON	Wal	69	69	77	69	284	-4	2,382.00	1,670.44
79	Titch MOORE	SA	71	70	74	70	285	-3	2,373.00	1,664.13
	Rolf MUNTZ	NL	73	67	75	70	285	-3	2,373.00	1,664.13
	Graeme MCDOWELL	N.Ire	73	68	73	71	285	-3	2,373.00	1,664.13
82	Emanuele CANONICA	It	72	67	71	76	286	-2	2,365.50	1,658.87
	Nick DOUGHERTY	Eng	71	70	71	74	286	-2	2,365.50	1,658.87
84	Jean-François LUCQUIN	Fr	71	70	75	71	287	-1	2,359.50	1,654.66
	Johan RYSTRÖM	Swe	69	72	76	70	287	-1	2,359.50	1,654.66
86	Ben MASON	Eng	73	68	75	72	288	0	2,355.00	1,651.51

US PGA Championship Oak Hill Country Club · Rochester · New York · USA

path to glory

Shaun Micheel

1	Shaun MICHEEL USA	276	-4
2	Chad CAMPBELL USA	278	-2
3	Tim CLARK SA	279	-1
4	Alex CEJKA Ger	280	0
5	Ernie ELS SA	282	2
	Jay HAAS USA	282	2
7	Fred FUNK USA	284	4
	Loren ROBERTS USA	284	4
	Mike WEIR Can	284	4
10	Billy ANDRADE USA	285	5
	Niclas FASTH Swe	285	5
	Charles HOWELL III USA	285	5
	Kenny PERRY USA	285	5

I n the aftermath of Curtis Strange's victory in the 1989 US Open Championship at Oak Hill Country Club, the Virginian began his press conference by uttering the words: "Move over, Ben!"

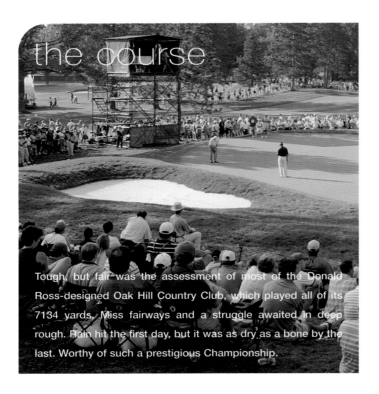

the course

Tough, but fair was the assessment of most of the Donald Ross-designed Oak Hill Country Club, which played all of its 7134 yards. Miss fairways and a struggle awaited in deep rough. Rain hit the first day, but it was as dry as a bone by the last. Worthy of such a prestigious Championship.

It was a reference, of course, to the fact he had just become the first golfer since the legendary Ben Hogan in 1950-51 to win successive US Open Championship titles. Little did we realise that 14 years later, at the same venue, another winner's press conference could have begun with the same words.

A month earlier, Ben Curtis had stunned the world of golf by choosing the 132nd Open Golf Championship at Royal St George's as his maiden European Tour victory, never mind Major success. Now we had Curtis's equally unheralded countryman Shaun Micheel producing a similar feat in the 85th US PGA Championship.

Move over Ben indeed!

In the run-up to the tournament there was a great deal of anticipation about the arrival of Tiger Woods in Rochester. The World Number One was attempting to stop 2003 being a barren year in terms of Major victories, the belief being that his name

Luke Donald

José Maria Olazábal

would sit perfectly next to the likes of Jack Nicklaus, Lee Trevino and Strange, other giants of the game to have won Majors at Oak Hill Country Club.

But Shaun Micheel?

His name may not roll off the tongue with the same reverence just yet, but the shot he hit under the most immense pressure at the 72nd hole, will be remembered for generations as one of the greatest in a Major Championship. It was one of which even Woods, who eventually tied for 39th, his worst performance in a Major as a professional, would have been proud,

"I really can't believe that this has happened to me," he said, minutes after ripping a seven iron from 174 yards to within two inches from the cup that secured his dramatic and unlikely victory.

He wasn't alone.

Like Curtis the previous month at Royal St George's, odds are

you could have got very long odds on Micheel to win when the Championship began and he would not have dropped a dime on himself even at a generous price.

"I showed up on the Tuesday to play a practice round and saw how difficult the course was. After that, my main goal then was just to make the cut," said the man from Memphis. "I probably would have been happy with that."

It goes without saying the 34 year old is a little happier now. In the final round he traded birdies and bogeys with playing partner Chad Campbell for four tension-packed hours and emerged with a par round of 70 for a four under par total of 276, two strokes better than Campbell.

Elsewhere, it proved another successful week for The European Tour contingent in New York State, seven Members – Tim Clark, Luke Donald, Ernie Els, Niclas Fasth, Padraig Harrington, Peter Lonard and Adam Scott – alongside Germany's Alex Cejka, finishing in the top 30.

Niclas Fasth

South African Clark, subsequently named by Gary Player as a wild card pick for the International Team in The Presidents Cup, fared best, superb under par rounds of 68-69 at the weekend giving him third place on 279, one shot ahead of Cejka, who matched Clark's weekend performance. But the day, and the week, belonged to Micheel.

The cheque for 953,979 euro (£671,641) ensured world wide recognition as well as a very healthy bank account. "It's kinda scary really," he admitted. "This time a year ago I was trying to win the BC Open (where he surrendered a three shot lead on the final day) and even up to a month ago I was trying to keep my card. To now have my name on this trophy, I don't know what to think. I look down the list and see all those names, and I just hope I can produce a career like a lot of those guys have."

Who says it cannot happen? When Trevino won the US Open Championship at Oak Hill Country Club in 1968, no-one outside his immediate family and the guys he used to hustle with down in Texas knew who he was. Four decades later, he remains one of the icons of the game.

Micheel's path to glory might be off to a late start, but what a start it was. However, he is not a stranger to the limelight.

Earlier in his career, while playing in a tournament in North Carolina, he saved two people from a sinking car, a selfless act which earned him an award for bravery. This time, his reward for being centre stage was the glittering Wanamaker Trophy.

Both were truly deserved.

Tony Stenson

final results

Oak Hill Country Club · Rochester · New York · USA
August 14 - 17 · 2003 · Par 70 · 7134 yards · 6524 metres

Pos.	Name		Rd1	Rd2	Rd3	Rd4	Total	Par	Prize Money Euro	£
1	Shaun MICHEEL	USA	69	68	69	70	276	-4	953,979.80	671,641.76
2	Chad CAMPBELL	USA	69	72	65	72	278	-2	572,387.90	402,985.07
3	Tim CLARK	SA	72	70	68	69	279	-1	360,392.40	253,731.35
4	Alex CEJKA	Ger	74	69	68	69	280	0	254,394.60	179,104.46
5	Jay HAAS	USA	70	74	69	69	282	2	189,029.30	133,084.55
	Ernie ELS	SA	71	70	70	71	282	2	189,029.30	133,084.55
7	Loren ROBERTS	USA	70	73	70	71	284	4	155,168.90	109,245.41
	Fred FUNK	USA	69	73	70	72	284	4	155,168.90	109,245.41
	Mike WEIR	Can	68	71	70	75	284	4	155,168.90	109,245.41
10	Billy ANDRADE	USA	67	72	72	74	285	5	119,689.10	84,266.14
	Kenny PERRY	USA	75	72	70	68	285	5	119,689.10	84,266.14
	Niclas FASTH	Swe	76	70	71	68	285	5	119,689.10	84,266.14
	Charles HOWELL III	USA	70	72	70	73	285	5	119,689.10	84,266.14
14	Rodney PAMPLING	Aus	66	74	73	73	286	6	86,785.66	61,100.74
	Tim HERRON	USA	69	72	74	71	286	6	86,785.66	61,100.74
	Scott MCCARRON	USA	74	70	71	71	286	6	86,785.66	61,100.74
	Robert GAMEZ	USA	70	73	70	73	286	6	86,785.66	61,100.74
18	Toshimitsu IZAWA	Jpn	71	72	71	73	287	7	64,481.97	45,398.01
	Jim FURYK	USA	72	74	69	72	287	7	64,481.97	45,398.01
	Carlos Daniel FRANCO	Par	73	73	69	72	287	7	64,481.97	45,398.01
	Rocco MEDIATE	USA	72	74	71	70	287	7	64,481.97	45,398.01
	Kevin SUTHERLAND	USA	69	74	71	73	287	7	64,481.97	45,398.01
23	Stuart APPLEBY	Aus	74	73	71	70	288	8	45,932.36	32,338.31
	Phil MICKELSON	USA	66	75	72	75	288	8	45,932.36	32,338.31
	Luke DONALD	Eng	73	72	71	72	288	8	45,932.36	32,338.31
	Adam SCOTT	Aus	72	69	72	75	288	8	45,932.36	32,338.31
27	Woody AUSTIN	USA	72	73	69	75	289	9	37,982.53	26,741.29
	Geoff OGILVY	Aus	71	71	77	70	289	9	37,982.53	26,741.29
29	Padraig HARRINGTON	Ire	72	76	69	73	290	10	32,329.32	22,761.20
	Peter LONARD	Aus	74	74	69	73	290	10	32,329.32	22,761.20
	Todd HAMILTON	USA	70	74	73	73	290	10	32,329.32	22,761.20
	David TOMS	USA	75	72	71	72	290	10	32,329.32	22,761.20
	Frank LICKLITER	USA	71	72	71	76	290	10	32,329.32	22,761.20
34	Jesper PARNEVIK	Swe	73	72	72	74	291	11	25,616.13	18,034.83
	Fred COUPLES	USA	74	71	72	74	291	11	25,616.13	18,034.83
	Vijay SINGH	Fiji	69	73	70	79	291	11	25,616.13	18,034.83
	Lee JANZEN	USA	68	74	72	77	291	11	25,616.13	18,034.83
	J.L. LEWIS	USA	71	75	71	74	291	11	25,616.13	18,034.83
39	Tiger WOODS	USA	74	72	73	73	292	12	19,432.92	13,681.59
	Joe DURANT	USA	71	76	75	70	292	12	19,432.92	13,681.59
	Mark CALCAVECCHIA	USA	73	71	76	72	292	12	19,432.92	13,681.59
	Hal SUTTON	USA	75	71	67	79	292	12	19,432.92	13,681.59
	Robert ALLENBY	Aus	70	77	73	72	292	12	19,432.92	13,681.59
	Briny BAIRD	USA	73	71	67	81	292	12	19,432.92	13,681.59
45	Angel CABRERA	Arg	71	76	72	74	293	13	15,458.01	10,883.09
	Duffy WALDORF	USA	70	75	72	76	293	13	15,458.01	10,883.09
	Tom PERNICE	USA	70	71	72	80	293	13	15,458.01	10,883.09
48	Shigeki MARUYAMA	Jpn	75	72	73	74	294	14	13,014.17	9,162.52
	Trevor IMMELMAN	SA	74	70	77	73	294	14	13,014.17	9,162.52
	Ben CRANE	USA	73	73	76	72	294	14	13,014.17	9,162.52
51	José Maria OLAZÁBAL	Sp	74	74	76	71	295	15	11,765.75	8,283.58
	Gary EVANS	Eng	74	74	71	76	295	15	11,765.75	8,283.58
	José COCERES	Arg	73	68	78	76	295	15	11,765.75	8,283.58
	Len MATTIACE	USA	74	70	75	76	295	15	11,765.75	8,283.58
	Brian GAY	USA	74	74	75	72	295	15	11,765.75	8,283.58
56	Chris DIMARCO	USA	74	71	78	73	296	16	11,218.10	7,898.01
57	Bernhard LANGER	Ger	75	72	75	75	297	17	10,997.27	7,742.54
	Bob ESTES	USA	71	76	73	77	297	17	10,997.27	7,742.54
	Scott HOCH	USA	75	72	73	77	297	17	10,997.27	7,742.54
	Aaron BADDELEY	Aus	69	77	73	78	297	17	10,997.27	7,742.54
61	Eduardo ROMERO	Arg	77	71	76	74	298	18	10,599.78	7,462.69
	Ian POULTER	Eng	72	75	72	79	298	18	10,599.78	7,462.69
	Billy MAYFAIR	USA	76	72	78	72	298	18	10,599.78	7,462.69
	Philip TATAURANGI	NZ	72	71	78	77	298	18	10,599.78	7,462.69
	Jonathan KAYE	USA	74	73	72	79	298	18	10,599.78	7,462.69
66	Paul CASEY	Eng	79	69	75	76	299	19	10,334.78	7,276.12
67	Bob BURNS	USA	72	76	70	82	300	20	10,246.45	7,213.93
68	Rory SABBATINI	SA	71	75	75	81	302	22	10,158.12	7,151.74
69	Kyoung-Ju CHOI	Kor	74	74	80	76	304	24	10,069.79	7,089.55
	Michael CAMPBELL	NZ	74	71	80	79	304	24	10,069.79	7,089.55

Marcus Fraser

1	Marcus FRASER Aus	269	-19
2	Martin WIEGELE Aut	269	-19
3	Peter HANSON Swe	272	-16
4	José Manuel CARRILES Sp	274	-14
	Andrew COLTART Scot	274	-14
	Tim MILFORD Eng	274	-14
	Graeme STORM Eng	274	-14
8	Mads VIBE-HASTRUP Den	275	-13
9	Kalle BRINK Swe	276	-12
	Robert ROCK Eng	276	-12

action not words

The Russian proverb, 'A man is judged by his deeds, not by his words' could have been written with Marcus Fraser in mind.

The 25 year old winner of the dual ranking BMW Russian Open - the first event on The European Tour International Schedule to be played in the former Soviet state - won a sudden-death play-off with Austrian Martin Wiegele at the second extra hole, fuelled by an inner drive and determination that is impossible to detect when you listen to his softly spoken Australian accent.

Fraser comes across as modest, almost shy, in the clubhouse, but on the fairways he is a different animal altogether.

He opened the tournament at Le Meridien Moscow Country Club with a four under par 68 to lie two shots behind Nicolas Vanhootegem. Many believed the Belgian's fine six under par effort might be the round of the week until it was bettered by a stroke on day two by Englishmen Jamie Elson and James Hepworth and, more tellingly, Fraser.

Following his wonderful round on the excellent Robert Trent Jones Jnr-designed course, Fraser remained quiet and unassuming in the interview room - and gave the first indication that he prefers to let his actions, not words, do the talking.

"I just need to keep plugging away and see what happens at the end of the week," was his reasoned response to the excitement he had generated amongst reporters with his bogey-free round in only his fourth appearance on The European Tour International Schedule.

However, those who had followed his progress earlier in the year on the European Challenge Tour would not have been surprised at his prominence. He had already won twice in his rookie season- at the Nykredit Danish Open in June and in a play-off for the Talma Finnish Challenge, only a fortnight before he arrived in Moscow.

That latter experience served him well, but his battle with Wiegele was different to the tussle for glory he had come through against Sweden's Tony Edlund two weeks previously in Scandinavia.

Andrew Coltart

the course

Set in glorious woodlands just 40 km from Moscow, the course is summed up by its signature hole - the par five fifth. Not overly long, but fraught with the difficulty of a dogleg, water hazards and a tricky sloping green - features that appear throughout the 7174 yard terrain.

Then, Fraser had won the shoot-out by holing a nine iron for an eagle two at the third extra hole. This time, at the second extra hole, he was in trouble after pulling his drive into the trees, and found himself having to search deep down to find the resolve that would take him to the title.

The Australian composed himself, stayed cool, and picked his spot through the trees to find safety on the fairway. He was still some 90 yards from the flag and could see his Austrian opponent at the side of the green when he pitched his ball to 16 feet and then proceeded to hole the most courageous par putt of his career to date.

Wiegele could not emulate the feat from the greenside rough, allowing Fraser to secure his first European Tour victory and an automatic exemption to the 2004 season.

For the BMW Russian Open and all those involved in the organisation and running of the tournament, it was a thrilling ending to what had been, at times, a frustrating week due to the adverse weather conditions over Moscow and the surrounding area. However, the crowds which turned up proved that interest in the sport, in a nation where the game is still at its developmental stage, is very much alive and kicking.

Mads Vibe-Hastrup

Martin Wiegele

final results

Le Meridien Moscow Country Club • Moscow • Russia
August 14 - 17 • 2003 • Par 72 • 7174 yards • 6560 metres

Pos.	Name		Rd1	Rd2	Rd3	Rd4	Total	Par	Prize Money Euro	£
1	Marcus FRASER	Aus	68	65	68	68	269	-19	66,660.00	46,931.43
2	Martin WIEGELE	Aut	68	66	67	68	269	-19	44,440.00	31,287.62
3	Peter HANSON	Swe	71	68	67	66	272	-16	25,040.00	17,629.21
4	José Manuel CARRILES	Sp	68	67	70	69	274	-14	15,740.00	11,081.62
	Tim MILFORD	Eng	72	68	67	67	274	-14	15,740.00	11,081.62
	Andrew COLTART	Scot	69	67	69	69	274	-14	15,740.00	11,081.62
	Graeme STORM	Eng	71	69	69	65	274	-14	15,740.00	11,081.62
8	Mads VIBE-HASTRUP	Den	70	70	67	68	275	-13	10,000.00	7,040.42
9	Kalle BRINK	Swe	69	66	71	70	276	-12	8,480.00	5,970.28
	Robert ROCK	Eng	68	69	70	69	276	-12	8,480.00	5,970.28
11	Jesus Maria ARRUTI	Sp	68	69	69	71	277	-11	6,893.33	4,853.20
	Michele REALE	It	72	68	71	66	277	-11	6,893.33	4,853.20
	Richard MCEVOY	Eng	70	68	71	68	277	-11	6,893.33	4,853.20
14	Damien MCGRANE	Ire	70	68	69	71	278	-10	5,422.86	3,817.92
	Garry HOUSTON	Wal	74	66	66	72	278	-10	5,422.86	3,817.92
	Shaun P WEBSTER	Eng	73	66	68	71	278	-10	5,422.86	3,817.92
	Johan EDFORS	Swe	67	68	72	71	278	-10	5,422.86	3,817.92
	Ian GARBUTT	Eng	69	70	69	70	278	-10	5,422.86	3,817.92
	David ORR	Scot	68	72	67	71	278	-10	5,422.86	3,817.92
	Steven O'HARA	Scot	67	72	70	69	278	-10	5,422.86	3,817.92
21	Alvaro SALTO	Sp	72	68	70	69	279	-9	4,400.00	3,097.78
	Jamie LITTLE	Eng	71	68	72	68	279	-9	4,400.00	3,097.78
	Sion E BEBB	Wal	69	69	69	72	279	-9	4,400.00	3,097.78
	Markus BRIER	Aut	72	68	71	68	279	-9	4,400.00	3,097.78
	Sebastian FERNANDEZ	Arg	69	69	71	70	279	-9	4,400.00	3,097.78
26	Michael ARCHER	Eng	68	71	71	70	280	-8	3,800.00	2,675.36
	Richard DINSDALE	Wal	69	70	71	70	280	-8	3,800.00	2,675.36
	James HEPWORTH	Eng	73	65	72	70	280	-8	3,800.00	2,675.36
	Erol SIMSEK	Ger	70	68	73	69	280	-8	3,800.00	2,675.36
	Oskar BERGMAN	Swe	68	71	71	70	280	-8	3,800.00	2,675.36
31	Renaud GUILLARD	Fr	70	66	71	74	281	-7	3,160.00	2,224.77
	Nicolas VANHOOTEGEM	Bel	66	72	68	75	281	-7	3,160.00	2,224.77
	Andrew RAITT	Eng	70	72	68	71	281	-7	3,160.00	2,224.77
	Joakim RASK	Swe	67	69	73	72	281	-7	3,160.00	2,224.77
	Ivo GINER	Sp	70	71	72	68	281	-7	3,160.00	2,224.77
	Jamie ELSON	Eng	69	65	78	69	281	-7	3,160.00	2,224.77
37	Chris GANE	Eng	73	69	70	70	282	-6	2,680.00	1,886.83
	Massimo FLORIOLI	It	71	70	67	74	282	-6	2,680.00	1,886.83
	Didier DE VOOGHT	Bel	71	71	69	71	282	-6	2,680.00	1,886.83
	Ben MASON	Eng	73	69	71	69	282	-6	2,680.00	1,886.83
	David RYLES	Eng	68	66	68	80	282	-6	2,680.00	1,886.83
42	Fredrik OREST	Swe	69	72	71	71	283	-5	2,200.00	1,548.89
	Mark DAVIS	Eng	67	69	74	73	283	-5	2,200.00	1,548.89
	Sven STRÜVER	Ger	70	70	73	70	283	-5	2,200.00	1,548.89
	Pasi PURHONEN	Fin	71	66	71	75	283	-5	2,200.00	1,548.89
	Benoit TEILLERIA	Fr	71	70	72	70	283	-5	2,200.00	1,548.89
	Marco BERNARDINI	It	68	72	72	71	283	-5	2,200.00	1,548.89
	Steven BOWDITCH	Aus	71	69	66	77	283	-5	2,200.00	1,548.89
49	Euan LITTLE	Scot	70	72	73	69	284	-4	1,640.00	1,154.63
	Stuart LITTLE	Eng	74	66	71	73	284	-4	1,640.00	1,154.63
	Jan-Are LARSEN	Nor	71	69	70	74	284	-4	1,640.00	1,154.63
	Mark PILKINGTON	Wal	69	73	71	71	284	-4	1,640.00	1,154.63
	Jean Louis GUEPY	Fr	67	73	72	72	284	-4	1,640.00	1,154.63
	John MELLOR	Eng	73	68	70	73	284	-4	1,640.00	1,154.63
	Brad KENNEDY	Aus	69	70	70	75	284	-4	1,640.00	1,154.63
56	Kalle VAINOLA	Fin	70	71	74	70	285	-3	1,165.71	820.71
	Scott DRUMMOND	Scot	71	71	70	73	285	-3	1,165.71	820.71
	Ilya GORONESKOUL	Fr	70	68	73	74	285	-3	1,165.71	820.71
	Stefano REALE	It	71	70	71	73	285	-3	1,165.71	820.71
	Thomas BESANCENEZ	Fr	68	70	74	73	285	-3	1,165.71	820.71
	Pehr MAGNEBRANT	Swe	67	74	74	70	285	-3	1,165.71	820.71
	Sebastien DELAGRANGE	Fr	71	71	73	70	285	-3	1,165.71	820.71
63	Mark MOULAND	Wal	69	72	72	73	286	-2	960.00	675.88
	Dominique NOUAILHAC	Fr	73	69	72	72	286	-2	960.00	675.88
	Bjorn PETTERSSON	Swe	70	70	74	72	286	-2	960.00	675.88
66	Paul DWYER	Eng	69	70	75	73	287	-1	820.00	577.31
	Federico BISAZZA	It	71	71	70	75	287	-1	820.00	577.31
	Thomas NORRET	Den	70	72	70	75	287	-1	820.00	577.31
	Paul MCKECHNIE	Scot	71	69	73	74	287	-1	820.00	577.31
70	Philip ARCHER	Eng	69	71	73	75	288	0	618.33	435.33
	Marcello SANTI	It	67	72	74	75	288	0	618.33	435.33
	Gianluca BARUFFALDI	It	67	73	73	75	288	0	618.33	435.33
	Lee S JAMES	Eng	69	70	75	74	288	0	618.33	435.33
	Sam WALKER	Eng	73	69	75	71	288	0	618.33	435.33
	Regis GUSTAVE	St.L	70	71	71	76	288	0	618.33	435.33
76	Lionel ALEXANDRE	Fr	71	71	74	75	291	3	585.00	411.86
77	Hennie WALTERS	SA	71	70	77	75	293	5	582.00	409.75

Most certainly the quality of the play came to the fore and the leaderboard swiftly took shape. By the time the tense and exciting denouement arrived on Sunday, the crowds were visibly gripped by a classic example of competitive sport as they witnessed Fraser and Wiegele battle it out over extra holes for the first prize of 66,660 euro (£46,931) after moving clear of challengers including Andrew Coltart and Peter Hanson.

That Fraser emerged victorious is definitive proof that the softly spoken Australian will always let his golf do his talking for him - it is up to everyone else to shout about it.

Michael Gibbons

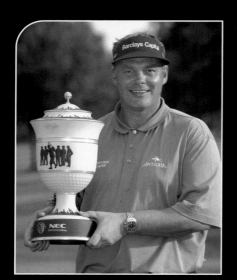

Darren Clarke

1	Darren CLARKE N.Ire	268	-12
2	Jonathan KAYE USA	272	-8
3	Davis LOVE III USA	273	-7
4	Chris RILEY USA	274	-6
	Tiger WOODS USA	274	-6
6	Robert ALLENBY Aus	275	-5
	Jim FURYK USA	275	-5
	Vijay SINGH Fiji	275	-5
9	Trevor IMMELMAN SA	276	-4
	Brad FAXON USA	276	-4

family values

	PAR	4	5	4	4	3	4	3	4	4	4	4	3	4	4	3	5
	LEADERS	1	2	3	4	5	6	7	8	9	10	11	12	13	14	15	16
9	CLARKE	9	11	11	12	11	11	11	11	12	12	13	13	14	14	13	12
	WOODS	7	7	7	7	7	7	8	9	9	9	9	8	7	7	7	7
	KAYE	8	7	7	6	7	6	7	7	7	7	7	8	9	9	9	8
18	LOVE III	6	7	6	7	7	6	6	7	7	7	7	7	6	7	7	7
4	SINGH	5	6	6	5	4	4	3	4	4	5	6	6	6	6	6	5
4	ALLENBY	4	5	5	5	5	5	5	5	6	6	7	7	7	7	7	6
4	FURYK	3	5	5	5	5	5	5	4	4	5	5	5	5	5	5	5
7	RILEY	7	8	8	7	6	5	5	5	5	4	4	4	4	4	5	6

When the International Federation of PGA Tours came together in 1999, their aim, in formulating the concept of the World Golf Championships, was to create a global golfing family.

That they have succeeded is testimony to the hard work and dedication of all concerned, but surely no-one involved could have envisaged a tournament such as the 2003 WGC - NEC Invitational at Firestone Country Club, won magnificently by Northern Ireland's Darren Clarke, where the theme of the family would take such a central role in the entire week.

It began with Ben Curtis, the affable young American who was the centre of attention on his competitive return to his home state of Ohio, following his sensational win in the 132nd Open Golf Championship at Royal St George's four weeks previously.

Before events in England changed his golfing life forever, Curtis believed he had organised his private life perfectly, planning his wedding for the Saturday of NEC Invitational week, when he would be nowhere near a golf course, far less Firestone.

But, instead of sneaking off from rehearsals for a quick afternoon's viewing of the world's best, Curtis found himself inside the ropes and in a tie for the first round lead with Sergio Garcia after a flawless six under par 64.

Suddenly the old song, 'Get Me To The Church On Time' had new meaning for Curtis and his bride-to-be Candace Beatty for, if he carried on in similar vein, he had no chance of making his 6.00pm Saturday appointment at Akron United Methodist Church.

As it was, fate took over and Curtis's second round 76 saw him drop sufficiently far down Saturday's playing order, that he was able to meet both his family commitments on Saturday night and his golfing commitments on Sunday afternoon, finishing with rounds of 72-70 to share 30th place, ironically alongside Garcia.

Next up was Clarke's countryman Padraig Harrington, a married man of six years, but standing on the threshold of the next stage of family life - fatherhood. With the baby late and with the blessing of wife Caroline, Harrington decided to play, but never had the mobile telephone far from his grasp.

After completing three and a half rounds, the Irishman received a text message on the 13th fairway in the final round to tell him events were beginning to move apace back home and sure enough

Trevor Immelman

they did, Harrington returning to Dublin on Monday morning, the proud father of baby Patrick Daniel.

And so to Clarke. The biggest talking point surrounding the larger-than-life Irishman at the start of the week was his fitness, which he himself had pinpointed as an area for consideration after huffing and puffing his way out of contention in the Masters Tournament in April.

If anything was going to test his new found stamina it would be the cloying humidity of the opening rounds which led the local paper, the wonderfully named 'Akron Plain Dealer' to report that people were feeling the need to 'chew the air before attempting to breathe in.'

It was an examination that Clarke passed with flying colours. His emerald green shirt might have been darkened with perspiration but his 65 saw him tie for third with World Number One Tiger Woods before a 70 saw him sit fifth at the halfway point.

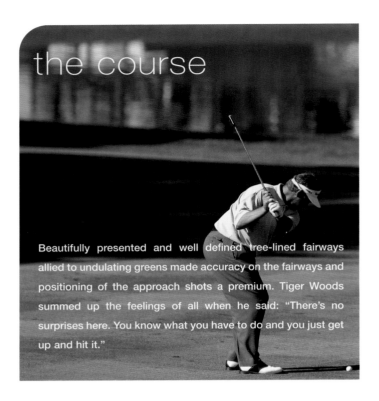

the course

Beautifully presented and well defined tree-lined fairways allied to undulating greens made accuracy on the fairways and positioning of the approach shots a premium. Tiger Woods summed up the feelings of all when he said: "There's no surprises here. You know what you have to do and you just get up and hit it."

Temperatures might have cooled at the weekend but Clarke got hotter, a third round 66 outscoring playing partner Woods, who was looking for his fourth consecutive NEC Invitational victory at Firestone, by a shot and taking him to pole position, his playing partner for the final day, the unheralded American Jonathan Kaye.

With Curtis having won the Open Golf Championship and Shaun Micheel having taken the US PGA Championship, it would have been no surprise if another little known American had stepped into the limelight, but Clarke's authority put paid to that.

Kaye, who harvests jalapeno peppers in his spare time, failed to get as hot as his hobby, three bogeys in his first six holes putting paid to his chances of victory although the 32 year old from Denver battled back bravely to post a 70 for second place, one shot clear of Davis Love III in third, but four adrift of Clarke.

Woods whipped the crowd into a frenzy in the final round with birdies at the first, seventh and eighth holes to reduce Clarke's one

Angel Cabrera

Bernhard Langer

time five stroke advantage to two, but if it was meant to unsettle the Irishman, all it succeeded in doing was lighting the leader's touchpaper.

Clarke found another gear and birdies of his own at the ninth, 11th and 13th finished the tournament as a contest, allowing The European Tour Member the luxury of enjoying the closing holes content in the knowledge that, with his 67 for a 12 under par total of 268, he had become only the second player in history, after Woods, to have won more than one WGC event, following his success in the 2000 Accenture Match Play.

With the dignitaries waiting on the 18th green to begin the prize giving, Clarke requested a moment to himself to do one very important thing, namely pop behind the Recorder's Hut, flip open his mobile phone, and call his wife Heather and sons Tyrone and Conor back home to share the moment.

His very own version, one supposes, of keeping it in the family.

Scott Crockett

final results

Firestone Country Club • Akron • Ohio • USA
August 21 - 24 • 2003 • Par 70 • 7283 yards • 6660 metres

Pos.	Name		Rd1	Rd2	Rd3	Rd4	Total	Par	Prize Money Euro	£
1	Darren CLARKE	N.Ire	65	70	66	67	268	-12	932,919.60	657,977.23
2	Jonathan KAYE	USA	68	69	65	70	272	-8	488,672.10	344,654.69
3	Davis LOVE III	USA	66	70	68	69	273	-7	319,858.10	225,592.16
4	Tiger WOODS	USA	65	72	67	70	274	-6	208,796.30	147,261.58
	Chris RILEY	USA	66	67	70	71	274	-6	208,796.30	147,261.58
6	Jim FURYK	USA	69	69	68	69	275	-5	145,120.80	102,352.00
	Vijay SINGH	Fiji	69	65	72	69	275	-5	145,120.80	102,352.00
	Robert ALLENBY	Aus	69	69	68	69	275	-5	145,120.80	102,352.00
9	Brad FAXON	USA	68	67	70	71	276	-4	103,731.80	73,160.82
	Trevor IMMELMAN	SA	70	68	70	68	276	-4	103,731.80	73,160.82
11	Bernhard LANGER	Ger	71	73	65	68	277	-3	81,445.36	57,442.46
	Steve FLESCH	USA	71	67	67	72	277	-3	81,445.36	57,442.46
	Dan FORSMAN	USA	69	68	70	70	277	-3	81,445.36	57,442.46
14	Peter JACOBSEN	USA	73	64	71	70	278	-2	66,637.11	46,998.37
	Fred FUNK	USA	72	62	72	72	278	-2	66,637.11	46,998.37
	Toshimitsu IZAWA	Jpn	70	71	68	69	278	-2	66,637.11	46,998.37
17	Jay HAAS	USA	72	69	73	65	279	-1	52,643.32	37,128.72
	Ernie ELS	SA	67	70	71	71	279	-1	52,643.32	37,128.72
	Retief GOOSEN	SA	67	69	69	74	279	-1	52,643.32	37,128.72
	Paul CASEY	Eng	72	66	71	70	279	-1	52,643.32	37,128.72
21	Fred COUPLES	USA	67	71	71	71	280	0	46,645.98	32,898.86
	Charles HOWELL III	USA	72	68	74	66	280	0	46,645.98	32,898.86
23	Justin LEONARD	USA	75	69	69	68	281	1	42,647.75	30,078.96
	Mike WEIR	Can	71	72	69	69	281	1	42,647.75	30,078.96
	Colin MONTGOMERIE	Scot	68	70	70	73	281	1	42,647.75	30,078.96
	Angel CABRERA	Arg	70	71	70	70	281	1	42,647.75	30,078.96
	Peter LONARD	Aus	70	73	72	66	281	1	42,647.75	30,078.96
	Phil MICKELSON	USA	68	73	70	70	281	1	42,647.75	30,078.96
	Shaun MICHEEL	USA	71	69	70	71	281	1	42,647.75	30,078.96
30	Sergio GARCIA	Sp	64	76	69	73	282	2	38,205.28	26,945.74
	Len MATTIACE	USA	72	69	69	72	282	2	38,205.28	26,945.74
	Ben CURTIS	USA	64	76	72	70	282	2	38,205.28	26,945.74
33	Eduardo ROMERO	Arg	70	74	68	71	283	3	34,281.09	24,178.05
	Justin ROSE	Eng	72	73	69	69	283	3	34,281.09	24,178.05
	Ian POULTER	Eng	73	68	67	75	283	3	34,281.09	24,178.05
	Hal SUTTON	USA	68	69	68	78	283	3	34,281.09	24,178.05
	David TOMS	USA	66	67	76	74	283	3	34,281.09	24,178.05
	Chris DIMARCO	USA	71	68	73	71	283	3	34,281.09	24,178.05
39	Jeff SLUMAN	USA	67	74	75	68	284	4	31,541.56	22,245.89
	Padraig HARRINGTON	Ire	73	71	70	70	284	4	31,541.56	22,245.89
	Paul AZINGER	USA	72	69	67	76	284	4	31,541.56	22,245.89
42	Robert-Jan DERKSEN	NL	73	70	70	72	285	5	29,986.70	21,149.27
	Nick PRICE	Zim	73	67	71	74	285	5	29,986.70	21,149.27
	Alex CEJKA	Ger	72	68	71	74	285	5	29,986.70	21,149.27
	Ben CRANE	USA	71	75	68	71	285	5	29,986.70	21,149.27
46	Stuart APPLEBY	Aus	70	75	68	73	286	6	27,987.59	19,739.32
	Scott VERPLANK	USA	66	73	70	77	286	6	27,987.59	19,739.32
	Bob ESTES	USA	68	74	70	74	286	6	27,987.59	19,739.32
	Stephen ALLAN	Aus	74	68	76	68	286	6	27,987.59	19,739.32
	Lee WESTWOOD	Eng	70	70	73	73	286	6	27,987.59	19,739.32
51	Scott HOCH	USA	69	72	72	74	287	7	26,432.72	18,642.69
	Rory SABBATINI	SA	73	72	70	72	287	7	26,432.72	18,642.69
53	Kyoung-Ju CHOI	Kor	73	71	71	73	288	8	25,011.13	17,640.06
	Jerry KELLY	USA	68	71	76	73	288	8	25,011.13	17,640.06
	Mark CALCAVECCHIA	USA	70	68	73	77	288	8	25,011.13	17,640.06
	Kenny PERRY	USA	72	76	68	72	288	8	25,011.13	17,640.06
	Chad CAMPBELL	USA	73	71	72	72	288	8	25,011.13	17,640.06
58	Kaname YOKOO	Jpn	73	71	70	75	289	9	23,989.36	16,919.41
	Paul MCGINLEY	Ire	70	71	73	75	289	9	23,989.36	16,919.41
	Niclas FASTH	Swe	67	76	74	72	289	9	23,989.36	16,919.41
61	Stewart CINK	USA	70	71	74	75	290	10	23,322.99	16,449.43
	Philip GOLDING	Eng	70	75	73	72	290	10	23,322.99	16,449.43
	Thomas BJÖRN	Den	72	72	75	71	290	10	23,322.99	16,449.43
64	Craig PARRY	Aus	69	75	71	76	291	11	22,656.62	15,979.45
	Adam SCOTT	Aus	72	70	69	80	291	11	22,656.62	15,979.45
	Tim CLARK	SA	73	69	73	76	291	11	22,656.62	15,979.45
67	Phillip PRICE	Wal	68	75	75	74	292	12	21,879.18	15,431.13
	Pierre FULKE	Swe	72	72	75	73	292	12	21,879.18	15,431.13
	Rich BEEM	USA	69	69	78	76	292	12	21,879.18	15,431.13
	John ROLLINS	USA	75	72	71	74	292	12	21,879.18	15,431.13
71	Jesper PARNEVIK	Swe	69	72	75	77	293	13	20,768.57	14,647.83
	Stephen LEANEY	Aus	75	69	72	77	293	13	20,768.57	14,647.83
	Steen TINNING	Den	71	74	76	72	293	13	20,768.57	14,647.83
	Michael CAMPBELL	NZ	74	71	70	78	293	13	20,768.57	14,647.83
	Kevin NA	Kor	71	80	69	73	293	13	20,768.57	14,647.83
	Jonathan BYRD	USA	71	77	73	72	293	13	20,768.57	14,647.83
77	Hennie OTTO	SA	72	69	75	78	294	14	19,546.88	13,786.18
	Robert KARLSSON	Swe	72	72	77	73	294	14	19,546.88	13,786.18
	Ignacio GARRIDO	Sp	74	74	72	74	294	14	19,546.88	13,786.18
	Rocco MEDIATE	USA	78	73	69	74	294	14	19,546.88	13,786.18
	Bob BURNS	USA	74	70	75	75	294	14	19,546.88	13,786.18
82	Nick FALDO	Eng	74	67	79	75	295	15	18,769.45	13,237.87
	Jarrod MOSELEY	Aus	76	74	72	73	295	15	18,769.45	13,237.87
84	Fredrik JACOBSON	Swe	75	71	77	73	296	16	18,436.27	13,002.88
85	Gene SAUERS	USA	73	76	77	82	308	28	18,214.14	12,846.22

Lee Westwood

1	Lee WESTWOOD Eng	269	-19
2	Alex CEJKA Ger	272	-16
3	Paul CASEY Eng	273	-15
	Andrew COLTART Scot	273	-15
	Gary EVANS Eng	273	-15
	Peter HEDBLOM Swe	273	-15
	Raphaël JACQUELIN Fr	273	-15
8	John BICKERTON Eng	274	-14
	Robert KARLSSON Swe	274	-14
	Marcel SIEM Ger	274	-14

blood, sweat and tears

The peak came in 2000 when he won seven times worldwide, including a record equalling six victories in one year on The European Tour International Schedule, to bring to an end Colin Montgomerie's seven year reign at the top of the Volvo Order of Merit.

That same year Westwood rose to Number Four in the Official World Golf Ranking, but by the time he arrived for his first visit to the beautiful Bavarian course, he could only lay claim to the 215th spot, leaving bookmakers rating him no better than a 66-1 outsider for the 300,000 euro (£207,000) first prize.

Furthermore, after he three putted the seventh green during the final round to fall four shots behind the then tournament leader Robert Karlsson, the best he could hope for was a top ten finish, surely?

However, a birdie four at the ninth lifted his spirits and with the greens, after three days of rain, receptive to the accurate approach play that has always been his strength, Westwood made a remark to his veteran caddie Pete Coleman that turned out to be a remarkable prediction.

He recalled: "As I walked off the tenth tee I turned to Pete and said: 'If I can get it round this nine in 30, I will have a chance.'" Within an hour and a half he was to prove true to his word.

Martin Maritz

I f timing really is everything, then in winning the BMW International Open, Lee Westwood could not have chosen a more opportune moment to remind the golfing world of his immense talent and strong, yet calm, personality in the face of adversity.

It was his first victory on The European Tour International Schedule in almost three years and coincided with Bernhard Langer's first appearance back in his native land since accepting the role of European Captain for The 35th Ryder Cup Matches at Oakland Hills Country Club, Michigan, USA, in September 2004.

When Langer addressed the media at Golfclub München Nord-Eichenried at the end of his second round to outline some of his campaign plans, the name of Westwood was, understandably, not high on his list of potential Team Members bound for the United States.

Despite playing a key role in the memorable European victories at Valderrama in 1997 and again at The De Vere Belfry in 2002, the 30 year old Englishman had suffered an unpredictable decline in form and had become a part of the supporting cast rather than having been centre-stage, courtesy of 24 superb tournament wins world-wide, during the previous five years.

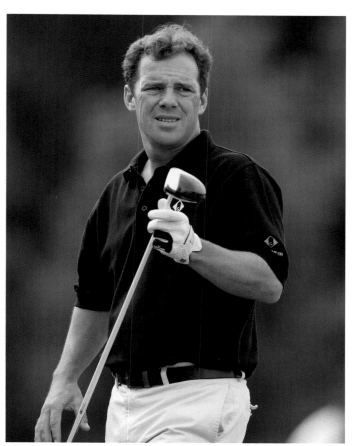

Malcolm Mackenzie

the course

Once again Golfclub München Nord-Eichenried won a universal accolade from all those who played throughout the week. Even with the rain which fell on the last three tournament days, the greens were good and true and the abundance of water hazards on the course called for accuracy to be the players' main watchword.

Ryder Cup Captain Bernhard Langer of Germany with The Ryder Cup during his press conference at the BMW International Open.

A run of three more birdies, starting at the 11th, coincided with a three putt for Karlsson on the tenth green, which stalled the towering Swede's challenge. A furtive glance at the leaderboard told Westwood he had a chance and it was then that his memory of how to win from a contending position kicked in.

In the dash to the winners' podium, Westwood's play over the final three holes was of a standard that those who had followed his career were well aware that he could produce once he turned the corner and propelled himself back into the heat of the battle.

He spun back his approach to the 16th green to within 18 inches of the flag, chipped in from the fringe at the 17th and, having wisely not tried to reach the green at the par five final hole in two, chipped to four feet to clinch a closing hat-trick of birdies, and meet his target of 30 strokes.

It was an emotionally charged Westwood who explained later the extent of his misery at times during the previous three years when he had kept his own council and refused to be intimidated by the adversity thrust upon him.

"Things had been written in the papers and magazines about me never coming back and winning again. I read those articles and it was hard to keep picking myself up and putting a positive edge on it," he admitted.

"There were times when I thought about putting my clubs away, not ever getting them out again and calling it a day. But that would have been the easy thing to do – I battled it out.

"What kept me going was pride. Pride in what I had achieved. Pride in the fact that I wasn't going down without a fight. I'm a working class lad who made good and I wasn't going to let that disappear without some sweat."

In Westwood's victory there was more than just a touch of irony, too, for his caddie Coleman had spent more than 20 years working for Langer with many a visit to Golfclub München Nord-Eichenried without celebrating victory there, yet he had succeeded with his new employer at the first attempt.

It did mean, however, there was no one better qualified to inform the new Ryder Cup Captain that one of the most prodigious talents on The European Tour had finally rediscovered his magical touch, and sent a message to all that the "holiday" was over. Lee Westwood was smiling again and the entire world of golf was uplifted by his return to the winners' enclosure.

Graham Otway

final results

Golfclub München Nord-Eichenried • Munich • Germany
August 28 - 31 • 2003 • Par 72 • 6957 yards • 6361 metres

Pos.	Name		Rd1	Rd2	Rd3	Rd4	Total	Par	Prize Money Euro	£
1	Lee WESTWOOD	Eng	65	68	70	66	269	-19	300,000.00	207,000.77
2	Alex CEJKA	Ger	69	66	70	67	272	-16	200,000.00	138,000.51
3	Raphaël JACQUELIN	Fr	62	69	71	71	273	-15	79,200.00	54,648.20
	Peter HEDBLOM	Swe	66	66	74	67	273	-15	79,200.00	54,648.20
	Gary EVANS	Eng	66	68	68	71	273	-15	79,200.00	54,648.20
	Andrew COLTART	Scot	70	70	65	68	273	-15	79,200.00	54,648.20
	Paul CASEY	Eng	65	69	70	69	273	-15	79,200.00	54,648.20
8	Marcel SIEM	Ger	64	70	68	72	274	-14	40,440.00	27,903.70
	Robert KARLSSON	Swe	65	64	71	74	274	-14	40,440.00	27,903.70
	John BICKERTON	Eng	67	68	68	71	274	-14	40,440.00	27,903.70
11	David HOWELL	Eng	64	71	70	70	275	-13	29,412.00	20,294.36
	Brian DAVIS	Eng	68	69	65	73	275	-13	29,412.00	20,294.36
	Trevor IMMELMAN	SA	69	67	72	67	275	-13	29,412.00	20,294.36
	Gary EMERSON	Eng	64	68	73	70	275	-13	29,412.00	20,294.36
	Stephen GALLACHER	Scot	67	66	72	70	275	-13	29,412.00	20,294.36
16	Carlos RODILES	Sp	71	69	69	67	276	-12	25,380.00	17,512.26
17	Søren KJELDSEN	Den	69	67	71	70	277	-11	22,110.00	15,255.96
	Miguel Angel JIMÉNEZ	Sp	71	65	68	73	277	-11	22,110.00	15,255.96
	Paul MCGINLEY	Ire	69	66	70	72	277	-11	22,110.00	15,255.96
	Ernie ELS	SA	68	71	74	64	277	-11	22,110.00	15,255.96
	Thomas BJÖRN	Den	64	70	70	73	277	-11	22,110.00	15,255.96
	Andrew RAITT	Eng	70	69	68	70	277	-11	22,110.00	15,255.96
23	Bernhard LANGER	Ger	67	72	72	67	278	-10	18,180.00	12,544.25
	Robert-Jan DERKSEN	NL	75	65	68	70	278	-10	18,180.00	12,544.25
	Maarten LAFEBER	NL	68	72	68	70	278	-10	18,180.00	12,544.25
	Søren HANSEN	Den	68	67	74	69	278	-10	18,180.00	12,544.25
	Stephen DODD	Wal	71	69	67	71	278	-10	18,180.00	12,544.25
	Charl SCHWARTZEL	SA	70	64	74	70	278	-10	18,180.00	12,544.25
	Kevin NA	Kor	71	69	71	67	278	-10	18,180.00	12,544.25
30	Peter FOWLER	Aus	74	66	70	69	279	-9	14,940.00	10,308.64
	Alessandro TADINI	It	73	67	68	71	279	-9	14,940.00	10,308.64
	Ignacio GARRIDO	Sp	71	68	69	71	279	-9	14,940.00	10,308.64
	Markus BRIER	Aut	68	71	69	71	279	-9	14,940.00	10,308.64
	Jamie DONALDSON	Wal	74	65	68	72	279	-9	14,940.00	10,308.64
35	Mårten OLANDER	Swe	69	69	70	72	280	-8	12,420.00	8,569.83
	Joakim HAEGGMAN	Swe	71	65	71	73	280	-8	12,420.00	8,569.83
	Ian GARBUTT	Eng	69	67	72	72	280	-8	12,420.00	8,569.83
	Gary ORR	Scot	71	68	70	71	280	-8	12,420.00	8,569.83
	Stephen SCAHILL	NZ	68	68	71	73	280	-8	12,420.00	8,569.83
	Simon DYSON	Eng	69	68	70	73	280	-8	12,420.00	8,569.83
	Martin MARITZ	SA	66	71	69	74	280	-8	12,420.00	8,569.83
42	Malcolm MACKENZIE	Eng	69	66	72	74	281	-7	10,260.00	7,079.43
	Barry LANE	Eng	72	65	71	73	281	-7	10,260.00	7,079.43
	Simon HURD	Eng	70	69	74	68	281	-7	10,260.00	7,079.43
	Raymond RUSSELL	Scot	69	68	70	74	281	-7	10,260.00	7,079.43
	Lee S JAMES	Eng	71	69	68	73	281	-7	10,260.00	7,079.43
47	Gordon BRAND JNR.	Scot	69	70	70	73	282	-6	8,280.00	5,713.22
	Roger CHAPMAN	Eng	71	68	73	70	282	-6	8,280.00	5,713.22
	Darren FICHARDT	SA	71	67	71	73	282	-6	8,280.00	5,713.22
	Andrew MARSHALL	Eng	72	67	74	69	282	-6	8,280.00	5,713.22
	Charlie WI	Kor	69	70	69	74	282	-6	8,280.00	5,713.22
	Nicolas VANHOOTEGEM	Bel	69	70	70	73	282	-6	8,280.00	5,713.22
53	Steen TINNING	Den	67	72	71	73	283	-5	6,840.00	4,719.62
	David LYNN	Eng	69	71	70	73	283	-5	6,840.00	4,719.62
55	Tobias DIER	Ger	69	68	70	77	284	-4	6,300.00	4,347.02
56	Greg OWEN	Eng	69	70	69	77	285	-3	5,760.00	3,974.41
	Brett RUMFORD	Aus	70	67	72	76	285	-3	5,760.00	3,974.41
58	Shaun P WEBSTER	Eng	68	70	76	72	286	-2	5,220.00	3,601.81
	Johan RYSTRÖM	Swe	68	70	74	74	286	-2	5,220.00	3,601.81
	Miles TUNNICLIFF	Eng	70	70	69	77	286	-2	5,220.00	3,601.81
	Martin KAYMER (AM)	Ger	69	69	76	72	286	-2		
62	Santiago LUNA	Sp	71	68	75	73	287	-1	4,680.00	3,229.21
	Paul BROADHURST	Eng	72	67	73	75	287	-1	4,680.00	3,229.21
	Russell CLAYDON	Eng	70	69	73	75	287	-1	4,680.00	3,229.21
65	Klas ERIKSSON	Swe	67	73	75	73	288	0	4,140.00	2,856.61
	David PARK	Wal	74	66	76	72	288	0	4,140.00	2,856.61
	Fredrik ANDERSSON	Swe	66	70	75	77	288	0	4,140.00	2,856.61
68	Gustavo ROJAS	Arg	69	69	72	79	289	1	3,780.00	2,608.21
69	Benn BARHAM	Eng	68	71	76	79	294	6	3,600.00	2,484.01
70	Simon WAKEFIELD	Eng	71	68	83	74	296	8	3,420.00	2,359.81
71	José Manuel LARA	Sp	68	66	78	W/D	212	-4	3,280.00	2,263.21

Ernie Els

1	Ernie ELS SA	267	-17
2	Michael CAMPBELL NZ	273	-11
3	Eduardo ROMERO Arg	274	-10
4	Emanuele CANONICA It	275	-9
	Andrew COLTART Scot	275	-9
	Robert KARLSSON Swe	275	-9
7	Peter HEDBLOM Swe	276	-8
8	Paul CASEY Eng	277	-7
	Brian DAVIS Eng	277	-7
	Paul EALES Eng	277	-7
	David HOWELL Eng	277	-7
	Miguel Angel JIMÉNEZ Sp	277	-7
	David LYNN Eng	277	-7
	Jarrod MOSELEY Aus	277	-7

good timing

A golfing masterpiece to blend with the majestic canvas of the Swiss Alps was required to win the Omega European Masters and Ernie Els was the man with the artistry to match the occasion at Crans-sur-Sierre.

Els was in that familiar sweet-swinging groove, appropriately timing his shots to absolute perfection, which met with the approval of the sponsors and ensured that he swept to a six shot victory with metronomic ease. It was an irresistible performance that drew the spectators to whichever tree-lined fairway he happened to grace.

The course, at an altitude of 5,000 feet, is the most picturesque on Tour, and Els only enhanced the attractiveness as he resisted the persistent probings of Michael Campbell, Emanuele Canonica, Andrew Coltart, Robert Karlsson and Eduardo Romero, all of whom came with challenges that Els imperiously rebuffed.

Romero, twice a winner of the event in this ski resort, posed the greatest danger when he led by two shots going into the final day, but Els was on the prowl and as he closed the show he could hardly suppress his delight. Els said: "I made the perfect start in the final round with four birdies, but the par at the fifth was a career best."

Eduardo Romero

That hole, a 341 yard par four that Els was capable of driving and was a definitive birdie hole, could have been a nightmare. He drove into the trees and had three free drops under the gaze of the referee as first a bench and then an aerial caused him line-of-sight problems. He eventually found the green and holed a 25 footer. That set the scene for a tumultuous final afternoon when the applause echoed through the mountain air.

Karlsson, going for back-to-back wins at the venue, took a double bogey at the second, and saw his hopes begin to slip away with another bogey at the fourth. Romero's normally reliable putting suddenly became a thing of the past. Although Karlsson made a charge, he could not apply any real pressure and when he and Romero both veered into the water at the 14th, their prospects of glory sunk with them as the irresistible Els rose to the top.

Campbell found a streak of form that sent him surging up the field only to be undone by bogeys at the ninth and 11th, although his 66 was yet another reminder of his immense talent as he took the runners-up berth. As he observed: "The bogeys stopped me in my tracks. I hoped I could birdie three of the last four holes but it wasn't to be and Ernie certainly showed his class."

Patrik Sjöland

the course

The scenery makes Crans-sur-Sierre one of the most spectacular courses on The European Tour International Schedule. With the ball flying extra distances at altitude, all four par fives are reachable in two and some of the par fours are driveable.

Romero, that man of superstition, had spoken boldly on the eve of the final round of how his study of yoga had given him mental and physical strength. He started four years ago with the Indian mystic Rhami Hayat. Hayat died in 2002 but Romero has continued to practise the discipline. He was confident even though his superstition of eating at the same table with the same people every night had been broken when he discovered the restaurant had closed down. He was the only player in the field unable to take a birdie from the course on the final day.

Until that time the burly and moustachioed Argentine, one of the game's genuine characters, had played with all the guile that has earned him the soubriquet 'El Gato' or 'The Cat'. There had been much talk of him becoming, at 49 years and 52 days, the oldest winner in European Tour history being, as he was, one year and 18 days older than Des Smyth who, in 2001, coincidentally, climbed a mountain and won the Maderia Island Open. A last round 74, however, relegated him to third place. He said: "I putted terribly. Nothing happened for me. I tried my hardest, but it wasn't to be."

So it came that supermodel Cindy Crawford, ambassador for sponsors Omega, helped Els into the winner's red jacket – little more then 24 hours after the pair had combined in a celebrity 18th hole shoot-out with Sergio Garcia and French model Estelle Lefebure. The American said: "I mentioned to Ernie that it would be nice to fit him with the champions jacket. I'm just glad they were able to find a size XL!"

Els had good reason to puff out his chest with pride. It was his sixth win of the year, and his fourth on The 2003 European Tour International Schedule. He had shared the lead after a first round 65, remained in contention with scores of 69 and 68 and then compiled another 65 to firmly shut the door on his rivals.

Patrik Sjöland enjoyed a memorable moment on the first day, holing in one at the eighth to win a gold watch worth £7,500, but it was Ernie Els who headed back down the mountain as champion following a victory achieved with timeless precision.

James Mossop

Emanuele Canonica

final results

Crans-sur-Sierre • Crans Montana • Switzerland
September 4 - 7 • 2003 • Par 71 • 6857 yards • 6239 metres

Pos.	Name		Rd1	Rd2	Rd3	Rd4	Total	Par	Prize Money Euro	£
1	Ernie ELS	SA	65	69	68	65	267	-17	266,660.00	185,730.01
2	Michael CAMPBELL	NZ	67	67	73	66	273	-11	177,770.00	123,817.68
3	Eduardo ROMERO	Arg	66	67	67	74	274	-10	100,160.00	69,761.93
4	Robert KARLSSON	Swe	65	67	71	72	275	-9	67,946.66	47,325.18
	Emanuele CANONICA	It	70	68	67	70	275	-9	67,946.66	47,325.18
	Andrew COLTART	Scot	70	72	66	67	275	-9	67,946.66	47,325.18
7	Peter HEDBLOM	Swe	67	68	71	70	276	-8	48,000.00	33,432.24
8	David HOWELL	Eng	68	69	67	73	277	-7	30,720.00	21,396.63
	Brian DAVIS	Eng	70	66	68	73	277	-7	30,720.00	21,396.63
	Miguel Angel JIMÉNEZ	Sp	69	69	72	67	277	-7	30,720.00	21,396.63
	Paul EALES	Eng	66	69	75	67	277	-7	30,720.00	21,396.63
	Jarrod MOSELEY	Aus	71	68	68	70	277	-7	30,720.00	21,396.63
	David LYNN	Eng	70	69	69	69	277	-7	30,720.00	21,396.63
	Paul CASEY	Eng	68	70	67	72	277	-7	30,720.00	21,396.63
15	Marc FARRY	Fr	66	73	66	73	278	-6	22,080.00	15,378.83
	Raphaël JACQUELIN	Fr	69	67	68	74	278	-6	22,080.00	15,378.83
	Mårten OLANDER	Swe	70	70	70	68	278	-6	22,080.00	15,378.83
	Nathan FRITZ	USA	70	66	74	68	278	-6	22,080.00	15,378.83
19	Mark FOSTER	Eng	71	70	67	71	279	-5	18,920.00	13,177.87
	Sergio GARCIA	Sp	67	70	72	70	279	-5	18,920.00	13,177.87
	Mattias ELIASSON	Swe	68	71	72	68	279	-5	18,920.00	13,177.87
	Erol SIMSEK	Ger	70	70	67	72	279	-5	18,920.00	13,177.87
23	Carlos RODILES	Sp	68	74	69	69	280	-4	17,120.00	11,924.16
	Henrik BJORNSTAD	Nor	66	72	71	71	280	-4	17,120.00	11,924.16
	Richard BLAND	Eng	67	71	71	71	280	-4	17,120.00	11,924.16
26	Andrew OLDCORN	Scot	74	68	68	71	281	-3	14,480.00	10,085.39
	Alvaro SALTO	Sp	71	70	67	73	281	-3	14,480.00	10,085.39
	Shaun P WEBSTER	Eng	69	72	70	70	281	-3	14,480.00	10,085.39
	Trevor IMMELMAN	SA	68	66	75	72	281	-3	14,480.00	10,085.39
	Colin MONTGOMERIE	Scot	70	68	72	71	281	-3	14,480.00	10,085.39
	Miles TUNNICLIFF	Eng	70	69	68	74	281	-3	14,480.00	10,085.39
	Patrik SJÖLAND	Swe	67	68	73	73	281	-3	14,480.00	10,085.39
	Matthew CORT	Eng	68	71	71	71	281	-3	14,480.00	10,085.39
34	Roger CHAPMAN	Eng	71	68	72	71	282	-2	11,680.00	8,135.18
	Ronan RAFFERTY	N.Ire	69	71	73	69	282	-2	11,680.00	8,135.18
	Jean-François LUCQUIN	Fr	71	67	71	73	282	-2	11,680.00	8,135.18
	Eduardo DE LA RIVA	Sp	70	70	70	72	282	-2	11,680.00	8,135.18
	Richard STERNE	SA	71	64	73	74	282	-2	11,680.00	8,135.18
39	Jesus Maria ARRUTI	Sp	72	70	71	70	283	-1	9,600.00	6,686.45
	Mathias GRÖNBERG	Swe	75	67	72	69	283	-1	9,600.00	6,686.45
	Christian CÉVAËR	Fr	71	71	72	69	283	-1	9,600.00	6,686.45
	Simon HURD	Eng	69	73	70	71	283	-1	9,600.00	6,686.45
	Iain PYMAN	Eng	71	70	72	70	283	-1	9,600.00	6,686.45
	Simon DYSON	Eng	69	69	74	71	283	-1	9,600.00	6,686.45
	Felipe AGUILAR	Chi	73	67	71	72	283	-1	9,600.00	6,686.45
	Marcus FRASER	Aus	69	72	68	74	283	-1	9,600.00	6,686.45
47	Barry LANE	Eng	68	74	72	70	284	0	7,200.00	5,014.84
	Jamie SPENCE	Eng	68	70	76	70	284	0	7,200.00	5,014.84
	Joakim HAEGGMAN	Swe	69	73	69	73	284	0	7,200.00	5,014.84
	Benn BARHAM	Eng	72	69	71	72	284	0	7,200.00	5,014.84
	Fredrik ANDERSSON	Swe	72	70	69	73	284	0	7,200.00	5,014.84
	Henrik NYSTROM	Swe	73	68	72	71	284	0	7,200.00	5,014.84
	Mikael LUNDBERG	Swe	70	71	73	70	284	0	7,200.00	5,014.84
54	Malcolm MACKENZIE	Eng	70	72	70	73	285	1	5,000.00	3,482.52
	Philip WALTON	Ire	71	69	74	71	285	1	5,000.00	3,482.52
	Bradford VAUGHAN	SA	69	69	74	73	285	1	5,000.00	3,482.52
	Hennie OTTO	SA	72	68	71	74	285	1	5,000.00	3,482.52
	Søren HANSEN	Den	72	69	73	71	285	1	5,000.00	3,482.52
	Ricardo GONZALEZ	Arg	67	73	70	75	285	1	5,000.00	3,482.52
	Adam MEDNICK	Swe	68	70	72	75	285	1	5,000.00	3,482.52
	Nick DOUGHERTY	Eng	73	65	76	71	285	1	5,000.00	3,482.52
62	Maarten LAFEBER	NL	67	74	69	76	286	2	3,760.00	2,618.86
	Titch MOORE	SA	72	69	74	71	286	2	3,760.00	2,618.86
	Ian GARBUTT	Eng	72	68	72	74	286	2	3,760.00	2,618.86
	Gustavo ROJAS	Arg	70	72	69	75	286	2	3,760.00	2,618.86
	Paul LAWRIE	Scot	68	72	74	72	286	2	3,760.00	2,618.86
	Tobias DIER	Ger	72	70	72	72	286	2	3,760.00	2,618.86
68	Jarmo SANDELIN	Swe	71	71	71	74	287	3	3,200.00	2,228.82
69	Charl SCHWARTZEL	SA	69	71	68	80	288	4	3,040.00	2,117.38
70	Alessandro TADINI	It	67	72	78	72	289	5	2,930.00	2,040.76
71	Klas ERIKSSON	Swe	70	71	79	71	291	7	2,398.50	1,670.57
	Darren FICHARDT	SA	70	72	74	75	291	7	2,398.50	1,670.57
73	Alexandre CHOPARD	Swi	73	68	78	74	293	9	2,394.00	1,667.43
74	Gary EMERSON	Eng	70	72	73	79	294	10	2,391.00	1,665.34
75	Miguel Angel MARTIN	Sp	67	74	75	79	295	11	2,388.00	1,663.25
76	Mark MCNULTY	Zim	66	75	DISQ		141	4		

Retief Goosen

1	Retief GOOSEN SA	266	-18
2	Paul McGINLEY Ire	270	-14
3	Raphaël JACQUELIN Fr	271	-13
	Ian POULTER Eng	271	-13
5	Nicolas COLSAERTS Bel	272	-12
	Hennie OTTO SA	272	-12
7	Jean-Francois REMESY Fr	273	-11
8	David HOWELL Eng	274	-10
	Carlos RODILES Sp	274	-10
10	Peter FOWLER Aus	275	-9
	Damien McGRANE Ire	275	-9
	Mårten OLANDER Swe	275	-9

fashion statement

Golf and fashion have, on occasion, not enjoyed the best of relationships over the years. The sartorially challenged Simon Hobday famously wrote to one clothing manufacturer demanding £200 a week or he would start wearing their clothes!

And who can forget, despite his best efforts, the lime green shirt and checked trouser combination of Tom Watson in the famous 'Duel in the Sun' with Jack Nicklaus during the Open Golf Championship at Turnberry in 1977?

Thankfully the Trophée Lancôme is one event where the worlds of golf and fashion meet without a garish clash of colours, and where, quite often, a glance into the crowd is almost as entertaining as the golf itself.

Fittingly, then, it was the elegant Retief Goosen who proved himself a cut above the rest in the 34th and final edition of the tournament which has graced The European Tour International Schedule over the years.

From the moment he posted a first round 63, denied a share of the course record only by a last hole bogey five, Goosen looked set fair for a fourth victory on French soil following his Open de France victories of 1997 and 1999 and his previous Trophée Lancôme triumph in 2000.

"It must be the red wine," joked the South African when asked for the recipe for such sustained success across the Channel from his English base in Ascot. Indeed, the winner of the Volvo Order of Merit in both 2001 and 2002 might well have had the rest of the field seeking a comforting drop of the vin rouge themselves after a second round 65 stretched his lead to four shots at halfway.

That it was not ultimately a cakewalk in front of the catwalk cognoscenti, however, was down to the determined challenges of Ryder Cup hero Paul McGinley and young Belgian Nicolas Colsaerts, at only 20, surely a star of the future.

McGinley posted a third round 66 but was still praying for a "helping hand" from Goosen to give the chasing pack hope going into the final day. Barely had the words come out of his mouth before his prayers were answered, the 2001 US Open Champion dropping a shot on the treacherous 18th to see his lead reduced to three shots.

Goosen remained confident, however, pointing out that the majority of his victories, including that memorable Major win

Matthew Blackey

at Southern Hills Country Club, had come when leading from the front.

Surely there would be no repeat of the dramatic conclusion to the 2001 Trophée Lancôme when he let slip a four shot lead over the last four holes to a charging Sergio Garcia? There was not, despite first Colsaerts then McGinley causing Goosen a few anxious moments early in the round.

Colsaerts, who turned professional on his 18th birthday in November 2000 and later that same month became the youngest player to achieve his card through the Qualifying School by battling through all three stages, twice trimmed Goosen's five

the course

A testing composite lay-out made up of the two courses at Saint-Nom-la-Bretèche, the tournament venue demanded total concentration from start to finish, with the closing stretch in particular ready to catch the unwary.

shot lead back to just two with an eagle on the sixth and a birdie on the eighth.

But it was McGinley who was to get closest to the reigning European Number One on the pivotal 11th hole, the Irishman holing from eight feet for birdie while Colsaerts found water to the back of the green to take six, and Goosen bogeyed after a wayward drive.

Was the 34 year old's Goose cooked? Not a chance.

A birdie on the 12th calmed his nerves before the shot of the week, a beautifully controlled approach to the 13th which spun back to within inches of the hole, effectively sealed the deal.

"It was tough because I was struggling all day, especially with my driver," admitted Goosen after a closing 70 gave him an 18 under par total of 266, a four shot winning margin over McGinley and his first victory of the year. "I was hitting it all over the golf course and used most of the golf course to get it done.

Peter Baker

Simon Wakefield

"But it's a special victory as this is the last Trophée Lancôme and if they don't want the trophy, definitely one of the great trophies in golf, I'll be happy to find a place for it at home!"

Local favourite Raphaël Jacquelin was unable to provide the fairytale home victory for the final tournament, but four rounds in the 60s gave the crowd plenty to cheer as he claimed third place alongside Ian Poulter, who knows a thing or two about fashion given the amount of column inches his hairstyle attracts.

With the weather even playing its part by bathing the final two days in glorious sunshine, it all added up to a fitting farewell to a wonderful event.

Phil Casey

final results

Saint-Nom-la-Bretèche • Paris • France
September 11 - 14 • 2003 • Par 71 • 6903 yards • 6311 metres

Pos.	Name		Rd1	Rd2	Rd3	Rd4	Total		Prize Money Euro	£
1	Retief GOOSEN	SA	63	65	68	70	266	-18	300,000.00	209,043.21
2	Paul MCGINLEY	Ire	66	67	66	71	270	-14	200,000.00	139,362.14
3	Raphaël JACQUELIN	Fr	69	67	68	67	271	-13	101,340.00	70,614.80
	Ian POULTER	Eng	67	69	65	70	271	-13	101,340.00	70,614.80
5	Hennie OTTO	SA	69	65	70	68	272	-12	69,660.00	48,539.83
	Nicolas COLSAERTS	Bel	66	66	68	72	272	-12	69,660.00	48,539.83
7	Jean-Francois REMESY	Fr	72	65	70	66	273	-11	54,000.00	37,627.78
8	David HOWELL	Eng	69	70	67	68	274	-10	42,660.00	29,725.94
	Carlos RODILES	Sp	66	66	73	69	274	-10	42,660.00	29,725.94
10	Peter FOWLER	Aus	67	69	73	66	275	-9	33,360.00	23,245.60
	Mårten OLANDER	Swe	71	66	67	71	275	-9	33,360.00	23,245.60
	Damien MCGRANE	Ire	68	68	67	72	275	-9	33,360.00	23,245.60
13	Ian WOOSNAM	Wal	70	67	70	69	276	-8	25,980.00	18,103.14
	Padraig HARRINGTON	Ire	68	68	71	69	276	-8	25,980.00	18,103.14
	Maarten LAFEBER	NL	68	70	70	68	276	-8	25,980.00	18,103.14
	Euan LITTLE	Scot	71	69	69	67	276	-8	25,980.00	18,103.14
	Richard BLAND	Eng	68	71	68	69	276	-8	25,980.00	18,103.14
	Simon WAKEFIELD	Eng	65	74	70	67	276	-8	25,980.00	18,103.14
19	Eduardo ROMERO	Arg	68	67	70	72	277	-7	20,988.00	14,624.66
	Steve WEBSTER	Eng	69	71	68	69	277	-7	20,988.00	14,624.66
	Nick O'HERN	Aus	69	70	69	69	277	-7	20,988.00	14,624.66
	Gary EVANS	Eng	73	68	66	70	277	-7	20,988.00	14,624.66
	David LYNN	Eng	69	69	66	73	277	-7	20,988.00	14,624.66
24	Mark MCNULTY	Zim	68	67	72	71	278	-6	17,640.00	12,291.74
	Henrik STENSON	Swe	70	68	68	72	278	-6	17,640.00	12,291.74
	Peter BAKER	Eng	71	66	72	69	278	-6	17,640.00	12,291.74
	Jarrod MOSELEY	Aus	68	71	71	68	278	-6	17,640.00	12,291.74
	Jesus Maria ARRUTI	Sp	70	68	73	67	278	-6	17,640.00	12,291.74
	Markus BRIER	Aut	68	70	69	71	278	-6	17,640.00	12,291.74
	John BICKERTON	Eng	71	67	68	72	278	-6	17,640.00	12,291.74
31	Robert-Jan DERKSEN	NL	68	73	71	67	279	-5	14,940.00	10,410.35
	Nicolas VANHOOTEGEM	Bel	69	70	69	71	279	-5	14,940.00	10,410.35
	Marcus FRASER	Aus	67	73	71	68	279	-5	14,940.00	10,410.35
34	Gary MURPHY	Ire	71	69	72	68	280	-4	13,320.00	9,281.52
	Ricardo GONZALEZ	Arg	69	69	71	71	280	-4	13,320.00	9,281.52
	Stephen GALLACHER	Scot	71	68	69	72	280	-4	13,320.00	9,281.52
	Mikael LUNDBERG	Swe	64	70	73	73	280	-4	13,320.00	9,281.52
38	Mark FOSTER	Eng	71	69	67	74	281	-3	11,520.00	8,027.26
	Soren KJELDSEN	Den	70	71	72	68	281	-3	11,520.00	8,027.26
	Philip GOLDING	Eng	69	70	69	73	281	-3	11,520.00	8,027.26
	Jorge BERENDT	Arg	67	73	69	72	281	-3	11,520.00	8,027.26
	Gustavo ROJAS	Arg	70	70	69	72	281	-3	11,520.00	8,027.26
	David DRYSDALE	Scot	72	69	67	73	281	-3	11,520.00	8,027.26
44	Titch MOORE	SA	68	72	71	71	282	-2	9,000.00	6,271.30
	Colin MONTGOMERIE	Scot	68	72	70	72	282	-2	9,000.00	6,271.30
	Patrik SJÖLAND	Swe	70	70	69	73	282	-2	9,000.00	6,271.30
	Mads VIBE-HASTRUP	Den	72	68	68	74	282	-2	9,000.00	6,271.30
	Fredrik WIDMARK	Swe	71	65	71	75	282	-2	9,000.00	6,271.30
	Simon DYSON	Eng	71	67	77	67	282	-2	9,000.00	6,271.30
	Charl SCHWARTZEL	SA	68	70	69	75	282	-2	9,000.00	6,271.30
	Hunter MAHAN	USA	73	68	71	70	282	-2	9,000.00	6,271.30
52	Andrew RAITT	Eng	70	71	70	72	283	-1	6,660.00	4,640.76
	Terry PRICE	Aus	66	73	74	70	283	-1	6,660.00	4,640.76
	Brett RUMFORD	Aus	68	70	72	73	283	-1	6,660.00	4,640.76
	Jamie DONALDSON	Wal	68	69	70	76	283	-1	6,660.00	4,640.76
	Martin MARITZ	SA	71	70	70	72	283	-1	6,660.00	4,640.76
57	Peter O'MALLEY	Aus	69	72	70	73	284	0	5,400.00	3,762.78
	Murray URQUHART	Scot	74	63	74	73	284	0	5,400.00	3,762.78
	Mark PILKINGTON	Wal	67	71	74	72	284	0	5,400.00	3,762.78
60	Santiago LUNA	Sp	68	73	75	69	285	1	4,410.00	3,072.94
	Darren FICHARDT	SA	68	71	74	72	285	1	4,410.00	3,072.94
	Kenneth FERRIE	Eng	68	73	73	71	285	1	4,410.00	3,072.94
	Ian GARBUTT	Eng	71	70	74	70	285	1	4,410.00	3,072.94
	Bradley DREDGE	Wal	68	70	72	75	285	1	4,410.00	3,072.94
	Henrik NYSTROM	Swe	72	68	69	76	285	1	4,410.00	3,072.94
	David CARTER	Eng	69	70	74	72	285	1	4,410.00	3,072.94
	Thomas NORRET	Den	75	66	73	71	285	1	4,410.00	3,072.94
68	Stephen SCAHILL	NZ	70	71	75	70	286	2	3,510.00	2,445.81
	Matthew BLACKEY	Eng	71	70	72	73	286	2	3,510.00	2,445.81
70	Klas ERIKSSON	Swe	71	68	74	74	287	3	2,812.40	1,959.71
	Shaun P WEBSTER	Eng	70	71	72	74	287	3	2,812.40	1,959.71
	Raymond RUSSELL	Scot	70	71	72	74	287	3	2,812.40	1,959.71
	Eddie LEE	NZ	70	71	75	71	287	3	2,812.40	1,959.71
	Ben CURTIS	USA	69	72	74	72	287	3	2,812.40	1,959.71
75	Gregory HAVRET	Fr	71	69	73	75	288	4	2,688.00	1,873.03
76	Jonathan LOMAS	Eng	69	71	71	78	289	5	2,683.50	1,869.89
	Matthew CORT	Eng	71	69	71	78	289	5	2,683.50	1,869.89
78	Philip ARCHER	Eng	70	71	73	76	290	6	2,679.00	1,866.76
79	Marc FARRY	Fr	71	70	72	78	291	7	2,674.50	1,863.62
	Fernando ROCA	Sp	69	71	75	76	291	7	2,674.50	1,863.62
81	Andrew COLTART	Scot	68	73	78	76	295	11	2,670.00	1,860.48

Linde German Masters Gut Lärchenhof · Cologne · Germany
golfing nirvana

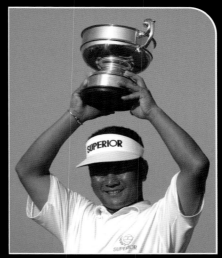

K J Choi

1	**K J CHOI** Kor	262	-26
2	Miguel Angel JIMÉNEZ Sp	264	-24
3	Niclas FASTH Swe	265	-23
	Ian POULTER Eng	265	-23
5	Darren CLARKE N.Ire	268	-20
	Anders HANSEN Den	268	-20
	Carlos RODILES Sp	268	-20
8	Michael CAMPBELL NZ	269	-19
	Mathias GRÖNBERG Swe	269	-19
	David HOWELL Eng	269	-19
	Jarrod MOSELEY Aus	269	-19

What would Jack Nicklaus have thought? On a course of his making, some of the world's finest players made hay while the sun shone down on Gut Lärchenhof and there was little that could be done to stop them. But why try? This, after all, was golf at its most entertaining, if not its most examining.

the course

A thoroughly modern, long, parkland course with generous fairways, large, well protected greens and an abundance of water. In the twelve years since it was built, the course has matured well and received universal praise from the players, with the immaculate greens particularly lauded.

After four days of extraordinary scoring, KJ Choi, of Korea, emerged an electrifying winner of the superbly organised Linde German Masters - his first event in Continental Europe - with a 26 under par total of 262. Appropriately, the man nicknamed 'The Tank', had steamrollered to victory.

It is hard to imagine many tournaments quite like this one. The scores were low, yes, but in reality the 156 players that started the week had found golfing Nirvana: a beautifully manicured course with exceptional greens - by common consent the best of the year - combined with plenty of sunshine and hardly a breath of wind.

At 7,289 yards and with a par of 72, Gut Lärchenhof is no tiddler, but its generous fairways and receptive greens encouraged and rewarded aggressive play. With temperatures into the 80s, becalmed conditions, and plenty of roll on the fairways, all the par fives were reachable in two, while approach shots to many of the par fours were with nine irons and wedges. The greens, soft enough to allow players to aim directly at the flags, were as smooth and true as snooker tables and rare was the putt that bobbled off line.

In such conditions the players, to some extent, had the course at their mercy, despite some tricky pin positions, and by the end of the week they had claimed an incredible 1,798 birdies and 66 eagles - among them holes-in-one for Paul Lawrie and Lee Westwood - with the leading seven finishers an astounding 156 under par for the week.

Mark McNulty

Throughout, there was also one intriguing sideshow that captured the imagination. Were we about to witness a 59 in a European Tour event for the first time? Three times it looked a distinct possibility with Anders Hansen, Fredrik Jacobson and Westwood all moving within range, only for the opportunity to slip agonisingly from their grasp.

Jacobson, already a two time winner on The 2003 European Tour International Schedule, will probably never get a better chance to claim a slice of golfing history. Playing with Colin Montgomerie and Ian Poulter on the first day, the Swede was in imperious form during a round that included ten birdies, an eagle and a paltry 21 putts.

Approaching the par four ninth, his last hole of the day, Jacobson needed only one more birdie to break the 60 barrier, a situation which even attracted the attention of Darren Clarke in the group behind, who asked to be kept up-to-date by the on-course television commentators.

It was not to be, however. After pulling his tee shot into a rotten lie, Jacobson came up short and left of the green with his second shot, chipped beyond the hole with his third and eventually did extremely well to save par with a tricky 12 foot downhill putt to become only the tenth player in history to officially score 60 in European Tour competition.

Hansen began his second round with six successive birdies and started his back nine with four more. But with five holes to go, the 2002 Volvo PGA Champion could not conjure up another birdie and had to settle for a not-inconsiderable round of 62, while Westwood reached eight under par after ten holes of his final round before losing momentum slightly and finishing with a 63. A one kilogramme bar of gold, worth around £7,500, for a hole-in-one at the eighth, compensated for his disappointment.

With a five year exemption for the winner, and a healthy 500,000 euro (£351,978) first prize, the field was a strong one. On the final day though, it was left to four players to vie for the title.

Anders Hansen

TECHNIQUE FOR PROFESSIONALS

More often it is the right technique that decides on the level of your success – in the game of golf as much as in business. In the same way that golf pro Bernhard Langer continually works at perfecting his play, we at Linde daily take up the technical challenge anew. With our aim set on innovations enabling Linde customers to do an increasingly professional and successful job.

www.linde.de

At one stage, each of Choi, who had two victories on the US PGA Tour in 2002, eventual runner-up Miguel Angel Jiménez, Niclas Fasth and Poulter, who shared third, had a taste of the lead. But in the end it was Choi's consistency that won the day. After starting the week with a 63, he followed up with rounds of 68-64-67 to make history by becoming the first Korean golfer to win on The European Tour.

Peter Dixon

Darren Clarke

final results

Gut Lärchenhof • Cologne • Germany
September 18 - 21 • 2003 • Par 72 • 7289 yards • 6662 metres

Pos.	Name		Rd1	Rd2	Rd3	Rd4	Total	Par	Prize Money Euro	£
1	K J CHOI	Kor	63	68	64	67	262	-26	500,000.00	351,978.82
2	Miguel Angel JIMÉNEZ	Sp	67	62	67	68	264	-24	333,330.00	234,650.20
3	Ian POULTER	Eng	65	63	69	68	265	-23	168,900.00	118,898.45
	Niclas FASTH	Swe	68	67	65	65	265	-23	168,900.00	118,898.45
5	Anders HANSEN	Den	69	62	72	65	268	-20	107,400.00	75,605.05
	Carlos RODILES	Sp	65	65	67	71	268	-20	107,400.00	75,605.05
	Darren CLARKE	N.Ire	65	71	65	67	268	-20	107,400.00	75,605.05
8	David HOWELL	Eng	66	69	69	65	269	-19	64,350.00	45,299.67
	Jarrod MOSELEY	Aus	68	65	67	69	269	-19	64,350.00	45,299.67
	Mathias GRÖNBERG	Swe	68	69	68	64	269	-19	64,350.00	45,299.67
	Michael CAMPBELL	NZ	69	67	66	67	269	-19	64,350.00	45,299.67
12	Gary ORR	Scot	65	66	70	69	270	-18	51,600.00	36,324.21
13	Henrik STENSON	Swe	72	65	68	66	271	-17	46,100.00	32,452.45
	Alex CEJKA	Ger	70	69	67	65	271	-17	46,100.00	32,452.45
	Lee WESTWOOD	Eng	71	67	70	63	271	-17	46,100.00	32,452.45
16	Justin ROSE	Eng	69	66	70	67	272	-16	40,500.00	28,510.28
	Retief GOOSEN	SA	68	67	66	71	272	-16	40,500.00	28,510.28
	Adam SCOTT	Aus	66	69	67	70	272	-16	40,500.00	28,510.28
19	Mark MCNULTY	Zim	68	67	66	73	274	-14	32,640.00	22,977.18
	Nick O'HERN	Aus	67	70	72	65	274	-14	32,640.00	22,977.18
	Thomas LEVET	Fr	70	68	68	68	274	-14	32,640.00	22,977.18
	Joakim HAEGGMAN	Swe	72	68	64	70	274	-14	32,640.00	22,977.18
	Paul MCGINLEY	Ire	67	72	69	66	274	-14	32,640.00	22,977.18
	Ricardo GONZALEZ	Arg	71	67	68	68	274	-14	32,640.00	22,977.18
	Fredrik JACOBSON	Swe	60	71	70	73	274	-14	32,640.00	22,977.18
	Raymond RUSSELL	Scot	68	71	69	66	274	-14	32,640.00	22,977.18
	Paul CASEY	Eng	65	67	67	75	274	-14	32,640.00	22,977.18
	Marcus FRASER	Aus	66	70	72	66	274	-14	32,640.00	22,977.18
29	Maarten LAFEBER	NL	67	69	69	70	275	-13	26,700.00	18,795.67
	Miles TUNNICLIFF	Eng	67	63	71	74	275	-13	26,700.00	18,795.67
	Mikael LUNDBERG	Swe	69	67	70	69	275	-13	26,700.00	18,795.67
32	Eduardo ROMERO	Arg	69	69	74	64	276	-12	23,280.00	16,388.13
	Darren FICHARDT	SA	69	67	72	68	276	-12	23,280.00	16,388.13
	Ian GARBUTT	Eng	69	70	66	71	276	-12	23,280.00	16,388.13
	Bradley DREDGE	Wal	67	69	69	71	276	-12	23,280.00	16,388.13
	David PARK	Wal	67	70	68	71	276	-12	23,280.00	16,388.13
37	Hennie OTTO	SA	72	66	69	70	277	-11	20,400.00	14,360.74
	Emanuele CANONICA	It	69	68	70	70	277	-11	20,400.00	14,360.74
	Stephen DODD	Wal	68	69	69	71	277	-11	20,400.00	14,360.74
	David LYNN	Eng	74	65	71	67	277	-11	20,400.00	14,360.74
41	Trevor IMMELMAN	SA	71	69	70	68	278	-10	18,600.00	13,093.61
	Paul LAWRIE	Scot	69	67	72	70	278	-10	18,600.00	13,093.61
43	Ian WOOSNAM	Wal	67	67	71	74	279	-9	15,900.00	11,192.93
	Philip GOLDING	Eng	71	69	70	69	279	-9	15,900.00	11,192.93
	Marcel SIEM	Ger	71	66	70	72	279	-9	15,900.00	11,192.93
	Charlie WI	Kor	69	71	70	69	279	-9	15,900.00	11,192.93
	Jonathan LOMAS	Eng	69	71	71	68	279	-9	15,900.00	11,192.93
	Brett RUMFORD	Aus	66	72	68	73	279	-9	15,900.00	11,192.93
	Richard STERNE	SA	69	69	68	73	279	-9	15,900.00	11,192.93
50	Peter FOWLER	Aus	69	67	73	71	280	-8	11,400.00	8,025.12
	David GILFORD	Eng	66	71	69	74	280	-8	11,400.00	8,025.12
	Brian DAVIS	Eng	71	69	71	69	280	-8	11,400.00	8,025.12
	Anthony WALL	Eng	67	70	71	72	280	-8	11,400.00	8,025.12
	Robert KARLSSON	Swe	68	68	72	72	280	-8	11,400.00	8,025.12
	Simon DYSON	Eng	70	67	73	70	280	-8	11,400.00	8,025.12
	Martin MARITZ	SA	73	66	71	70	280	-8	11,400.00	8,025.12
	Charl SCHWARTZEL	SA	72	66	67	75	280	-8	11,400.00	8,025.12
58	Santiago LUNA	Sp	72	66	71	72	281	-7	8,700.00	6,124.43
	José Maria OLAZÁBAL	Sp	72	68	72	69	281	-7	8,700.00	6,124.43
	John BICKERTON	Eng	67	68	72	74	281	-7	8,700.00	6,124.43
61	Sandy LYLE	Scot	67	72	73	70	282	-6	7,950.00	5,596.46
	Greg OWEN	Eng	72	68	75	67	282	-6	7,950.00	5,596.46
63	Jamie SPENCE	Eng	68	70	74	71	283	-5	7,500.00	5,279.68
64	Peter HEDBLOM	Swe	68	65	80	71	284	-4	7,050.00	4,962.90
	Graeme MCDOWELL	N.Ire	70	70	69	75	284	-4	7,050.00	4,962.90
66	Raphaël JACQUELIN	Fr	71	67	77	70	285	-3	6,600.00	4,646.12
67	Andrew OLDCORN	Scot	69	69	75	73	286	-2	5,867.50	4,130.47
	Klas ERIKSSON	Swe	72	68	73	73	286	-2	5,867.50	4,130.47
	Barry LANE	Eng	70	70	78	68	286	-2	5,867.50	4,130.47
	Richard PORTER	Ger	70	70	73	73	286	-2	5,867.50	4,130.47
71	Tobias DIER	Ger	71	68	75	73	287	-1	4,500.00	3,167.81
72	Henrik NYSTROM	Swe	69	71	78	73	291	3	4,497.00	3,165.70

Daniel and Sam Torrance

1	Lee WESTWOOD Eng	267	-21
2	Ernie ELS SA	268	-20
3	Raphaël JACQUELIN Fr	270	-18
4	Darren CLARKE N.Ire	271	-17
	Maarten LAFEBER NL	271	-17
6	Brian DAVIS Eng	272	-16
	David HOWELL Eng	272	-16
	Nick O'HERN Aus	272	-16
	Henrik STENSON Swe	272	-16
	Richard STERNE SA	272	-16

application and appreciation

Lee Westwood

t was five time Open Golf Champion Peter Thomson who said of St Andrews that if one part of a player's game was off, "this great course will find you out, no matter how hard you try to hide it."

After Lee Westwood had defeated Ernie Els by one shot to win the dunhill links championship, he admitted that his game had stood up better than he would have believed possible. With the win coming, as it did, only a month after he had emerged from a near three year barren spell to capture the BMW International Open in Germany, he felt that it served as the final confirmation of his comeback.

Laurae Westwood, though she set great store by the help her husband had had from coach David Leadbetter, had her own take on why things had suddenly come right.

To her, it was also down to the time her other half had spent in America for the US PGA Championship and the World Golf Championships - NEC Invitational. He was not alone in finding the American courses long and tough and he was also not alone in feeling that the workout had left him in good shape for the excellent challenge presented by Golfclub München Nord-Eichenried on his return in late August for the BMW International Open.

"The course in Germany was a little shorter than the courses he had been playing in the States but he knew he could handle it," said Mrs Westwood, talking during the final afternoon in Scotland. She then

Henrik Stenson

recalled the scene at their Nottingham home four weeks earlier as her husband set about returning to winning ways. "My family and I were all in the house on the Sunday afternoon and Lee's parents joined us," Laurae explained. "Even the gardener came in to watch! It was amazing..."

On the subject of what was happening in front of her at St Andrews, she saw the 12th and 13th as crucial. Though Westwood would eventually have to be more aware of Els, he was, at that point, locked in battle with his good friend and playing partner, Darren Clarke.

Westwood was 19 under par to Clarke's 17 as they played the 12th but, after the Englishman had driven through the green on the 314 yard par four and the Irishman had found the putting surface, there was a possibility of a two shot swing. As it was, each player left the green with a birdie three and Westwood made a 25 footer for another birdie at the 13th to move to 21 under par and three ahead.

Moments later, when the International Sports Management stablemates were on the 16th fairway, there was an almighty roar across the links which Westwood knew, instinctively, had something to do with Els up ahead on the 17th.

Richard Sterne

the courses

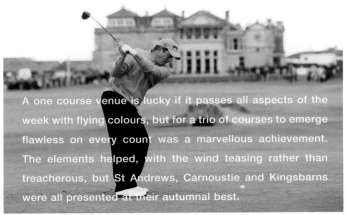

A one course venue is lucky if it passes all aspects of the week with flying colours, but for a trio of courses to emerge flawless on every count was a marvellous achievement. The elements helped, with the wind teasing rather than treacherous, but St Andrews, Carnoustie and Kingsbarns were all presented at their autumnal best.

Mark James and Dan Quayle

In fact, the South African, who had landed on the 18th tee with his second to the famous Road Hole, had holed for an improbable birdie three to move to 19 under. Buoyed by the stroke of fortune, The Big Easy made another birdie at the 18th to sign off with a 64 for a 20 under par total of 268, giving Westwood the target which would make for such riveting viewing all around the world.

Many a man, from David Duval to Tommy Nakajima, has found difficulty negotiating his way safely through the 17th on the Old Course, and Westwood, who needed two pars to win, was more than a little vulnerable as he addressed his second at the penultimate hole. He was in a position where he could have taken any one of a five, six or seven iron for the shot. Which was it to be?

At times like this, it is always advisable to seek wise counsel and in the caddie world they do not come any more judicious than Pete Coleman, the former bagman of Bernhard Langer, whose colours are now firmly fixed to Westwood's mast. Taking Coleman's advice, Westwood opted for the five iron, "because I could go straight at it." It proved a wise choice as the ball landed safely aboard the green to set up the first of two memorable closing fours.

The 705,093 euro (£490,346) first prize, in itself, was one good reason for Westwood to speak graciously of a golf course whose delights, like many of the golfing greats to have trodden the famous links in the past, the Englishman had taken time to savour.

"I've learned to like it," he said. "I've grasped what kind of course it is. It has taken me a few years to appreciate St Andrews, but finally it has happened and I can now see why everyone loves it so much and regards it as such a fantastic test."

Fifteen year old Daniel Torrance, on the other hand, had hit it off at once with the legendary links, thanks not least to the guidance of his father. He and Sam finished at 37 under par 251 to collect the team prize from a field in which the amateur contingent was peppered with celebrities such as Ian Botham, Sir Bobby Charlton, Hugh Grant, Samuel L Jackson, Jodie Kidd and Dan Quayle.

There was a trophy for Daniel and Sam and 44,068 euro (£30,646) for Torrance Snr which, as was lightly pointed out, would almost certainly cover the rest of Torrance Jnr's school fees before his plan to turn professional at 16, like his father did in 1970, comes to fruition. There was

pro-am team results

Pos.	Name	Rd1	Rd2	Rd3	Rd4	Total	Prize Money	
							Euro	£
1	SAM TORRANCE and Daniel Torrance	67	63	59	62	251	44,068.34	30,646.64
2	RAPHAËL JACQUELIN and Guy East	64	62	63	65	254	19,096.28	13,280.21
	ROBERT-JAN DERKSEN and Pieter van Doorne	65	62	60	67	254	19,096.28	13,280.21
	ERNIE ELS and Neels Els	68	62	63	61	254	19,096.28	13,280.21
5	FREDRIK JACOBSON and Rurik Gobel	66	62	63	65	255	8,813.67	6,129.33
6	SIMON DYSON and John Mikkelsen	65	64	62	65	256	4,406.83	3,064.66
	RICHARD STERNE and Alex Martin	68	62	60	66	256	4,406.83	3,064.66
	DARREN CLARKE and Dermot Desmond	63	65	61	67	256	4,406.83	3,064.66

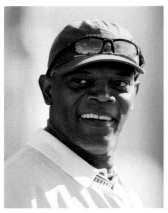

Samuel L Jackson

Sir Bobby Charlton

Sam, Daniel and Bob Torrance

also a wonderful picture to treasure as Bob Torrance, Daniel and Sam sat side by side on the Swilcan Bridge.

For the winning Captain of The European Ryder Cup Team in 2002, this golfing week had been all about his offspring, whose individual rounds were approximately 73-70-68-67. "I feel pride and joy because he's my son, but what he did was incredible for a 15 year old. He played like God every day," he said.

As befits a young man whose mother was a celebrated actress, Daniel was in his element in front of a record 14,620 last day crowd, only feeling a touch cheated, perhaps, that, due to the vagaries of the draw, he and his father had to start at the tenth and finish at the ninth, rather than in front of the packed stands at the 18th.

Bearing in mind his age, the Golfing Gods may have felt they had to hold something back. It could be a wise move because, like Westwood, there is definitely more to come.

Lewine Mair

Jodie Kidd

final results

September 25 - 28 • 2003
St Andrews • Fife • Scotland
Par 72 • 7115 yards • 6506 metres
Carnoustie • Angus • Scotland
Par 72 • 7112 yards • 6504 metres
Kingsbarns • Fife • Scotland
Par 72 • 7059 yards • 6456 metres

Pos.	Name		Rd1	Rd2	Rd3	Rd4	Total	Par	Prize Money Euro	£
1	Lee WESTWOOD	Eng	70	68	62	67	267	-21	705,093.48	490,346.31
2	Ernie ELS	SA	72	65	67	64	268	-20	470,059.38	326,895.49
3	Raphaël JACQUELIN	Fr	69	68	64	69	270	-18	264,833.11	184,174.07
4	Darren CLARKE	N.Ire	67	68	66	70	271	-17	195,451.91	135,924.00
	Maarten LAFEBER	NL	68	69	67	67	271	-17	195,451.91	135,924.00
6	Henrik STENSON	Swe	71	66	67	68	272	-16	112,025.25	77,906.22
	Nick O'HERN	Aus	73	67	67	65	272	-16	112,025.25	77,906.22
	Richard STERNE	SA	71	67	65	69	272	-16	112,025.25	77,906.22
	David HOWELL	Eng	67	68	69	68	272	-16	112,025.25	77,906.22
	Brian DAVIS	Eng	74	70	66	62	272	-16	112,025.25	77,906.22
11	Michael CAMPBELL	NZ	68	68	66	71	273	-15	77,842.32	54,134.23
12	Peter LAWRIE	Ire	67	68	71	68	274	-14	66,948.63	46,558.38
	Simon YATES	Scot	66	71	66	71	274	-14	66,948.63	46,558.38
	Phillip PRICE	Wal	68	71	66	69	274	-14	66,948.63	46,558.38
	Mark MCNULTY	Zim	71	66	68	69	274	-14	66,948.63	46,558.38
16	Charlie WI	Kor	71	70	66	68	275	-13	57,112.57	39,718.05
	Vijay SINGH	Fiji	72	66	69	68	275	-13	57,112.57	39,718.05
	Ian POULTER	Eng	69	69	68	69	275	-13	57,112.57	39,718.05
19	Julien CLEMENT	Swi	72	68	70	66	276	-12	49,328.34	34,304.63
	Paul LAWRIE	Scot	69	67	68	72	276	-12	49,328.34	34,304.63
	Mark JAMES	Eng	70	71	67	68	276	-12	49,328.34	34,304.63
	Fredrik JACOBSON	Swe	71	68	65	72	276	-12	49,328.34	34,304.63
	Stephen SCAHILL	NZ	70	73	67	66	276	-12	49,328.34	34,304.63
24	John BICKERTON	Eng	70	70	70	67	277	-11	42,728.66	29,714.99
	Joakim HAEGGMAN	Swe	69	73	69	66	277	-11	42,728.66	29,714.99
	Trevor IMMELMAN	SA	71	71	68	67	277	-11	42,728.66	29,714.99
	Kenneth FERRIE	Eng	71	72	68	66	277	-11	42,728.66	29,714.99
	David PARK	Wal	70	70	66	71	277	-11	42,728.66	29,714.99
29	Ian WOOSNAM	Wal	72	69	70	67	278	-10	35,748.24	24,860.56
	Richard GREEN	Aus	74	72	64	68	278	-10	35,748.24	24,860.56
	Jamie DONALDSON	Wal	67	74	69	68	278	-10	35,748.24	24,860.56
	Nick PRICE	Zim	68	70	70	70	278	-10	35,748.24	24,860.56
	Glen DAY	USA	69	73	67	69	278	-10	35,748.24	24,860.56
	Nick FALDO	Eng	71	70	70	67	278	-10	35,748.24	24,860.56
35	Anders HANSEN	Den	74	67	69	69	279	-9	27,921.70	19,417.71
	Padraig HARRINGTON	Ire	72	69	67	71	279	-9	27,921.70	19,417.71
	Santiago LUNA	Sp	73	68	70	68	279	-9	27,921.70	19,417.71
	Darren FICHARDT	SA	73	70	67	69	279	-9	27,921.70	19,417.71
	Nick DOUGHERTY	Eng	70	70	67	72	279	-9	27,921.70	19,417.71
	David GLEESON	Aus	70	71	67	71	279	-9	27,921.70	19,417.71
	Shaun MICHEEL	USA	73	69	67	70	279	-9	27,921.70	19,417.71
	Angel CABRERA	Arg	73	70	67	69	279	-9	27,921.70	19,417.71
	Robert-Jan DERKSEN	NL	70	72	65	72	279	-9	27,921.70	19,417.71
	Klas ERIKSSON	Swe	69	69	69	72	279	-9	27,921.70	19,417.71
45	Gary EVANS	Eng	70	69	68	73	280	-8	21,998.92	15,298.80
	Patrik SJÖLAND	Swe	70	70	70	70	280	-8	21,998.92	15,298.80
	Raymond RUSSELL	Scot	73	70	66	71	280	-8	21,998.92	15,298.80
	Mathias GRÖNBERG	Swe	71	73	66	70	280	-8	21,998.92	15,298.80
49	Ricardo GONZALEZ	Arg	69	70	66	76	281	-7	17,345.30	12,062.52
	Thomas BJÖRN	Den	71	73	65	72	281	-7	17,345.30	12,062.52
	Terry PRICE	Aus	71	70	68	72	281	-7	17,345.30	12,062.52
	Fredrik ANDERSSON	Swe	72	72	66	71	281	-7	17,345.30	12,062.52
	Simon DYSON	Eng	68	70	70	73	281	-7	17,345.30	12,062.52
	James KINGSTON	SA	70	69	70	72	281	-7	17,345.30	12,062.52
	Adam SCOTT	Aus	72	67	70	72	281	-7	17,345.30	12,062.52
56	Peter O'MALLEY	Aus	69	70	70	73	282	-6	13,537.79	9,414.65
	Henrik BJORNSTAD	Nor	68	68	68	78	282	-6	13,537.79	9,414.65
58	Miles TUNNICLIFF	Eng	72	72	66	73	283	-5	11,845.57	8,237.82
	Soren HANSEN	Den	66	71	74	72	283	-5	11,845.57	8,237.82
	Thomas LEVET	Fr	73	67	70	73	283	-5	11,845.57	8,237.82
	Mark PILKINGTON	Wal	72	71	67	73	283	-5	11,845.57	8,237.82
	Steen TINNING	Den	74	71	65	73	283	-5	11,845.57	8,237.82
63	Andrew COLTART	Scot	73	69	69	74	285	-3	10,364.87	7,208.09
	Miguel Angel MARTIN	Sp	69	72	70	74	285	-3	10,364.87	7,208.09
65	Alastair FORSYTH	Scot	69	72	70	75	286	-2	9,730.29	6,766.78
66	Markus BRIER	Aut	73	70	69		212	-4	7,160.51	4,979.66
	Gregory HAVRET	Fr	74	70	68		212	-4	7,160.51	4,979.66
	Peter FOWLER	Aus	73	67	72		212	-4	7,160.51	4,979.66
	Sam TORRANCE	Scot	76	68	68		212	-4	7,160.51	4,979.66
	Miguel Angel JIMÉNEZ	Sp	74	70	68		212	-4	7,160.51	4,979.66
	Justin ROSE	Eng	73	70	69		212	-4	7,160.51	4,979.66
	Emanuele CANONICA	It	71	70	71		212	-4	7,160.51	4,979.66
	Adam CRAWFORD	Aus	73	71	68		212	-4	7,160.51	4,979.66
	Gary MURPHY	Ire	66	70	76		212	-4	7,160.51	4,979.66
	Simon KHAN	Eng	75	67	70		212	-4	7,160.51	4,979.66
	Jyoti RANDHAWA	Ind	72	70	70		212	-4	7,160.51	4,979.66
	Colin MONTGOMERIE	Scot	73	74	65		212	-4	7,160.51	4,979.66
	Robert KARLSSON	Swe	74	71	67		212	-4	7,160.51	4,979.66

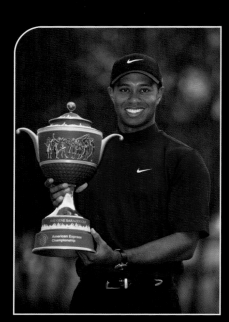

Tiger Woods

1	Tiger WOODS USA		274	-6
2	Stuart APPLEBY Aus		276	-4
	Tim HERRON USA		276	-4
	Vijay SINGH Fiji		276	-4
5	David TOMS USA		277	-3
6	K J CHOI Kor		279	-1
	Padraig HARRINGTON Ire		279	-1
8	Paul CASEY Eng		281	1
	Retief GOOSEN SA		281	1
10	Fred COUPLES USA		282	2
	Ignacio GARRIDO Sp		282	2

as good as it gets

any golfers achieve greatness but shed their humility along the way. Others remain modest without ever scaling the peaks of global success. Tiger Woods has managed to strike the perfect balance of remaining utterly self-effacing while, at the same time, ascending to the apex of his chosen profession.

Woods is as far removed as it is possible to find from a braggart. At the climax of another successful campaign in the World Golf Championships - American Express Championship at the Capital City Club in Atlanta, the World Number One had every reason to be boastful. Typically, he elected to praise not himself, but a fundamental member of his 'Team Tiger' entourage, caddie Steve Williams.

He had just completed his eighth victory in the World Golf Championships series in the 15 events played since their inception in 1999, only Northern Ireland's Darren Clarke, with two victories, having also won more than once.

It was also Woods's 39th win in 143 professional starts on the US PGA Tour - equalling the career records of luminaries such as Gene Sarazen and Tom Watson - and his 52nd worldwide in a career barely

into its eighth year. It was his fifth win of the season and the fifth year he had attained that level of excellence.

The list went on and on but Woods chose to gloss over that catalogue of achievement to focus instead on New Zealand-born Williams, a man who had been over the course before, and for whom Woods's victory represented his 100th as a bag-carrier par excellence.

Williams is one of the game's most respected caddies, and employer and employee have long enjoyed a relationship more akin to brothers. Woods said proudly: "I was trying to get it done for him at one of the Majors. I thought it would be pretty sweet to make it the 100th win at the 'British' but that didn't quite happen.

"That's why the Open was so disappointing. I was right in there with a chance of winning and helping Stevie get that 100th win," continued Woods, adding with a sly grin: "That being said, perhaps the WGC - American Express Championship was the next best thing."

The Capital City Club, opened only 16 months prior to the event, proved to be a demanding test for the best players in the world, which is exactly the way Woods liked it. He added: "It's fun when

Ignacio Garrido

the course

The Capital City Club in the Atlanta district tested the entire bag. The cloying rough and the hard, fast-running greens, along the lines of a Major Championship, ensured that the challenge was a demanding one, from which the best prevailed.

you have a chance to play against the best. This field is right off the Official World Golf Ranking — it can't get any better than that."

Woods said the way the Crabapple Course was set up reminded him of a Major Championship. "It's so much work when you have to play a golf course that's this difficult. It's like in a US Open where every shot is relevant. I like courses where I can make par at every hole and be in contention."

Australian Stuart Appleby, Tim Herron of the United States and Fiji's Vijay Singh all shared second place on a four under par total of 276, two shots behind Woods, who carved out an inexorable route towards his third WGC - American Express Championship crown with scores of 67-66-69-72.

There were many notable performances by European Tour Members who, in common with the vast majority of the 72-strong field, were unable to get close enough to Woods to land a telling punch.

Ireland's Padraig Harrington was one of five Members in the top ten alongside co-runner-up Singh, England's Paul Casey and South

Padraig Harrington

Sergio Garcia

African Retief Goosen (joint eighth) and Ignacio Garrido of Spain (joint tenth). Harrington found his game over the weekend after a modest first 36 holes, closing with rounds of 69 and 66 for a final total of 279.

The Irish Ryder Cup player consolidated his position well inside the top ten by reeling off three birdies to conclude his week, even chipping in at the last from the deep fringe rough for a satisfying three. In addition to those performances, first round leader Sergio Garcia of Spain finished in a share of 12th place alongside, amongst others, South Africa's Ernie Els, who closed with an excellent 67.

However, the week belonged to the double act of Woods and Williams, a partnership familiar with the practiced art of winning titles. What could be better than making a successful defence of the title Woods won at Mount Juliet in Ireland 12 months earlier? Well, actually, the news that he will get the opportunity to defend once more at that glorious Irish venue in 2004. A good week indeed.

Gordon Simpson

final results

Capital City Club · Atlanta · Georgia · USA
October 2 - 5 · 2003 · Par 70 · 7189 yards · 6575 metres

Pos.	Name		Rd1	Rd2	Rd3	Rd4	Total	Par	Prize Money Euro	£
1	Tiger WOODS	USA	67	66	69	72	274	-6	914,474.90	632,644.45
2	Tim HERRON	USA	66	72	67	71	276	-4	352,726.00	244,019.98
	Stuart APPLEBY	Aus	71	68	69	68	276	-4	352,726.00	244,019.98
	Vijay SINGH	Fiji	70	70	64	72	276	-4	352,726.00	244,019.98
5	David TOMS	USA	73	72	67	65	277	-3	204,668.20	141,591.86
6	Padraig HARRINGTON	Ire	71	73	69	66	279	-1	158,944.40	109,959.60
	K J CHOI	Kor	67	71	68	73	279	-1	158,944.40	109,959.60
8	Retief GOOSEN	SA	73	69	67	72	281	1	119,752.70	82,846.32
	Paul CASEY	Eng	73	71	66	71	281	1	119,752.70	82,846.32
10	Fred COUPLES	USA	71	73	70	68	282	2	96,890.79	67,030.18
	Ignacio GARRIDO	Sp	68	71	69	74	282	2	96,890.79	67,030.18
12	Sergio GARCIA	Sp	65	73	70	75	283	3	77,839.23	53,850.09
	Jim FURYK	USA	70	74	69	70	283	3	77,839.23	53,850.09
	Alex CEJKA	Ger	70	76	72	65	283	3	77,839.23	53,850.09
	Ernie ELS	SA	71	74	71	67	283	3	77,839.23	53,850.09
16	Loren ROBERTS	USA	69	75	70	70	284	4	61,835.92	42,778.81
	Brad FAXON	USA	75	71	66	72	284	4	61,835.92	42,778.81
	Rocco MEDIATE	USA	66	72	73	73	284	4	61,835.92	42,778.81
	Niclas FASTH	Swe	68	76	70	70	284	4	61,835.92	42,778.81
20	Jonathan KAYE	USA	73	69	73	70	285	5	56,610.35	39,163.70
21	Steve FLESCH	USA	71	75	72	68	286	6	52,255.71	36,151.11
	Jerry KELLY	USA	70	72	69	75	286	6	52,255.71	36,151.11
	Robert ALLENBY	Aus	72	76	73	65	286	6	52,255.71	36,151.11
	Charles HOWELL III	USA	76	75	65	70	286	6	52,255.71	36,151.11
25	Eduardo ROMERO	Arg	72	74	68	73	287	7	46,159.21	31,933.48
	Toshimitsu IZAWA	Jpn	70	74	72	71	287	7	46,159.21	31,933.48
	Bob ESTES	USA	77	74	68	68	287	7	46,159.21	31,933.48
28	David HOWELL	Eng	74	75	71	68	288	8	40,124.92	27,758.89
	Justin ROSE	Eng	75	69	74	70	288	8	40,124.92	27,758.89
	Mike WEIR	Can	69	73	72	74	288	8	40,124.92	27,758.89
	Thomas BJÖRN	Den	74	73	67	74	288	8	40,124.92	27,758.89
	Fredrik JACOBSON	Swe	75	74	70	69	288	8	40,124.92	27,758.89
	Kenny PERRY	USA	70	74	70	74	288	8	40,124.92	27,758.89
	Chris RILEY	USA	74	73	70	71	288	8	40,124.92	27,758.89
35	Brian DAVIS	Eng	71	77	68	73	289	9	36,143.53	25,004.52
	Lee WESTWOOD	Eng	72	71	71	75	289	9	36,143.53	25,004.52
37	Peter LONARD	Aus	75	74	70	71	290	10	34,837.14	24,100.74
38	Darren CLARKE	N.Ire	69	82	72	68	291	11	33,530.75	23,196.97
	Phil MICKELSON	USA	73	77	70	71	291	11	33,530.75	23,196.97
40	Fred FUNK	USA	73	74	69	76	292	12	31,571.16	21,841.30
	Davis LOVE III	USA	74	77	70	71	292	12	31,571.16	21,841.30
	Alastair FORSYTH	Scot	71	77	71	73	292	12	31,571.16	21,841.30
	Adam SCOTT	Aus	70	73	75	74	292	12	31,571.16	21,841.30
44	Trevor IMMELMAN	SA	70	77	71	75	293	13	29,829.30	20,636.26
	Ian POULTER	Eng	73	74	68	78	293	13	29,829.30	20,636.26
	Peter O'MALLEY	Aus	69	74	70	80	293	13	29,829.30	20,636.26
	Shaun MICHEEL	USA	72	75	71	75	293	13	29,829.30	20,636.26
48	Nick PRICE	Zim	71	73	73	77	294	14	28,305.18	19,581.86
	Arjun ATWAL	Ind	76	72	72	74	294	14	28,305.18	19,581.86
	Hennie OTTO	SA	76	73	73	72	294	14	28,305.18	19,581.86
51	Taichi TESHIMA	Jpn	77	75	70	73	295	15	27,071.36	18,728.28
	Colin MONTGOMERIE	Scot	74	75	70	76	295	15	27,071.36	18,728.28
	Scott VERPLANK	USA	75	75	68	77	295	15	27,071.36	18,728.28
54	Jyoti RANDHAWA	Ind	69	77	74	76	296	16	26,127.85	18,075.55
	Jay HAAS	USA	74	72	75	75	296	16	26,127.85	18,075.55
	Craig PARRY	Aus	76	72	75	73	296	16	26,127.85	18,075.55
	Phillip PRICE	Wal	70	79	72	75	296	16	26,127.85	18,075.55
	Len MATTIACE	USA	70	74	74	78	296	16	26,127.85	18,075.55
59	Raphaël JACQUELIN	Fr	77	80	68	72	297	17	24,930.33	17,247.09
	Søren KJELDSEN	Den	70	75	74	78	297	17	24,930.33	17,247.09
	Bob TWAY	USA	73	80	70	74	297	17	24,930.33	17,247.09
	Chad CAMPBELL	USA	74	76	73	74	297	17	24,930.33	17,247.09
	Rich BEEM	USA	76	75	73	73	297	17	24,930.33	17,247.09
	J.L. LEWIS	USA	72	74	77	74	297	17	24,930.33	17,247.09
65	Kirk TRIPLETT	USA	74	72	70	82	298	18	24,168.26	16,719.89
66	Thongchai JAIDEE	Thai	73	72	72	82	299	19	23,841.67	16,493.95
	Ben CURTIS	USA	76	76	72	75	299	19	23,841.67	16,493.95
68	Mark FOSTER	Eng	76	77	73	74	300	20	23,406.20	16,192.68
	Michael CAMPBELL	NZ	82	76	75	67	300	20	23,406.20	16,192.68
70	Scott HOCH	USA	75	79	75	72	301	21	22,970.74	15,891.43
	Chris DIMARCO	USA	76	74	76	75	301	21	22,970.74	15,891.43
72	Todd HAMILTON	USA	78	81	72	71	302	22	22,644.14	15,665.48

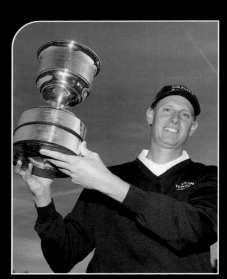

Maarten Lafeber

fever pitch

1	Maarten LAFEBER NL	267	-13
2	Mathias GRÖNBERG Swe	268	-12
	Søren HANSEN Den	268	-12
4	Jamie DONALDSON Wal	270	-10
	Steen TINNING Den	270	-10
6	Gary EVANS Eng	271	-9
	Alastair FORSYTH Scot	271	-9
	Gary MURPHY Ire	271	-9
9	Fredrik ANDERSSON Swe	272	-8
	Stephen DODD Wal	272	-8
	Gary EMERSON Eng	272	-8
	Kenneth FERRIE Eng	272	-8
	Miguel Angel JIMÉNEZ Sp	272	-8
	Adam MEDNICK Swe	272	-8

Costantino Rocca

Derksen, who claimed the Dubai Desert Classic in March 2003, there came the first home winner of the Dutch Open in 56 years. Lafeber had, at last, found the key to open the door to victory, a door on which he had been knocking with increasing intent.

In March 2002 he had finished one stroke short of a play-off against eventual Madeira Island Open champion Diego Borrego when the title at Santo da Serra had been well within his grasp. He also knew, realistically, that he should have made his breakthrough in the Trophée Lancôme later that same year. He was leading after two rounds and still on top going into the final day at Saint-Nom-la-Bretèche before slipping back in the final 18 holes.

W ilhelmina was Queen of The Netherlands and King George VI ruled Britain. Both countries were finding their feet, two years after the end of World War II. Charlton Athletic beat Burnley 1-0 at Wembley in the FA Cup Final in England and Dutch golf celebrated its first home winner in 17 years when Joop Rühl lifted the Dutch Open trophy at Eindhoven.

The year was 1947.

Twenty seven years later there was another auspicious occasion for Dutch golf in Eindhoven, although it was not fully appreciated at the time. The occurrence? The birth of Maarten Lafeber.

A little less than three decades on and, thanks to Lafeber, Dutch golf celebrated another golden moment. Following in the footsteps of Rolf Muntz, who won the Qatar Masters in 2000, and Robert-Jan

Steen Tinning

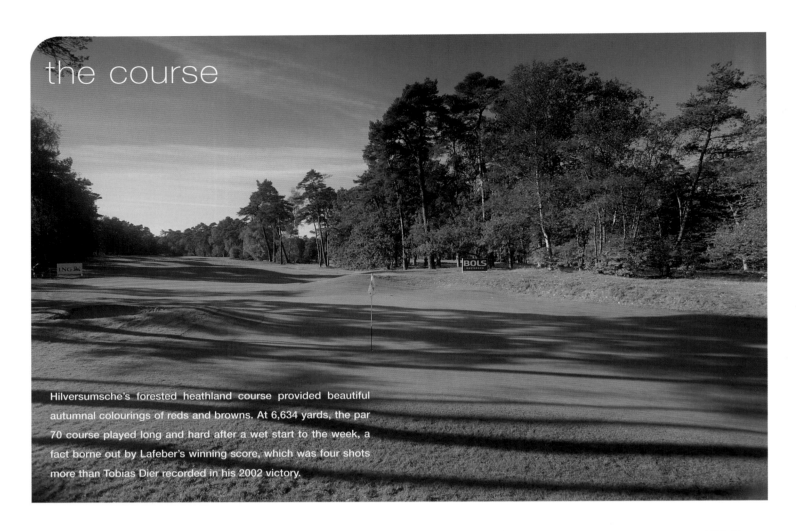

the course

Hilversumsche's forested heathland course provided beautiful autumnal colourings of reds and browns. At 6,634 yards, the par 70 course played long and hard after a wet start to the week, a fact borne out by Lafeber's winning score, which was four shots more than Tobias Dier recorded in his 2002 victory.

Markus Brier

The start of the 2003 season brought more of the same. A share of third place in the BMW Asian Open was followed by a tie for fourth in the Caltex Masters, presented by Carlsberg, Singapore 2003. Advised by his coaches to stay patient, Lafeber began to wonder if patience really was a virtue.

In the end, though, the ability to not panic when a rival threatened to show him a clean pair of heels on the final day in Hilversum, earned Lafeber his maiden title in front of a thronging gallery in a glorious autumnal setting at one of the most traditional venues in The Netherlands.

When the experienced Dane, Søren Hansen, accelerated three strokes in front of him, Lafeber refused to be fazed and lifted the crowd to ecstatic heights with a display of calm, typical of winners. Showing hardly a flicker of stress, Lafeber began the process of rewriting the Dutch golfing history books.

Patience certainly did have to be observed at the start of the week as he trailed behind the early front-runners, Jamie Donaldson of Wales, Alastair Forsyth of Scotland and Ireland's Gary Murphy on Thursday and Fredrik Widmark of Sweden on Friday.

A glorious opening nine on Saturday, however, had the Sunday tabloid writers musing over the usual cliches: 'A Dutch Treat' and 'Flying Dutchman'. But a flying Lafeber stalled slightly over the back nine to allow in a 'Great Dane' by a stroke.

Unruffled by Hansen extending his lead early in the final round, Lafeber pressed on doggedly, trying to blot out the frenzy of the home fans. Then came the hole that changed the destiny of the 2003 Dutch Open title, the ninth, a wooded and potentially deadly tunnel through the russet leaves of the Hilversum forest.

Lafeber's ball refused to be drawn into the arborial trap. Hansen's toyed with the idea and just escaped its clutches off the tee but then embedded itself in the undergrowth when it dived into the forest on his second shot. As if grateful of the cover, it failed to break clear. The Dutch crowd's anticipation reached fever pitch. Their man went to the top at last, and there he would stay.

Just as Joop had Rühl-ed all those years ago, Dutch golf had a new crown prince.

Norman Dabell

final results

Hilversumsche Golf Club • Hilversum • The Netherlands
October 9 - 12 • 2003 • Par 70 • 6634 yards • 6067 metres

Pos.	Name		Rd1	Rd2	Rd3	Rd4	Total	Par	Prize Money Euro	£
1	Maarten LAFEBER	NL	67	69	64	67	267	-13	166,660.00	116,211.45
2	Søren HANSEN	Den	68	65	66	69	268	-12	86,855.00	60,563.69
	Mathias GRÖNBERG	Swe	70	66	67	65	268	-12	86,855.00	60,563.69
4	Steen TINNING	Den	66	67	69	68	270	-10	46,200.00	32,215.10
	Jamie DONALDSON	Wal	64	70	67	69	270	-10	46,200.00	32,215.10
6	Gary MURPHY	Ire	64	70	67	70	271	-9	30,000.00	20,918.90
	Gary EVANS	Eng	70	68	65	68	271	-9	30,000.00	20,918.90
	Alastair FORSYTH	Scot	64	72	68	67	271	-9	30,000.00	20,918.90
9	Kenneth FERRIE	Eng	70	67	68	67	272	-8	18,233.33	12,714.04
	Gary EMERSON	Eng	68	68	67	69	272	-8	18,233.33	12,714.04
	Miguel Angel JIMÉNEZ	Sp	69	69	68	66	272	-8	18,233.33	12,714.04
	Stephen DODD	Wal	67	70	68	67	272	-8	18,233.33	12,714.04
	Adam MEDNICK	Swe	68	67	73	64	272	-8	18,233.33	12,714.04
	Fredrik ANDERSSON	Swe	67	66	69	70	272	-8	18,233.33	12,714.04
15	Brian DAVIS	Eng	69	71	67	66	273	-7	14,100.00	9,831.88
	David CARTER	Eng	65	70	72	66	273	-7	14,100.00	9,831.88
	Simon DYSON	Eng	69	66	69	69	273	-7	14,100.00	9,831.88
18	Santiago LUNA	Sp	69	70	66	69	274	-6	11,537.50	8,045.06
	Mårten OLANDER	Swe	70	68	66	70	274	-6	11,537.50	8,045.06
	Steve WEBSTER	Eng	67	73	67	67	274	-6	11,537.50	8,045.06
	Jamie SPENCE	Eng	69	69	65	71	274	-6	11,537.50	8,045.06
	Pierre FULKE	Swe	68	69	72	65	274	-6	11,537.50	8,045.06
	Christian CÉVAËR	Fr	70	69	67	68	274	-6	11,537.50	8,045.06
	David LYNN	Eng	65	69	71	69	274	-6	11,537.50	8,045.06
	Markus BRIER	Aut	68	65	70	71	274	-6	11,537.50	8,045.06
26	Anthony WALL	Eng	67	70	68	70	275	-5	10,100.00	7,042.70
27	Mark ROE	Eng	67	72	67	70	276	-4	9,350.00	6,519.72
	Warren BENNETT	Eng	70	70	71	65	276	-4	9,350.00	6,519.72
	Gary ORR	Scot	71	67	68	70	276	-4	9,350.00	6,519.72
	Benn BARHAM	Eng	69	66	72	69	276	-4	9,350.00	6,519.72
31	Gordon BRAND JNR.	Scot	67	66	72	72	277	-3	7,900.00	5,508.64
	Malcolm MACKENZIE	Eng	68	70	68	71	277	-3	7,900.00	5,508.64
	Nicolas COLSAERTS	Bel	67	69	66	75	277	-3	7,900.00	5,508.64
	David PARK	Wal	68	67	67	75	277	-3	7,900.00	5,508.64
	Patrik SJÖLAND	Swe	67	71	70	69	277	-3	7,900.00	5,508.64
	Brad KENNEDY	Aus	68	71	69	69	277	-3	7,900.00	5,508.64
37	Andrew OLDCORN	Scot	71	67	74	66	278	-2	6,800.00	4,741.62
	Henrik STENSON	Swe	66	71	70	71	278	-2	6,800.00	4,741.62
	Ian GARBUTT	Eng	70	67	71	70	278	-2	6,800.00	4,741.62
	Andrew COLTART	Scot	69	70	71	68	278	-2	6,800.00	4,741.62
41	Costantino ROCCA	It	70	65	73	71	279	-1	5,500.00	3,835.13
	Ian WOOSNAM	Wal	70	70	72	67	279	-1	5,500.00	3,835.13
	Marc FARRY	Fr	70	70	69	70	279	-1	5,500.00	3,835.13
	Jean-Francois REMESY	Fr	71	68	67	73	279	-1	5,500.00	3,835.13
	Carlos RODILES	Sp	70	69	67	73	279	-1	5,500.00	3,835.13
	Peter HEDBLOM	Swe	70	68	71	70	279	-1	5,500.00	3,835.13
	Raymond RUSSELL	Scot	70	70	68	71	279	-1	5,500.00	3,835.13
	John BICKERTON	Eng	67	71	71	70	279	-1	5,500.00	3,835.13
	Tobias DIER	Ger	69	71	70	69	279	-1	5,500.00	3,835.13
50	Roger CHAPMAN	Eng	71	68	69	72	280	0	3,711.11	2,587.75
	Mark JAMES	Eng	67	72	70	71	280	0	3,711.11	2,587.75
	David HOWELL	Eng	70	69	70	71	280	0	3,711.11	2,587.75
	Barry LANE	Eng	69	71	69	71	280	0	3,711.11	2,587.75
	Andrew MARSHALL	Eng	68	67	73	72	280	0	3,711.11	2,587.75
	Robert KARLSSON	Swe	70	70	69	71	280	0	3,711.11	2,587.75
	Bradley DREDGE	Wal	67	70	68	75	280	0	3,711.11	2,587.75
	Stephen GALLACHER	Scot	72	68	71	69	280	0	3,711.11	2,587.75
	Richard STERNE	SA	71	65	69	75	280	0	3,711.11	2,587.75
59	Peter BAKER	Eng	67	72	70	72	281	1	2,600.00	1,812.97
	Paul EALES	Eng	69	65	72	75	281	1	2,600.00	1,812.97
	Jonathan LOMAS	Eng	67	72	73	69	281	1	2,600.00	1,812.97
	Rolf MUNTZ	NL	66	73	73	69	281	1	2,600.00	1,812.97
	Stephen SCAHILL	NZ	66	71	71	73	281	1	2,600.00	1,812.97
	Fredrik WIDMARK	Swe	65	66	75	75	281	1	2,600.00	1,812.97
	Martin MARITZ	SA	73	67	70	71	281	1	2,600.00	1,812.97
66	Simon WAKEFIELD	Eng	70	69	72	72	283	3	2,200.00	1,534.05
67	Tony JOHNSTONE	Zim	66	70	71	77	284	4	2,050.00	1,429.46
	Mark PILKINGTON	Wal	67	72	68	77	284	4	2,050.00	1,429.46
	Jan-Willem VAN HOOF (AM)	NL	74	65	73	72	284	4		
70	Søren KJELDSEN	Den	72	68	73	72	285	5	1,681.75	1,172.68
	Jean-François LUCQUIN	Fr	71	66	75	73	285	5	1,681.75	1,172.68
	Nicolas VANHOOTEGEM	Bel	67	71	75	72	285	5	1,681.75	1,172.68
	Nick DOUGHERTY	Eng	70	68	73	74	285	5	1,681.75	1,172.68
74	Inder VAN WEERELT	NL	70	70	74	72	286	6	1,494.00	1,041.76
75	Joost STEENKAMER	NL	67	72	73	76	288	8	1,491.00	1,039.67

HSBC World Match Play Championship Wentworth Club · Surrey · England

seventh heaven

Ernie Els

Champion - Ernie ELS SA
Runner-Up - Thomas BJÖRN Den

As weekends go, it was not a bad one for Ernie Els.

On Friday, he celebrated his 34th birthday with a two hole victory over fellow South African Tim Clark in the quarter-finals of the HSBC World Match Play Championship at Wentworth Club. On Saturday he celebrated being confirmed as winner of the Volvo Order of Merit for the first time with a 5 and 4 semi-final victory over old adversary Vijay Singh. And on Sunday, he celebrated a 4 and 3 victory in the 36 hole final over Denmark's Thomas Björn with a £1 million first prize, the largest ever in Europe or America.

the course

Just half an inch of rain had fallen on this corner of Surrey from the middle of July leaving the immaculately presented West Course playing, in the words of champion Ernie Els, "more like a links." The greens, running at 12.5 on the stimpmeter, also drew widespread praise.

Thomas Björn

The win, his seventh around the globe in 2003, saw Els move alongside his fellow South African Gary Player and Spain's Seve Ballesteros as a five time winner of the prestigious title.

Indeed it was Ballesteros, commenting on the final for BBC Television, who helped present the gleaming new Mark McCormack Trophy, in honour of the event's late founder figure, and who paid Els the ultimate accolade. "Ernie is simply fantastic," said the Spaniard. "He has more natural ability and talent than Tiger Woods. If he wants to be World Number One, he will be."

These were sentiments that stirred 'The Big Easy'. "Those are big words from one of my all time heroes," said the South African. "But I do now feel that I can take my game to a new level."

Certainly Els has few equals in the match play sphere at Wentworth Club, having collected his five titles in just ten years, during which time he has played 22 matches, winning 18 of them.

Highlight of his earlier rounds this year undoubtedly came in the semi-final against 1997 champion Singh. Four down after 15 holes, Els set a new World Match Play Championship record by winning eight holes in succession, the last three of the morning round and

Vijay Singh

Stephen Leaney

WENTWORTH, WHERE ELS?

Wentworth

WENTWORTH CLUB, WENTWORTH DRIVE, VIRGINIA WATER, SURREY GU25 4LS
WWW.WENTWORTHCLUB.COM

Fredrik Jacobson

His four iron tee shot at the 179 yard 14th arrowed for the flag, took one bounce and rolled into the cup to win the doughty Dane a gleaming £37,000 Toyota Land Cruiser to go with his not inconsiderable runners-up cheque of £400,000.

Björn, who immediately promised the vehicle to his faithful caddie Billy Foster, challenged Els with a smile to "follow that." Not surprisingly he did not manage the feat but at the next hole a curling 25 foot putt, one of many Els had sunk all week, finally settled an always good natured tussle between two close friends.

Their homes lie just 300 yards apart on the Wentworth Estate, their wives Liezl and Pernilla are friends, and their daughters Samantha and Filippa attend the same class at nursery school.

"Usually you want to go out there and get in a certain mood with an opponent," said Els. "But that's hard to do when your opponent is a close friend." Björn was quick to agree and added: "It's no shame to lose to such a great player."

John Whitbread

the first five of the afternoon, beating the seven hole sequence set by Tony Lema against Gary Player in 1965. In the process, Els turned the match on its head and gave himself the impetus to go on and win.

At the same time as Els was making imperious progress to the final through the top half of the draw, in the bottom half, Björn, who had never progressed more than one round in his three previous appearances, went about putting that record straight with a determined 4 and 3 first round win over American Len Mattiace, an excellent 5 and 4 dismissal of Masters Tournament Champion Mike Weir in the quarter-finals and a final green ousting of Open Golf Champion Ben Curtis in the semi-finals.

Although a fit man, Björn admitted that, perhaps, the demands of playing one more 36 hole match than Els over the course of the week had left him with just too few reserves in the tank to outgun the King of the Burma Road in the final.

The Dane was never in front and when Els went six up at the 29th it seemed the end would come quickly. Even when Björn won the 30th with a superb eagle three, it seemed only to be delaying the inevitable. As it turned out, that was the case, but not before Björn produced a moment of pure magic to thrill the thousands of spectators and the millions watching on television.

final results

Wentworth Club · Surrey · England
October 16 - 19 · 2003 · Par 72 · 7072 yards · 6468 metres

FIRST ROUND		Euro	£
Tim Clark (SA) (9) beat Stephen Leaney (Aus) (8)	3 and 2	105,744	75,000
Vijay Singh (Fij) (5) beat Alex Cejka (Ger) (12)	8 and 7	105,744	75,000
Chad Campbell (USA) (6) beat Fredrik Jacobson (Swe) (11)	6 and 5	105,744	75,000
Thomas Björn (Den) (10) beat Len Mattiace (USA) (7)	4 and 3	105,744	75,000
		422,976	300,000
QUARTER-FINALS			
Ernie Els (SA) (1) beat Tim Clark	2 holes	126,892	90,000
Vijay Singh beat Shaun Micheel (USA) (4)	at the 38th hole	126,892	90,000
Ben Curtis (USA) (3) beat Chad Campbell	5 and 3	126,892	90,000
Thomas Björn beat Mike Weir (Can) (2)	5 and 4	126,892	90,000
		507,568	360,000
SEMI-FINALS			
Ernie Els beat Vijay Singh	5 and 4	169,190	120,000
Thomas Björn beat Ben Curtis	2 holes	169,190	120,000
		338,380	240,000
FINAL			
Ernie Els beat	4 and 3	1,409,920	1,000,000
Thomas Björn		563,968	400,000
		1,973,888	1,400,000
Figures in brackets indicate seeding			
Exchange Rate: £1 = 1.40992 euro	Total:	3,242,812	2,300,000

simply a genius

t was the dream assignment: three weeks filming Mark McCormack in planes and limos, at his homes and offices in Cleveland, New York, Orlando and London, for a one-hour TV documentary. "Film anything you like," said the man acknowledged worldwide as The Most Powerful Figure in Sport. "I have nothing to hide."

So we did, almost to the point of vulgar intrusion. There was the amazing wall in his Cleveland office covered from ceiling to floor with the room keys from hotels in which he had stayed. "I had to give that up," he said ruefully, "when I was eventually accused of theft." In the dressing room of one of his homes there were 34 cashmere jackets, immaculately spaced. Alongside his four sets of golf clubs stood a tall wicker basket containing at least 2,000 tee-pegs.

We recognised a compulsive accumulator, confirmed when he showed us his pocket book. It recorded every mile he travelled, every hour he slept. These were few - on average four a night - for he started work every day at 4.30am.

Throughout those three weeks I kept one question up my sleeve for the final interview which I felt sure would floor the man unkindly known to his jealous detractors as Mark the Shark. It concerned the annual World Match Play Championship at Wentworth Club in Surrey, England.

"Mark", I said, "here's a tournament in which you make money out of the sponsors, the television rights and the players, most of whom are your clients. You even commentate on it for the BBC. Isn't this what is known as the unacceptable face of monopoly?" Devastating question, or what ?

McCormack considered it for all of two seconds. "Do you enjoy it ?" he asked. I replied that I did.

"Well," he said, "if I hadn't invented it, it wouldn't be there."

It was worth being flattened because it was while making this documentary that I met Sarah, his first personal assistant when he opened his London office with a staff of four in 1966. We have now been married for 23 years. At the time of his shocking death at the age of 72 in May 2003 his International Management Group and its television arm, Transworld International, had 80 offices in 32 countries. It was literally a business empire on which the sun never set.

I say his death was shocking with good reason. In January he was given a clean bill of health after his regular check-up at the Mayo Clinic. Shortly afterwards he had minor surgery for the cosmetic removal of a small blemish on his cheek. Under anaesthetic he went into a coma from which he never emerged.

There were memorial celebrations of his remarkable life in New York and at Hampton Court Palace, outside London, following its summer music festival, another of Mark's inventions. The theme at both was loyalty: Mark's loyalty to his clients and employees and, mostly, their reciprocated loyalty to him.

Never was this better illustrated than the deal which launched his career. After Yale and a stint in the US Army, he found himself stifled in a law firm which promised little more than a lingering death. His true interest was golf. He was a fine amateur player but conceded he was always two strokes short of turning professional. Then he met Arnold Palmer, the game's most charismatic player in the late 50s and early 60s.

Palmer was earning peanuts. "Let me handle your business affairs," said McCormack. They shook hands on the deal. Within a year Palmer's income from endorsements and business deals had vaulted by 100 per cent. Today, long after his last tournament victory, he is still reputed to make ten million dollars a year. There was never a written contract. It became the most famous handshake in the history of sport.

Within a year Jack Nicklaus and Gary Player had joined the circus with Palmer to become The Big Three. Mark didn't come cheap. His cut was mostly 25 per cent of prize money and endorsement earnings but since they were all piling money into the bank, no-one complained.

Reputation established, Mark then spread his wings: Rod Laver in tennis, Jackie Stewart in motor racing, Jean-Claude Killy in skiing and eventually persuading stolid institutions like the Royal and Ancient Golf Club and Wimbledon that they were missing out on millions in marketing, sponsorship and hospitality deals. Patiently, in face of plenty of antediluvian suspicion, he won them over.

Barley able to distinguish a Beethoven concerto from a Mozart opera, he then turned to music, recruiting many of the world's finest orchestras and soloists to his stable. Two of them, Kiri Te Kanawa and José Carreras, sang to his memory at the Hampton Court celebration.

Mark McCormack's impact on sport was incomparable. "I have always told anyone who had dealings with him," said Ken Schofield, Executive Director of The European Tour, "that his word is his bond. As anything on paper."

I deeply regret the premature death of the man I met making that TV documentary more than 20 years ago. There is one abiding memory: the night he invited my wife and myself to join him for dinner at a Mexican restaurant in New York.

It threatened to be a disaster because I detest Mexican food and Mark, without a business deal over the table, could look as distracted as the Dali Lama at prayers.

Thus, since I had no business deal to offer, I was delighted but surprised when he announced that we would have a drinking contest. Something that evening had to be competitive. Mark chose Margaritas, I chose equally lethal dry martinis. I fancied my chances because Mark was never a big drinker and I had had many years training in the bars of Fleet Street.

After two each we were mutually happy. After three I felt the words slipping out sideways. Half way down the fourth one I was within a trice of admitting defeat when Mark stood bolt upright and without a word walked out of the restaurant. He never mentioned the episode afterwards. Mark McCormack, I'd discovered, was actually human.

He transformed sport globally by the shrewd exploitation of exceptional talent. Behind the scenes he had helped many who had fallen on hard times. He wasn't a paragon, simply a genius.

Tribute by Ken Schofield CBE
Executive Director of The European Tour

"Mark McCormack's legacy is international sport as we know it. I would not go as far to say that without Mark McCormack golf and tennis would not have developed as international sports - Mark would not have expected that - but the reality is that they would not have developed as quickly and efficiently without him. He saw the bigger picture for his company and his athletes and I can think of no greater tribute.

"Just a matter of months before I succeeded John Jacobs as Executive Director of The European Tour on January 1, 1975, John, who gave me so much wonderful advice, suggested that I should meet Mark McCormack as soon as possible.

"John said I would find him extremely challenging and very dominating in that he would argue for what he believed in and in what he wants, but to argue how I saw things with Mark in the room because when he made an agreement it would never be broken. John was right. It never was.

"Mark would drive the ultimate bargain because I think he started with the ultimate drawing card in Arnold, before very quickly adding Gary and Jack to form the 'Big Three'. I feel he is rightly credited with making athletes worthy of their hire, and, in the case of Arnold, for playing a large part in driving, making and aiding the image of a guy who was a combination of Dwight D Eisenhower and John Wayne!

"He was both intuitive and calculating in business, in that he followed his instincts, but at the same time had the ability to calculate the odds and make sure that the table was stacked in his favour.

"His sheer force of presence was, certainly for me, very inspiring. The name and reputation went before him and he was no disappointment in reality. He was larger than life, an icon in our lives."

Mark McCormack and Nick Faldo

José Maria Olazábal and Miguel Angel Jiménez

tale of the unexpected

One of golf's most seductive traits is its ability to throw up the unexpected. Human nature means that we rarely predict the unpredictable, no matter how many times we are shocked by the live theatre of professional sport – allowing most observers to feel that unique sense of surprised confusion every time the unexpected occurs before us.

In 2003, the great game of golf threw up one of the most unbelievable tales in its illustrious history. No one expected the unheralded Ben Curtis to capture the 132nd Open Golf Championship at Royal St George's, but the image will live long in the memories of golf fans from all corners of the globe who watched the American lift the Claret Jug on the south east coast of England.

By the same token, those who were there to bear witness to Miguel Angel Jiménez's victory in the inaugural Turespaña Mallorca Classic, the third dual ranking event between The European Tour and the Challenge Tour in 2003, left the delightful Pula Golf Club with that same mixture of excitement and confusion that leaves its mark on the mind of any sports fan when events take an unforeseen turn.

The spectators had been frustrated by the lightning and rain storms that engulfed Mallorca, reducing the tournament to 54 holes, but they were to be equally stimulated by the events on the testing 6,568 yard course that led to the tournament's thrilling climax.

Even Jiménez himself was startled. Like Curtis on the last day in Kent, the Spaniard posted a clubhouse total, that was eventually to prove the winning aggregate, long before the tournament was over.

Jiménez started the final round on one under par 139 in a tie for 25th place, five strokes behind leader David Park, of Wales, who was playing alongside Ireland's Damien McGrane, and the man who would finally provide that element of surprise, José Maria Olazábal.

Olazábal, twice a winner of the Masters Tournament, picked up three birdies in his first 11 holes to move to eight under par and into what looked like a comfortable lead. But, just as Jiménez appeared in the clubhouse showered and changed in preparation to

Jamie Spence

the course

All players were tested by the tight fairways and small, undulating greens of Pula Golf Club, which more than compensated for the lack of length on the 6568 yard, par 70 layout.

James Hepworth

receive second prize for his six under par total of 204, the unexpected happened.

Olazábal put his tee shot out of bounds on the 17th and made double bogey six, dropping him back level with Jiménez with the tough 203 yard par three, 18th to play. He found the putting surface at the last, but an awkward position meant he had to chip instead of putt the ball over the undulating green, leaving himself a tricky 12 foot par effort back towards the hole. He knew he had to hole to force a play-off with his compatriot, but could only watch the ball slide agonisingly wide of the cup.

So Jiménez collected the trophy and his seventh European Tour International Schedule victory in his 350th Tour event. His last victory had come in the 1999 Volvo Masters Andalucia, and he was as delighted as he was surprised to take the plaudits again.

"I'm obviously very happy to have won," he said after the biggest final round comeback by any of the champions on The 2003 European Tour. "But it was a surprise to me. I had finished my round and had gotten changed because José Maria, eight under at one point, had been solid all week.

Stuart Little

"But, after I had changed, the Tournament Director told me of the situation and I went to get ready for a play-off. I thought there would at least be a play-off, but that is golf for you – you never know what to expect."

Indeed.

Jiménez had gone out for the final round and was rewarded for his strategic aggression. The 39 year old from Malaga picked up final round birdies at the par four fifth and seventh holes on his way to the turn in 33, before four birdies in six holes - between the 11th and 16th - rendered his solitary bogey on the 17th insignificant to his ultimately successful quest for first place.

For Olazábal, there was obvious disappointment, but the 37 year old Spaniard was heartened by his superb play throughout the week and the collection of valuable Ryder Cup points. For the watching galleries, however, it was another sporting moment when the unexpected took place, leaving an indelible mark on a highly successful week.

Michael Gibbons

final results

Pula Golf Club · Mallorca · Spain
October 16 - 19 · 2003 · Par 70 · 6568 yards · 6006 metres

Pos.	Name		Rd1	Rd2	Rd3	Rd4	Total	Par	Prize Money Euro	£
1	Miguel Angel JIMÉNEZ	Sp	72	67	65		204	-6	66,660.00	47,279.28
2	José Maria OLAZÁBAL	Sp	66	69	70		205	-5	44,440.00	31,519.52
3	Jamie SPENCE	Eng	71	66	69		206	-4	22,520.00	15,972.54
	Gary EMERSON	Eng	73	64	69		206	-4	22,520.00	15,972.54
5	Paul BROADHURST	Eng	68	70	69		207	-3	12,384.00	8,783.48
	Tomas Jesus MUÑOZ	Sp	72	66	69		207	-3	12,384.00	8,783.48
	Simon KHAN	Eng	69	72	66		207	-3	12,384.00	8,783.48
	James HEPWORTH	Eng	70	67	70		207	-3	12,384.00	8,783.48
	Benn BARHAM	Eng	68	68	71		207	-3	12,384.00	8,783.48
10	Miguel Angel MARTIN	Sp	70	67	71		208	-2	6,960.00	4,936.45
	Klas ERIKSSON	Swe	74	65	69		208	-2	6,960.00	4,936.45
	José Manuel LARA	Sp	69	68	71		208	-2	6,960.00	4,936.45
	Maarten LAFEBER	NL	68	68	72		208	-2	6,960.00	4,936.45
	Marcel SIEM	Ger	68	68	72		208	-2	6,960.00	4,936.45
15	Mark FOSTER	Eng	69	68	72		209	-1	5,211.43	3,696.26
	José Manuel CARRILES	Sp	68	68	73		209	-1	5,211.43	3,696.26
	Mattias ELIASSON	Swe	74	69	66		209	-1	5,211.43	3,696.26
	Damien MCGRANE	Ire	64	71	74		209	-1	5,211.43	3,696.26
	Jonathan LOMAS	Eng	71	69	69		209	-1	5,211.43	3,696.26
	Gustavo ROJAS	Arg	68	70	71		209	-1	5,211.43	3,696.26
	David CARTER	Eng	71	70	68		209	-1	5,211.43	3,696.26
22	Andrew MARSHALL	Eng	73	70	67		210	0	4,280.00	3,035.63
	Ricardo GONZALEZ	Arg	70	66	74		210	0	4,280.00	3,035.63
	Sion E BEBB	Wal	68	69	73		210	0	4,280.00	3,035.63
	Markus BRIER	Aut	71	66	73		210	0	4,280.00	3,035.63
	Michael JONZON	Swe	67	71	72		210	0	4,280.00	3,035.63
27	Euan LITTLE	Scot	72	70	69		211	1	3,620.00	2,567.52
	Charlie WI	Kor	71	66	74		211	1	3,620.00	2,567.52
	David PARK	Wal	70	64	77		211	1	3,620.00	2,567.52
	Francois DELAMONTAGNE	Fr	70	69	72		211	1	3,620.00	2,567.52
	Simon DYSON	Eng	72	69	70		211	1	3,620.00	2,567.52
	Jamie ELSON	Eng	73	70	68		211	1	3,620.00	2,567.52
33	Santiago LUNA	Sp	68	75	69		212	2	2,885.00	2,046.22
	Titch MOORE	SA	72	69	71		212	2	2,885.00	2,046.22
	Henrik STENSON	Swe	68	68	76		212	2	2,885.00	2,046.22
	Fernando ROCA	Sp	71	71	70		212	2	2,885.00	2,046.22
	Christian CÉVAËR	Fr	71	71	70		212	2	2,885.00	2,046.22
	Lee S JAMES	Eng	71	70	71		212	2	2,885.00	2,046.22
	Michael KIRK	SA	70	71	71		212	2	2,885.00	2,046.22
	Louis OOSTHUIZEN	SA	71	67	74		212	2	2,885.00	2,046.22
41	Marc FARRY	Fr	75	68	70		213	3	2,320.00	1,645.48
	Jan-Are LARSEN	Nor	72	71	70		213	3	2,320.00	1,645.48
	Eduardo DE LA RIVA	Sp	69	73	71		213	3	2,320.00	1,645.48
	Gary CLARK	Eng	69	74	70		213	3	2,320.00	1,645.48
	Patrik SJÖLAND	Swe	71	68	74		213	3	2,320.00	1,645.48
	Mads VIBE-HASTRUP	Den	71	71	71		213	3	2,320.00	1,645.48
47	José RIVERO	Sp	73	70	71		214	4	1,720.00	1,219.93
	Shaun P WEBSTER	Eng	71	70	73		214	4	1,720.00	1,219.93
	Paul EALES	Eng	71	71	72		214	4	1,720.00	1,219.93
	Jorge BERENDT	Arg	72	69	73		214	4	1,720.00	1,219.93
	James KINGSTON	SA	72	68	74		214	4	1,720.00	1,219.93
	Simon HURD	Eng	69	73	72		214	4	1,720.00	1,219.93
	Matthew BLACKEY	Eng	68	72	74		214	4	1,720.00	1,219.93
	Lee WESTWOOD	Eng	72	69	73		214	4	1,720.00	1,219.93
	Fredrik WIDMARK	Swe	72	69	73		214	4	1,720.00	1,219.93
56	Mark MOULAND	Wal	72	69	74		215	5	1,124.44	797.52
	Alvaro SALTO	Sp	72	70	73		215	5	1,124.44	797.52
	Warren BENNETT	Eng	71	66	78		215	5	1,124.44	797.52
	Stuart LITTLE	Eng	67	72	76		215	5	1,124.44	797.52
	Jean-François LUCQUIN	Fr	70	70	75		215	5	1,124.44	797.52
	Olivier DAVID	Fr	72	70	73		215	5	1,124.44	797.52
	David J GEALL	Eng	76	67	72		215	5	1,124.44	797.52
	Christopher HANELL	Swe	69	71	75		215	5	1,124.44	797.52
	Ben MASON	Eng	69	74	72		215	5	1,124.44	797.52
65	Roger CHAPMAN	Eng	77	66	73		216	6	823.33	583.96
	Scott DRUMMOND	Scot	68	72	76		216	6	823.33	583.96
	Michael ARCHER	Eng	73	70	73		216	6	823.33	583.96
	Jesus Maria ARRUTI	Sp	73	69	74		216	6	823.33	583.96
	David DRYSDALE	Scot	70	71	75		216	6	823.33	583.96
	Matthew CORT	Eng	73	70	73		216	6	823.33	583.96
71	Adam MEDNICK	Swe	71	72	74		217	7	598.50	424.49
	Martin LEMESURIER	Eng	68	72	77		217	7	598.50	424.49
73	Sam WALKER	Eng	70	70	78		218	8	594.00	421.30
74	Johan EDFORS	Swe	75	68	77		220	10	591.00	419.17
75	Mark PILKINGTON	Wal	71	71	79		221	11	588.00	417.04
76	Didier DE VOOGHT	Bel	66	74	83		223	13	585.00	414.92

Ricardo Gonzalez

question and answer

With Ernie Els already installed as 'el numero uno', the fight for top Volvo Order of Merit honours was already over but there were still many battles to be won and lost in the Telefonica Open de Madrid.

Could Padraig Harrington, Ian Poulter or Lee Westwood – all multiple winners on The 2003 European Tour International Schedule – close on Darren Clarke, who was not playing, in the chase for second place behind Els?

Would anyone force his way out of the pack into the Volvo Order of Merit top 60 to snatch a coveted place in the end-of-term Volvo Masters Andalucia the following week at Valderrama?

Who would emerge successful in the last ditch scramble for Tour playing privileges for 2004?

Could Sandy Lyle, winner of the 1985 Open Golf Championship and the 1988 Masters Tournament, win enough prize money to preserve his exempt status through The European Tour Career Official Earnings table?

Who would join the four Official World Ranking qualifiers in this last counting event to complete the Continental Europe and Great Britain and Ireland teams to contest The Seve Trophy at Campo de Golf Parador El Saler in Valencia a fortnight later?

Would Denmark's Steen Tinning repeat his 2002 victory in Madrid and delay his retirement from tournament golf for one more week?

Questions aplenty on day one at Club de Campo with its spectacular Royal Palace backdrop.

Poulter (wrist strain) and Westwood (stiff neck) bowed out of the race to close on Clarke with last day retirements, but Harrington continued his 'love affair' with the course.

It was at Club de Campo that he triumphed for the first time on The European Tour, winning the 1996 Open de España, and to where he returned four years later to win the Masters de Madrid.

Now, as he took the lead on the final afternoon with a birdie at the 14th, the Irishman appeared poised to keep the pressure on Ulsterman Clarke for that second place. This he would have achieved if birdie putts of six feet and 15 feet had disappeared at the 17th and 18th respectively.

Harrington, however, was compelled to rue the ones that got away

Paul Lawrie

for as Argentina's Ricardo Gonzalez swooped past him to secure the title so Harrington found himself sharing second place with England's Paul Casey, Australia's Nick O'Hern and Sweden's Mårten Olander. Instead of winning the 233,330 euro (£162,288) first prize, Harrington collected 93,137 euro (£64,780) and the absent Clarke knew as he prepared for the Volvo Masters Andalucia that he would finish second in the Volvo Order of Merit for a third time in his career.

Meanwhile Gonzalez had earned himself another week in Spain. The Argentinian had celebrated his 34th birthday two days late by coming from 11 shots behind Casey at the halfway stage, and from six behind entering the final round. So with his first win on The European Tour since the 2001 Omega European Masters, Gonzalez lifted himself from 87th to 46th in the Volvo Order of Merit. He had secured his place in the Volvo Masters Andalucia at Valderrama.

Sergio Garcia, who opened with a 64 and closed with a 67 to tie sixth three behind Gonzalez, Ireland's Gary Murphy and Denmark's Anders Hansen hung on to their Valderrama spots – the last two by the skin of their teeth – but although Iain Pyman did not have the Volvo Masters Andalucia in his sights, he, too, had good reason to celebrate.

the course

The great Javier Arana laid out the course in the sweeping, plunging wooded hillside acres of Club de Campo where Max Faulkner won the Spanish Open in 1957. The steeply downhill first and steeply uphill 18th are feature holes on a course affording dramatic views of the Spanish capital.

Robert Karlsson

Yorkshireman Pyman had missed the cut. He had started the tournament in 117th place in the Volvo Order of Merit, and that is where he finished. The top 115 Members plus affiliate Members earn Category 7 Membership for the following year, and with both Luke Donald and Robert Rock, in 115th and 116th places respectively, the final card for 2004 went to the player in 117th place – Iain Pyman.

Veteran Scot Lyle teed off 144th in the table and pinned his hopes on finishing in the top 40 in the Career Official Earnings table, but he was sadly forced to retire with flu during round two.

Seve Ballesteros, as Captain for Continental Europe in The Seve Trophy, welcomed compatriots Miguel Angel Jiménez and José Maria Olazábal on to his team to take on Colin Montgomerie's Great Britain and Ireland team.

Jiménez, who had finished 20th, overtook Swede Mathias Grönberg and Dane Søren Kjeldsen as the last Order of Merit qualifier while Olazábal, who followed his second place to Jiménez in Mallorca with joint 13th in Madrid after a closing 67, was Seve's 'wild card' choice.

Peter Fowler

Alistair Forsyth finished with a brave 66 to tie 15th in the championship but could not catch David Howell or Brian Davis. So Davis claimed the last qualifying spot, and Howell was left on standby to replace Clarke. Montgomerie went for 1999 Open Champion Paul Lawrie, who battled to joint sixth in Madrid, as his Captain's pick.

Defending champion Tinning's opening 68 hinted an action-replay could be on the cards but he took 79 the next day and confirmed persistent back trouble would sadly force him on to the sidelines.

So, the questions had been unanswered, in a fascinating denouement that provided the enthusiastic spectators with much to enjoy, but as for many the curtain came down on The 2003 European Tour International Schedule so for the champion Gonzalez the play went on for another week with that late place in the Volvo Masters Andalucia.

Gordon Richardson

final results

Club de Campo · Madrid · Spain
October 23 - 26 · 2003 · Par 71 · 6967 yards · 6371 metres

Pos.	Name		Rd1	Rd2	Rd3	Rd4	Total	Par	Prize Money Euro	£
1	Ricardo GONZALEZ	Arg	69	70	66	65	270	-14	233,330.00	162,288.30
2	Padraig HARRINGTON	Ire	65	73	68	65	271	-13	93,137.50	64,780.04
	Mårten OLANDER	Swe	69	65	70	67	271	-13	93,137.50	64,780.04
	Nick O'HERN	Aus	67	67	69	68	271	-13	93,137.50	64,780.04
	Paul CASEY	Eng	63	65	71	72	271	-13	93,137.50	64,780.04
6	Peter FOWLER	Aus	67	66	70	70	273	-11	39,340.00	27,362.20
	Sergio GARCIA	Sp	64	71	71	67	273	-11	39,340.00	27,362.20
	Paul LAWRIE	Scot	69	64	70	70	273	-11	39,340.00	27,362.20
	Matthew BLACKEY	Eng	70	70	68	65	273	-11	39,340.00	27,362.20
10	Pierre FULKE	Swe	71	65	70	68	274	-10	26,880.00	18,695.88
	Adam SCOTT	Aus	72	69	68	65	274	-10	26,880.00	18,695.88
	Gonzalo FERNANDEZ-CASTANO (AM)	Sp	67	70	70	67	274	-10		
13	José Maria OLAZÁBAL	Sp	70	68	70	67	275	-9	23,310.00	16,212.83
	Patrik SJÖLAND	Swe	69	70	69	67	275	-9	23,310.00	16,212.83
15	Anders HANSEN	Den	71	67	70	68	276	-8	19,740.00	13,729.79
	Jarrod MOSELEY	Aus	70	69	68	69	276	-8	19,740.00	13,729.79
	Greg OWEN	Eng	72	66	71	67	276	-8	19,740.00	13,729.79
	Niclas FASTH	Swe	71	71	69	65	276	-8	19,740.00	13,729.79
	Alastair FORSYTH	Scot	70	71	69	66	276	-8	19,740.00	13,729.79
20	Brian DAVIS	Eng	70	68	70	69	277	-7	16,100.00	11,198.05
	Maarten LAFEBER	NL	69	67	69	72	277	-7	16,100.00	11,198.05
	Thomas LEVET	Fr	66	71	72	68	277	-7	16,100.00	11,198.05
	Miguel Angel JIMÉNEZ	Sp	70	67	71	69	277	-7	16,100.00	11,198.05
	Robert KARLSSON	Swe	65	67	74	71	277	-7	16,100.00	11,198.05
	Andrew COLTART	Scot	69	68	68	72	277	-7	16,100.00	11,198.05
26	José Manuel LARA	Sp	69	70	72	67	278	-6	13,090.00	9,104.50
	Jamie SPENCE	Eng	71	70	70	67	278	-6	13,090.00	9,104.50
	Carlos RODILES	Sp	72	70	68	68	278	-6	13,090.00	9,104.50
	Gregory HAVRET	Fr	67	70	70	71	278	-6	13,090.00	9,104.50
	Ignacio GARRIDO	Sp	68	71	68	71	278	-6	13,090.00	9,104.50
	Bradley DREDGE	Wal	69	71	68	70	278	-6	13,090.00	9,104.50
	David PARK	Wal	74	63	73	68	278	-6	13,090.00	9,104.50
	Stephen GALLACHER	Scot	69	64	72	73	278	-6	13,090.00	9,104.50
34	Andrew OLDCORN	Scot	71	69	68	71	279	-5	10,826.67	7,530.29
	Klas ERIKSSON	Swe	71	70	69	69	279	-5	10,826.67	7,530.29
	Stephen DODD	Wal	68	73	69	69	279	-5	10,826.67	7,530.29
37	Jean-Francois REMESY	Fr	71	71	70	68	280	-4	9,660.00	6,718.83
	Raphaël JACQUELIN	Fr	71	68	71	70	280	-4	9,660.00	6,718.83
	Christian CÉVAËR	Fr	76	66	69	69	280	-4	9,660.00	6,718.83
	Angel CABRERA	Arg	67	68	71	74	280	-4	9,660.00	6,718.83
	David LYNN	Eng	73	69	68	70	280	-4	9,660.00	6,718.83
42	Miguel Angel MARTIN	Sp	69	70	68	74	281	-3	7,980.00	5,550.34
	Ian WOOSNAM	Wal	68	72	70	71	281	-3	7,980.00	5,550.34
	David HOWELL	Eng	71	69	70	71	281	-3	7,980.00	5,550.34
	Jesus Maria ARRUTI	Sp	71	68	74	68	281	-3	7,980.00	5,550.34
	Miles TUNNICLIFF	Eng	67	70	73	71	281	-3	7,980.00	5,550.34
	Simon DYSON	Eng	74	66	72	69	281	-3	7,980.00	5,550.34
	Martin MARITZ	SA	69	70	70	72	281	-3	7,980.00	5,550.34
49	Warren BENNETT	Eng	69	71	72	70	282	-2	6,580.00	4,576.60
	Barry LANE	Eng	67	74	69	72	282	-2	6,580.00	4,576.60
	Gary ORR	Scot	72	67	72	71	282	-2	6,580.00	4,576.60
52	Mark ROE	Eng	68	74	72	69	283	-1	5,320.00	3,700.23
	Kenneth FERRIE	Eng	72	66	70	75	283	-1	5,320.00	3,700.23
	Richard BLAND	Eng	71	69	70	73	283	-1	5,320.00	3,700.23
	Søren HANSEN	Den	69	70	74	70	283	-1	5,320.00	3,700.23
	Peter O'MALLEY	Aus	70	68	74	71	283	-1	5,320.00	3,700.23
	David DRYSDALE	Scot	72	69	70	72	283	-1	5,320.00	3,700.23
58	Santiago LUNA	Sp	71	71	71	71	284	0	4,130.00	2,872.54
	Jean-François LUCQUIN	Fr	72	70	73	69	284	0	4,130.00	2,872.54
	Rolf MUNTZ	NL	71	68	73	72	284	0	4,130.00	2,872.54
	Jarmo SANDELIN	Swe	67	73	72	72	284	0	4,130.00	2,872.54
62	Søren KJELDSEN	Den	69	69	74	73	285	1	3,780.00	2,629.11
63	Eduardo DE LA RIVA	Sp	73	69	73	71	286	2	3,570.00	2,483.05
	Nick DOUGHERTY	Eng	69	71	72	74	286	2	3,570.00	2,483.05
65	Gary MURPHY	Ire	71	68	74	74	287	3	3,360.00	2,336.98
66	Costantino ROCCA	It	75	67	71	76	289	5	3,150.00	2,190.92
	Gary EMERSON	Eng	74	68	75	72	289	5	3,150.00	2,190.92
68	Carlos BALMASEDA SANCHEZ	Sp	72	69	71	78	290	6	2,940.00	2,044.86
69	Raymond RUSSELL	Scot	71	70	74	76	291	7	2,800.00	1,947.49
	Mikko ILONEN	Fin	73	68	75	75	291	7	2,800.00	1,947.49
71	Ian POULTER	Eng	72	70	76	W/D	218	5	1,280.00	890.28
	Lee WESTWOOD	Eng	68	68	77	RETD	213	0	1,280.00	890.28

Volvo Masters Andalucia Club de Golf Valderrama · Sotogrande · Spain

burgeoning ambition

Fredrik Jacobson

1	Fredrik JACOBSON	Swe	276	-12
2	Carlos RODILES	Sp	276	-12
3	Brian DAVIS	Eng	279	-9
4	John BICKERTON	Eng	282	-6
5	Stephen LEANEY	Aus	284	-4
	Greg OWEN	Eng	284	-4
7	Michael CAMPBELL	NZ	286	-2
	Sergio GARCIA	Sp	286	-2
9	Ian POULTER	Eng	287	-1
10	Colin MONTGOMERIE	Scot	288	0
	José Maria OLAZÁBAL	Sp	288	0
	Adam SCOTT	Aus	288	0

Determination to succeed and better himself has always been a feature of Fredrik Jacobson's life. Aged ten, he picked up his first set of golf clubs, was given a handicap of 40, and set himself the target of getting down to single figures; within five years, he had surpassed that and was a scratch player.

Therefore when he stood on the threshold of The 2003 European Tour International Schedule with a sizeable wish list, it was no surprise that each and every item revealed something more about his burgeoning ambition as a professional golfer.

"At the start of the year, I wanted to make the top 50 in the world," said the 29 year Swede. "I also wanted to be in the top 15 in Europe, have two wins and score under 63."

Come the end of the season, just as in his formative years, each and every one had been eclipsed in considerable style.

Prior to his maiden victory in the Omega Hong Kong Open he was 107th on the Official World Golf Ranking. After adding the Algarve Open de Portugal in April - following a ten week lay-off with a wrist injury - he came to the Volvo Masters Andalucia in 41st position. By winning it in dramatic fashion at Club de Golf Valderrama, Jacobson leapt to 19th.

As far as the Volvo Order of Merit was concerned, the achievement was just as meritorious. After ending the 2002 campaign in 30th place, his triumph in southern Spain saw him sweep to fourth place

behind Ernie Els, Darren Clarke and Padraig Harrington with hugely impressive winnings of 1,521,302 euro (£1,060,666). Terrific company to keep indeed.

In the process, he also carved himself a niche in golf's record books. Not only did his fourth place finish on the Volvo Order of Merit equal the highest placed finish by a Swedish player in the history of The European Tour, namely Anders Forsbrand's fourth place finish in 1992, his trio of successes, eclipsing the target of two he had set, saw him become the first Swedish golfer to win three official events in the same season.

All that was left was the desire to post his lowest round as a professional, his previous best being the eight under par 63 he carded in the 2000 Murphy's Irish Open and which he matched with a six under par 63 on his way to victory in Hong Kong.

Not only did Jacobson better the mark, he smashed his personal best with a stunning performance in the opening round of the Linde German Masters at Gut Lärchenhof in September, ten birdies and an eagle seeing him become only the tenth player in history to score 60 in official European Tour competition.

Barry Lane

Volvo Masters Andalucia Club de Golf Valderrama · Sotogrande · Spain

the course

Consistently voted continental Europe's top course, Valderrama is one of golf's sternest tests. Always in immaculate condition, it places a premium on accuracy and stretches even the best players like few others.

The next target for the Swede is Major Championship success and the former ice hockey player broke the ice in spectacular fashion in his debut in the US Open Championship at Olympia Fields Country Club in June where he tied for fifth. A month later and a tie for sixth place in the 132nd Open Golf Championship at Royal St George's suggested that his next wish could be about to be attained too.

Not a bad year's work, all in all, for someone who had waited 161 events for his first victory and had six runners-up finishes along the way. But, boy, how he had to work for his third title.

The record books will show that he became the first wire-to-wire winner in the history of the Volvo Masters Andalucia. But there was abundant drama before he added his name to the illustrious list of winners of an event open to the leading 60 on the 2003 Volvo Order of Merit.

From the time Jacobson and the gallant Spaniard Carlos Rodiles occupied first and second place at the halfway stage, the contest for the main spoils developed into an intriguing and exhilarating head-to-head battle between the pair.

Not that theirs was the only performance of note. Far from it. Before the thrilling denouement, the final round was illuminated by Brian Davis whose closing 66 was the best score of the day, elevating the

Carlos Rodiles

29 year old Englishman to third place, and bringing a thoroughly satisfying end to a season which yielded 11 top ten finishes in total, including four in a row from mid March to mid May.

As Davis finished out his tournament, in the match behind, the leading duo approached Valderrama's final two holes, the Swede one stroke in front of his Spanish rival. However a double bogey seven for Jacobson at the 17th, after his pitch rolled back into the water, allied to Rodiles's birdie four produced a three shot swing.

Two ahead with one to play is never safe at Valderrama, however, especially when your opponent produces the shot of the tournament. With Rodiles in the trees and on his way to a bogey five, Jacobson ensured extra time with a majestic nine iron from 151 yards to two feet for a brilliant birdie three.

Having played the last 54 holes in regulation together, the pair set off in tandem for even more, Rodiles making his debut in the nerve-wracking realm of the play-off, while Jacobson's two previous experiences - in the 1998 Belgacom Open and The 2002 Barclays Scottish Open - had both ended in defeat.

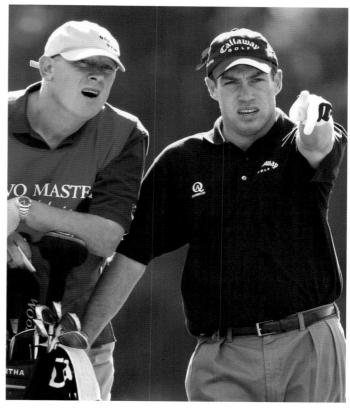

Brian Davis

Thomas Björn

Angel Cabrera

final results

Club de Golf Valderrama • Sotogrande • Spain
October 30 - November 2 • 2003 • Par 72 • 7006 yards • 6406 metres

Pos.	Name		Rd1	Rd2	Rd3	Rd4	Total	Par	Prize Money Euro	£
1	Fredrik JACOBSON	Swe	64	71	71	70	276	-12	583,330.00	406,702.97
2	Carlos RODILES	Sp	68	69	69	70	276	-12	388,880.00	271,130.66
3	Brian DAVIS	Eng	71	73	69	66	279	-9	227,500.00	158,615.06
4	John BICKERTON	Eng	71	72	70	69	282	-6	175,000.00	122,011.59
5	Stephen LEANEY	Aus	77	72	67	68	284	-4	142,000.00	99,003.69
	Greg OWEN	Eng	73	67	73	71	284	-4	142,000.00	99,003.69
7	Sergio GARCIA	Sp	71	71	73	71	286	-2	105,000.00	73,206.95
	Michael CAMPBELL	NZ	75	69	74	68	286	-2	105,000.00	73,206.95
9	Ian POULTER	Eng	74	72	73	68	287	-1	87,500.00	61,005.79
10	José Maria OLAZÁBAL	Sp	70	75	70	73	288	0	67,313.34	46,931.47
	Colin MONTGOMERIE	Scot	71	74	70	73	288	0	67,313.34	46,931.47
	Adam SCOTT	Aus	72	75	68	73	288	0	67,313.34	46,931.47
13	Nick O'HERN	Aus	70	78	69	72	289	1	50,925.00	35,505.37
	Jarrod MOSELEY	Aus	73	72	70	74	289	1	50,925.00	35,505.37
	Darren CLARKE	N.Ire	77	72	68	72	289	1	50,925.00	35,505.37
	Angel CABRERA	Arg	71	74	73	71	289	1	50,925.00	35,505.37
	Bradley DREDGE	Wal	72	73	71	73	289	1	50,925.00	35,505.37
	Paul CASEY	Eng	77	70	73	69	289	1	50,925.00	35,505.37
19	Padraig HARRINGTON	Ire	76	74	70	70	290	2	45,150.00	31,478.99
	Anders HANSEN	Den	66	73	73	78	290	2	45,150.00	31,478.99
21	Peter FOWLER	Aus	72	79	70	70	291	3	41,650.00	29,038.76
	Darren FICHARDT	SA	73	72	74	72	291	3	41,650.00	29,038.76
	Miguel Angel JIMÉNEZ	Sp	75	72	73	71	291	3	41,650.00	29,038.76
24	David HOWELL	Eng	73	77	72	71	293	5	37,275.00	25,988.47
	Raphaël JACQUELIN	Fr	74	75	72	72	293	5	37,275.00	25,988.47
	Phillip PRICE	Wal	75	71	75	72	293	5	37,275.00	25,988.47
	Thomas BJÖRN	Den	71	73	74	75	293	5	37,275.00	25,988.47
28	Barry LANE	Eng	75	76	71	72	294	6	33,600.00	23,426.22
	Ricardo GONZALEZ	Arg	77	70	74	73	294	6	33,600.00	23,426.22
	Stephen GALLACHER	Scot	71	75	76	72	294	6	33,600.00	23,426.22
31	Nick FALDO	Eng	74	71	73	77	295	7	28,350.00	19,765.88
	Mark MCNULTY	Zim	74	75	71	75	295	7	28,350.00	19,765.88
	Trevor IMMELMAN	SA	77	70	76	72	295	7	28,350.00	19,765.88
	Philip GOLDING	Eng	76	73	76	70	295	7	28,350.00	19,765.88
	Paul MCGINLEY	Ire	75	73	76	71	295	7	28,350.00	19,765.88
	Gary EVANS	Eng	74	75	69	77	295	7	28,350.00	19,765.88
	Niclas FASTH	Swe	71	77	74	73	295	7	28,350.00	19,765.88
38	Eduardo ROMERO	Arg	73	73	72	78	296	8	23,625.00	16,471.56
	Robert KARLSSON	Swe	74	75	73	74	296	8	23,625.00	16,471.56
40	Robert-Jan DERKSEN	NL	74	71	73	79	297	9	21,525.00	15,007.43
	Paul LAWRIE	Scot	75	75	72	75	297	9	21,525.00	15,007.43
42	Peter LAWRIE	Ire	72	77	77	72	298	10	19,950.00	13,909.32
	Lee WESTWOOD	Eng	75	72	76	75	298	10	19,950.00	13,909.32
44	Maarten LAFEBER	NL	77	75	71	77	300	12	18,200.00	12,689.21
	Justin ROSE	Eng	73	74	77	76	300	12	18,200.00	12,689.21
	Ignacio GARRIDO	Sp	79	76	75	70	300	12	18,200.00	12,689.21
47	Peter HEDBLOM	Swe	78	72	73	78	301	13	16,100.00	11,225.07
	Alastair FORSYTH	Scot	82	75	71	73	301	13	16,100.00	11,225.07
	Jamie DONALDSON	Wal	81	74	74	72	301	13	16,100.00	11,225.07
50	Gary MURPHY	Ire	74	78	76	75	303	15	14,750.00	10,283.83
51	Mathias GRÖNBERG	Swe	73	80	78	73	304	16	14,300.00	9,970.09
52	Kenneth FERRIE	Eng	74	77	74	80	305	17	13,850.00	9,656.35
53	David LYNN	Eng	82	82	70	72	306	18	13,175.00	9,185.73
	Andrew COLTART	Scot	82	82	70	72	306	18	13,175.00	9,185.73
55	Søren KJELDSEN	Den	75	73	78	82	308	20	12,600.00	8,784.83
56	Nick DOUGHERTY	Eng	78	78	80	76	312	24	12,250.00	8,540.81
57	Søren HANSEN	Den	74	W/D					11,900.00	8,296.79

Someone had to win a play-off for the first time and in the end it was Jacobson, at the fourth extra hole, but only after a titanic struggle which saw Rodiles, who was supported by his fellow European Tour colleague and Malaga resident Miguel Angel Jiménez amongst the huge galleries, have putts to win at each of the first three holes, only to agonise as the ball stayed above ground on each occasion.

With the light beginning to fade and memories echoing of 12 months earlier when Bernhard Langer and Colin Montgomerie shared the title after dusk put an end to their extra time tussle, Jacobson made the vital breakthrough.

Back on the 18th tee for the fourth time in the day, Rodiles pushed his drive into the trees from where he could do no better than a bogey five. It left Jacobson, in the middle of the green in regulation, with two putts for the title and he wisely took them both.

Mark Garrod

Colin Montgomerie and Seve Ballesteros

The arrival of The Seve Trophy on The European Tour International Schedule in 2000 provided a fascinating opportunity for Europe's finest players to showcase their match play skills in an enthralling contest.

At Sunningdale Golf Club in England the inaugural Seve Trophy proved to be a memorable week, climaxed when Seve Ballesteros himself moved past Colin Montgomerie, the opposing captain, in the lead singles match of the final day, as Continental Europe beat Great Britain and Ireland 13 $^1/_2$ - 12 $^1/_2$.

That the two teams should deliver another feast of high-octane competition two years later at Druids Glen in Ireland was as

predictable as Ballesteros, recovering from all kinds of unlikely spots, forging another win against Montgomerie, although this time Great Britain and Ireland triumphed 14 $^1/_2$ - 11 $^1/_2$.

So it was inevitable that, on the eve of the third Seve Trophy, there would be much speculation again about the coming together of the respective captains on the closing day, even before a single shot had been struck.

Montgomerie insisted that it was "a very daunting task to play Seve," as he made plans for himself and his team mates to watch Valencia play Maccabi Haifa in a UEFA Cup match, kicking off at 10pm! Ballesteros retorted that in match play "all you have to do

There were others in Valencia whose thoughts would, in time, turn to the prospect of a Ryder Cup debut, players such as Paul Casey, Alex Cejka, Brian Davis, David Howell, Raphaël Jacquelin, Ian Poulter and Justin Rose, but inevitably the spotlight on the first day focused on two players well versed as companions in the art of match play.

Ballesteros and Olazábal first played together in The Ryder Cup in 1987. They won three points out of four. They went on to take 12 points out of 15, a truly remarkable record. Now they were back in tandem as they launched the third Seve Trophy against Lee Westwood and Howell in the opening fourballs.

A typically gritty Spanish rearguard action saw the match go to the last green where Howell's four iron from 209 yards to three feet ended the resistance of the Spaniards. Yet the glory belonged to Westwood who had given a display of driving, iron play and putting that was awe-inspiring. "He played fantastically well," said Howell.

David Howell and Lee Westwood

is try and beat your opponent somehow." He added: "Sometimes both players play brilliantly and sometimes they don't produce any great things on the course. What counts is to win."

However, there was no questioning the abilities of all 20 players who assembled at Campo de Golf Parador El Saler Valencia.

The two captains had won 87 and 36 tournaments respectively world wide while José Maria Olazábal and Paul Lawrie, the two players chosen as captain's picks, had both enjoyed Major Championship glory. What is more, the 16 players who qualified to compete had, between them, won no fewer than 14 tournaments on The 2003 European Tour International Schedule on the way to earning 17,185,351 euro (£11,981 783).

For some, however, the match represented a first opportunity to demonstrate their match play skills in a team arena. Fredrik Jacobson, of Sweden, who played in the HSBC World Match Play Championship at Wentworth Club in October, fell into that category as he teed-up in his first Seve Trophy. However, his victory only a few days earlier at the Volvo Masters Andalucia had not only been his third of the year, but was also an indication that he was on-course to graduate to Ryder Cup honours in the near future.

Raphaël Jacquelin and Alex Cejka

the course

Campo de Golf Parador El Saler, designed by Javier Arana, was sculpted out of rugged links land beside the Mediterranean and presented a gem of a test.

Fredrik Jacobson and Niclas Fasth

Great Britain and Ireland ended the first day ahead by 3 1/2 - 1 1/2, and it was a similar story in the second series of fourballs. Howell and Westwood led the way again, winning the opening match 5 and 3 against Thomas Björn and Sergio Garcia, while Ballesteros and Olazábal, this time in the last match, succumbed 3 and 1 to Poulter and Rose. At the end of the session, Great Britain and Ireland were 6 1/2 - 3 1/2 in front, but as these matches tend to do, new partnerships emerge that augur well for the future.

Niclas Fasth had made his Ryder Cup debut at The De Vere Belfry in 2002. Now he was paired with Swedish compatriot Jacobson. They had halved their first fourball match against Paul Lawrie and Montgomerie, and won the second against Padraig Harrington and Phillip Price.

On day three, Fasth and Jacobson beat Harrington and Lawrie 5 and 4 in the greensomes before overcoming Casey and Lawrie in the afternoon foursomes by 3 and 2. They had contributed three and a half points to Continental Europe's cause, but not even they could match the outstanding achievement of Germany's Alex Cejka and France's Jacquelin, who won each of their four matches together.

These two partnerships gave Ballesteros hope, despite the fact that Great Britain and Ireland led 10-8 entering the final singles, as the time came for him to face Montgomerie again. This time, however, the Scot emerged victorious 5 and 4 after being two down in the early stages.

Although Fasth and Jacobson kept their unbeaten records, Jacobson's 2 and 1 victory over Westwood seeing him emerge as the most prolific points scorer of the week with four and a half out of five, The Seve Trophy remained in Montgomerie's hands.

Mitchell Platts

Ian Poulter and Justin Rose

Great Britain and Ireland: Left to right: Top row: Ian Poulter, Padraig Harrington, David Howell, Colin Montgomerie, Paul Lawrie and Phillip Price.
Front row: Paul Casey, Lee Westwood, Justin Rose and Brian Davis.

final results
Campo de Golf Parador El Saler · Valencia · Spain
November 6 - 9 · 2003 · Par 72 · 6950 yards · 6355 metres

CONTINENTAL EUROPE
Captain: Seve Ballesteros

Thursday November 6: Fourballs
Seve Ballesteros & José Maria Olazábal	0	David Howell & Lee Westwood (2 holes)	1
Ignacio Garrido & Miguel Angel Jiménez	0	Paul Casey & Brian Davis (2 and 1)	1
Alex Cejka & Raphaël Jacquelin (4 and 3)	1	Ian Poulter & Justin Rose	0
Niclas Fasth & Fredrik Jacobson (Halved)	1/2	Paul Lawrie & Colin Montgomerie (Halved)	1/2
Thomas Björn & Sergio Garcia	0	Padraig Harrington & Phillip Price (2 holes)	1
Score:	**11/2**		**31/2**

Friday November 7: Fourballs
Thomas Björn & Sergio Garcia	0	David Howell & Lee Westwood (5 and 3)	1
Alex Cejka & Raphaël Jacquelin (2 and 1)	1	Paul Lawrie & Colin Montgomerie	0
Ignacio Garrido & Miguel Angel Jiménez	0	Paul Casey & Brian Davis (2 holes)	1
Niclas Fasth & Fredrik Jacobson (1 hole)	1	Padraig Harrington & Phillip Price	0
Seve Ballesteros & José Maria Olazábal	0	Ian Poulter & Justin Rose (3 and 1)	1
Score:	**2**		**3**

Saturday November 8: Greensomes
Niclas Fasth & Fredrik Jacobson (5 and 4)	1	Padraig Harrington & Paul Lawrie	0
Thomas Björn & José Maria Olazábal (Halved)	1/2	Colin Montgomerie & Justin Rose (Halved)	1/2
Alex Cejka & Raphaël Jacquelin (3 and 2)	1	Paul Casey & Brian Davis	0
Seve Ballesteros & Sergio Garcia	0	Ian Poulter & Lee Westwood (3 and 1)	1
Score:	**21/2**		**11/2**

Saturday November 8: Foursomes
Ignacio Garrido & Miguel Angel Jiménez	0	Padraig Harrington & Colin Montgomerie (2 and 1)	1
Niclas Fasth & Fredrik Jacobson (3 and 2)	1	Paul Casey and Paul Lawrie	0
Alex Cejka & Raphaël Jacquelin (5 and 3)	1	David Howell & Lee Westwood	0
Thomas Björn & Sergio Garcia	0	Ian Poulter & Justin Rose (2 and 1)	1
Score:	**2**		**2**

Sunday November 9: Singles
Seve Ballesteros	0	Colin Montgomerie (5 and 4)	1
Alex Cejka	0	David Howell (1 hole)	1
Ignacio Garrido (3 and 2)	1	Paul Lawrie	0
Fredrik Jacobson (2 and 1)	1	Lee Westwood	0
José Maria Olazábal (Halved)	1/2	Padraig Harrington (Halved)	1/2
Niclas Fasth (Halved)	1/2	Ian Poulter (Halved)	1/2
Thomas Björn (Withdrew)	0	Paul Casey (W/O)	1
Raphaël Jacquelin	0	Justin Rose (3 and 2)	1
Miguel Angel Jiménez (2 and 1)	1	Brian Davis	0
Sergio Garcia (4 and 3)	1	Phillip Price	0
Score:	**5**		**5**

| **Match Result:** | **13** | | **15** |

GREAT BRITAIN AND IRELAND
Captain: Colin Montgomerie

2003 Seve Trophy Points Record

	P	W	H	L	Pts
Continental Europe					
Ballesteros	4	0	0	4	0
Björn	4	0	1	3	1/2
Cejka	5	4	0	1	4
Fasth	5	3	2	0	4
Garcia	5	1	0	4	1
Garrido	4	1	0	3	1
Jacobson	5	4	1	0	41/2
Jacquelin	5	4	0	1	4
Jiménez	4	1	0	3	1
Olazábal	4	0	2	2	1
Great Britain and Ireland					
Montgomerie	5	2	2	1	3
Casey	5	3	0	2	3
Davis	4	2	0	2	2
Harrington	5	2	1	2	21/2
Howell	4	3	0	1	3
Lawrie	5	0	1	4	1/2
Poulter	5	3	1	1	31/2
Price	3	1	0	2	1
Rose	5	3	1	1	31/2
Westwood	5	3	0	2	3

place in history

Toshimitsu Izawa and Shigeki Maruyama

The World Golf Championships – World Cup, which was first played as the Canada Cup in 1953, has been contested on many of the great courses around the world. In 2003 it was the turn of the United States to play host to this two man team competition, featuring 24 countries, and, more specifically, at a venue which has swiftly earned a place in the history books.

For the Ocean Course at Kiawah Island, where the United States won The 29th Ryder Cup Matches in 1991, was for a second time host to The World Cup. In 1997, Ireland's Padraig Harrington and Paul McGinley pulled off an outstanding victory when the tournament was a 72 hole stroke play team event named the World Cup of Golf.

However, since 2000, the event has come under the umbrella of the World Golf Championships and undergone a title and format change. Now known as the WGC - World Cup, a new format was introduced in 2001 comprising two rounds each of fourballs and foursomes.

Paul Casey and Justin Rose

Designed by Pete Dye, the Ocean Course is a 7,296 yard par 72 layout which also hosted, in 2001, the inaugural UBS Cup. Since then minor changes to the second and fourth holes have been made with Dye also repositioning the 18th green, moving it closer to the Atlantic Ocean.

When first played as one of the World Golf Championships in 2000, David Duval and Tiger Woods linked together at the Buenos Aires Golf Club in Argentina to retain the famous trophy for the United States following the victory of Mark O'Meara and Woods at The Mines Resort & Golf Club in Kuala Lumpur, Malaysia, in 1999.

Then at The Taiheiyo Club, Gotemba, Japan, in 2001, Woods, again in partnership with Duval, gave the Americans the chance of a third successive win, and their 24th triumph in all, when he chipped in for an eagle at the final hole. It meant that Duval and Woods had played the closing four holes in five under par to become the fourth team in a play-off. Denmark's Thomas Björn and Søren Hansen had set the target. They were caught on the 24 under par 264 mark first by the South African duo of Ernie Els and Retief Goosen then by New Zealand, represented by Michael Campbell and David Smail, and finally by the United States.

Els had tasted victory before, winning The World Cup with Wayne Westner in 1996 at Erinvale Golf Club in his native South Africa, and now he did so again with Goosen as they overcame Denmark at the second extra hole after New Zealand and the United States had been eliminated at the first.

In 2002 on the Vista Vallarta course at Puerto Vallarta in Mexico, Toshimitsu Izawa and Shigeki Maruyama ended a 45 year drought for

Paul McGinley and Padraig Harrington

Japan when, with a 36 under par total of 252, they won by two shots from Americans Phil Mickelson and David Toms. Paul Casey and Justin Rose claimed a share of third place for England, and Rose insisted: "We stayed positive throughout and we were determined to do England as proud as possible."

Unquestionably, the World Golf Championships have become a truly global experience since the launch in February 1999. They feature the game's leading players competing against one another in a variety of formats. The World Cup joined the Accenture Match Play, NEC Invitational and American Express Championship in the World Golf Championships line-up, with the events rotating through a variety of outstanding venues.

Mitchell Platts

Kiawah Island

The 35th Ryder Cup Matches
The South Course · Oakland Hills Country Club · Michigan · USA

steeped in tradition

16th Hole at Oakland Hills Country Club

Oakland Hills Country Club, where The 35th Ryder Cup Matches will unfold on September 17-19, 2004, is located 15 miles northwest of Detroit at 3951 West Maple Road, Bloomfield, Michigan, in the United States. Christened 'The Monster' when Ben Hogan won his third US Open Championship in 1951, Oakland Hills has hosted no fewer than six US Open Championships, two US PGA Championships, two US Senior Open Championships, one US Women's Amateur and one 'Ryder Cup' although you will not find that in the record books.

Over eighteen holes, anything is possible.

Every two years, the greatest European and
American golfers do battle for the world's
most coveted golf trophy – The Ryder Cup.

It's a competition that rouses a rare passion.
And when there is passion on a golf course
– anything is possible. In 2006 The Ryder Cup
will be played at The K Club. At AIB, we're
delighted to play our part in making it possible.

AIB, proud partner to The 2006 Ryder Cup in Ireland.

Be with AIB.

In 1940, Samuel Ryder's elegant golden chalice was proudly displayed at Oakland Hills. The United States held the trophy, courtesy of an 8-4 winning margin at Southport & Ainsdale in 1937, and with World War II nearly ten months old, and with the British Ryder Cup Team otherwise occupied, it seemed like a good idea for the United States team to exhibit their world class skills and to raise money for charity.

The seventh edition of The Ryder Cup Matches had been scheduled to unfold at the Ponte Vedra Club in Jacksonville, Florida, in 1939 and, as had happened two years earlier when Henry Cotton won the Open Golf Championship in the week following the match with all the Americans in the field, there was a genuine hope that the Cup would be brought home. Indeed the first eight places in the British team had been announced with Cotton at the helm as Captain alongside Jimmy Andrews, Dick Burton, Sam King, Alf Padgham, Dai Rees, Charles Whitcombe and Reg Whitcombe. The remaining places were never filled because on September 3, 1939, war broke out, although 'caps' were still awarded.

Walter Hagen had also been installed as the United States Captain and his team comprised of Vic Ghezzi, Ralph Guldahl, Jimmy Hines, Harold McSpaden, Dick Metz, Byron Nelson, Henry Picard, Paul Runyan, Horton Smith and Sam Snead. It was decided they should face a 'top-flight' squad of American professionals who had been overlooked in The Ryder Cup selection process! So Gene Sarazen was made Captain with Tommy

Armour, Billy Burke, Harry Cooper, Jimmy Demaret, Ben Hogan, Lawson Little, Ed Oliver, Jimmy Thompson, Al Watrous and Craig Wood in his squad. The match was billed as 'Hagen's Ryder Cuppers' against 'Sarazen's Challengers.'

The bill of fare on July 16-17, 1940, was made up of a first day of four foursomes played over 36 holes and a second day of eight singles also over 36 holes. Demaret and Hogan birdied their first hole and eventually won by one hole after a classic match against Guldahl and Snead, but Hagen's men won the other three matches to lead 3-1. The spoils were shared in the singles so 'Hagen's Ryder Cuppers' had won 7-5.

Just for the record The Matches produced more than $10,000 for The Red Cross. The newspapers gave the event strong support and it became a community enterprise. The players received railroad fares, a small gift and little else. Their expenses totalled $1,146.25!

For Oakland Hills, The 35th Ryder Cup Matches will mark another milestone in its wonderful history as, of course, will the playing of the 90th US Open Championship on the course in 2008.

It was in 1916 - coincidently the same year that the PGA of America was founded - that Donald Ross looked out across the rolling, tree-clad parcel of land and declared: "The Lord intended this for a golf links." Ross had already

Captain Sam Torrance and the winning European Team at The 34th Ryder Cup Matches at The De Vere Belfry, Sutton Coldfield, England

IRELAND

A Natural Home for the
RYDER CUP 2006

RYDER CUP 2006

IRELAND

Ireland, a golfer's paradise, with every shape, size and shade of green and the friendliest 19th watering hole on the circuit. Ireland has produced more than her share of Ryder Cup players and welcomed many of the world's top golfers. The 2006 Ryder Cup. Ireland, a perfect venue, an ideal host.

www.ireland.ie

Fáilte Ireland

Ireland
THE FOOD ISLAND

WATERFORD
CRYSTAL

AIB

Mid-life crisis? What mid-life crisis?

Life begins at forty, or so they say. But for many men, it's just the start of their troubles. At precisely the time when all their years of experience in a loving relationship should add up to a better sex life, one in twenty men in their forties will begin to experience problems maintaining an erection.

And the more you worry about it, the worse it's likely to get.

But why worry? Erection problems are a medical condition and treatments are available.

So return the coupon or call us today.

Our free, confidential information pack explaining the causes and treatment options available for this common medical problem could help you keep the life in your love life.

Call now on 0845 378 0144
Or visit www.informED.org.uk

Keep the life in your love life.

Pelé

MHF
MEN'S HEALTH
FORUM

The Impotence Association

Please complete the questions below. Completing them fully will enable us to send you the most relevant information

Are you currently taking a prescription treatment for erection problems? yes ☐ no ☐

If yes, this treatment is _____

If no, please tick the reason that best describes your situation:

I have not been to see my GP yet ☐

I have seen my GP but have not been prescribed a treatment yet ☐

I was prescribed a treatment but I am not using it any more ☐

This treatment was _____

I am taking a non-prescription treatment ☐

So we can now send you a tailored information pack within the next few weeks please complete your details below:

Title: _____ Forename: _____

Surname: _____

Address: _____

_____ Postcode: _____

Email: _____

Once you have filled in your details please place the coupon into an envelope and post to: **informED, FREEPOST SEA11874, Crawley RH10 9BR.** You don't need a stamp.

Privacy: By returning this coupon you agree that your information will be held on a database (within the EU or outside the EU where data privacy laws may be less strict) administered by Pfizer Limited, Walton Oaks, Dorking Road, Tadworth, Surrey KT20 7NS. The information will be used to send you information as part of the informED programme.

948 09/03

designed the acclaimed No.2 course at Pinehurst, North Carolina, and Norval Hawkins and Joseph Mack, the two men behind the birth of Oakland Hills, had already hired Ross ahead of calling on October 17, 1916, what, in effect, was the club's first board meeting. Hawkins, the first sales Manager for the Ford Motor Company, and Mack, who ran his own printing and advertising business, invited 46 friends and acquaintances to that meeting at the Detroit Athletic Club and determined that there would be 140 chartered members each paying $250 to join.

The press knew soon enough about the venture! On Saturday, October 21, 1916, the front page of the Pontiac Press Gazette ran an article announcing that: "Another golf course is soon to be laid out in Bloomfield Township, two and a half miles west of Birmingham." The group had purchased the Spicer and Miller farms of 250 acres, and taken options on 160 acres comprising the German and Leach farms off dusty Maple Road in south-eastern Oakland County.

Hawkins and Mack wanted only the best. By engaging the services of Ross, who would eventually design more than 100 golf courses in the United States, they knew from the start that they had the right man to make the South Course a true examination and by April 1917, there were 30 men working on the site.

Ross remains one of golf's most revered architects, and the reason is easy to understand at Oakland Hills. His superb routing of the South Course is a legacy of his genius. Two nine hole loops, each starting and finishing at the clubhouse, provides for a complete test of the game. The first loop runs clockwise while the second follows almost a figure-of-eight, although some prefer to call it kidney-shaped because the holes do not cross, with the main topographical features being two dramatic ridges that run across the property

with a lot of the holes playing off or over one or both. Ross's dictum was simple: "To build each hole in such a manner that it wastes none of the ground at my disposal and takes advantage of every possibility that I can see."

The course opened formally in July 1918, and Walter Hagen, who had already won the 1914 US Open Championship, was taken on not only as the club's first professional – his shop was an old chicken coop! – but also as a public relations man. His task? To teach Detroiters how to play golf, and romance them into becoming members. Hagen would not remain long in the role, but through the boom and bust years of the 'Roaring Twenties' Oakland Hills matured, playing host to a number of tournaments, and grew its membership and reputation.

Cyril Walker won when first the US Open Championship was played at Oakland Hills in 1924. Walter Hagen and Bobby Jones were among the giants of the game who strode the elegant fairways that year. Hagen had been the club's first professional although two years earlier he had refused to participate when the inaugural event to be played at Oakland Hills – the 1922 Western Open – was won by Mike Brady. The selection of the South Course, then only five years old, as a US Open Championship course in 1924 was a tribute to Ross.

With the likes of Jim Barnes, Leo Diegel and Sarazen also in the field, a high profile winner appeared assured, but a 118lbs, feisty Englishman destroyed that theory. Cyril Walker told a group of sportswriters on the eve of the Championship that a "rank outsider" would win, and he was right! He shot 74-74-74-75 for a nine over par total of 297 – three ahead of Jones. This Championship marked the use of the steel-shafted putter for the first time. Ralph Guldahl's win in 1937 in the US Open Championship – Glenna Collett had won the 1929 Women's Amateur – was overshadowed by some

There's
Average Golf...

and there's Golf in Wales.

There's
Stuffy Golf...

and there's Golf in Wales.

For a free copy of the Wales Tourist Board's official Golf Wales guide,
telephone **08701 211252** quoting reference **GO100** or visit **www.golfasitshouldbe.com**

Undiscovered Golf Destination of the Year.

WALES CYMRU

Golf as it should be.

A view of the 18th green and clubhouse at Oakland Hills

of the comments about the course. A great deal of publicity had been given to the South Course which measured a "back-breaking" 7,037 yards. It had, in fact, been lengthened by 100 yards. There was a question about the rough, too, and that was cut back on two holes. Then, under pressure, the tee markers were moved forward. H.G. Salsinger, the nationally-known Detroit News sports editor, did not like it and wrote: "Oakland Hills was made an easier course by moving up the markers on a majority of the tees and placing the cups in the most accessible spots on the greens. It was an easier one than the course over which the 1924 tournament was played."

Nevertheless in depression-riddled Michigan there were record-breaking crowds with record takings. The first day revenue was reported at $22,000 which was only $4,000 short of the total receipts at Baltusrol one year earlier.

The South Course had been lengthened to counter three major advancements in golf equipment - the wound-centre ball, the steel shaft and the sand wedge - by moving the tees back. Technology was the winner though with Guldahl's 71-69-72-69 for a seven under 281 winning him the first of successive US Open Championship titles. Incidentally it was said that Guldahl was so obsessed with his swing that he practiced in a room where the walls were covered entirely by full-length mirrors. After 1940, he did not win again.

For the record, Texan Guldahl, who had almost given up the game one year earlier, received $1,000, but Sam Snead, then a 25 year old rookie and, who was never to win the US Open Championship, earned more - he took home $800 for runner-up spot plus $500 for being voted "the best dressed golfer."

Oakland Hills was remodelled for the 1951 US Open Championship with the deliberate intent of making it the most difficult challenge anywhere. Some said fairness was a secondary consideration. Robert Trent Jones, then just coming into his own as a premier golf architect, was retained by the club for the specific purpose of toughening an already acknowledged quality course. Nevertheless with continued advances in clubs and balls it had become clear that the grand old layout that had tested Bobby Jones and company would not test Ben Hogan and the class of the 1950s. The USGA decided that if it was going to return to its favourite courses then they would have to be updated. The era of the narrow fairway had arrived and when the

players arrived at Oakland Hills the course had a new name. William Mullin of the New York World Telegram, had christened it 'The Monster.'

It was Jones's first US Open Championship course. His remodelling of the Ross masterpiece stood the test of time. He designed, enlarged and re-contoured the greens. Jones actually shortened the course by 110 yards to 6,927 yards but he converted the par five eighth and 18th holes to 458 yard and 459 yard par fours respectively. The par was reduced from 72 to 70. Jones also set out to "pinch" the landing areas for the professional drives - which he calculated at the time to be 230 to 260 yards of carry - by moving the bunkers and strategically locating them in the driving target area. The average score in the first round was 78.4! Walter Hagen, a spectator, observed: "The players aren't playing the course; the golf course is playing them." There had been cries of anguish from the contestants as they played their practice rounds; and those cries were audible throughout. Golf World wrote: "Golf's greatest tournament reached a new peak in public interest." Indeed officials and writers called those that were on Hogan's heels every step of his final round "the biggest mob in history to ever follow a golfer." It also marked the 250th Anniversary celebration of Detroit, and Jones had guaranteed the future. Now drives were directed not to fairways but to landing areas; approaches were played not to greens but to targets. And for the first time a golf course was receiving more attention than the players.

Hogan, the eventual champion, lunched on a roast beef sandwich between rounds on the final day - 36 holes were played on the Saturday at that time - and spoke of the course as a personality, as a formidable and dangerous opponent, as an intricate problem which had to be solved. The 'Iceman' did so with a closing 67 on a course where no one had broken 70. He called the win "most satisfying!"

For Oakland Hills it represented a place on the map. Hogan, who had opened with scores of 76-73-71, finished two in front of Clayton Heafner, whose closing 69 represented the only other sub-par round by the field of 162 throughout the Championship. Hogan said: "I'm glad I brought this course, this monster, to its knees." Whether or not Hogan joined in the ovation Jones received at the closing ceremony is not known. He did, however, turn to Jones's wife, Ione, and say: "If your husband had to make a living on the courses he builds, your family would be on the breadline."

In 1961, the South Course was not deemed to be the same challenge. The element of surprise was gone, some bunkering which was more frightening than strategic had been removed, and a late spring had inhibited the growth of what normally would have been thick, lush rough. In truth the course had been softened immediately after the 1951 US Open Championship so that at least a few club members could break 90! By now Arnold Palmer, the defending Champion, and Jack Nicklaus were on the scene although Hogan, now aged 48, was back. He said: "The course is magnificent. They've widened the fairways and the rough isn't brutal." Jack Fleck claimed: "The spray gun artists aren't going to be penalised sufficiently here." The more favourable west wind switched to the north east for the opening day, and when it was all over there was only one sub-par round!

Official Mobile Telecommunications Sponsor to the Ryder Cup 2006

See what you can do.

O₂

Gene Littler had arrived with winnings of only $116 from his first five tournaments of the year. He returned home to California as the US Open Champion after scores of 73-68-72-68 for a one over par 281 - one ahead of Bob Goalby and Doug Sanders.

The US PGA Championship was first played at Oakland Hills in 1972. Nicklaus was the defending Champion. He had won the Masters Tournament and the US Open Championship that year, and finished one shot behind Lee Trevino in the Open Golf Championship at Muirfield. Heavy rain softened the greens, and there were seven sub-par rounds on the first day, but as the Championship unfolded with intermittent rain and muggy heat, so at one time on the front nine on the final day no fewer than seven players were tied for the lead at one over par. Gary Player won and declared: "This is the best and toughest American course I've ever played. It is certainly quite humbling." There was a lovely finale, too, as Sam Snead who had returned at the age of 60, closed with a 69 and finished tied third just three shots behind Player, who scored 71-71-67-72 for 281.

Then came the 1979 US PGA Championship. They called it 'The Monster Massacre.' The Championship left Oakland Hills golfing enthusiasts in a state of shock and set a once near-invincible course awash in the proverbial red numbers. When it was all over there had been no fewer than 140 sub-par or even-par rounds and 15 players had beaten or tied Player's 1972 winning total of 281. Unseasonably heavy rainfall played a major role. Billy Casper, then the new Ryder Cup Captain, said: "I don't think the greens will dry out. There's too much moisture in the ground." Jack Berry of the Detroit News wrote: "Downhill putts aren't reaching the cup. More rain and Oakland Hills will be a soft touch." Tom Watson was the favourite; Jack Nicklaus, without a win all year, had to succeed or miss the US Ryder Cup Team for the first time in 11 years. Nicklaus opened with a 73 and said: "This is as much of a piece of cake as you'll ever get at Oakland Hills, and I didn't get to the icing."

The eventual winner was Australian David Graham. He captured his first Major Championship by beating Ben Crenshaw in a play-off. They had tied on a record low Oakland Hills score of 272 - Graham storming through at the end by following rounds of 67-68-70 with a 65. Bud Erickson, the Oakland Hills Tournament Director, offered a philosophical palliative. "No one thinks any less of Augusta National because Jack Nicklaus and Ray Floyd have scored 17 under par victories there." No fewer than 145,102 spectators paid to see the Championship unfold and after Oakland Hills had, in 1981, hosted the first US Senior Open to be played at the 50-and-over level and Arnold Palmer wrote his name indelibly into the Club's history by winning an 18-hole play-off, so the US Open Championship returned in 1985. The USGA had invited Oakland Hills to host the Championship again and set a total yardage of 6,996 - 90 yards longer than it was in 1961 and 69 yards longer than in 1951. Some type of change was made to all holes, with the exception of two of the par threes, with Trent Jones once again making the revisions. Andy North won with 70-65-70-74 for a one under par 279 - becoming the only man to break 280 in a US Open Championship at Oakland Hills.

Since Arnold Palmer had won the first US Senior Open at Oakland Hills, it seemed only logical that when the Championship returned there ten years later that Jack Nicklaus should triumph. Many observers recognise the Oakland Hills greens as the most fearsome that Ross ever designed, and Nicklaus, before winning, said: "They represent the most difficult combination of speed and contour of any course we play." The greens, of course, have changed since Ross first laid them out. Jones added 'wings' to many of them prior to the 1951 US Open Championship, and following the 1991 US Senior Open the designer Arthur Hills added additional wings to the first and 14th hole to accommodate more hole locations and he also enlarged areas on the fourth, fifth, ninth and 11th holes in readiness for the 1996 US Open when the course played longer because of another very wet spring. In addition to that a monsoon-like storm hit Oakland Hills at noon on the day prior to the start of the Championship. When the storm abated, officials looked out over a course which, in places, lay under two or three feet of water and shook their heads in dismay. Then the green staff got down to work and, miracle of miracles, play began on schedule at 7am on Thursday! American Steve Jones scored 74-66-69-69 for a two under par 278 - one ahead of Tom Lehman and Davis Love III. Significantly Tiger Woods was in the field. Two months later he had turned professional and by the end of the year he had won twice on the US PGA Tour.

Now "The Monster" awaits the greatest golf show on earth. This time, of course, it will be the genuine article but as anyone will know who witnessed the exhibition in 1940, or for that matter any of the great Championships to have been played at Oakland Hills, the South Course that fulfilled a dream off dusty Maple Road will provide a wonderful examination for all at The 35th Ryder Cup Matches.

Mitchell Platts

FORTHCOMING VENUES FOR THE RYDER CUP MATCHES

2004   The 35th Ryder Cup Matches, Oakland Hills CC
Bloomfield Hills, Michigan, USA
17-19 September

2006   The 36th Ryder Cup Matches
The K Club, Straffan, Ireland

2008   The 37th Ryder Cup Matches
Valhalla GC, Louisville, Kentucky, USA

2010   The 38th Ryder Cup Matches
The Celtic Manor Resort, City of Newport, Wales

2012   The 39th Ryder Cup Matches
Medinah CC, Medinah, Illinois, USA

2014   The 40th Ryder Cup Matches
Gleneagles Hotel, Perthshire, Scotland

2016   The 41st Ryder Cup Matches
Hazeltine National GC, Chaska, Minnesota, USA

Hole 1

Hole 1   435 Yards - 398 Metres   Par 4

An excellent starting hole for The 35th Ryder Cup Matches. The opening tee shots will be hit from an elevated tee to a landing area framed by bunkers left and right. The hole usually plays downwind, leaving a short iron approach to one of many undulating greens at Oakland Hills. The most difficult hole locations are front left (behind bunker) and the back right plateau.

Hole 2   519 Yards - 475 Metres   Par 5

Birdie is very possible on this slight dogleg left if the drive avoids the fairway bunkers that guard both sides of the fairway 240 to 290 yards from the tee. The green is protected by four bunkers and has a centre crown that makes for a treacherous putting surface. The most difficult hole locations are back and middle right.

Hole 3   198 Yards - 181 Metres   Par 3

The first par three on the South Course is a classic. The green runs diagonally from right to left and is surrounded by five bunkers. The farther back the hole location, the more difficult the shot because the green narrows to a small terrace.

Hole 4   430 Yards - 393 Metres   Par 4

This is a slight dogleg to the left with four bunkers protecting the inside of the dogleg and two bunkers right. Players who carry the inside bunker will be left with a short iron approach to a green protected by bunkers at the front. A small ridge runs from front left to back left making any left side hole locations very difficult.

Hole 5   455 Yards - 416 Metres   Par 4

This is another tight driving hole, with trees guarding the left side of the fairway and bunkers guarding the right. The fairway runs downhill to the creek, which crosses diagonally and is about 300 yards from the tee. The green is one of the most difficult on the course and is very fast from back to front. The front right is the most difficult hole location protected by a bunker and an overhanging elm tree.

Hole 6   356 Yards - 326 Metres   Par 4

This is the shortest par four on the course. Most players will keep their drivers in the bag and hit a long iron from the tee, thereby taking the bunkers to the left of the fairway landing area out of play. Although this hole has the deepest green on the course, the putting surface is split into two tiers, with the higher portion demanding an accurate short iron to a terrace that is only 12 yards wide. The option of using a shorter tee to

allow the players to try to drive the green would provide for a very exciting hole for The Ryder Cup Matches.

Hole 7   411 Yards - 376 Metres   Par 4

This hole is a slight dogleg with three bunkers on the upper left hand side of the fairway. From there the fairway slopes downhill to the pond on the right starting at 250 yards and extending 300 yards from the tee. The green is long and narrow, set diagonally with bunkers flanking both sides of the green. The most difficult hole locations are front and back left.

Hole 8   482 Yards - 441 Metres   Par 4

The toughest driving hole on the front nine has bunkers pinching the fairway on each side of the landing area 250 to 300 yards from the tee. The uphill approach demands a long iron to a large green, bunkered left and right. Par will be a good score on the most difficult hole on the front nine.

Hole 9   220 Yards - 201 Metres   Par 3

The longest of Oakland Hills's excellent par threes, requires a long iron to a large undulating green. The green slopes severely from back to front and the contouring is very severe. Both the front left plateau and back right make for difficult hole locations and are protected by bunkers.

Hole 9

Hole 10 453 Yards - 414 Metres   Par 4

Donald Ross started his routing of Oakland Hills with the tenth & 11th holes. The tee shot from the elevated tenth tee, probably a three wood, should avoid not only the three bunkers that line the landing area (one left, two right), but also a steep slope beyond the bunkers that could 'kick' the ball into the thick rough. The second shot is uphill to a green guarded by a shallow bunker left and a deep bunker right. The green has a crown in the middle and slopes severely downhill to the right hand bunker. The hole will require a mid-iron and the right side hole location behind the bunker will be the most difficult.

Hole 11 423 Yards - 387 Metres   Par 4

This hole has an elevated tee to a valley below. There is a hill at 270 yards from the tee that must be carried. Three fairway bunkers on the right side protect the landing area. The second shot will be a short iron and club selection will be crucial, as the back tier is four feet higher than the front.

Hole 12 560 Yards - 512 Metres   Par 5

The tee on the South Course's longest hole stands 40 feet above the landing area, with bunkers left of the fairway and trees guarding the right. To go for the green in two, you must favour the left side of the fairway off the tee. Three deep bunkers protect the front of the green and the putting surface has a steep ridge running from back left to front right. The most difficult hole location is front right.

Hole 13

Hole 13 170 Yards - 155 Metres   Par 3

This is one of the finest short holes that offers a multitude of interesting problems. The tee and green are both slightly elevated with the tee being higher than the green. The green contours are classic Donald Ross, with a distinct hollow in the front approximately four feet below the upper surface. All hole locations on the top plateau and behind the front right pot bunker make this a difficult short par three.

Hole 14 473 Yards - 433 Metres   Par 4

The first of five difficult finishing holes, this hole is without a single fairway bunker, but is guarded on both sides by trees to a wide landing area. The hole features a fall away green with a large swale running from front right to back left. Front bunkers protect both the front left terrace and the right terrace with the front right hole location being the most difficult on the golf course.

Hole 15 400 Yards - 366 Metres   Par 4

A severe dogleg from right to left with trees protecting the entire left side. There is a bunker located directly in the centre of the fairway starting at 240 yards from the tee. Some players may gamble and try to cut through the gap between the trees and fairway bunker. The reward is a shorter approach than those who lay up short of the bunker. The inverted saucer shaped green has crowns, contours and is flanked by five bunkers, three on the left and two on the right.

Hole 16 406 Yards - 371 Metres   Par 4

This dogleg-right is the signature hole at Oakland Hills. The player must keep the ball in the fairway by avoiding water right and trees left. Like the 18th hole at The De Vere Belfry, this second shot will be one of the most intimidating with the match on the line. A short iron approach will be one to a wide, shallow green that has a ridge running from front to back with water protecting the green along the front and right side. Some players may be tempted to use one extra club and take the water out of play, but they run the risk of catching one of the four rear bunkers and leaving a difficult sand shot.

Hole 17 200 Yards - 183 Metres   Par 3

Robert Trent Jones Sr. considered this one of the country's great short holes. The players will probably hit a four or five iron to a green that is 30 feet above the tee and is protected on all sides by deep bunkers. The green has severe slopes with a ridge running from front right to back centre A hole location on the back right makes for one of the most demanding tee shots in Championship golf.

Hole 18 493 Yards - 451 Metres   Par 4

The most demanding tee shot on the South Course. The fairway slopes to the left on this dogleg-right making it difficult to hit with bunkers on both sides and out of bounds left. The mid-iron second shot is slightly uphill to a shallow green protected by four bunkers. A mound through the centre separates the contour of the green, where the ball must end up on the same side of the pin, otherwise the putt over the mound will be difficult.

Pat Croswell
Host PGA of America Golf Professional

card of the course

**Oakland Hills Country Club · South Course ·
Bloomfield Hills · Michigan · USA**

Hole	Par	Yards	Metres
1	4	435	398
2	5	519	475
3	3	198	181
4	4	430	393
5	4	455	416
6	4	356	326
7	4	411	376
8	4	482	441
9	3	220	201
Out:	**35**	**3,506**	**3,207**
10	4	453	414
11	4	423	387
12	5	560	512
13	3	170	155
14	4	473	433
15	4	400	366
16	4	406	371
17	3	200	183
18	4	493	451
In:	**35**	**3,578**	**3,272**
Total:	**70**	**7,084**	**6,479**

bernhard langer

2004 European Team Captain

Bernhard Langer's leadership qualities never have been in doubt. Yet his modesty is such that long before he realised he would rather like to be European Ryder Cup Captain, most aficionados of the game knew that here was, perhaps, the perfect skipper.

That he has been handed this vital role sooner rather than later is further, and eloquent, testimony to the German's unique standing within a professional circuit that can judge a man harshly at times. Put simply, Langer is the professionals' professional.

"Bernhard leaves very little to chance and even the bit he does will have been carefully analysed at some point," said his long-time friend and former caddie Pete Coleman. "I have never known him not be focused and ready for whatever he is doing, wherever he is playing. He expects others to work as hard as he does but he is an instinctively fair man."

Coleman's own back carries the scars of Langer's commitment to a work ethic that might bring a donkey to its knees prematurely, for it is he who had to bear the weight not just of his employer's

expectations, but of the 17 golf clubs Bernhard frequently required him to haul over 18 holes of a practice round.

Eventually he will decide on 'this' driver and 'that' putter but not before he is convinced the right choice has been made. "I don't see the point in doing anything unless you try to do it the very best that you can," said Langer. "We are very fortunate to be able to play this game for a living and I am always aware of this good fortune."

Working hard, staying focused and doing the right thing comes easily to Langer, however, for it is the way he was brought up in the village of Anhausen, a short train journey from Munich.

His father was a bricklayer, his mother a waitress, and his brother Erwin was caddieing at the local club as soon as he could. By eight years of age Bernhard, too, had caught the golfing bug.

Every day he would cycle five miles to Augsburg Golf Club where his talent for the game was first unearthed. It was here that he studied a faded sepia magazine clipping of a Jack Nicklaus instruction session, and where he earned his first few Deutschmarks.

It was a tough but loving upbringing that made Langer the man he is today. His desire for perfection is still vivid and it is this which fuels his ambition to an extent that, although now approaching middle-age, he is still comfortably within the top 100 on the Official World Golf Ranking. Two Masters Tournament victories (in 1985 and 1993) are the highlights of a CV which includes 42 European Tour titles.

Deeply religious, he lists his priorities in life as "God, then my family and then golf." It is a pecking order that reflects a man of rare judgement, sensitivity and decency, but one which should not disguise the steel within this civilised exterior.

What happens at Oakland Hills Country Club under his Captaincy remains to be seen, but be certain of one thing: if Europe win The 35th Ryder Cup Matches, Langer's eye for even the smallest detail will have played a vital part.

"I remember as a little boy, pressing my face against the sweet shop window and wishing I could go inside and buy some," he said. Now, here he is with the keys to the biggest 'sweet shop' in the game. Don't be surprised if his charges fill their pockets.

Bill Elliott

hal sutton

2004 United States Team Captain

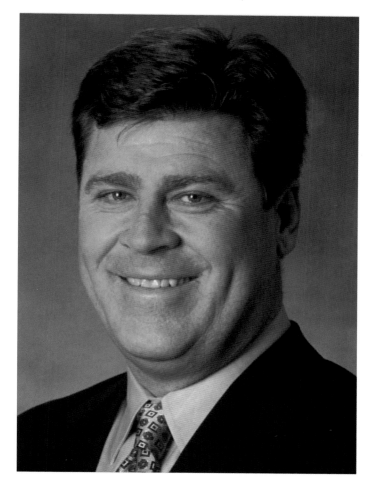

al Evan Sutton is the sort of man who commands respect even before he opens his mouth and delivers his version of sense in a voice so deep it starts somewhere around his ankles and rarely rises above knee level even when real excitement encourages a squeak.

For a start the American, who will be 46 when The Matches unfold, has the sort of forearms that suggest his childhood was largely spent chomping on spinach while his neck is thick enough to encourage even Fred Flintstone to drop his gaze quickly.

Yet, though Sutton has a real physical presence, it is his natural inclination to engage eye contact and then to hold it that encourages the thought that the PGA of America chose wisely when it came to picking The United States 2004 Ryder Cup Captain.

"It goes without saying that this is a real honour for me but the whole point now is to win back The Ryder Cup when we play at Oakland Hills. Of course we know it's going to be close - and that's

a lot of the fun of it - but I've played in The Matches four times and won once (1999) and I know which one was the most fun for me," he said, his easy grin failing to disguise the determination lying underneath.

Sutton's personal Ryder Cup record reflects a career that has, more than anyone else, been a game of two halves. When he turned professional in 1981 he carried with him the title College Player of The Year and the first of his 14 US PGA Tour victories was carved out just 12 months later. By 1986 he had added another five, made his Ryder Cup debut at The De Vere Belfry in 1985, and seemed set to move ever onward and upward.

Few things in life are predictable, however, and from this apparently secure position Sutton's professional career was affected by a series of personal setbacks even as he played in his second Ryder Cup in 1987.

After winning The Memorial Tournament in the spring of 1986 it was to be nine long, hard seasons before he announced his return to genuine action when he won the B.C. Open, closing the deal with a record final round of 61. Since then there have been another six wins, a series of 40 years-plus victories that ties him alongside Greg Norman and Loren Roberts for the 'older champion' tag among active players.

The best of these was his second Players Championship title in 2000 - his first was back in 1983 - when he fought toe-to-toe with Tiger Woods on the last day and emerged the champion by one stroke. And nearly 18 years.

So now this Business Graduate has a new challenge. He is ready for it. To make sure, he resigned from the all-powerful PGA Tour Policy Board explaining that "being Captain will take up too much of my time and energy". His study back home in Shreveport, Louisiana, where any worries over his golf game have been somewhat diluted by the success of the family oil business, is already a command centre as he studies the form and character of various potential Team Members.

For relaxation he says he hunts, fishes and breeds horses. This, however, is something of a front because for Hal Sutton one suspects the only true relaxation is competing hard, doing his best and then looking up to see where he has finished. A man used to adversity and, of course, a natural leader.

Bill Elliott

worldly wise

Vijay Singh

f ever proof were needed about the impact that European Tour Members have on the global stage, a glance around the world of golf in January 2003 provided all the evidence required.

In six tournaments spanning three continents, five European Tour Members - Ernie Els, Trevor Immelman, Hennie Otto, Mahal Pearce and Vijay Singh - stood tall with gleaming silverware in their hands, a testimony to the international strength in depth of the Tour itself and the versatility of the Members within it.

Leading the way in some considerable style was Els who got the 2003 US PGA Tour season off to a scintillating start in Hawaii with a record breaking success in the Mercedes Championships on the Plantation Course at Kapalua, before following it a week later with another triumph in the Sony Open at the Waialae Country Club in Honolulu.

The victories could not have been more contrasting, the former by eight shots and in the process setting a new US PGA Tour scoring record of 31 under par 261, the latter the culmination of a thrilling play-off with Australian Aaron Baddeley, 'The Big Easy' winning thanks to a 40 foot birdie putt at the second extra hole.

It represented the first time since Steve Jones achieved the feat in 1989 that a player had captured the first two events on the US PGA Tour and reaffirmed Els's credentials as one of the world's truly great golfing talents.

With the South African foregoing the chance of a title hat-trick in favour of a return to The European Tour International Schedule, the winner's circle on the US PGA Tour was left vacant until it was filled, the following week, by another European Tour representative, Singh.

The Fijian went into the final round of the Phoenix Open at the TPC of Scottsdale course in Arizona two shots off the lead but grabbed the tournament he had previously won in 1995 by the scruff of the neck with a blistering start, five birdies in his first six holes helping him to the turn in 29.

"When you are hitting it that close and making the putts you can have a good score and that's what I did on the front nine. That's what won the golf tournament for me," said Singh, who eventually closed with a 63 for a 23 under par total of 261, three strokes clear of John Huston. It was to be the start of an electrifying year for the irrepressible Singh.

Ernie Els

Wins Around The World

Mahal Pearce

"That was superb, you can't get any better than that – that is what you play the game for," said the New Zealander, who finished two shots ahead of fellow European Tour Member, Australian Brett Rumford.

Across in South Africa, the beginning of January had already proved to be memorable for Immelman, who claimed his maiden victory on The European Tour International Schedule in the South African Airways Open at his home Erinvale Golf Club in Cape Town.

Buoyed by the success, the 23 year old returned to the Sunshine Tour a fortnight later and won again, this time in the Dimension Data Pro-Am, continuing a proud tradition of European Tour success in the event, Immelman following in the footsteps of previous winners Lee Westwood (2000), Darren Clarke (2001) and Retief Goosen (2002).

However, it was not just in the United States that European Tour Members were making their presence felt in January. In the southern hemisphere too, success was being gleaned on both the Australasian Tour and the Sunshine Tour.

As Els was bagging his second consecutive success in Hawaii, down under at Auckland Golf Club in New Zealand, host nation favourite Pearce completed an emotional maiden professional victory in front of a host of friends and family at the Holden New Zealand Open.

The 27 year old from Dunedin clinched a two shot victory on ten under par 278 with a largely blemish free final round 70, allowing him to truly appreciate the standing ovation he was accorded all the way up the 18th fairway.

Trevor Immelman

Hennie Otto

Zimbabwe's Marc Cayeux led the way in the 54 hole Limpopo Industrelek Classic at the Pietersburg Golf Club with a winning 19 under par total of 197, ten days before South Africa's Des Terblanche captured the Capital Alliance Royal Swazi Sun Open at the Royal Swazi Sun Country Club, beating Brazil's Adilson da Silva in a play-off after both men had finished with 36 points in the modified stableford competition. The success did not stop there as, in October, Doug McGuigan, of Scotland, won the Platinum Classic at Mooinooi Golf Club.

Back in the United States, Singh took his second title of the year on the US PGA Tour with victory in the EDS Byron Nelson Championship at the Cottonwood Valley Golf Club in Irving, Texas, in May.

Unlike earlier in the season in Phoenix, where he approached the final round in a challenging position, this time Singh held the lead going into the last 18 holes but he proved he was equally as effective in both roles, a final round 66 for a 15 under par total of 265, seeing the two time Major Champion home by two strokes from Nick Price.

In September, when Taiwan's Yeh Wei-Tze won the ANA Open at the Sapporo Golf Club on the Japan Golf Tour, Singh won for a third time on the 2003 US PGA Tour when, with rounds of 66-68-69 and 65 for a 16 under par 268, he captured the John Deere Classic at the TPC at Deere Run in Illinois. Another win in the Funai Classic at the Walt Disney World Resort, Lake Buena Vista, Florida, in October, took Singh to the top of the US PGA Tour money list, and he consolidated his position the following week

A final round 71 at the Gary Player Country Club gave Immelman a 17 under par total of 271 and a one shot victory over fellow countryman Andrew McLardy and Bruce Vaughan of the United States. More importantly, it also put him in an unassailable position as Number One on the Sunshine Tour Order of Merit.

Immelman nearly rounded the Sunshine Tour season off in style the following week in The Tour Championship at the Leopard Creek Country Club, but this time he had to accept the runners-up spot as fellow European Tour Member Otto triumphed, a final round 68 giving him a 17 under par total of 271 and a two stroke winning margin over Immelman, who finished strongly with a 63.

Into May and South Africa continued to be a fertile hunting ground for European Tour Members in search of silverware.

Des Terblanche

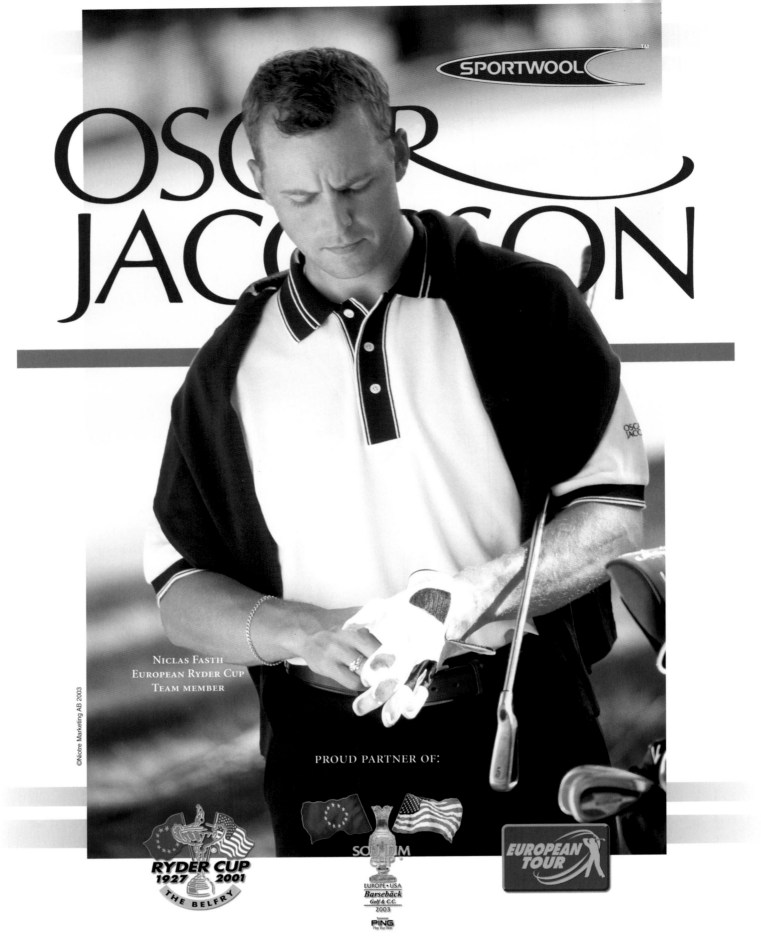

when he was runner-up to South Africa's Retief Goosen in the Chrysler Championship at the Westin Innisbrook Resort, Palm Harbor, Florida. "My goal was to win the money list just once before I retired," he said. A tie for fifth place the following week in the season-ending Tour Championship, presented by Coca-Cola, saw the Fijian achieve his quest with winnings of $7,573,907, relegating World Number One Tiger Woods to second.

Singh became the first European Tour member to win the US PGA Tour money list since Greg Norman in 1995, "I'm really proud of what I've accomplished," he said.

While Els and Singh are both proven winners on the US PGA Tour, the 2003 season saw another European Tour Member take his first step up onto the winners' podium Stateside.

England's Luke Donald had won the Southern Farm Bureau Classic at the end of the 2002 season, and now Australia's Adam Scott took the lead into the final round of the inaugural Deutsche Bank Championship at the Tournament Players Club of Boston in September and withheld the pressure superbly to triumph.

A final round 66 saw Scott complete all four rounds in the 60s and his 20 under par total of 264 proved to be four shots better than runner-up Rocco Mediate, who was glowing in his praise of the 23 year old Australian. "He's as good as you can get," said the American.

Colin Montgomerie

When Colin Montgomerie headed east in October, to tee-up in the Macau Open - one week after John Daly had won the Kolon Cup Korean Open at Woo Jung Hills Country Club in Seoul, and four weeks before India's Arjun Atwal won the Hero Honda Masters at Delhi Golf Club on the Asian PGA Tour - his one and only thought was of winning.

The Scot had won on his previous visit to Asia in 2002, reigning victorious in the TCL Classic in China, and now he did so again at the Macau Golf & Country Club. "This was very much a case of mission accomplished," said Montgomerie. "I had had two seconds previously in the year - in Italy and Denmark - but I wanted to keep the streak alive of winning in each year since 1993."

Montgomerie, however, was compelled to go to a play-off. He had opened with scores of 66, 72 and 67, and he birdied the final hole in a closing 68 to draw level with Australian Scott Barr on 11 under par 273. He immediately birdied the same hole again to claim the title at the first extra hole, and added; "I keep leaving winning later and later each year. Too late! I would rather win in January."

Adam Scott

Scott Crockett

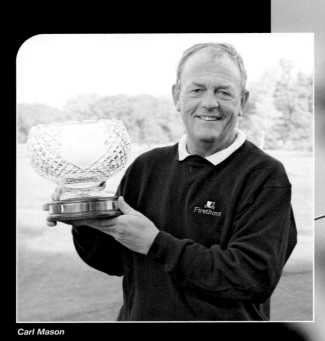

Carl Mason

statement of intent

The 2003 European Seniors Tour Order of Merit

1 Carl MASON Eng
2 Bill LONGMUIR Scot
3 Terry GALE Aus
4 John CHILLAS Scot
5 Denis DURNIAN Eng
6 Guillermo ENCINA Chi
7 David OAKLEY USA
8 Denis O'SULLIVAN Ire
9 Jerry BRUNER USA
10 David GOOD Aus
11 Nick JOB Eng
12 Delroy CAMBRIDGE Jam
13 Noel RATCLIFFE Aus
14 Brian JONES Aus
15 Bob CAMERON Eng

f anything told Carl Mason that the 2003 European Seniors Tour season was to be one to remember, it was the dream start he made to his rookie year amongst the over 50s. He won on only his second appearance to set the ball rolling, but it was the three victories he achieved in consecutive appearances at the end of the year which turned the amiable Englishman into a record breaker.

Mason became the quickest player in European Seniors Tour history to win four times, his run of successes, in 11 events, beating the previous best of four in 12 by Brian Huggett in the period covering the end of the 1992 season and the beginning of 1993.

In topping the Order of Merit and winning the John Jacobs Trophy, in addition, of course, to becoming Ping Rookie of the Year, Mason also amassed record earnings in a single season of 350,241 euro, 20,031 euro more than the previous best set by Japan's Seiji Ebihara in the 2002 season.

The Englishman, a former European Tour regular, also played a central role in a sensational Senior British Open, presented by MasterCard, that did much to enhance the burgeoning European Seniors Tour's profile on the world stage.

Mason took almost 20 years to win the first of his two European Tour titles in 1994 but a mere two weeks to achieve his maiden victory on the Seniors Tour. That came when he closed with a 68 to pip Bob Cameron in The Mobile Cup, Stoke Park, England, a victory which was to mark the start of an incredible summer for the man known affectionately to his friends and colleagues as, simply, 'Mace'.

The win in Buckinghamshire might have been a statement of intent, but it was two weeks later, in the Senior British Open, presented by MasterCard, at the Westin Turnberry Resort, Scotland, that he made his mark on a global stage.

Bill Longmuir

The advance publicity for the Championship, the first to be officially sanctioned by the US Champions Tour, had understandably focused on Jack Nicklaus and Tom Watson replaying their famous 'Duel in the Sun' of the 1977 Open Golf Championship at the renowned Scottish links.

Paired together for the first two rounds, the headline writers had their ideal opportunity, but they had not counted on the intervention of the third member of the group, Mason. The Englishman was immense as he outscored both his illustrious playing partners to lead the field at halfway.

Denis O'Sullivan

Noel Ratcliffe

A leader in Europe for the production of exquisite print

Titles have included The European Tour Yearbooks, Volvo PGA Championship Programmes, Hotels of Distinction Books, Les Routiers Guides and Mizuno Golf Consumer Catalogues.

London Print & Design

TC COMMUNICATIONS PLC

01344 622280
timl@tc-comms.co.uk
www.tc-comms.co.uk

020 7242 6051
pdane@londonprint.com
www.londonprint.com

Terry Gale

Six weeks later he won The Daily Telegraph/Turismo Andaluz Seniors Match Play Championship at Los Flamingos, Spain, beating Ireland's Denis O'Sullivan on the last green of an enthralling final, before claiming the Merseyside English Seniors Open at Hillside Golf Club, England, the following week. He then rounded off the season in sumptuous style in the Estoril Seniors Tour Championship at Oitavos Golf Club, Portugal, an opening 64 and a closing 65, either side of a 73, helping him to an eight shot win and cementing his Number One status.

Incredibly, given the length and difficulty of many of the Seniors Tour venues, the Englishman failed to break par in just five of the 32 stroke play rounds he played during the year, posting a superb stroke average of 68.87. Not surprisingly, in the circumstances, he also set a new Seniors Tour record for average earnings per tournament, winning an average of 31,840 euro each time he teed up.

For a long while it looked as if he might go all the way until he came cruelly unstuck on the 72nd hole. Holding a two shot lead, Mason had hit what he thought was a good tee shot but the ball finished in an horrendous lie in a fairway bunker. He took a double bogey six and in the process handed the initiative to the fast finishing Watson. "I thought I had lost," said the five time Open Golf Champion. "Carl was playing so well that I didn't expect him to slip. Unfortunately, it happens sometimes. That's golf, I'm afraid."

Mason was understandably disappointed by the reversal but showed immense courage and application to bounce back.

Mason was a deserved winner of the John Jacobs Trophy, awarded annually to the leader of the Order of Merit, but he was by no means the only newcomer to shine.

Scotland's Bill Longmuir won twice to finish second on the Order of Merit and, like Mason, earn a place in Tony Jacklin's Rest of the World Cup team which faced the United States in the UBS Cup match at Sea Island Golf Club, Georgia, USA, in November.

Longmuir had spent the winter practising at the Florida home of his great friend and former European Tour colleague, Greg Norman,

Neil Coles became the first recipient of the Lawrence Batley International Trophy, to be awarded annually to the leading player aged 60 and over on the Seniors Tour Order of Merit. Rita Firth, the daughter of the late Lawrence Batley OBE, made the presentation.

Hank Woodrome

The European Seniors Tour

Guillermo Encina

Tom Watson

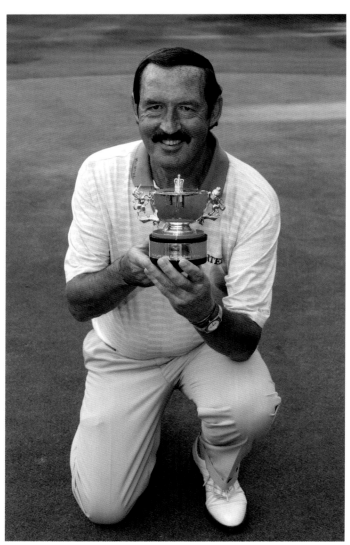

Paul Leonard

and the hard work paid off when he won on just his third start in the Ryder Cup Wales Seniors Open at Royal St David's Golf Club, Wales. He also went on to collect the title in the De Vere PGA Seniors Championship at De Vere Carden Park, England, where Mason was runner-up.

The following week another rookie, Horacio Carbonetti, the medallist at the 2002 Seniors Tour Qualifying School, became the first Argentine golfer to win on the European Seniors Tour when he captured the Bad Ragaz PGA Seniors Open at Bad Ragaz Golf Club, Switzerland.

Carbonetti, Longmuir and Mason, however, were not the only first-time winners to emerge from a 2003 season that started in the steamy heat of a Caribbean spring and ended, seven months later, in the balmy breezes of a Portuguese autumn.

America's Hank Woodrome led the way when he defeated Northern Ireland's Eddie Polland in a play-off for the Wallonia Open at Pierpont Golf Club, Belgium. Scotland's Mike Miller won the inaugural Nigel Mansell Classic, presented by Sunseeker International, at Woodbury Park, England, the week after compatriot, John Chillas, collected his first title at the Travis Perkins Senior Masters on the Edinburgh Course at Wentworth Club, England.

Chillas, a former club professional, has made a huge impact since turning 50 in the summer of 2001. The Scot posted three top five finishes in his first five starts that season and then cemented his playing privileges by finishing fourth at the subsequent Qualifying School. His 2002 season started in fine fashion when he finished second at the Tobago Plantations Seniors Classic and he was to go on to post six further top ten finishes on his way to claiming eighth place on the Order of Merit.

During 2003, the Scot continued in much the same vein, finishing second twice before relegating Ireland's Eamonn Darcy into second place after a fascinating duel at Wentworth Club. Altogether Chillas amassed 11 top ten finishes, one more than Australia's Terry Gale, who elicited slight revenge by pipping him for third place on the Order of Merit thanks to his tied fifth place finish in the Estoril Seniors Tour Championship.

If Chillas is to be regarded as the most consistent golfer of the year, then Gale, a 56 year old from Perth, Western Australia, must go down as the most improved. During 2002 he had brought a six year winless drought to an end when he captured the GIN Monte Carlo Invitational but that hardly prepared his peers for what he was to achieve in 2003.

Gale started his season with back-to-back wins in the Royal Westmoreland Barbados Open at Royal Westmoreland, Barbados,

Malcolm Gregson and Tommy Horton

Denis Durnian

David Creamer

Hardys Super Seniors Final Order of Merit

	Name	Country	Points
1	David Creamer	(Eng)	10,875
2	Liam Higgins	(Ire)	7,000
3	Neil Coles	(Eng)	6,250
4	Tommy Horton	(Eng)	5,875
5	Malcolm Gregson	(Eng)	3,500

David Oakley

Horacio Carbonetti

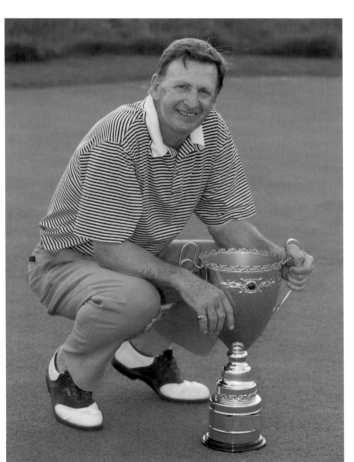

David Good

and the Tobago Plantations Seniors Classic at the Tobago Plantations Golf & Beach Resort, Tobago. Some five months later, he became just the sixth man to win three events in a single season, when he defeated England's Nick Job and New Zealand's Barry Vivian by two shots to take the Charles Church Scottish Seniors Open at The Roxburghe, Scotland.

The Australian was by no means the only experienced campaigner to win on the 2003 Seniors Tour. Indeed, for a while at least, before the emergence of Longmuir and Mason, the proceedings were dominated by golfers in their mid 50s.

That process started when 56 year old American, Ray Carrasco, won the opening event of the season, the Digicel Jamaica Classic, in association with Sony Ericsson, at Half Moon, Montego Bay, Jamaica. Subsequently, further victories were achieved by 58 year old Australian Noel Ratcliffe in the AIB Irish Seniors Open at Adare Manor Hotel & Golf Resort, Ireland; 59 year old Englishman Malcolm Gregson in the Irvine Whitlock Jersey Seniors Classic at La Moye Golf Club, Jersey; 58 year old American John Jacobs in the US PGA Seniors Championship at Aronimink Golf Club, Newton Square, Pennsylvania, USA; 56 year old American Jerry Bruner in the De Vere Northumberland Seniors Classic at De Vere Slaley Hall,

The European Seniors Tour

Ray Carrasco

Mike Miller

England; 58 year old Irishman Paul Leonard in the Bovis Lend Lease European Senior Masters at Woburn Golf & Country Club, England; and 55 year old Australian David Good in the Tunisian Seniors Open at Port El Kantaoui Golf Club, Tunisia.

One player to break the mould, so to speak, was American Bruce Leitzke, who was a mere 51 years young when he captured his first Senior Major, the US Senior Open, at the Inverness Club, Toledo, Ohio, USA, in June.

However, it was entirely appropriate that in the final week it was to be Mason who won the season's grand finale in Portugal. "It is hard

to believe what I have managed to do in the four months since I turned 50," said an elated Mason after recording his breathtaking, eight shot victory, the largest winning margin of the 2003 season.

"When I started, I thought that with a bit of luck I might be able to win once before the end of the season but to win four times is beyond my wildest dreams. It took me almost 20 years to win the first of my two European Tour titles but here I am winning four times in as many months on the Seniors Tour. It really is quite remarkable."

Colin Callander

Jerry Bruner

John Chillas

Bill Longmuir and Carl Mason

Bernard Gallacher was accorded Honorary Life Membership of The European Tour and received the Tour's Silver Membership Card from Ken Schofield, Executive Director of The European Tour, at the European Seniors Tour's Annual Dinner at Wentworth Club.

The 2003 European Seniors Tour Order of Merit

Pos.	Name & Country	Tournaments Played	Prize Money Euro	£	Pos.	Name & Country	Tournaments Played	Prize Money Euro	£
1	Carl MASON (Eng)	(11)	350,241.61	244,222.27	51	John MASHEGO (SA)	(14)	33,934.42	23,662.35
2	Bill LONGMUIR (Scot)	(15)	253,666.95	176,881.10	52	Ian STANLEY (Aus)	(17)	33,318.32	23,232.75
3	Terry GALE (Aus)	(18)	195,726.57	136,479.47	53	John MCTEAR (Scot)	(15)	30,784.46	21,465.90
4	John CHILLAS (Scot)	(21)	190,002.99	132,488.43	54	Tommy HORTON (Eng)	(19)	28,581.06	19,929.48
5	Denis DURNIAN (Eng)	(21)	146,603.95	102,226.44	55	Christy O'CONNOR JNR (Ire)	(7)	28,079.45	19,579.70
6	Guillermo ENCINA (Chi)	(19)	145,388.21	101,378.70	56	Bob SHEARER (Aus)	(8)	28,005.31	19,528.01
7	David OAKLEY (USA)	(20)	142,932.98	99,666.68	57	Jeff VAN WAGENEN (USA)	(17)	27,387.37	19,097.12
8	Denis O'SULLIVAN (Ire)	(20)	130,427.08	90,946.36	58	Robbie STEWART (SA)	(14)	25,602.88	17,852.80
9	Jerry BRUNER (USA)	(20)	128,039.44	89,281.46	59	Neville CLARKE (SA)	(13)	23,188.50	16,169.26
10	David GOOD (Aus)	(19)	125,316.26	87,382.60	60	Sam TORRANCE (Scot)	(3)	19,781.86	13,793.82
11	Nick JOB (Eng)	(20)	124,647.51	86,916.28	61	Bill HARDWICK (Can)	(17)	19,657.57	13,707.16
12	Delroy CAMBRIDGE (Jam)	(21)	124,031.40	86,486.67	62	George BURNS (USA)	(6)	19,538.56	13,624.17
13	Noel RATCLIFFE (Aus)	(18)	120,140.75	83,773.73	63	Alberto CROCE (It)	(14)	18,021.19	12,566.12
14	Brian JONES (Aus)	(20)	111,479.97	77,734.60	64	Peter TOWNSEND (Eng)	(18)	16,352.28	11,402.39
15	Bob CAMERON (Eng)	(19)	109,333.17	76,237.65	65	Bernard GALLACHER (Scot)	(13)	14,557.72	10,151.05
16	Horacio CARBONETTI (Arg)	(16)	104,280.32	72,714.31	66	Craig MALTMAN (Scot)	(4)	14,424.44	10,058.12
17	Giuseppe CALI (It)	(19)	101,364.81	70,681.33	67	David JONES (N.Ire)	(5)	13,000.98	9,065.54
18	Jim RHODES (Eng)	(18)	89,007.36	62,064.53	68	Martin FOSTER (Eng)	(13)	12,648.06	8,819.45
19	Keith MACDONALD (Eng)	(20)	83,675.62	58,346.72	69	John BENDA (USA)	(10)	12,644.29	8,816.82
20	John MORGAN (Eng)	(20)	78,938.39	55,043.47	70	Noboru SUGAI (Jpn)	(6)	12,624.86	8,803.27
21	Alan TAPIE (USA)	(13)	78,301.65	54,599.47	71	Steve WILD (Eng)	(14)	12,585.11	8,775.55
22	Paul LEONARD (N.Ire)	(14)	74,511.85	51,956.86	72	Hisao INOUE (Jpn)	(5)	12,434.72	8,670.69
23	Ian MOSEY (Eng)	(20)	72,696.02	50,690.68	73	Keith ASHDOWN (Eng)	(8)	12,422.79	8,662.37
24	Mike MILLER (Scot)	(19)	68,592.25	47,829.14	74	Craig DEFOY (Wal)	(15)	12,174.13	8,488.98
25	Eamonn DARCY (Ire)	(5)	66,152.98	46,128.25	75	John FOURIE (SA)	(17)	11,722.11	8,173.79
26	Baldovino DASSU (It)	(20)	62,918.53	43,872.88	76	Joe MCDERMOTT (Ire)	(11)	10,663.21	7,435.42
27	Manuel PIÑERO (Sp)	(13)	62,717.51	43,732.71	77	Geoff TICKELL (Wal)	(16)	10,587.02	7,382.30
28	Ray CARRASCO (USA)	(16)	62,034.91	43,256.73	78	Bill BRASK (USA)	(12)	9,176.65	6,398.85
29	Martin GRAY (Scot)	(16)	61,464.73	42,859.14	79	David HUISH (Scot)	(12)	9,173.00	6,396.30
30	Simon OWEN (NZ)	(17)	60,240.19	42,005.28	80	Antonio GARRIDO (Sp)	(16)	8,807.76	6,141.62
31	Malcolm GREGSON (Eng)	(17)	60,038.80	41,864.85	81	Ross METHERELL (Aus)	(14)	7,958.57	5,549.48
32	Dragon TAKI (Jpn)	(19)	57,855.91	40,342.73	82	Peter DAWSON (Eng)	(14)	7,453.09	5,197.01
33	Steve STULL (USA)	(20)	56,284.08	39,246.70	83	Wayne WRIGHT (USA)	(6)	7,149.45	4,985.29
34	David CREAMER (Eng)	(20)	54,360.59	37,905.45	84	Juan JIMÉNEZ(Sp)	(13)	6,899.88	4,811.27
35	Gary WINTZ (USA)	(20)	54,043.80	37,684.56	85	Renato CAMPAGNOLI (It)	(14)	6,620.60	4,616.52
36	John GRACE (USA)	(12)	53,265.37	37,141.76	86	Bobby VERWEY (SA)	(8)	5,930.24	4,135.14
37	Maurice BEMBRIDGE (Eng)	(18)	49,781.64	34,712.57	87	Mike FERGUSON (Aus)	(5)	4,999.76	3,486.31
38	Neil COLES (Eng)	(8)	48,349.48	33,713.93	88	Jay HORTON (USA)	(6)	4,926.11	3,434.96
39	Russell WEIR (Scot)	(19)	47,717.55	33,273.28	89	Joey COMBS (USA)	(9)	4,570.31	3,186.86
40	Barry VIVIAN (NZ)	(10)	46,051.02	32,111.22	90	Jay DOLAN III (USA)	(8)	4,539.93	3,165.68
41	Eddie POLLAND (N.Ire)	(19)	44,504.12	31,032.57	91	Tony ALLEN (Eng)	(4)	4,377.75	3,052.59
42	Priscillo DINIZ (Bra)	(20)	43,905.27	30,615.00	92	Gery WATINE (Fr)	(3)	4,110.05	2,865.92
43	Bob LENDZION (USA)	(16)	41,052.93	28,626.07	93	Lawrence FARMER (Wal)	(6)	3,908.30	2,725.24
44	Hank WOODROME (USA)	(14)	40,495.95	28,237.68	94	Adriano MORI (It)	(6)	3,392.38	2,365.49
45	Seiji EBIHARA (Jpn)	(6)	39,349.43	27,438.22	95	David SNELL (Eng)	(8)	2,616.39	1,824.40
46	John IRWIN (Can)	(19)	38,446.93	26,808.91	96	TR JONES (USA)	(4)	2,438.30	1,700.22
47	Manuel VELASCO (Sp)	(16)	37,856.18	26,396.99	97	Victor GARCIA (Sp)	(5)	1,628.76	1,135.73
48	Bob LARRATT (Eng)	(17)	36,282.18	25,299.44	98	David OJALA (USA)	(6)	1,447.23	1,009.15
49	Liam HIGGINS (Ire)	(13)	34,933.48	24,358.99	99	Mike GALLAGHER (Eng)	(6)	1,382.12	963.75
50	Alan MEW (T&T)	(12)	34,875.96	24,318.88	100	David CHILLAS (Scot)	(5)	1,347.25	939.43
					101	Kenny STEVENSON (N.Ire)	(3)	244.29	170.34

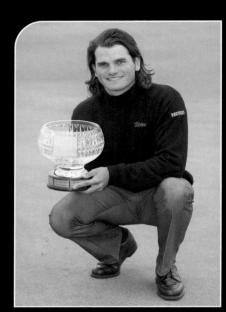

Johan Edfors

setting standards

The 2003 European Challenge Tour Rankings

1 Johan EDFORS Swe

2 Martin LeMESURIER Eng

3 José Manuel CARRILES Sp

4 Martin WIEGELE Aut

5 Peter HANSON Swe

6 Martin ERLANDSSON Swe

7 Scott DRUMMOND Scot

8 Stuart LITTLE Eng

9 Sebastian FERNANDEZ Arg

10 Jamie ELSON Eng

11 James HEPWORTH Eng

12 Michael JONZON Swe

13 Robert COLES Eng

14 Ivo GINER Sp

15 Ben MASON Eng

There were points during the Challenge Tour season where standards became so good and the golf so impressive, that course records were seemingly broken every other week by some searingly hot golf under the European sunshine.

This was highlighted at the end of July at the Golf Club Padova Terme Euganee International Open at Padova Golf Club, Valsansibio, Italy, where Spain's Ivo Giner picked up his second title of the season, his first having come two weeks previously in the Open des Volcans Challenge de France at Golf des Volcans, France.

In Italy, the talented Spaniard, who played the bulk of his amateur golf alongside compatriot Sergio Garcia, won with a performance The Ryder Cup golfer would have been proud of himself, a record breaking 72 hole total of 29 under par 259 - the lowest in the 15 year history of the European Challenge Tour.

By that point in the season, exceptional levels of performance had become commonplace – ever since Sweden's Johan Edfors, who would go on to be crowned Challenge Tour Champion 2003, had seized the early season initiative and surged to the top of the Rankings with two victories and two top ten finishes during the opening months of the Schedule.

Ivo Giner

José Manuel Carriles

With such standards being set, it was no surprise to see the Challenge Tour regulars faring well against their counterparts from The European Tour in the dual ranking BMW Russian Open at Le Meridien Moscow Country Club, Russia, in August. The tournament was one of three dual ranking events of the season and, for the Challenge Tour professionals, offered the chance of an increased prize fund alongside the even greater prize of a year's exemption to The European Tour.

In Russia, Australia's Marcus Fraser and his Challenge Tour colleague Martin Wiegele of Austria successfully fended off the likes of European Tour representative Andrew Coltart, of Scotland, by posting respective 19 under totals of 269 to take the tournament into extra time before Fraser triumphed at the second extra hole.

For Fraser, it was the end of his short, but impressive stay on the Challenge Tour. In his maiden season, he won three times in eight months and proved that he is a devastating talent when on top of his game.

His first win of the year came in the Nykredit Danish Open at Gilleleje Golf Club, Helsingor, Denmark, before his second success, a week before his Russian adventure, came in a play-off for the Talma Finnish Challenge at Talma Golf, Finland, against Tony Edlund of Sweden. Fraser won, spectacularly, at the third extra hole by holing his nine iron approach.

Martin Erlandsson

Earlier in the season, the first of the three dual ranking events, the Aa St Omer Open at Aa St Omer Golf Club, France, had also gone the way of Australia, in the hands of Brett Rumford, while the third, the Turespaña Mallorca Classic, at Pula Golf, Mallorca, Spain, in October went to Miguel Angel Jiménez, of Spain.

One of the most satisfying aspects of life on the Challenge Tour is seeing the birth and early trajectory of the future stars of the game. Season after season, the Challenge Tour officials see players who are improving the standards every year. That is why it will be no surprise to those who know the Challenge Tour if any of the 15 graduates from the class of 2003 make a big impression on The European Tour in 2004.

Included among those who are vying to make their mark alongside illustrious former Challenge Tour players such as Denmark's Thomas Björn, and Englishmen Ian Poulter and Justin Rose were the season's multiple winners.

The Swedish pair of Johan Edfors and Michael Jonzon, alongside Englishman Martin LeMesurier, emulated Giner by picking up two wins each on the 2003 Schedule – with LeMesurier

Robert Coles

The European Challenge Tour

Stuart Little

Sebastian Fernandez

exploding onto the scene as he pipped André Bossert, of Switzerland, and England's Sam Walker to first place by winning a play-off for the Tessali - Metaponto Open di Puglia e Basilicata at Riva dei Tessali and Metaponto, Italy, in May. He did not look back after securing what was his first victory as a professional.

His next stop was Spain where he guaranteed second spot, behind eventual winner Martin Erlandsson of Sweden, in the Izki Challenge de España at Izki Golf, Urturi, Vittoria, Spain, before finishing tied fourth in the Fortis Challenge Open at Burggolf Purmerend, Purmerend, The Netherlands. He went on to share eighth place in the Aa St Omer Open before achieving his second victory of the year in the Clearstream International Luxembourg Open at Kikuoka Golf & Country Club, Canach, Luxembourg, in June.

That glorious six week spell took LeMesurier to the top of the Rankings, ahead of Edfors, who had won the Stanbic Zambia Open at Lusaka Golf Club, Zambia, in March, two months before his success in the Fortis Challenge Open in The Netherlands.

LeMesurier would hold the lead entering the Challenge Tour Grand Final at Golf du Médoc, Bordeaux, France, in late October but such was the consistency of the Challenge Tour players in 2003 that the leading three players were separated by 1,631 euro and the leading 15 by only 28,815 euro. Spain's José Manuel

Edfors's fellow countryman, Jonzon, who has six years experience on The European Tour, got his first victory of the season in June in the Galeria Kaufhof Pokal Challenge at Rittergut Birkhof Golf Club, Germany, before picking up the Rolex Trophy, two months later at the Golf Club de Genève, Switzerland.

The Swedish golf production line continued to bear fruit on the European Challenge Tour – with no less than four players finishing the season in the top 15. The Scandinavian country

Martin Wiegele

Carriles would win the title with a closing 66 and a wonderful seven iron approach at the first extra hole, but the man he beat in the play-off – Edfors – was able to celebrate being Number One.

Edfors, who in all had nine top ten finishes, had taken his earnings to 94,509 euro to finish ahead of LeMesurier (88,643 euro), Carriles (86,603 euro) and Wiegele (86,057 euro). He said: "It was a brilliant season for me, and the competition was tough every week. So to finish Number One meant so much. I was absolutely delighted by my achievement."

Scott Drummond

- TOP 10* - WHY CHANGE? -

Padraig Harrington, armed with his Wilson Deep Red driver broke into the world's top 10 during 2002. So why change? Because he wants to be in the top 5! That's the confidence he has in the new Deep Red II driver from Wilson. The new 400cc Wilson Deep Red II has 40% more weight low and deep in the heel, making it easier to square the face at impact. The squarer the face the greater the velocity on the ball and the farther it goes! Easy. However, the new 350cc Tour model has a lower centre of gravity giving it the same hot face but with better shot-shaping ability. That's why pros like Padraig play with them. Visit <u>wilson.com</u> or call +44 (0) 1294 316270 to find details of the new Deep Red II Drivers and Fairway Woods and your nearest Approved Wilson Retailer.

- THE NEW -
WILSON DEEP RED II
DRIVERS AND
FAIRWAY WOODS

*World Rankings as at 15th December 2002

wilson

Martin LeMesurier

also hosted two events on the 2003 schedule, with South African Titch Moore picking up the Skandia PGA Open at Falsterbo Golf Club, Sweden, and Scotsman Euan Little taking the Telia Grand Prix at Ljunghusens Golf Club, Sweden.

The other Challenge Tour champions in 2003 emerged from all corners of the globe – from Argentinian Sebastian Fernandez's victory in the first event of 2003, the Costa Rica Open presented by Credomatic MasterCard at Cariari Country Club, San Jose, Costa Rica, to the more experienced duo of Welshman Bradley Dredge and Ulsterman Darren Clarke who respectively won the Madeira Island Open at Santo da Serra, Madeira, in March, and the inaugural Benmore Developments Northern Ireland Masters at Clandeboye Golf Club, Belfast, Northern Ireland, in September.

Elsewhere, the sweet taste of success was savoured by Argentine Daniel Vancsik in the Telefonica Centro America Abierto de Guatemala at Club Hacienda Nueva, Guatemala; Englishman James Hepworth in the American Express Los Encinos Open at the Los Encinos Golf Club, Toluca, Mexico; Greig Hutcheon, of Scotland, in the Panalpina Bank Commerciale du Maroc Classic

Michael Jonzon

The European Challenge Tour

Peter Hanson

Ben Mason

at Royal Golf Dar Es Salam, Rabat, Morocco; England's Jamie Elson in the Volvo Finnish Open at Espoon Golfseura, Finland; England's David J Geall in the Kitzbühel Golf Alpin Open at Kitzbühel-Schwarzsee, Kitzbühel, Austria; England's Robert Coles in the BA CA Golf Open, presented by Telekom Austria, at Fontana Golf Club, Vienna, Austria; Scott Drummond, of Scotland, in the Open de Toulouse at Golf de Toulouse-Palmola, Toulouse, France; and Craig Williams, of Wales, in the Ryder Cup Wales Challenge at Northop Country Park Golf Club, Wales.

In all eight players – Johan Edfors, Martin LeMesurier, Martin Wiegele, Martin Erlandsson, Scott Drummond, Sebastian Fernandez, Jamie Elson and James Hepworth – earned through finishing in the top 15 the chance to compete on The European Tour for the first time. This further endorsed the view that the European Challenge Tour continues to play an integral part in the professional golfing community by emphasising the long-term policy of opportunity and incentive operated by The European Tour.

Michael Gibbons

Jamie Elson

James Hepworth

The 2003 European Challenge Tour Rankings

Pos.	Name & Country	Tournaments Played	Prize Money Euro	Pos.	Name & Country	Tournaments Played	Prize Money Euro
1	Johan EDFORS (Swe)	(22)	94,509.47	51	Erol SIMSEK (Ger)	(17)	22,100.87
2	Martin LEMESURIER (Eng)	(15)	88,643.77	52	Alvaro SALTO (Sp)	(10)	21,393.30
3	José Manuel CARRILES (Sp)	(18)	86,603.76	53	Marco SOFFIETTI (It)	(21)	21,311.17
4	Martin WIEGELE (Aut)	(19)	86,057.15	54	Juan ABBATE (Arg)	(14)	21,100.43
5	Peter HANSON (Swe)	(22)	83,662.93	55	Jesus Maria ARRUTI (Sp)	(6)	20,878.48
6	Martin ERLANDSSON (Swe)	(22)	80,426.41	56	Michele REALE (It)	(17)	20,307.56
7	Scott DRUMMOND (Scot)	(21)	79,773.85	57	Edward RUSH (Eng)	(22)	20,279.43
8	Stuart LITTLE (Eng)	(23)	73,553.96	58	Chris GANE (Eng)	(21)	19,122.30
9	Sebastian FERNANDEZ (Arg)	(24)	72,115.27	59	Didier DE VOOGHT (Bel)	(23)	19,027.93
10	Jamie ELSON (Eng)	(15)	70,551.29	60	Benoit TEILLERIA (Fr)	(16)	18,998.69
11	James HEPWORTH (Eng)	(25)	67,970.74	61	Tony EDLUND (Swe)	(8)	17,810.00
12	Michael JONZON (Swe)	(22)	66,307.99	62	David PATRICK (Scot)	(10)	17,589.83
13	Robert COLES (Eng)	(16)	65,869.03	63	André BOSSERT (Swi)	(13)	17,423.39
14	Ivo GINER (Sp)	(22)	60,635.94	64	Olivier DAVID (Fr)	(20)	17,416.80
15	Ben MASON (Eng)	(13)	59,828.68	65	Ryan REID (SA)	(14)	17,111.69
16	Cesar MONASTERIO (Arg)	(24)	57,782.08	66	Oskar BERGMAN (Swe)	(15)	16,945.44
17	Greig HUTCHEON (Scot)	(27)	55,664.76	67	Paul DWYER (Eng)	(22)	16,800.23
18	Sion E BEBB (Wal)	(23)	51,399.49	68	Philip ARCHER (Eng)	(11)	16,663.76
19	Richard MCEVOY (Eng)	(24)	51,259.18	69	Hennie OTTO (SA)	(9)	16,519.03
20	Michael KIRK (SA)	(24)	51,010.69	70	Neil CHEETHAM (Eng)	(18)	16,466.83
21	Peter GUSTAFSSON (Swe)	(23)	45,631.28	71	Stephen BROWNE (Ire)	(20)	16,398.25
22	Damien MCGRANE (Ire)	(8)	44,667.76	72	Massimo FLORIOLI (It)	(22)	16,329.29
23	Marc PENDARIES (Fr)	(23)	37,944.19	73	Leif WESTERBERG (Swe)	(10)	16,205.66
24	Kalle BRINK (Swe)	(22)	37,229.89	74	Gianluca BARUFFALDI (It)	(17)	15,719.41
25	Louis OOSTHUIZEN (SA)	(18)	36,382.62	75	Marcello SANTI (It)	(14)	15,222.65
26	Graeme STORM (Eng)	(16)	36,293.18	76	Allan HOGH (Den)	(22)	15,144.72
27	Sam WALKER (Eng)	(23)	35,888.70	77	Daren LEE (Eng)	(19)	14,284.57
28	Euan LITTLE (Scot)	(10)	35,287.57	78	Raphael PELLICIOLI (Fr)	(14)	14,146.48
29	Daniel VANCSIK (Arg)	(24)	35,028.77	79	Fredrik HENGE (Swe)	(8)	14,031.66
30	Sam LITTLE (Eng)	(25)	34,726.35	80	Pehr MAGNEBRANT (Swe)	(17)	13,456.01
31	Titch MOORE (SA)	(13)	34,664.81	81	Jimmy KAWALEC (Swe)	(12)	13,281.03
32	Garry HOUSTON (Wal)	(25)	34,588.80	82	Magnus PERSSON ATLEVI (Swe)	(9)	12,885.27
33	Gregory BOURDY (Fr)	(20)	34,261.02	83	Marcel HAREMZA (Ger)	(14)	12,738.39
34	Steven O'HARA (Scot)	(22)	31,946.13	84	Regis GUSTAVE (St.L)	(17)	12,522.44
35	Mark SANDERS (Eng)	(24)	31,879.68	85	Gareth PADDISON (NZ)	(15)	12,472.02
36	David J GEALL (Eng)	(21)	31,619.84	86	Carlos QUEVEDO (Sp)	(13)	11,615.53
37	Federico BISAZZA (It)	(12)	31,127.81	87	Johan SKOLD (Swe)	(11)	11,410.14
38	Mattias ELIASSON (Swe)	(12)	30,050.74	88	Marco BERNARDINI (It)	(16)	11,203.30
39	Craig WILLIAMS (Wal)	(15)	29,261.01	89	Ilya GORONESKOUL (Fr)	(18)	11,051.66
40	Pasi PURHONEN (Fin)	(14)	29,236.80	90	Thomas NORRET (Den)	(16)	11,010.88
41	Christopher HANELL (Swe)	(19)	29,038.34	91	Sebastien DELAGRANGE (Fr)	(12)	10,980.26
42	Joakim RASK (Swe)	(17)	28,393.82	92	Jose TRAUWITZ (Mex)	(7)	10,337.01
43	Jamie LITTLE (Eng)	(25)	28,392.53	93	Fredrik OREST (Swe)	(8)	10,236.42
44	Alexandre BALICKI (Fr)	(14)	27,083.86	94	Francesco GUERMANI (It)	(13)	10,068.24
45	Tim MILFORD (Eng)	(24)	26,541.27	95	Paolo TERRENI (It)	(15)	9,791.05
46	Steven BOWDITCH (Aus)	(16)	25,100.80	96	Joakim KRISTIANSSON (Swe)	(20)	9,641.31
47	Gary CLARK (Eng)	(21)	24,973.64	97	Richard DINSDALE (Wal)	(21)	9,463.18
48	Mark MOULAND (Wal)	(18)	24,437.14	98	Stefano REALE (It)	(17)	9,327.98
49	Kariem BARAKA (Ger)	(22)	23,412.93	99	Adam CRAWFORD (Aus)	(12)	9,152.56
50	David RYLES (Eng)	(22)	23,216.08	100	Paul MCKECHNIE (Scot)	(20)	9,070.96

ROBERT-JAN DERKSEN
March

FREDRIK JACOBSON
April & October

PAUL CASEY
May

PHILIP GOLDING
June

Asprey Golfer of the Month Awards 2003

The Asprey Golfer of the Month Awards
are presented throughout the year
followed by an Annual Award.

Previous winners have been:

2002 Ernie Els

2001 Retief Goosen

2000 Lee Westwood

1999 Colin Montgomerie

1998 Lee Westwood

1997 Colin Montgomerie

1996 Colin Montgomerie

1995 Colin Montgomerie

1994 Ernie Els

1993 Bernhard Langer

1992 Nick Faldo

1991 Severiano Ballesteros

1990 Nick Faldo

1989 Nick Faldo

1988 Severiano Ballesteros

1987 Ian Woosnam

1986 Severiano Ballesteros

1985 Bernhard Langer

PHILLIP PRICE
July

DARREN CLARKE
August

LEE WESTWOOD
September

Ernie Els, Asprey Golfer of the Month in January and February, receives his alms dish after the second round of the Volvo PGA Championship at Wentworth Club, from Edward Asprey, New Business Director of Asprey, the ultimate authentic British luxury lifestyle house.

DARREN CLARKE
August

Darren Clarke, The Royal Bank of Scotland Shot of the Month winner for August, receives his Award from Jim Bellany, Head of Sponsorship, The Royal Bank of Scotland.

The Royal Bank of Scotland

The European Tour International Schedule was enhanced by an exciting new addition in 2003, The Royal Bank of Scotland Shot of the Month Award, an innovatory award which recognised the shot-making skills of European Tour Members across the globe.

An outstanding repertoire of shots executed by European Tour Members throughout the season provided hours of fascinating debate for The Royal Bank of Scotland Shot of the Month judging panel, comprising representatives of both the Media and The European Tour.

Players of the calibre of Paul Casey, Darren Clarke, Robert-Jan Derksen, Sergio Garcia, Ignacio Garrido, Philip Golding, Trevor Immelman, Fredrik Jacobson and Lee Westwood were judged to have played the outstanding shot of each month, while many others featured in the discussions.

Each of the above named players received The Royal Bank of Scotland Shot of the Month Award, beautifully crafted by Waterford Crystal, in addition to a cheque for £1000 which was donated to a charity of their choice.

From a wide initial choice of shots each calendar month from tournaments played on The European Tour International Schedule, the judging panel selected their top three, before deciding in which order to place them.

The three shots were then featured during Sky Television's golf coverage and viewers asked to place the shots in the same order as the panel to win a variety of golf related prizes. In addition to the Sky Sports package, golf enthusiasts received another chance to register a telephone vote through Golf Weekly magazine, for a further selection of prizes.

The winning shots from each month were entered towards The Royal Bank of Scotland Shot of the Year Award and the candidates in 2003 delivered a superb array of shot-making from which the panel would make the annual Award.

In January, South African Trevor Immelman played a brilliant wedge to the last hole at Erinvale Golf Club in Cape Town to secure a birdie three and a place in a play-off which he subsequently won against compatriot Tim Clark in the South African Airways Open.

TREVOR IMMELMAN
January

PAUL CASEY
February

ROBERT-JAN DERKSEN
March

FREDRIK JACOBSON
April

IGNACIO GARRIDO
May

PHILIP GOLDING
June

SERGIO GARCIA
July

LEE WESTWOOD
September

Shot of the Month Award

February's Award went to England's Paul Casey's approach to the final hole on his way to winning the ANZ Championship in Australia, while the 72nd hole was also the scene of a glorious wedge played by Robert-Jan Derksen, of The Netherlands, setting up a birdie, to edge out South African Ernie Els for the Dubai Desert Classic and claim the honours in March.

Sweden's Fredrik Jacobson sank his chip for an eagle three en route to landing the Algarve Open de Portugal in April while May saw Spain's Ignacio Garrido collect the Award for his delicate chip at the first play-off hole of the Volvo PGA Championship at Wentworth Club, where he took the title from Immelman.

The quality of shots continued into the summer months with England's Philip Golding hitting a glorious six iron onto the last green at the Open de France to claim his first title on The European Tour and the Award for June.

The 132nd Open Golf Championship at Royal St George's in July was the setting for a typically flamboyant chip and run from 67 yards by Spain's Sergio Garcia which dropped into the hole for an unlikely par four in the third round and took July's Award, while Northern Ireland's Darren Clarke took the plaudits in August for his unerring 40 foot birdie putt at the 13th hole at Firestone Country Club which effectively sealed his superb victory in the WGC-NEC Invitational.

England's Lee Westwood captured the September Award with the first albatross of his life – he holed his 224 yard four iron second shot at the 558 yard ninth hole at Kingsbarns where his course record 62 set him on the way to winning the dunhill links championship.

Gordon Simpson

The Royal Bank of Scotland

Sponsors of the 2003 Shot of the Month and 2003 Shot of the Year Awards

STROKE AVERAGE

#	Player		Avg
1	Ernie ELS (SA)	(60)	68.95
2	Marcus FRASER (Aus)	(33)	69.85
3	Paul CASEY (Eng)	(81)	70.06
4	Retief GOOSEN (SA)	(53)	70.15
5	Brian DAVIS (Eng)	(110)	70.35
6	Miguel Angel JIMÉNEZ (Sp)	(82)	70.37
7	Thomas LEVET (Fr)	(36)	70.39
8	Padraig HARRINGTON (Ire)	(70)	70.46
9	Darren CLARKE (N.Ire)	(64)	70.48
10	Nick O'HERN (Aus)	(64)	70.50
11	Thomas BJÖRN (Den)	(72)	70.51
12	David HOWELL (Eng)	(96)	70.58
13	Peter FOWLER (Aus)	(87)	70.69
14	Dean ROBERTSON (Scot)	(33)	70.70
15	Maarten LAFEBER (NL)	(98)	70.72
16	John BICKERTON (Eng)	(91)	70.73
17	Fredrik JACOBSON (Swe)	(65)	70.77
	Bradley DREDGE (Wal)	(87)	70.77
19	Gary ORR (Scot)	(67)	70.79
20	Sergio GARCIA (Sp)	(40)	70.83
21	Trevor IMMELMAN (SA)	(78)	70.86
22	Brad KENNEDY (Aus)	(33)	70.97
23	Thongchai JAIDEE (Thai)	(35)	71.00
24	José Maria OLAZÁBAL (Sp)	(62)	71.02
	Paul MCGINLEY (Ire)	(90)	71.02
26	Søren KJELDSEN (Den)	(98)	71.03
	Niclas FASTH (Swe)	(65)	71.03
	James KINGSTON (SA)	(63)	71.03
29	Colin MONTGOMERIE (Scot)	(69)	71.06
	David PARK (Wal)	(97)	71.06
31	Joakim HAEGGMAN (Swe)	(28)	71.07
32	Andrew COLTART (Scot)	(103)	71.10
	Stephen GALLACHER (Scot)	(91)	71.10
	Ian POULTER (Eng)	(98)	71.10
	Søren HANSEN (Den)	(88)	71.10
36	Carlos RODILES (Sp)	(89)	71.11
37	Nick FALDO (Eng)	(54)	71.13
38	Alastair FORSYTH (Scot)	(93)	71.15
	Ricardo GONZALEZ (Arg)	(65)	71.15
	David LYNN (Eng)	(97)	71.15
41	Raphaël JACQUELIN (Fr)	(100)	71.16
42	Stephen SCAHILL (NZ)	(82)	71.17
43	Stephen LEANEY (Aus)	(52)	71.21
44	Peter O'MALLEY (Aus)	(60)	71.22
	Jamie DONALDSON (Wal)	(87)	71.22
46	Paul LAWRIE (Scot)	(62)	71.23
	Mårten OLANDER (Swe)	(87)	71.23
	Jamie SPENCE (Eng)	(73)	71.23
49	Peter HEDBLOM (Swe)	(79)	71.24
50	Patrik SJÖLAND (Swe)	(84)	71.25
	Mathias GRÖNBERG (Swe)	(76)	71.25
52	Miles TUNNICLIFF (Eng)	(78)	71.26
	Richard GREEN (Aus)	(74)	71.26
	Martin MARITZ (SA)	(89)	71.26
	Brett RUMFORD (Aus)	(57)	71.26
56	Gary EVANS (Eng)	(78)	71.27
57	Nicolas COLSAERTS (Bel)	(89)	71.28
58	Fredrik ANDERSSON (Swe)	(90)	71.29
59	Jarrod MOSELEY (Aus)	(87)	71.30
	Erol SIMSEK (Ger)	(30)	71.30
61	Robert KARLSSON (Swe)	(85)	71.31
	Barry LANE (Eng)	(98)	71.31
	Phillip PRICE (Wal)	(68)	71.31
64	Justin ROSE (Eng)	(69)	71.32
65	Richard STERNE (SA)	(72)	71.33
66	Anders HANSEN (Den)	(83)	71.34
67	Jean-Francois REMESY (Fr)	(83)	71.35
68	Eduardo ROMERO (Arg)	(61)	71.36
	Lee WESTWOOD (Eng)	(80)	71.36
	Stephen DODD (Wal)	(88)	71.36
71	Simon KHAN (Eng)	(71)	71.37
72	Ian WOOSNAM (Wal)	(65)	71.38
73	Mark MCNULTY (Zim)	(62)	71.39
74	Steen TINNING (Den)	(60)	71.40
75	Stuart LITTLE (Eng)	(35)	71.43
76	Hennie OTTO (SA)	(48)	71.44
	Raymond RUSSELL (Scot)	(88)	71.44
78	Robert-Jan DERKSEN (NL)	(82)	71.45
79	Greg OWEN (Eng)	(78)	71.46
	Adam SCOTT (Aus)	(56)	71.46
81	Damien MCGRANE (Ire)	(57)	71.51
82	Peter LONARD (Aus)	(34)	71.53
83	Andrew MARSHALL (Eng)	(79)	71.54
84	Charl SCHWARTZEL (SA)	(81)	71.57
	Darren FICHARDT (SA)	(82)	71.57
86	Anthony WALL (Eng)	(78)	71.59
87	Greg TURNER (NZ)	(38)	71.61
	Santiago LUNA (Sp)	(87)	71.61
89	Eddie LEE (NZ)	(26)	71.62
90	Angel CABRERA (Arg)	(48)	71.63
91	Steve WEBSTER (Eng)	(83)	71.64
92	Emanuele CANONICA (It)	(71)	71.68
	Marcel SIEM (Ger)	(78)	71.68
94	Markus BRIER (Aut)	(86)	71.71
95	Terry PRICE (Aus)	(69)	71.74
	Arjun ATWAL (Ind)	(70)	71.74
97	Gary MURPHY (Ire)	(87)	71.76
98	David GILFORD (Eng)	(69)	71.77
99	José Manuel LARA (Sp)	(60)	71.82
	Shaun P WEBSTER (Eng)	(79)	71.82
101	Simon DYSON (Eng)	(85)	71.84
	Henrik BJORNSTAD (Nor)	(75)	71.84
103	Ian GARBUTT (Eng)	(93)	71.85
104	Rolf MUNTZ (NL)	(76)	71.86
105	Kenneth FERRIE (Eng)	(86)	71.87
	Jarmo SANDELIN (Swe)	(71)	71.87
107	Peter BAKER (Eng)	(90)	71.88
108	Matthew BLACKEY (Eng)	(94)	71.91
109	Graeme MCDOWELL (N.Ire)	(71)	71.92
	Andrew RAITT (Eng)	(63)	71.92
111	Paul BROADHURST (Eng)	(74)	71.93
	David CARTER (Eng)	(76)	71.93
113	Michael CAMPBELL (NZ)	(56)	71.95
114	Peter LAWRIE (Ire)	(92)	71.96
	Charlie WI (Kor)	(73)	71.96
	Mikko ILONEN (Fin)	(79)	71.96
	Marc FARRY (Fr)	(83)	71.96
118	Bernhard LANGER (Ger)	(38)	71.97
	Henrik STENSON (Swe)	(77)	71.97
120	Jesus Maria ARRUTI (Sp)	(53)	71.98
121	Ignacio GARRIDO (Sp)	(68)	71.99
122	Julien CLEMENT (Swi)	(72)	72.00
123	Roger CHAPMAN (Eng)	(77)	72.01
124	Philip GOLDING (Eng)	(99)	72.03
125	Christian CÉVAËR (Fr)	(80)	72.04
126	Mark FOSTER (Eng)	(60)	72.07
	Ivo GINER (Sp)	(28)	72.07
128	Mattias ELIASSON (Swe)	(47)	72.09
129	Klas ERIKSSON (Swe)	(93)	72.12
130	Mikael LUNDBERG (Swe)	(76)	72.16
	Richard BLAND (Eng)	(80)	72.16
132	Gordon BRAND JNR. (Scot)	(66)	72.24
133	Jorge BERENDT (Arg)	(68)	72.25
134	Henrik NYSTROM (Swe)	(73)	72.26
	Robert ROCK (Eng)	(34)	72.26
136	Mads VIBE-HASTRUP (Den)	(75)	72.27
137	Pierre FULKE (Swe)	(49)	72.29
138	Miguel Angel MARTIN (Sp)	(68)	72.32
139	Mark ROE (Eng)	(75)	72.33
	Jonathan LOMAS (Eng)	(90)	72.33
	Matthew CORT (Eng)	(48)	72.33
142	Fredrik OREST (Swe)	(50)	72.34
143	Ben MASON (Eng)	(69)	72.35
144	Gary EMERSON (Eng)	(76)	72.36
	Nicolas VANHOOTEGEM (Bel)	(76)	72.36
	Gustavo ROJAS (Arg)	(75)	72.36
147	Jean-François LUCQUIN (Fr)	(87)	72.37
	Nick DOUGHERTY (Eng)	(97)	72.37
149	Mark JAMES (Eng)	(49)	72.39
150	Alvaro SALTO (Sp)	(53)	72.40

DRIVING ACCURACY (%)

#	Player		%
1	Jarrod MOSELEY (Aus)	(77)	78.1
2	Richard GREEN (Aus)	(69)	74.2
3	Gary MURPHY (Ire)	(80)	73.5
4	Peter O'MALLEY (Aus)	(47)	73.4
5	Hennie OTTO (SA)	(24)	71.6
6	Simon WAKEFIELD (Eng)	(95)	71.1
7	Stephen LEANEY (Aus)	(37)	70.2
8	Ian GARBUTT (Eng)	(90)	70.1
9	Gary ORR (Scot)	(64)	70.0
	Dean ROBERTSON (Scot)	(32)	70.0
11	Miguel Angel JIMÉNEZ (Sp)	(77)	69.6
12	Simon KHAN (Eng)	(68)	69.3
13	Maarten LAFEBER (NL)	(92)	69.1
14	Diego BORREGO (Sp)	(28)	69.0
15	Paul EALES (Eng)	(65)	68.8
16	Mark MCNULTY (Zim)	(54)	68.6
	Matthew BLACKEY (Eng)	(91)	68.6
18	Paul MCGINLEY (Ire)	(77)	68.2
	David PARK (Wal)	(92)	68.2
	Pierre FULKE (Swe)	(36)	68.2
	Andrew MARSHALL (Eng)	(79)	68.2
22	Thomas LEVET (Fr)	(26)	68.1
23	Nicolas VANHOOTEGEM (Bel)	(73)	67.9
	Ernie ELS (SA)	(32)	67.9
25	Anders HANSEN (Den)	(74)	67.7
	Alastair FORSYTH (Scot)	(78)	67.7
	David GILFORD (Eng)	(66)	67.7
28	Stephen DODD (Wal)	(85)	67.5
29	Darren CLARKE (N.Ire)	(38)	66.7
	Jamie SPENCE (Eng)	(69)	66.7
	Marc FARRY (Fr)	(81)	66.7
32	Steen TINNING (Den)	(48)	66.6
	Søren KJELDSEN (Den)	(92)	66.6
34	Kenneth FERRIE (Eng)	(80)	66.4
35	Mark MOULAND (Wal)	(37)	66.2

DRIVING DISTANCE (YDS)

#	Player		Yds
1	Titch MOORE (SA)	(31)	316.7
2	Emanuele CANONICA (It)	(68)	316.5
3	Jean HUGO (SA)	(40)	314.5
4	Ernie ELS (SA)	(32)	310.0
5	Marcel SIEM (Ger)	(78)	307.0
6	Paul CASEY (Eng)	(62)	304.0
7	Francois DELAMONTAGNE (Fr)	(52)	303.0
8	Ricardo GONZALEZ (Arg)	(58)	302.9
9	Richard STERNE (SA)	(63)	302.5
10	Angel CABRERA (Arg)	(24)	301.7
11	Ivo GINER (Sp)	(28)	301.1
12	David DIXON (Eng)	(70)	300.7
	Adam SCOTT (Aus)	(32)	300.7
14	Robert KARLSSON (Swe)	(76)	300.6
15	Mattias ELIASSON (Swe)	(46)	300.0
	Darren CLARKE (N.Ire)	(38)	300.0
17	Stuart LITTLE (Eng)	(34)	299.8
18	Mark PILKINGTON (Wal)	(85)	299.7
19	Nicolas COLSAERTS (Bel)	(90)	299.6
20	Charl SCHWARTZEL (SA)	(74)	298.8
21	Hennie OTTO (SA)	(24)	298.7
22	Lucas PARSONS (Aus)	(32)	298.5
23	Klas ERIKSSON (Swe)	(87)	298.3
24	Justin ROSE (Eng)	(46)	297.7
25	Retief GOOSEN (SA)	(31)	297.4
26	Ryan REID (SA)	(33)	296.8
	Nick DOUGHERTY (Eng)	(93)	296.8
28	Steve WEBSTER (Eng)	(80)	296.6
29	José Manuel LARA (Sp)	(59)	295.8
	Martin MARITZ (SA)	(86)	295.8
31	Fredrik WIDMARK (Swe)	(80)	295.5
	Santiago LUNA (Sp)	(83)	295.5
33	Gary BIRCH JNR (Eng)	(45)	295.3
34	Raphaël JACQUELIN (Fr)	(87)	295.2
35	Søren HANSEN (Den)	(82)	294.6
	Stephen GALLACHER (Scot)	(88)	294.6

SAND SAVES (%)

1	Charlie WI (Kor)	(69)	73.3
	Sebastien DELAGRANGE (Fr)	(27)	73.3
3	Joakim HAEGGMAN (Swe)	(24)	70.0
4	Padraig HARRINGTON (Ire)	(44)	69.4
5	Mikael LUNDBERG (Swe)	(71)	69.2
6	Patrik SJÖLAND (Swe)	(80)	67.0
7	Warren BENNETT (Eng)	(59)	66.7
8	Justin ROSE (Eng)	(46)	66.1
9	Robert KARLSSON (Swe)	(76)	66.0
10	Ernie ELS (SA)	(32)	65.0
	Jorge BERENDT (Arg)	(64)	65.0
12	Robert COLES (Eng)	(29)	63.9
13	Erol SIMSEK (Ger)	(26)	63.2
14	Peter O'MALLEY (Aus)	(47)	62.5
	Andrew MARSHALL (Eng)	(79)	62.5
	Eduardo ROMERO (Arg)	(38)	62.5
17	Simon KHAN (Eng)	(68)	62.4
18	Andrew COLTART (Scot)	(100)	61.6
19	Peter HEDBLOM (Swe)	(77)	61.5
20	Trevor IMMELMAN (SA)	(53)	61.4
21	Gustavo ROJAS (Arg)	(75)	61.3
	Alessandro TADINI (It)	(53)	61.3
23	Andrew RAITT (Eng)	(60)	60.8
24	Peter BAKER (Eng)	(87)	60.4
25	Tony JOHNSTONE (Zim)	(49)	60.2
	Robert-Jan DERKSEN (NL)	(71)	60.2
27	Marcel SIEM (Ger)	(78)	60.0
28	Richard GREEN (Aus)	(69)	59.7
	Paul LAWRIE (Scot)	(49)	59.7
30	Mark JAMES (Eng)	(41)	59.6
31	Ian POULTER (Eng)	(76)	59.5
32	Simon HURD (Eng)	(69)	59.4
33	Bradley DREDGE (Wal)	(80)	59.3
34	Damien MCGRANE (Ire)	(53)	58.9
35	Raymond RUSSELL (Scot)	(84)	58.7

GREENS IN REGULATION (%)

1	Ernie ELS (SA)	(32)	80.2
2	Peter O'MALLEY (Aus)	(47)	78.3
3	Darren CLARKE (N.Ire)	(38)	76.8
4	Thomas LEVET (Fr)	(26)	76.5
5	Gary EVANS (Eng)	(66)	73.7
	Stephen LEANEY (Aus)	(37)	73.7
7	Richard GREEN (Aus)	(69)	72.9
8	Paul LAWRIE (Scot)	(49)	72.8
9	Stuart LITTLE (Eng)	(34)	72.7
10	Raymond RUSSELL (Scot)	(84)	72.4
11	Paul CASEY (Eng)	(62)	72.3
12	Stephen GALLACHER (Scot)	(88)	72.0
13	Steen TINNING (Den)	(48)	71.9
	Justin ROSE (Eng)	(46)	71.9
15	Raphaël JACQUELIN (Fr)	(87)	71.8
16	Paul MCGINLEY (Ire)	(77)	71.6
17	Ian GARBUTT (Eng)	(90)	71.4
18	Nicolas VANHOOTEGEM (Bel)	(73)	71.2
19	Retief GOOSEN (SA)	(31)	71.1
20	Greg OWEN (Eng)	(71)	71.0
	Martin MARITZ (SA)	(86)	71.0
22	Lee WESTWOOD (Eng)	(63)	70.9
	Roger WESSELS (SA)	(54)	70.9
24	Alastair FORSYTH (Scot)	(78)	70.8
25	Hennie OTTO (SA)	(24)	70.6
	Anders HANSEN (Den)	(74)	70.6
27	Jesus Maria ARRUTI (Sp)	(51)	70.5
28	Jarrod MOSELEY (Aus)	(77)	70.4
	Søren HANSEN (Den)	(82)	70.4
30	Mark MCNULTY (Zim)	(54)	70.2
31	Adam SCOTT (Aus)	(32)	70.1
	Maarten LAFEBER (NL)	(92)	70.1
33	Colin MONTGOMERIE (Scot)	(49)	70.0
34	Erol SIMSEK (Ger)	(26)	69.9
35	Niclas FASTH (Swe)	(42)	69.8
	Trevor IMMELMAN (SA)	(53)	69.8
	Fredrik JACOBSON (Swe)	(43)	69.8
	Jean-Francois REMESY (Fr)	(79)	69.8

AVERAGE PUTTS PER ROUND

1	Padraig HARRINGTON (Ire)	(44)	28.2
2	Pierre FULKE (Swe)	(36)	28.4
3	Robert KARLSSON (Swe)	(76)	28.5
4	Angel CABRERA (Arg)	(24)	28.6
5	Marcel SIEM (Ger)	(78)	28.7
	Richard BLAND (Eng)	(76)	28.7
7	Jarmo SANDELIN (Swe)	(68)	28.8
	Jamie SPENCE (Eng)	(69)	28.8
	David LYNN (Eng)	(88)	28.8
	Ian POULTER (Eng)	(76)	28.8
	Retief GOOSEN (SA)	(31)	28.8
	Michael CAMPBELL (NZ)	(32)	28.8
13	Joakim HAEGGMAN (Swe)	(24)	28.9
	Patrik SJÖLAND (Swe)	(80)	28.9
	Christian CÉVAËR (Fr)	(77)	28.9
	Andrew COLTART (Scot)	(100)	28.9
	Brian DAVIS (Eng)	(92)	28.9
	Darren FICHARDT (SA)	(78)	28.9
19	Thongchai JAIDEE (Thai)	(24)	29.0
	Simon DYSON (Eng)	(79)	29.0
	Alessandro TADINI (It)	(53)	29.0
	Niclas FASTH (Swe)	(42)	29.0
	Henrik BJORNSTAD (Nor)	(70)	29.0
	Peter FOWLER (Aus)	(80)	29.0
	David HOWELL (Eng)	(86)	29.0
	Thomas BJÖRN (Den)	(52)	29.0
	Miguel Angel JIMÉNEZ (Sp)	(77)	29.0
28	Bradley DREDGE (Wal)	(80)	29.1
	Matthew CORT (Eng)	(48)	29.1
	Fredrik JACOBSON (Swe)	(43)	29.1
	Brett RUMFORD (Aus)	(50)	29.1
	Nick O'HERN (Aus)	(58)	29.1
	Trevor IMMELMAN (SA)	(53)	29.1
	José Maria OLAZÁBAL (Sp)	(47)	29.1
	Robert-Jan DERKSEN (NL)	(71)	29.1
	Philip GOLDING (Eng)	(90)	29.1
	Fredrik ANDERSSON (Swe)	(86)	29.1

PUTTS PER GREEN IN REGULATION

1	Ernie ELS (SA)	(32)	1.699
2	Retief GOOSEN (SA)	(31)	1.718
3	Fredrik JACOBSON (Swe)	(43)	1.724
4	Niclas FASTH (Swe)	(42)	1.729
5	Thomas BJÖRN (Den)	(52)	1.733
6	Robert KARLSSON (Swe)	(76)	1.734
7	Padraig HARRINGTON (Ire)	(44)	1.736
8	Paul CASEY (Eng)	(62)	1.740
9	Ian POULTER (Eng)	(76)	1.742
10	Arjun ATWAL (Ind)	(63)	1.745
11	José Maria OLAZÁBAL (Sp)	(47)	1.746
12	Brian DAVIS (Eng)	(92)	1.747
13	Miguel Angel JIMÉNEZ (Sp)	(77)	1.748
	David HOWELL (Eng)	(86)	1.748
15	Michael CAMPBELL (NZ)	(32)	1.751
	Pierre FULKE (Swe)	(36)	1.751
17	Henrik BJORNSTAD (Nor)	(70)	1.752
18	Jamie SPENCE (Eng)	(69)	1.753
	Marcel SIEM (Ger)	(78)	1.753
	Ricardo GONZALEZ (Arg)	(58)	1.753
21	Andrew COLTART (Scot)	(100)	1.755
22	Angel CABRERA (Arg)	(24)	1.757
23	David PARK (Wal)	(92)	1.761
24	Carlos RODILES (Sp)	(81)	1.762
	Peter FOWLER (Aus)	(80)	1.762
26	Gary ORR (Scot)	(64)	1.763
	Dean ROBERTSON (Scot)	(32)	1.763
28	Jarmo SANDELIN (Swe)	(68)	1.764
	Phillip PRICE (Wal)	(50)	1.764
30	Trevor IMMELMAN (SA)	(53)	1.766
31	Jamie DONALDSON (Wal)	(83)	1.769
	Christian CÉVAËR (Fr)	(77)	1.769
	Jarrod MOSELEY (Aus)	(77)	1.769
34	John BICKERTON (Eng)	(87)	1.770
	Nick O'HERN (Aus)	(58)	1.770

REUTERS

Performance Data for The 2003 European Tour

EUROPEAN TOUR

OFFICIAL PERFORMANCE DATA

	Pos	Name & Country	Tournaments Played	Total Prize Money euro	£
	1	Ernie ELS (SA)	(16)	2,975,374.43	2,074,458.05
	2	Darren CLARKE (N.Ire)	(18)	2,210,051.09	1,540,867.67
	3	Padraig HARRINGTON (Ire)	(20)	1,555,623.00	1,084,594.47
	4	Fredrik JACOBSON (Swe)	(18)	1,521,302.69	1,060,666.04
	5	Ian POULTER (Eng)	(30)	1,500,855.27	1,046,409.91
	6	Paul CASEY (Eng)	(24)	1,360,455.86	948,522.17
	7	Lee WESTWOOD (Eng)	(25)	1,330,712.88	927,785.09
	8	Thomas BJÖRN (Den)	(22)	1,327,148.17	925,299.74
	9	Brian DAVIS (Eng)	(31)	1,245,512.65	868,382.72
	10	Phillip PRICE (Wal)	(20)	1,234,017.67	860,368.32
	11	Adam SCOTT (Aus)	(19)	1,152,526.60	803,552.00
	12	Retief GOOSEN (SA)	(16)	1,115,886.19	778,005.98
	13	Stephen LEANEY (Aus)	(16)	1,099,806.88	766,795.33
	14	Trevor IMMELMAN (SA)	(23)	1,007,777.56	702,631.66
	15	Michael CAMPBELL (NZ)	(16)	881,999.28	614,937.90
	16	David HOWELL (Eng)	(28)	881,640.24	614,687.57
	17	Ignacio GARRIDO (Sp)	(23)	854,004.13	595,419.43
	18	Peter LONARD (Aus)	(11)	850,491.56	592,970.43
	19	Alastair FORSYTH (Scot)	(26)	850,179.74	592,753.03
	20	Raphaël JACQUELIN (Fr)	(29)	834,814.40	582,040.17
	21	Greg OWEN (Eng)	(25)	808,179.24	563,469.90
	22	Niclas FASTH (Swe)	(20)	784,444.99	546,922.17
	23	Miguel Angel JIMÉNEZ (Sp)	(23)	781,351.84	544,765.59
	24	Carlos RODILES (Sp)	(28)	780,256.80	544,002.12
	25	Justin ROSE (Eng)	(21)	767,900.01	535,386.85
	26	Mathias GRÖNBERG (Swe)	(25)	748,117.42	521,594.25
	27	Søren KJELDSEN (Den)	(27)	743,484.07	518,363.84
	28	Colin MONTGOMERIE (Scot)	(22)	730,773.16	509,501.68
	29	Maarten LAFEBER (NL)	(31)	726,788.01	506,723.20
	30	Gary EVANS (Eng)	(26)	688,837.59	480,263.82
	31	Andrew COLTART (Scot)	(31)	647,277.50	451,287.75
#	32	Philip GOLDING (Eng)	(30)	647,258.26	451,274.33
	33	Paul MCGINLEY (Ire)	(27)	637,521.52	444,485.79
	34	Kenneth FERRIE (Eng)	(30)	628,539.15	438,223.19
	35	Peter HEDBLOM (Swe)	(25)	623,112.33	434,439.57
	36	Eduardo ROMERO (Arg)	(18)	607,761.04	423,736.51
	37	Nick O'HERN (Aus)	(18)	604,445.67	421,425.00
	38	John BICKERTON (Eng)	(27)	583,049.87	406,507.66
	39	Darren FICHARDT (SA)	(27)	574,137.60	400,293.94
#	40	Robert-Jan DERKSEN (NL)	(25)	547,721.38	381,876.32
	41	David LYNN (Eng)	(29)	545,315.76	380,199.09
	42	Bradley DREDGE (Wal)	(25)	543,050.41	378,619.67
	43	Mark MCNULTY (Zim)	(19)	540,047.46	376,525.99
	44	Jarrod MOSELEY (Aus)	(27)	532,631.53	371,355.53
	45	Peter FOWLER (Aus)	(24)	527,549.27	367,812.14
	46	Nick FALDO (Eng)	(16)	503,858.30	351,294.58
	47	Ricardo GONZALEZ (Arg)	(20)	503,752.71	351,220.96
	48	Robert KARLSSON (Swe)	(27)	501,593.59	349,715.60
	49	Sergio GARCIA (Sp)	(12)	496,521.05	346,178.98
	50	Stephen GALLACHER (Scot)	(29)	479,995.40	334,657.15
	51	Paul LAWRIE (Scot)	(20)	477,247.57	332,741.34
	52	José Maria OLAZÁBAL (Sp)	(19)	467,710.76	326,092.19
	53	Angel CABRERA (Arg)	(15)	463,541.21	323,185.14
	54	Barry LANE (Eng)	(30)	449,411.33	313,333.65
	55	Søren HANSEN (Den)	(28)	424,472.90	295,946.35
~$	56	Peter LAWRIE (Ire)	(32)	422,816.56	294,791.54
	57	Anders HANSEN (Den)	(27)	414,614.03	289,072.67
	58	Jamie DONALDSON (Wal)	(29)	397,806.18	277,354.08
#	59	Gary MURPHY (Ire)	(25)	386,419.50	269,415.18
	60	Nick DOUGHERTY (Eng)	(31)	385,077.28	268,479.37
	61	Mårten OLANDER (Swe)	(27)	349,701.38	243,814.98
	62	David PARK (Wal)	(29)	342,676.27	238,917.00
	63	Arjun ATWAL (Ind)	(24)	335,855.90	234,161.78
	64	Peter O'MALLEY (Aus)	(19)	335,122.41	233,650.39
#	65	Stephen SCAHILL (NZ)	(26)	313,986.03	218,913.91
^	66	James KINGSTON (SA)	(20)	312,081.36	217,585.95
	67	Mark FOSTER (Eng)	(21)	306,101.21	213,416.54
	68	Henrik STENSON (Swe)	(28)	300,463.25	209,485.70
	69	Christian CÉVAËR (Fr)	(28)	294,147.95	205,082.62
	70	Raymond RUSSELL (Scot)	(27)	293,201.23	204,422.55
#$	71	Charl SCHWARTZEL (SA)	(26)	291,533.96	203,260.12
	72	Rolf MUNTZ (NL)	(28)	288,132.25	200,888.42
	73	Hennie OTTO (SA)	(14)	286,522.80	199,766.30
	74	Jean-Francois REMESY (Fr)	(25)	281,579.37	196,319.69
	75	Ian WOOSNAM (Wal)	(20)	278,598.95	194,241.72
#$	76	Richard STERNE (SA)	(25)	277,634.34	193,569.18
~	77	Nicolas COLSAERTS (Bel)	(29)	275,331.70	191,963.76
	78	Thomas LEVET (Fr)	(11)	274,432.09	191,336.54
	79	Gary ORR (Scot)	(21)	267,138.15	186,251.14
	80	Stephen DODD (Wal)	(28)	261,591.90	182,384.24
	81	Santiago LUNA (Sp)	(26)	261,464.17	182,295.19
	82	Fredrik ANDERSSON (Swe)	(29)	256,701.80	178,974.83
	83	Richard GREEN (Aus)	(24)	254,775.34	177,631.68
	84	Martin MARITZ (SA)	(29)	251,664.64	175,462.87
	85	Jonathan LOMAS (Eng)	(33)	249,162.85	173,718.60
#	86	Simon KHAN (Eng)	(24)	246,718.55	172,014.41
	87	Anthony WALL (Eng)	(27)	243,514.99	169,780.86
	88	Pierre FULKE (Swe)	(16)	232,797.78	162,308.72
#	89	Paul BROADHURST (Eng)	(26)	232,041.23	161,781.25
	90	Bernhard LANGER (Ger)	(12)	231,139.81	161,152.77
	91	Mark ROE (Eng)	(26)	225,943.24	157,529.67
	92	Miles TUNNICLIFF (Eng)	(22)	225,191.86	157,005.81
#	93	José Manuel LARA (Sp)	(21)	225,165.25	156,987.26
~	94	Matthew BLACKEY (Eng)	(31)	223,475.68	155,809.27
#	95	Marcel SIEM (Ger)	(26)	223,159.07	155,588.53
	96	Graeme MCDOWELL (N.Ire)	(23)	221,909.08	154,717.02
	97	Patrik SJÖLAND (Swe)	(29)	219,455.92	153,006.65
	98	Steve WEBSTER (Eng)	(28)	217,129.14	151,384.41
~	99	Simon WAKEFIELD (Eng)	(33)	214,435.18	149,506.15
	100	Jarmo SANDELIN (Swe)	(22)	209,297.98	145,924.45

Pos	Name & Country	Tournaments Played	Total Prize Money	
			euro	£
101	Emanuele CANONICA (It)	(25)	206,834.89	144,207.16
102	Gregory HAVRET (Fr)	(28)	206,816.72	144,194.49
103	David GILFORD (Eng)	(23)	205,275.17	143,119.71
104	Mikko ILONEN (Fin)	(28)	197,802.62	137,909.78
105	Andrew OLDCORN (Scot)	(22)	196,788.02	137,202.39
#$ 106	Julien CLEMENT (Swi)	(23)	192,535.31	134,237.37
# 107	Andrew MARSHALL (Eng)	(25)	189,928.43	132,419.83
108	Jamie SPENCE (Eng)	(24)	188,081.76	131,132.31
109	Klas ERIKSSON (Swe)	(29)	180,493.48	125,841.69
# 110	Markus BRIER (Aut)	(28)	177,269.98	123,594.24
111	Henrik BJORNSTAD (Nor)	(27)	175,527.01	122,379.02
^ 112	Brett RUMFORD (Aus)	(18)	169,924.33	118,472.78
113	Roger CHAPMAN (Eng)	(25)	167,735.55	116,946.75
# 114	Mads VIBE-HASTRUP (Den)	(28)	166,796.65	116,292.14
* 115	Luke DONALD (Eng)	(4)	165,079.02	115,094.59
* 116	Robert ROCK (Eng)	(12)	165,036.07	115,064.65
~ 117	Iain PYMAN (Eng)	(27)	162,099.95	113,017.56
# 118	Shaun P WEBSTER (Eng)	(25)	160,527.58	111,921.29
# 119	Terry PRICE (Aus)	(24)	157,861.97	110,062.80
120	Jorge BERENDT (Arg)	(28)	154,195.03	107,506.18
121	Steen TINNING (Den)	(22)	152,807.97	106,539.10
122	Marc FARRY (Fr)	(29)	151,815.31	105,847.01
123	Charlie WI (Kor)	(27)	149,940.19	104,539.66
124	David CARTER (Eng)	(27)	149,599.93	104,302.42
* 125	Thongchai JAIDEE (Thai)	(10)	149,392.25	104,157.63
126	Peter BAKER (Eng)	(30)	149,378.26	104,147.88
127	Simon DYSON (Eng)	(29)	148,858.74	103,785.67
128	Gary EMERSON (Eng)	(25)	148,144.49	103,287.68
^$ 129	Marcus FRASER (Aus)	(10)	145,522.50	101,459.61
130	Henrik NYSTROM (Swe)	(26)	144,977.64	101,079.72
131	Paul EALES (Eng)	(25)	142,988.78	99,693.07
132	Richard BLAND (Eng)	(31)	142,535.10	99,376.76
133	Greg TURNER (NZ)	(13)	141,138.25	98,402.87
134	Miguel Angel MARTIN (Sp)	(26)	139,121.00	96,996.42
^ 135	Brad KENNEDY (Aus)	(10)	137,301.13	95,727.59
136	Sven STRÜVER (Ger)	(29)	137,052.55	95,554.28
137	Mikael LUNDBERG (Swe)	(27)	135,453.20	94,439.20
~ 138	Gustavo ROJAS (Arg)	(26)	132,225.61	92,188.90
139	Ian GARBUTT (Eng)	(31)	127,651.74	88,999.95
#$ 140	Damien MCGRANE (Ire)	(17)	126,363.97	88,102.11
#$ 141	Ben MASON (Eng)	(23)	126,112.75	87,926.95
# 142	Andrew RAITT (Eng)	(22)	124,920.36	87,095.61
143	Mark JAMES (Eng)	(19)	115,994.26	80,872.25
~$ 144	Jean-François LUCQUIN (Fr)	(30)	115,346.15	80,420.38
145	Sandy LYLE (Scot)	(18)	114,731.66	79,991.95
146	Gordon BRAND JNR. (Scot)	(22)	109,693.46	76,479.28
~$ 147	Fredrik WIDMARK (Swe)	(28)	108,573.94	75,698.73
148	David DRYSDALE (Scot)	(32)	101,945.58	71,077.38
149	Dean ROBERTSON (Scot)	(11)	100,122.34	69,806.20
~$ 150	Benn BARHAM (Eng)	(29)	98,021.03	68,341.15

$ = 2002 Challenge Tour Members
* = Affiliated Member
# = 2002 Qualifying School Graduates
~ = 2002 Challenge Tour Graduates

The 2003 Volvo Order of Merit

First time winners on The 2003 European Tour International Schedule. Left to right - Top Row: Fredrik Jacobson , Trevor Immelman , Mark Foster, Lian-Wei Zhang, Robert-Jan Derksen, Bradley Dredge, Kenneth Ferrie and Greg Owen. Bottom Row: Brett Rumford, Jim Furyk, Søren Kjeldsen, Philip Golding, Ben Curtis, Marcus Fraser, Shaun Micheel, KJ Choi and Maarten Lafeber.

The European Tour

DIRECTORS

N. C. Coles, MBE, *Chairman*

A. Gallardo, *Vice Chairman*
D. Cooper
T. A. Horton, MBE
M. H. James (alternate: K. J. Brown)

D. Jones
M. Lanner

R. Lee
J. E. O'Leary
D. J. Russell
O. Sellberg

Sir M. F. Bonallack, OBE *(Non Executive Tour Group Director)*
P. A. T. Davidson *(Non Executive Tour Group Director, Finance)*
B. Nordberg *(Non Executive Tour Group Director)*
K. S. Owen *(Non Executive Tour Group Director, Broadcasting)*

TOURNAMENT COMMITTEE

M. H. James, *Chairman* (Eng)

R. Chapman (Eng)
D. Clarke (N. Ire)
P. Eales (Eng)
A. Forsbrand (Swe)
M. A. Jiménez (Sp)
B. Langer (Ger)

R. Lee (Eng)
C. Montgomerie, MBE (Scot)
J. Spence (Eng)
G. Turner (NZ)
J. Van de Velde (Fr)

EXECUTIVE DIRECTOR ....K. D. Schofield CBE
DEPUTY EXECUTIVE DIRECTOR ....G. C. O'Grady
DIRECTOR OF TOUR OPERATIONS ....D. W. Garland
RYDER CUP DIRECTOR AND ASSISTANT TO EXECUTIVE DIRECTOR ....R. G. Hills
GROUP MARKETING DIRECTOR ....S. F. Kelly
CHIEF FINANCIAL OFFICER ....J. Orr
DIRECTOR OF CORPORATE AFFAIRS AND PUBLIC RELATIONS ....M. S. Platts
DIRECTOR OF INTERNATIONAL POLICY..K. Waters
CHIEF REFEREE ....J. N. Paramor
ASSISTANT DIRECTOR OF TOUR OPERATIONS...D. A. Probyn
SENIOR REFEREE ....A. N. McFee
SENIOR TOURNAMENT DIRECTOR AND QUALIFYING SCHOOL DIRECTOR ....M. R. Stewart
MANAGING DIRECTOR, EUROPEAN SENIORS TOUR...K. A. Stubbs
DIRECTOR OF CHALLENGE TOUR ....A. de Soultrait
CHAMPIONSHIP DIRECTOR, WORLD GOLF CHAMPIONSHIPS ....P. Adams
DIRECTOR OF TOURNAMENT DEVELOPMENT...J. Birkmyre
GROUP COMPANY SECRETARY...M. Bray
DIRECTOR OF TOURNAMENT SERVICES ....E. Kitson
DIRECTOR OF IT & NEW MEDIA..M. Lichtenhein
DIRECTOR, SPECIAL PROJECTS ....M. MacDiarmid
SALES DIRECTOR ....T. Shaw
DIRECTOR OF COMMUNICATIONS...G. Simpson

The Contributors

Mike Aitken *(The Scotsman)*
The Barclays Scottish Open

Colin Callander
European Seniors Tour

Phil Casey *(PA Sport)*
Scandic Carlsberg Scandinavian Masters
Trophée Lancôme

Peter Corrigan *(Independent)*
The Celtic Manor Resort Wales Open

Scott Crockett *(The European Tour)*
Omega Hong Kong Open
Caltex Masters, presented by Carlsberg,
Singapore 2003
60th Italian Open Telecom Italia
WGC – NEC Invitational
Wins Around the World

Norman Dabell
Madeira Island Open
Open de France
Dutch Open

Peter Dixon *(The Times)*
Linde German Masters

Bill Elliott *(The Observer/Golf Monthly)*
Volvo Order of Merit Winner
The Year in Retrospect
Benson and Hedges International Open
132nd Open Golf Championship
Bernhard Langer Profile
Hal Sutton Profile

Andy Farrell *(The Independent)*
WGC – Accenture Match Play

Mark Garrod *(PA Sport)*
Volvo Masters Andalucia

Michael Gibbons
BMW Russian Open
Turespaña Mallorca Classic
European Challenge Tour

Martin Hardy
The Daily Telegraph Damovo British Masters

John Hopkins *(The Times)*
Deutsche Bank – SAP Open TPC
of Europe

Renton Laidlaw *(The Golf Channel)*
Heineken Classic
ANZ Championship
Johnnie Walker Classic

Derek Lawrenson *(Daily Mail)*
Masters Tournament
US Open Championship

Jock MacVicar *(Scottish Daily Express)*
The Diageo Championship
at Gleneagles

Lewine Mair *(The Daily Telegraph)*
Dubai Desert Classic
dunhill links championship

James Mossop *(Sunday Telegraph)*
Omega European Masters

Graham Otway *(Freelance/Daily Mail)*
BMW International Open

Mitchell Platts *(The European Tour)*
BMW Asian Open
Volvo PGA Championship
The Seve Trophy
WGC – World Cup
The 35th Ryder Cup Matches

Gordon Richardson
Canarias Open de España
Telefonica Open de Madrid

Gordon Simpson *(The European Tour)*
South African Airways Open
dunhill championship
Qatar Masters
Nissan Irish Open
WGC – American Express Championship
The Royal Bank of Scotland Shot of the
Month Awards

Colm Smith
Smurfit European Open

Tony Stenson
US PGA Championship

Mel Webb *(The Times)*
Algarve Open de Portugal
Aa St Omer Open
Nordic Open

John Whitbread *(Surrey Herald)*
HSBC World Match Play Championship

Roddy Williams *(The European Tour)*
Carlsberg Malaysian Open

Ian Wooldridge *(Daily Mail)*
A Tribute to Mark McCormack

The Photographers